WAR AND MIGRATION

1860-2020

*The Ruin of Western Civilization
and
the American Way of War*

The Current Calamity in Historical Perspective:
A Narrative

JOHN HENRY EGAN

War and Migration 1860-2020
The Ruin of Western Civilization and the American Way of War

Copyright © 2020 by Joshua Tree Books

All rights reserved. No part of this book may be reproduced or transmitted in any form or by any means without written permission of the author.

ISBNs
978-1-7362285-0-0 (paperback)
978-1-7362285-1-7 (eBook)

Published by: Joshua Tree Books
www.joshuatreebooks.com

Contact the author @ www.warandmigration.com

Contents

Introduction 1
1 The Present Calamity in Historical Perspective 3
2 The Transformation of the West Into a Permanent War Economy . . 133
3 The Darwinian Revolution and the Politics of Mass-Murder 295
4 The Failure of Liberal Democracy 417
Some Sources 445

INTRODUCTION

The book's premise is that a *100 Years War* started in 1914 that rages ever onward onto the present day. It began as a *European Civil War* that eventually engaged Japan and the United States. It then evolved into a continuous *World War* with no end in sight. The war is a new sort where the primary targets are civilian non-combatants. Their deaths; the elderly, women and children mostly, far outstrip military ones. Every nation is now involved in it: either at war with a foreign foe or else in hostilities against their own people. In many cases both. The war began with soldiers in cloth caps using tactics from the Napoleonic Age. Four years later they had modern steel helmets, submachine guns and flamethrowers. Conditions like total war, weapons of mass destruction, regime change and ethnic cleansing were introduced and practiced. After a twenty year pause for rearmament, it began again and was worse than ever. On the day it ended, the Vietnam War began. One of the legends to emerge was that only the United States had the technical wizardry to produce *The Bomb*. The evidence indicates that Germany and possibly Japan produced nuclear weapons called *atom-splitting bombs*. Germany had a fleet of *Amerika Bombers* in Norway ready to hit New York when the war ended. The plot is a narrative told as a record of human greed, wrath, genius, stupidity and lust for power. Testimony is extremely complicated; compounded by institutionalized lies and deception. Many times, baffled by ignorance and pride, events overcame the best people with the finest intentions. Eventually though, in a world hardened by war, the worst sort of people necessarily rose to the top.

They stayed there. Its final argument is that in the prolonged trauma of perpetual war, Americans and Europeans lost their will to prosper and survive. Their civilization has run its course and its people, purposeless and despised, will soon disappear from history; like so many before them.

> John Henry Egan, Mojave California, 2020

PART I

THE PRESENT CALAMITY IN HISTORICAL PERSPECTIVE

It glows in the dark

IN 1898 MARIE Curie discovered the Radium that would kill her. She was born in the Kingdom of Poland, sometimes called *Congress Poland*, then a part of the Russian Empire. The Emperor of Russia was also the King of Poland by right of conquest. That same right made the King of England both King of Ireland and Emperor of India. Since Europe owned a good part of the world, their noble houses had all sorts of royal and imperial titles. The French *Emperor Napoleon I* briefly created the *Grand Duchy of Warsaw* in 1807. Napoleon Bonaparte was born of humble origins on the small island of Corsica. He had a genius for war in a way that some children intuitively grasp the game of chess. At a young age Bonaparte figured out how to move and motivate large military organizations all over the map. When his armies conquered most of Europe he literally crowned himself Emperor of France. This gave him and his family royal and noble pedigree. And who could dispute it? The *right of conquest* gave him title. The new Emperor (from Latin *imperium*) ruled most of Europe and he reasoned a renewed Poland would be a good ally. He was right. They would provide him with some crack

3

military units. Once the largest country in Europe, Poland wasn't able to defend itself from the large empires on their extensive borders. The Kingdom of Prussia; eastern Germans with a powerful army then conquered Poland along with Russia and Austria. Later on Prussia foolishly chose war with Napoleon who commanded the world's best army. They lost and he took a good slice of Prussian territory to renew Poland. In the next century, the German Empire would face a similar problem. Instead of creating an ally, they would first ignore Poland and then destroy it. Poland's brief revival under Napoleon was costly to Russia as well; both they and Prussia had divvied up Poland only a few years before. Neither of them wanted to see Poland restored, but they were under Napoleon's heel. Russia recaptured Poland when Napoleon was finally defeated in 1815. They still held it in 1867 when Marie was born in Warsaw. Although they were Russian territory, the Poles governed themselves. However, Russia made foreign policy verdicts for them and those decisions were binding. This too was not unusual. The Kingdom of Hungary joined the Austrian Empire voluntarily to bolster their defenses against Slavic peoples in general and Romania in particular. The Hungarians made Austria's emperor their king in a mutually beneficial arrangement. Like Poland, Hungary governed itself. In recognition of their power, the concord with Austria allowed Hungary its own large and powerful army. But Austria decided world affairs and would eventually drag the reluctant Hungarians into the coming *World War* with them. Marie; she just wanted to study math and physics at the University of Krakow. However she lacked a penis and wasn't allowed in. Had she one, the history of Poland as a center for nuclear research might have been different. Instead she settled in the slightly more enlightened French Republic. There she began the investigations that would ultimately lead to *The Bomb*. She couldn't have known it though. For her it was all about energy and progress. It seemed as though the two elements she isolated in her laboratory (Polonium and Radium) were their own source of energy. They were like the sun! She introduced the term *radioactivity*. X-Rays were already discovered but nobody knew what they were. She did and understood what nobody else could. When *the World War* started in 1914 the ever practical Marie invented mobile X-Ray machines to help heal wounded soldiers. She was a genius and anticipated a bright future when the new energy sources she discovered would light the world. An interesting film about her life is *Radioactive* (2019).

New Years Day 1900

It fell on a Monday, just as it did 900 years before in 1000 AD. Back then medieval Europe had no such thing as a weekend. In that agrarian society people had holidays; lots of them. When the harvest came they worked seven days a week. When it was Christmastime they took three months off. On January 1, 1000 they expected the end of the world. Interestingly the same thing happened on January 1, 2000. In both cases, nothing happened. The pious and even not so devout imagined *The Nazarene* would re-emerge and create paradise on that perfect Monday, an even 1000 years after His birth and *Resurrection*. He decided to wait. In 1900 almost everybody anticipated an enlightened new *inventive* century. It didn't work out that way either. That came as a profound cultural shock; one we still feel. The century before, 1800-1899, gave evidence that human society had indeed *evolved*. Wars were few, limited and of short duration, at least in Europe. It was a century of peace in Europe, and it seemed that the dreadful wars in the *Age of Napoleon* (1795-1815) were indeed a thing of the past. Northern Euro-American industrialized nation-states and its peoples seemed to be the apex of human development and ingenuity. That's why even today, millions want to migrate there. Modern ideas in agriculture, nutrition and medicine made life there longer and more fruitful. There was a belief in *modernity* centered about rationalism and decency. The supposed dark and dank medieval world was replaced by one of light and warmth. It was all very evident: electricity lit the streets and the electric light bulb was a wonder to behold. So too was the phonograph, the telephone, telegraphs, motion pictures and refrigerated railroad cars that delivered fresh food to industrialized cities all year round. What educator would dare to say, then or now, that *Medieval Agrarian Society* was more sensible? It's denigrated now, even though medieval life was self-sustaining, pollution free and organic. Nowadays, *Climate Change* alarmist hearken a return to that sort of pre-industrial society. But realistically who now knows how to maintain a hearth in a world without fossil fuels? Luckily the complete idiots are still in the minority. What we do have among the vast majority of people is a harmoniously erected reality that the modern world, despite its problems, is the best ever imagined. Modern Sociology calls this a *Social Construction of Reality*. However it is a consensual truth and not something tangible: *a belief system* erected as a certainty by what people *feel and think* about the world. Its foundation rests upon a series of ideas presented as undeniable truth in everyday life; *taken for granted assumptions*. One of them is that modern medicine is the best the world has ever seen. Who disputes that taken for granted assumption? Arguing against socially constructed realities make people public outcasts. We can see this today with the Wuhan virus or *Covid-19*. People willingly endure a self-imposed house arrest and mask themselves in public, all on the say so of a few celebrity doctors. Doctors wouldn't lie about it would they? A seemingly wondrous *modernity* has emerged and it's become an evident and irrefutable truth that there's never been anything better.

Retina scans

Few could know that *modernity* would be ever more complex and intimidating. On *New Year's Day 1900,* no one needed personal identification: it was evident by the way you lived, dressed and spoke how much wealth and influence you had. No one really cared about identifying you: personal connections and integrity was the only thing worth knowing. How could anyone have foreseen that by the next century it would be impossible to get anything done without multiple photo identification cards that could be electronically analyzed while another instrument scanned your eye's retina or thumbprint? Even now, it should be frightening that an electronic device can print out your entire life history for a nameless bureaucrat who has the power to imprison you literally at the touch of a button. To achieve this level of individual control and surveillance requires an enormous increase in bureaucracy. High taxation must pay for it. Westerners are now taxed at a higher rate than any people in the history of the world. A massive and expensive police presence enforces payment. We submit to it for comfort's sake. Nobody wants to be an inmate inside the newly emerged and massive world-wide *Prison Industrial Complex*. Even so, most people are utterly convinced that this is civilization in its highest form.

THE PRESENT CALAMITY IN HISTORICAL PERSPECTIVE

This belief is the practical application of a *socially constructed reality*. The truth may be the exact opposite.

Jonny Gutenberg has an idea

The invention of the printing press in 1450 set this process in motion. It sure seemed like a good idea at the time. The printed word initially gave people personal access to holy books. The word of God had hitherto remained secret knowledge in the hands of a priest caste. If anyone wanted to know *the Word* it had to come from a priest. *William Tyndale* and others were strangled and burnt to death for printing Bibles in English. *Purgatory* was gruesome but Tyndale demonstrated it is not mentioned anywhere in the *Holy Book*. This understanding created deep schisms in medieval society. Eventually sequestered knowledge and its inquisition did not prevail. Books for profit and propaganda gave people an insight into the human condition because after all, reading is something a child can do. What's more, ordinary people could place the present in historical perspective. What serf could do that? Prior to the printing press children dressed as their parents did and worked with them; girls with their mothers at home and boys with their fathers in the fields or mines. As novels, and later the internet gave people more insight into human nature, children often came to believe they were smarter than their parents. Events sometimes proved them right. Nowadays, at least in the cities where most people live, children seldom do what their parents do. They don't even talk to them very much. There is a new order in place and the dissolution of the family is a part of it. The United States has more single parents than any country in the world. Instead of human relations we now have *Apple Music*; just plug it in on your way to the fitness center. The modern technological world with its wondrous innovations and personal freedom is *unmistakably* a grand place to live. Things are better than ever; everybody says so. The development of the steam engine c. 1750 enhanced this revolution, not only in industry, but also in human thought. When it was discovered that a steam engine could be made progressively bigger and more powerful, Europeans thought that human societies could also be manipulated and made progressively better. *Utopia*, an idea and now a readable essay from the 16th century, came to influence political thinking in the 18th and 19th centuries. It convinced Europeans that humanity could be actively manipulated to create a perfect society.

Population reduction and war

James Watt, who patented but did not invent the first steam engine in 1776 was, interestingly enough, pals with Adam Smith who published *The Wealth of Nations*, also in 1776. This was the same year England's rebellious American colonies declared independence. Smith, the first sociologist, argued that economics should be viewed as the product of personal labor in the various strata and sub-strata of society. The true wealth of nations lay in the hands of its individuals, rich and poor alike; not in land, gold or military might. Smith was not an egalitarian. On the contrary, he argued that the ruling elite had a right and a duty to accumulate wealth. But Smith was himself a morally sound Christian who didn't recognize that many of the *Seven Deadly Sins*, especially greed and avarice, would negate his finely wrought *invisible hand*. Karl Marx would elaborate this in *Das Kapital*. So too would Thomas Malthus in *On Population* (1798) which would amazingly argue that *population reduction* would invigorate society; once its poorer moribund members were weeded out by Smith's ruthless invisible hand. The current world-wide *Climate Change* alarm and the notion that population decrease is its cure, is Malthus' argument. Of course, like modern governments, the *Goode Reverend Malthus* presented ways to help the invisible hand along the way; such as by introducing typhus to inner city ghettos. These arguments are presented today as genetics and population control. Most people argue that this is a good thing and are convinced that the world is *overpopulated* by people other than themselves. Malthus would influence Charles Darwin who was among the first of the atheists, or Agnostics as they called it then. Darwin would incredibly present the idea that sex, reproduction and death were the only essential creative forces in the universe. As a corollary God wasn't necessary; most likely did not exist, and indeed probably never existed. Soon, in the century to come, hundreds of millions of ordinary people would meet untimely deaths in what would seem to be an endless series of wars directed primarily against them. The victims were determined mostly by their ethnic identity; some deemed fit to survive, others not so much. But it would be difficult to foresee that on Monday, January 1, 1900. Western civilization was at its apex. The Indo-European Caucasian race ruled the world. One century later that civilization would begin its collapse from self-induced trauma and treason. In an astounding reversal, Caucasian Christians would be scheduled for extermination and extinction. This was the fate they often visited upon unfortunate races around the world. Now they stare in dumfounded disbelief as the tables turn upon them.

And the caissons go rolling along

There were signs of the decline to come. But they were often overlooked in 1900; like the invention of dynamite. Alfred Nobel was an intelligent young man who was also a chemist. He created a *high explosive* that had plenty of peaceful uses but devastating military ones as well. A peace prize is named after him now: amusingly enough after Alfred read a mistakenly published obituary about himself. It named him *The Merchant of Death*. That wasn't the legacy Alfred had in mind. He decided to use his wealth to promote peace and harmony. But, as much as he wished to avoid it, his discovery greatly increased the killing power of military weapons; even more so with the later invention of *TNT* by another chemist. High explosives could now be safely poured into artillery shells. Gun powder was the most powerful explosive before Alfred came along. It is a *low explosive* used primarily as propellant. Military organizations preferred to use it that way for solid metal cannon balls (and bullets) rather than as a shelled explosive. The *American Civil War* or *War Between the States* was the first large war that gave a glimpse of the destruction to come. Both armies, the Federal and the Confederate, had two types of large guns; the ones that shot low explosive shells or the ones that fired iron cannon balls. The shells filled with *low explosive* gun powder did kill some enemy troops. But the cannon balls were far more effective against enemy artillery. When those iron balls crashed into an artillery piece it was done for, while an explosive shell might most likely just kill the crew whose replacements could quickly fire the guns again. *TNT* meant that a compact high explosive fired from guns now had many times the explosive power of gunpowder. It could kill and maim dozens, even hundreds of men, and take out not just single guns but entire artillery batteries too, guns, caissons, horses and all. The machine gun was also introduced in the American war and it became lighter, more compact, more mobile and more destructive. By the end of the American war in 1865, two years before the invention of dynamite, the Americans had lost close to *one million men*. They reluctantly came to the conclusion that frontal assaults against accurate rifle fire, machine guns and cannons would always end badly. Europeans didn't pay attention. They regarded the Americans as slovenly amateurs at war and called their armies '*armed mobs.*' They didn't understand the assent of firepower. European war colleges continued to plan for massed offensives with cavalry charges into the teeth of enemy fire; fire that they either discounted or else felt could be overcome by personal valor. They couldn't have been more wrong, and it was just the beginnings of sorrow.

Manifest Destiny

The USA has always been an expansionist nation. This is how it got to be the way it is. They purchased the massive *Louisiana Territory* from France in 1803. It had been French, but was ceded to Spain by treaty. Then it was given back to France in another lost war. Ruled by General Napoleon Bonaparte, France decided to cash in. Back then, 15 million dollars in solid gold was some real money. The American offer convinced him to part with far away Louisiana to better feed his men with fresh guns and ammo. In 1810 the USA annexed the *West Florida Republic* that had revolted against Spanish rule. Then Spain ceded all of Florida in 1821. Filled with alligator infested swamps and with *Miami Beach* not yet invented, Spain just didn't want it anymore. Florida entered the USA as a *Free and Independent State* and would cite that when it seceded from the USA only 40 years later. The issue was slavery. Some states wanted it, others didn't. In fact, none of the states that joined the federal union would have done it if they thought they couldn't get out of the deal. As the United States expanded westward, adding more states, some slave and some free, inevitable conflicts arose with the native population. State and Federal power was then used to remove the natives further west. There was both legal and popular resistance to this but Andrew Jackson said to the Chief Justice:

when you put an army together you can stop me. Jackson personally felt sorry for the Cherokee but wasn't willing to risk civil war to protect them. That settled the issue as the southern states wanted native lands for their own slave empire. This set the USA on a violent expansionist course. The conquest of Mexico that followed made America a continental power from coast to coast. But it was a nation beset, as Lincoln said, *half slave and half free.*

Political warfare

The American Civil War, also known as *The War for Southern Independence*, was a political struggle between the Republican Party that sought the abolition of slavery and the Democrat Party that represented the slave owners. It is interesting that most Americans today think it was the other way around. That's the value of a nationally directed propaganda campaign that begins in grade school. In 1860 the Republican Presidential nominee Abraham Lincoln, who represented an *Abolitionist party*, was elected. Within a month, slave state South Carolina seceded from the USA. They argued that their compact agreed to upon joining the USA was not valid and no longer binding. More southern states would join them the next month. They argued that the states created the Federal Government and not the other way around. Federal power was severely limited by the *Constitution of the USA* and the Federal Government was ignoring those limitations. The southern states feared that if Federal powers were expanded at their expense, they would soon revert to the colonies they once were under British rule. Soon they would be. Foreseeing this, they revolted, unfortunately choosing the abomination of slavery as the cause they would fight for. On the wrong side of history and decency they were joined by ten other southern states that formed The *Confederate States of America* or *CSA*. The Confederacy was supported by London and British banks. Still miffed at their lost wars to the American bumpkins, they were ready to send troops as well but were leery. They had the troops in Canada, war plans in hand, but the Northern states were backed up by Tsarist Russia. They sent two fleets in support of the Unionists and were ready to send troops as well. This close relationship with Russia was the reason why they sold Alaska to the USA rather than possibly lose it to British Canada.

Those damn Yankees

Both sides thought the ensuing *Rebellion* or *Civil War* would be a quick and easy win. It turned out to be the most devastating war in the history of the United States. At the onset, Virginia was the 2nd largest, most populous and richest state in the USA. Its capitol Richmond was the grandest city in the country and of the first twelve US Presidents, seven were from Virginia. Four years later Richmond, the capitol of the CSA, lay in smoldering ruin and the state was split asunder never to regain its former glory. The first capitol of the CSA was in rustic Montgomery Alabama. Had the CSA kept its capitol there, the war might have taken a different course as it was far from Washington DC; a city that was very soon to become the most heavily fortified in the world. It still is; defended by missiles, Air Force bases, and dozens of *deep underground military bases, DUMB* in American military acronym. But the Southern diplomats preferred the elegant comforts of Richmond and so the war was fought between two powers whose capitols were 100 miles apart, slugging it out in Virginia and along the major rivers in the west.

Secession

There were plenty of elegant grand secession balls all through the South akin to the one in *Gone with the Wind* (1939) and dang, it was going to be *easy pickins* as everybody knew those sissified Yankees couldn't even ride a horse. Well they could, and Louisiana was the first Confederate state to fall. Like the rest of the Confederacy, the folks in Louisiana honestly thought those soft and fancy Yankees couldn't fight a lick. That was until the *Battle of Shiloh* in April 1862, when most of the Confederate losses were thousands of young men from Louisiana. The slaughter at Shiloh cost more men than all previous American wars combined. This devastated Louisiana's morale: few foresaw the death and destruction to come when the state gleefully seceded 15 months earlier, the sixth state to do so. A few weeks after Shiloh, New Orleans fell and Federal troops occupied the state until 1877. One by one, the Confederate states were defeated and occupied. The slaves were freed and given the opportunity to own some land and make a life for themselves. Their freedom was protected by

Federal troops. But by 1876 the Federal government in Washington was faced with massive strikes by workers in the north (*The Great Upheaval*) and mobile cavalry wars in the west against the natives (*The Great Sioux War of 1876*).

> *The consolidation of the states into one vast empire, aggressive abroad and despotic at home, will be the certain precursor of its ruin.* Robert E. Lee

The *Reconstruction Era* (1863-76) was a brief shining moment for the freed slaves. It was they who established the first public schools in the United States. General Grant's election as President insured that the Freedmen's rights would be protected. Northern workers were in a hard spot too. They had more rights than slaves but were brutally mistreated in a monopoly capital experiment run completely amok. It might be said that apologists for slavery like George Fitzhugh (*Sociology for the South* 1854) saw this coming and argued just this: that slaves as property would always be better treated than wage-slaves who were mere commodities easily replaced at no cost. This was written before the massive and abhorrent industrialization of the North in the Civil War and after it when the situation got even worse. Even so, Fitzhugh was too self-important to comprehend that workers, however badly treated, had *freedom and rights*. They could quit and move to another state. So too was it for the Freedmen. They couldn't be easily whipped and murdered at the whim of an owner. Very few people could see their way through any of these contradictions except that liberty was, and should always have been, the foundation of the American nation. After General Grant retired, the ruling Republican Party decided to withdraw its troops from the southern states to protect the magnates up north, thereby callously leaving the newly freed slaves to their own devices. Outnumbered, they would be terrorized by the defeated Confederates, the resurrected Democrat Party and its terror death squads called the *Ku Klux Klan*; all under the banner of *White Supremacy*. The defeat of *Reconstruction* was a loss for all workers and small farmers both black and white. They often united, notably in the *New Orleans General Strike* of 1892. But the notion of white supremacy, legitimized by Darwinist eugenics, divided both races. *Jim*

Crow Laws legally segregated them. The Federal Government and its judiciary would support this endeavor for the next 100 years.

Africa is dismembered

Following the defeat of the Confederacy, the Federals used their regular army to nearly exterminate the natives and drive the few survivors into reservations. All the while, an even larger private army named *The Pinkerton Detective Agency* was used to suppress the northern workers. By 1895 the natives were defeated and the workers temporarily subdued after two decades of massacres by a corporate elite whose private military forces operated outside any laws. At this point the Federal Government was completely controlled by people called *Captains of Industry*. They wanted more markets for their goods and used their influence to provoke a war with Spain, thinking it would be trouble-free. It was, at least initially. The *Spanish-American War* (1898) ended quickly and Spain happily ceded the remnants of their once vast empire. They handed over what was a problem for them to the Americans who were internally divided about foreign colonies and unable to completely see through the problems that imperialism would bring. At the same time Europe decided that they too needed more foreign markets for their industrial production. So they captured Africa. In 1875 Europeans controlled only 10% of Africa; a small region around Algeria owned by nearby France, land that actually became a *Departement of France* in 1848, like Texas is in America: a state. With France as the only African power, Europeans had the audacity to hold a conference in Berlin. They divided Africa like a piece of cherry pie. It was a brutal conquest. Within a few years 90% of Africa was conquered. The German subjugation of Southwest Africa was particularly wicked as they engaged in racial extermination policies replete with concentration camps. The British were no better, though a bit less evil. The French had already begun to populate Algeria with French immigrants for after all, *it was now France*. Of course they took all the prime real estate. Who then could have foreseen the social destruction this would bring to France? It would take awhile but the French would be driven out of Africa in 1963. Amazingly, France itself would be colonized and invaded by Algerians in the late 20th and early 21st century. The vast majority of modern Americans have no clue about any of this.

THE PRESENT CALAMITY IN HISTORICAL PERSPECTIVE

The Insular Cases

In South America, the descendants of the erstwhile Spanish rulers were quietly efficient in decimating the natives and, historically, they go unscathed. In America there were many who didn't want to go down this path. The *Treaty of Paris* (1898) gave America the Philippines, Guam, Puerto Rico and Cuba. It was ratified by only *one vote* in the American Senate. The Supreme Court decisions that gave the Federal Government the right to administer foreigners only passed 5-4. Andrew Carnegie, noted philanthropist, offered to personally hand over the twenty million dollars that America paid Spain for the Philippines. He wanted to buy back Philippine independence and set them free. All to no avail as the Federal Government was set on empire. They then conquered the *Kingdom of Hawaii* just because they could and it all began to be costly right away. The residents of the Philippines wanted independence and were suppressed with a brutality that matched the German conquest of Namibia. That war is called *The Philippine-American War* and hardly anyone in America even knows it ever happened. Cuba was given nominal freedom but it was actually ruled by the US Army and local mercenaries. American corporations moved into Cuba to exploit its resources and women with slave labor, gambling and prostitution. Ditto for Puerto Rico. The Americans then used this model of exploitation to subdue the rest of Central America for its fruit, coffee and sugar. The actions were disputed in the US Supreme Court. In a series of cases known as the *Insular Cases* and all by 5-4 decisions, and all in 1901, the court decided that the residents of the new American Empire did not have Constitutional rights. The consequences would manifest themselves in revolts, death squads, racial extermination policies and the massive emigration to the USA by people, ironically enough, fleeing American bombs and death squads for the only safe haven open to them: in the heart of the beast. Very little of this history is known inside the USA for if the people did know, and had the power to stop it, they would have. By the time of the 20th century, the various individual states that make up the *United States* had lost all power. Like the *Confederate States* predicted, they become mere colonies again, crushed under the weight of a Federal Government that knew no limitations. Europe was seemingly much more civilized, but beneath its genteel surface, it was beset by ethnic aggravations that would explode into unconstrained violence upon the first pretext given. In addition, Europe was not a completely Christian continent: there were large Islamic enclaves, the remnants of the vast Ottoman Empire that once almost conquered all of Europe and soon will again.

The Sick Man of Europe

Fourteen years after New Year's Day 1900, the *World War* broke out. Incredibly it still rages in the bleak and desolate remnants of the once great *Ottoman Empire*. Sporadically there is still shooting in Europe itself and the mighty *Twin Towers* in New York fell because of it. The wars that America, France and Britain still wage there are sometimes called *The Wars of the Ottoman Succession*. At present there is no end in sight as the victors, a century on, try to figure out what sort of political system can replace Ottoman rule. In 1914 the Ottoman Empire (before its dissolution) was not really a European power and nor was it sick; at least not anymore sick than the decrepit Austro-Hungarian Empire or the pathologically brutal Russian Empire. The phrase *Sick Man of Europe* was dreamed up by Russian Emperor Nicholas I when he looked in the mirror and tried to figure out a way to loot and pillage the place. Historians and commentators gleefully took him up on it. They named the Ottomans *sick* because they seemed to be in decline. But as it turned out, the Ottoman Empire managed to fight as long and as hard as did the German Empire in the vicious battle of nations we now call *World War One*. The biggest mistake the foolish victors made was to break the Empire up into small states that had no national identity. They still work at it; bombing Iraq, Syria, Lebanon and Libya to smithereens, the object of which is to steal their resources and depopulate them.

Thrace

When the war began, there were no celebrations in Istanbul (aka Constantinople) the Ottoman capital city. It lay on the *Dardanelles Strait* that connects the Black Sea to the Mediterranean Sea and from there to the Suez Canal and the *Pillars of Hercules*, now called Gibraltar. The *Dardanelles Strait*, a very narrow waterway, has long been the object of policy and war. Queen Helen of Sparta moved there because Troy controlled the waterway and its riches. She was a very hot date for Prince Paris heir to the Trojan throne. The Spartans had chosen her queen by her beauty and when he abducted her (with her consent and retinue) it was the greatest heroic act of the Age. She became a *cause célèbre* but the 10 year commercial war waged by Greek city states upon Troy was not about her. It was the waterway. Three thousand years later, the Dardanelles became the main reason Russia wouldn't quit the *World War* when it went badly against them in 1917. The straits were promised to them by the British and French who often guarantee much but seldom deliver. Russia never got it. For the folks in Istanbul this new war in 1914 was just another one of many. The Ottomans had recently lost a series of *Balkan Wars* (1912-13) that drove them out of Europe. They had one small foothold there in a place called *Thrace*. They still own it, the last remnant of their once extensive lands in Europe. Thrace was formerly inhabited by the Thracians who didn't call themselves that, but the Greeks did (*the Independent Thracians*), which is how we come know about them. Conquered by Alexander (335 BC) they served with him, later the Romans, and then came the Bulgarians who own some of it and want the rest of it. In 1352 AD Thrace and the Bulgarians were overrun by the *Ottoman Turks* who were headed north to Vienna. With the Turks on their way to conquer Europe they took Islam with them. They were only stopped when a Christian coalition of Hapsburg Germans, Poles and Lithuanians held onto Vienna in 1683. Driven back from there, they are left with only Thrace. *Bulgar* foreign policy aims at its conquest, along with that of *Macedonia* from whence Alexander set out on his way to India. But the Turks are still there in Thrace and have no intention of retreat.

The Ottoman Empire

The Ottoman Turks stayed in Europe for a long time and have in indelible stamp on places like Montenegro, Bosnia, Herzegovina, Serbia and Bulgaria itself, where they represent c. 10% of the population. The Ottomans were an empire modeled on Rome and had an imperial court ruled by the Sultan. Like Rome, the provinces governed themselves and paid taxes to the central government. Most Sultans were reasonable. Some weren't since the *Ottoman Sultan* ruled by whim and decree. That rule could be very brutal depending upon who he was. In the early days when a

Sultan died, the most ruthless of his possible successors rose to power by killing all the members of the dead Sultan's household. This was by design. Once there, a wicked Sultan like *Selim the Grim* (1512-1520) would have eight *Grand Viziers* (Prime Ministers) beheaded and 30,000 lesser officials lost their heads as well. There were no prisons in the Empire. The penalty for everything was either death or retribution. They were tolerant of all religions even though Islam and the word of God as transcribed by the Prophet Mohamed was the central tenant of their society. Their laws were not the deadly *Sharia Law*. Christians and Jews were not routinely tortured and brutally killed as they are in today's modern incarnation of the Islamic Empire. There were millions of Christians and Jews in the Ottoman Empire and they were all an integral part of it. Every one of them had to donate their 2nd son to the Sultan as a soldier, and they were taken at a young age to serve for life; as did all the soldiers of the Empire. Jews and Christians often became administrators. In this way they had a stake in the Ottoman Empire and pretty much like in Rome: if you paid your taxes and minded your own business, it didn't matter to the Sultan what you were. You could even build a synagogue, or a church, as long as it wasn't in the center of town ringing church bells and making a fuss trying to convert anyone (a crime punished by death). If a Christian or Jew committed an offense against another of their kind, the Ottomans left it up to them to settle the issue in their own tribunals. It was surely easier and much better to live in the Ottoman Empire as a Muslim but nobody was forced to do so. And it was too, easier to live as a Christian or Jew in the Empire than as a Jew or Muslim in Christian Europe. There; an early death often awaited you upon the whim of some local dignitary, or just as bad; a night ride by a band of drunken Cossacks looking to rape and murder some hapless Jews.

The Origins of the Turks

No one knows where the Ottoman Turks came from except that it was someplace far out east in western China or maybe Mongolia where some Turkic manuscripts were discovered in 1889 that date to the 11th century AD. Sometime around then the Turks began to migrate. Some went north to Siberia where they still live. Some went to Manchuria, while others headed west and settled in the rich and fertile lands of the Caucasus and Anatolia; or Turkey as it is now known. Some

Turks remained in China; the *Uyghur*, who are a subject minority in China. Years ago you could sometimes read about them attacking ethnic Chinese with knives and swords; people whom they regard as interlopers residing in their historical homeland. Now though, the *Uyghur* are often the unfortunate people that *Communist China* harvests internal organs from. More than a million of them are now interned in Chinese *re-education* camps. One thousand years ago, the migrating *Uyghur Turks* settled everywhere on a pathway between China and Turkey north of Persia, or Iran as it is called nowadays. Some of those places were later conquered by the Russian Empire and administered by its descendant, the *Soviet Union*. One of the reasons for the *breakup* of the old Soviet Union in 1989 was that the Russians who ran it didn't want to provide for the Turks in their union anymore. All that free and affordable housing, healthcare, food subsidies, energy, education and public transportation was a drain on the Russian economy. This was the difference between Soviet/Russian imperialism and that of the western powers: the West drew resources from the fringe but the Russians invested resources into the fringe. In the end, it was easier to just let economically disadvantaged Turkish provinces like Kazakhstan, Uzbekistan, and Kyrgyzstan go their own way, fend for themselves, and have their own *"republics"* that are now all depressed dictatorships.

The Wars of the Ottoman Succession

This too accounts for the present Turkish national agenda for the re-conquest of these regions. Present American foreign policy projects itself as if Turkey has no other interest than support of the American agenda. In fact, Turkish foreign policy is centered about the reconquest of the Turkish provinces of the old Soviet Union that lie to the east in the direction of the historic homeland. Their foreign policy also envisions a reconquest of Syria, Lebanon, Palestine and Iraq, regions that were all within the Ottoman Empire until 1922 when the temporarily victorious Europeans dismantled the Empire to their eventual sorrow. Right now, 2020, the Turks are moving south into Syria to re-conquer the Levant and have also invaded Libya, another former possession. This is why most educated Americans cannot grasp foreign affairs. They think that no other nation in the world has any agenda at all, except perhaps in relation to American needs. But American policy is not defined by its peoples but rather by its ruling elite; another term unfathomable to most Americans who incredibly believe that everyone is equal, or almost equal. They cannot grasp that their rulers are as unlike them as King David was to his ordinary subjects: dirt beneath his feet.

The Crimea

The Turks settled in what we now call Turkey and formed the core of the Ottoman Empire that was established by *Osman I* in 1299. Amazingly, using Islam as the central tenant of society, they subjugated an Empire that rivaled Rome and overran the capital of the Roman Empire, Constantinople, after a long Siege in 1453. It was not a wave of conquests but rather a population shift where the Balkans fell to the Turks before Constantinople did. At the height of their power at the gates of Vienna, they ruled Algeria, Morocco, Tunisia, Libya, Egypt, and Arabia, all of the Levant including Iraq and Syria, as well as the Balkans including Greece, Bulgaria, and Serbia. The Black Sea was their lake, hence their historical clashes and animosity towards Russia who took the Crimea, the jewel of the Black Sea, from them in 1783. Some present historical anomalies reveal themselves with the Russian reconquest of the Crimea in 2014. Crimea was never a part of Ukraine but only given to them by Nikita Khrushchev, a Ukrainian, in 1954 for administrative purposes. Americans cannot understand this, even though the situation is somewhat analogous to Texas; an erstwhile independent nation that once belonged to an utterly corrupt Mexico. Some Mexicans now sit quietly and patiently waiting for the *reconquista* of Texas by population shift.

Ethnic Cleansing

By 1900 it was all falling apart for the Ottomans as France had conquered North Africa and Christians reasserted their independence through various wars in Greece, Bulgaria, Romania and the Balkans. In this shift, a series of vicious race wars called *The Balkan Wars* (1912-13) broke out. These wars featured the unfortunate expulsion of Muslims on a massive scale: 400,000 of them were forced by the victors to leave their homes and emigrate to Anatolia, or Turkey as we now call it. This was nothing completely new. Muslims were also driven out of their ancestral homelands in the Caucasus Mountains by Russia's southward advance in the years preceding the Balkan wars. The names Azerbaijan, Georgia and Armenia emerge in the news as the fighting continues into the 21st century. What we see now is a reversal of these mass migrations as global banking interests seek the destabilization and destruction of Europe.

Libya was a nice place to live

By 1914 Egypt was also lost. The Empire essentially sold it because France and then later England wanted a canal at Suez. Significantly they were both willing to pay large bribes for it. That worked. Another blow came when Italy conquered Libya in 1912. No one knew there was oil there yet but the coast was very fertile in a nice Mediterranean climate rich in dates, nuts, olives and wine. There were also plenty of salt and other minerals too. The Italians could have lived peaceably with the natives but chose instead to brutally suppress them. They then lost Libya with a risky and short-sighted decision to attack British Egypt in 1940. They then lost all influence when Libyan *Muammar Khadafy* expelled the Italians after he took power in 1969. This was his biggest mistake as the Italians could have been a buffer against foreign aggression. Vito Corleone said; *Keep your friends close and your enemies even closer*. In the 21st Century, Gaddafi tried to mend fences with the Italians but it was too late. The Americans had Libya in their sights because he was a secular ruler who wanted to establish the *Gold Dinar*, a currency redeemable in gold. That was a threat to the United States. The *US Dollar* is not redeemable in anything except as an idea based upon American military might. The Americans also wanted Islamists to run Libya as a way of destabilizing it, and thus the entire region for their own ends. They brutally murdered Gaddafi in 2011 throwing the country into permanent chaos. That was the plan all along. Open slave markets now flourish there. The foolish Americans led by Hillary Clinton thought they would eventually subdue and control the Islamists and make Libya another American colony. They couldn't. Now Africans migrate by boat in an exodus across the narrows organized by the *European Union* that wants cheap labor to replace the more expensive and strike prone native whites. Their destination is, ironically enough, Italy; the erstwhile rulers of Libya. The destruction of the Italian nation and race is imminent. Most Italians begin to grasp their own eradication but without a real army they are disarmed and helpless.

The Young Turks

When 1914 began The Ottoman Islamic Empire was ruled by a group of reformers called the *Young Turks* who were mostly from the Balkans. They were led by fellows called *The Three Pashas*: *Mehmed Talaat Pasha* who was Prime Minister, *Enver Pasha*, Minister of War and *Ahmed Djmel Pasha* who ran the navy. Originally, in the flush of revolution in 1908, the *Young Turks* said they wanted to install a western style democratic republic. That was what most of the young, emerging political class wanted. But once they took power, they ruled by military decree. They ran into problems right away as Austria-Hungary annexed Bosnia-Herzegovina in 1908 and Bulgaria declared independence at the same time. Things weren't that bad under the Sultan's rule and the Empire thrived for 700 years on a policy of relative tolerance and low taxation. Newfound freedom from Ottoman rule didn't mean a better lifestyle for the masses either. When Bulgaria was unchained many of the locals reported that things got much worse; as the lax imperative of the Sultan was replaced with authoritarian decrees from the German princes who took over. Those snobbish brutes raised taxes to enrich themselves as soon as they could. The Sultan's government wanted taxes to be paid for sure, and woe onto a provincial governor who couldn't pay up. But other than that, the dozens of provinces that constituted the Empire ran themselves with little interference from Constantinople. The centralization was so lax, that when war began in 1914, Minister of War *Enver Pasha* found he had no maps of Syria and the Levant. It would have been best for the Ottomans had they remained neutral when *the World War* broke out. Many wanted to. But they were forced into a war they didn't want and got consumed by the fighting that eventually ruined Christian Europe as well. The Young Turks proceeded to wreck the Empire and led it into disastrous wars against Russia, France and England. They reversed the centuries old policy of religious and ethnic toleration through the Armenian, Greek and Assyrian genocides. All three Pashas came to a bad end:

Enver in combat in 1922 and the other two murdered by Armenian revenge squads in 1921 and 1922. Just because you sign a peace treaty doesn't always mean the war is over.

Armistice Day

We are still fighting the wars that the Young Turks started. The last five wars that the United States engaged were in Serbia, Iraq, Syria, Libya and Afghanistan; as well as interminable bloody skirmishes all over what was once the Ottoman Empire. Our modern social construction of reality tells us the *First World War* ended on November 11, 1918. The sociopaths that ruined the western world timed the end to be on the eleventh hour, of the eleventh day; the famous Armistice Day; still celebrated as a poetic melody after years of slaughter. Most people think the *World War I* ended that day. It didn't. The armistice only gave pause in France; but the war against German and Austrian children continued through a total starvation blockade. No matter to the winners though. They named it *The Great War* because the carnage was unprecedented. As the worldwide fighting continues to this day, civilian populations are the primary target as they always were, right from the get go. But we don't see it all as one war because our social construction of reality teaches us different. All the commentators, or most of them, tell us that the century of warfare that followed is but a series of different, unrelated wars. Primarily, the public cannot be allowed to know that western civilization is in a permanent war economy with apparently no way out. *The Great War*, they say, was long ago, and the media presents the war as one special event and so we accept that story as true. It becomes a consensus reality and anyone who disputes that, or any other social reality, is shunned and ridiculed. Yet when the same belligerents line up and begin fighting each other 20 years later, why is the continuation called *World War Two*, a different war? That war never ended either, as the fighting continued without a break in Asia, Africa and the Middle East with butchery that now includes biological weapons, poison gas, radioactive weapons as well as conventional bombing. We are in the midst of ongoing race war not only against poor non-industrialized indigenous peoples in Brazil, but also against advanced industrialized nations like Iraq, Lebanon and Syria; all now turned to rubble and chaos. It has reached the point where every nation on earth is now at war; either with a foreign *enemy* or else some internal threat deemed a foe. In some cases like the USA, the nation is mired in an extremely profitable external war against terrorists and an internal one against drug users and white Christians, incredibly defined as enemies of the state. What is even more amazing is that most Euro-Americans think this state of being, permanent war, is the normal human condition! This attitude took decades of cultural conditioning to manifest and promote, or as the Director of the CIA William Casey once remarked: *We will know that our disinformation is successful when the public has no concept of the truth.*

The Hundred Years War

When the war broke out in 1914 almost all the participants thought it would be short; six months at most. Very few foresaw a *Hundred Years World War* that would rage into the 21st Century. The original *Hundred Years War* (generally 1337-1453) was fought in the country we now call France. But *France* didn't exist then. The territory was a loose-knit confederation of duchies. The only unifying thread was that all the inhabitants spoke various languages all somewhat similar to the language we now refer to as *French*. This includes the country we now call *England* whose ruling elite spoke Norman French, while the inhabitants, who were under their thumb, spoke a colloquial language remotely akin to the language of Shakespeare, that is to say, a lingo essentially indecipherable to most modern speakers of the English tongue. Like now, the participants then didn't know that they were involved in a hundred years struggle. That series of wars was a dynastic dispute over who was or should be the King of France. This was difficult to discern because all the claimants spoke one sort of French dialect or another. It was all eventually decided when a young girl from Lorraine emerged who had a brain for war. She took command of an army paid for by one of the claimants to the throne. By the sheer force of her will she forged victory over the English claimants. This changed the course of European history forever and created the political structure we now see before us. The story of *Joan of Arc* is probably the most astounding one in the whole annals of western civilization precisely because it is so well documented by hundreds of witness who were called to testify at her two "*trials*." Most commentators go along with the notion that Joan had no real impact upon martial affairs except in morale. The direct testimony of her compatriots contradicts this; subordinate commanders who said quite unequivocally that she understood best among them the placement of artillery and the disposition of troops. And who can argue with the results? Surely one of the great geniuses in the thousand-year history of medieval agrarian civilization, Joan was a girl of nineteen able to cogently argue arcane points of theology with university Rectors intent to legally murder her as well as triumphantly command and maneuver an army in one of history's most remarkable campaigns. The evidence shows that while Joan was a paragon of chivalric and Christian virtue she could be as ruthless as any man in the storm of combat. Most of this is lost in modern history. But the results of her triumphs remain the eventual creation of the modern European national state system that is still in place and waging yet another *100 Years War*. However this war is a far more vicious and brutal one, unfortunately unleashed upon all of us in the summer of 1914.

Gerardus Mercator's Map

The modern world's history is determined by the very tiny continent of Europe, even though its landmass and population do not warrant it. Most westerners grow up with a Mercator projection map on their school room's wall. That map greatly distorts the size of Europe, and the USA, and makes them both appear much larger than they actually are. The two places are also at the center of the map and the rest of the world at the periphery. This is how a socially constructed reality subconsciously evolves. In fact the whole of Europe could neatly fit into the Sahara Desert, itself but a small part of Africa. Though tiny, Europe inherited much of the genius of Greek and Roman civilizations and the roots of those societies were entwined with Persian, Syrian, Iraqi and Egyptian culture. This gave European nations a cultural history of many thousands of years even though the countries that make it up have been nations for something less than 500; in the case of Germany and Italy, only 150 years. This great historical lineage gave Europe a firm basis in the past to confirm their hegemony over the rest of the world, notably Asia, Africa and the Americas. Europeans believed themselves to be superior to other cultures on the basis of their religion and the metallic weapons they used with unmatched brutality. Later on came a significant change in attitude when the Darwinian ethos triumphed. Very soon after the publication of *The Origins of Species* (1859) Darwin followed up with the lesser known *The Descent of Man, and Selection in Relation to Sex* (1871). This book first categorized some of the world's people as "*sub human.*" With this, Europeans approached life with a new core belief. Armed now with *steel and science* they came to see their superiority as inherently good; something *natural*. With Darwin's ideas as their guide, European notions of supremacy were based on scientific explanations. Their apparent dominance was not just a moral one solely centered upon Christian virtues. Those ideas were now scientifically rejected as superstition. European cultural superiority was to be centered upon the supposedly irrefutable discipline of *Genetics* and *Natural Law*. Quickly, they conquered the entire continent of Africa and all the Pacific island kingdoms. They established brutal economic torment over the inhabitants who couldn't grasp what hit them.

Science and Steel

Up until 1914 Europeans had done a bang up job, literally, of decimating the world's population to enhance their own greed: irrelevant of Darwin and science. Led by Spain and England they had pretty much wiped out the indigenous population of the Americas, Australia and New Zealand. In North America they left hardly anyone alive. That included the native buffalo species they replaced with dairy cows. European cows brought with them irreparable and disastrous environmental consequences. They are pollutant nightmares sold as a part of *global warming* to stoke more fear and taxes from an unwitting, hyper-drugged and shell-shocked society. The British also reduced the population of India by a few hundred million people through excessive taxation and starvation so as to completely rob that nation of its wealth.

THE PRESENT CALAMITY IN HISTORICAL PERSPECTIVE

The Opium Wars

In 1805 China and India were the world's two foremost economies. But with the wealth of those nations transferred to Europe through conquest, economic slavery, thievery and opium, they are now among the poorest. Most people don't give too much thought, nor is there any publicity about how the world's fabulously wealthy royal families get their loot. They steal it. All the jewels and landed estates are confiscated by their armed retainers; sometimes an armed private equity firm and other times the national army. In the early 19th century China had the world's leading economy. They exported the finest tea, silk and porcelain to the west and didn't need anything in return. The west had nothing to offer them. Nowadays they call this a 100% favorable balance of trade. The British wanted to export opium into China from India that was then a massive British owned slave labor colony. The Chinese said no. Opium addiction is destructive to humans as it dulls the body's self-defense instinct. People who are addicted to opium don't care if they or anyone else lives or dies. They cannot make rational decisions. This is why opioid drugs are now freely distributed in the USA. The Chinese knew this and outlawed it by penalty of death. When the British and French armies defeated China in the Opium Wars (1839-42, 1856-60) they forced the unwilling Chinese to allow internal opium markets. The highly destructive drug ruined the tightly structured and efficient Chinese social order. With their government unable to protect them, the Chinese people revolted in the bloody *Taiping Rebellion (1850-64)*. With disease and starvation factored in with mass killings, between 50 and 200 million people died, no one will ever know the truth. This event further destroyed traditional Chinese society. The opium profits went straight into the coffers of the German princes that ruled England and still do.

The Age of Imperialism

European civilization soon supplanted China and India. Meanwhile, Belgium raped and looted central Africa. Their agents murdered and enslaved ten million inhabitants of an orderly agricultural society that threw the Congo into the chaos that still reigns. The French and Italians did the same in

North Africa, while Indonesia was left to the Dutch and Southeast Asia to the French. These were old cultures with rich historical traditions. They were simply not prepared to deal with European ruthlessness and barbarism. There is no need to cite all the hundreds of sources about these atrocities as they are multitudinous and unimpeachable. What the Europeans had wasn't any kind of intellectual or moral pre-eminence but rather an industrial base that gave them more guns and ammo than any of these essentially agrarian societies could ever, or would ever, wish to acquire. To enforce their claims of racial preeminence, an incredibly powerful and advanced military machine was created. Europe's industrial might and scientific expertise was now directed towards war and killing rather than peace: plunder instead of trade and economic growth. Machine guns and large caliber rapid fire artillery with exploding TNT cartridges meant that the war engine was now the most devastating in history. In 1914 though, the Europeans, through pride and arrogance, directed the murder machine away from their colonies. Instead they unwisely turned it upon themselves.

Alliances

General George Washington , who never bought nor sold a slave, was the first President of the USA and politically the smartest guy in a room full of smart guys. He warned against foreign *entangling alliances* and for a long time the USA did so. However, it now finds itself, amazingly, in military alliances with over 60 countries around the world. Any American with even half a brain might ask what a defensive alliance with tiny Estonia, which lies 6000 miles away, might do for the United States. The answer is nothing; except as a launching pad for an attack upon Russia, the latest contrived and demonized foe. The situation in 1914 was equally grim for Europeans. There were a number of formal alliances and other natural alliances that bound their nations together. Because they shared similar foreign interests, the Ottoman Empire had such a natural alliance with England. They were both in eternal conflict with Russia. They had fought with England against the Russians in the *Crimean War* in 1854: scene of the famous *Charge of the Light Brigade.* Ever onward, British and Ottoman policy sought to limit Russian expansion that most often came at the expense of them; like in the *Crimea* which was lost by the Ottomans to Russia in 1783. They make fine sparkling wine there in the world's best climate. That was a big loss for the Ottomans and a ripe treasure for the Russians; not to mention a naval base that controls the Black Sea. That base, Sevastopol, was a key German objective in 1941 and an American one in the 21st Century through neo-Nazi Ukrainian proxies.

The Russian Empire parts with Alaska

With no more eastern lands to conquer Russia sold Alaska to the Americans. They feared the British Empire in Canada would expand westward and easily take it from them in the event of war. American President Andrew Johnson and his Secretary of State (foreign minister) William Seward liked the idea and negotiated a treaty to buy *Alyaska* or *Alyaksa*. The Americans renamed it. The Russians took an American check *in lieu* of gold for 7.2 million dollars. Their eastern flank now secure, Russia's great aim was surely India. This was England's most valued and exploited colony; the one that made England the richest nation in the world, and India the poorest. England's aim was to keep Russia bottled up in the Black Sea and away from warm water ports with access to the Atlantic Ocean. With Turkey in control of the Bosporus waterway and Constantinople, they did. Since Turkey wanted large swaths of Russia for their own, the natural alliance with England made sense for both. Unfortunately for the Ottoman Empire, the Young Turks chose to wage war against England in 1914; a serious mistake in policy that cost them most of their empire and their lives.

Battleships

There is always money to be made from war; lands to loot and plunder, and this formed the basis for historical or classical imperialism: like that waged by the Greeks and Romans way back when. *But in modern times, and this makes modern imperialism different from classical imperialism: most money is to be made from the industrialization of war; the production of vast stores of complicated and expensive articles of destruction with the profits lodged in an international banking system.* Modern shipbuilding was a key part of this system and still is; those nuclear submarines and attack carriers cost more than the nation's entire educational and infrastructure combined. In 1905 England invented a new kind of battleship; one that had 3 times the firepower of all other existing *men o' war*. Basically *HMS Dreadnaught* made every other battleship, and the fleets that had them, obsolete from one day to the next. Everybody that could afford a *Dreadnought type battleship* wanted one, including the Ottomans. Brazil wanted some too, and Argentina and Chile as well; so that the three of them could fight out wars against each other for lands still in dispute. They all paid England enormous sums to build them big-gunned battleships. British banks gleefully obliged and lent the South Americans the money to buy them. It's a racket. The Ottomans did likewise when they lost *Tripoli* (Libya) in 1911-12. They couldn't get troops there to defend the place on account of the Italian navy. They had to send reinforcements overland through Egypt by car! *Mustafa Kemal Atatürk* who would later be the first President of Turkey, as well as Enver Pasha both made the trip by automobile. Those fellows were patriots who didn't shirk from their duty. To get out of this mess they later organized the purchase of two fine and expensive ships from England. This created a mini-battleship race in the Black Sea as the Russians also felt they needed to keep pace. A major problem arose when England confiscated the ships before the Turks could take delivery. The war with Germany was paramount and the canny *City of London* bankers pocketed the Turkish cash as booty. This really riled up the people of the Ottoman Empire as the ships were partly paid for by subscription: school children had sacrificed their lunch money, women gave up their jewelry and sold their hair, ordinary people donated what little gold and silver they had to help pay for the two battleships. The ships quickly became an issue of national pride. At the time of the confiscation, the Empire was still neutral. Winston Churchill called the shots as First Sea Lord and decided that two battleships had more worth then the entire Ottoman Empire. What a fool. Ordinarily, England had no strategic need for the Ottomans. But with them allied with Germany in a major war against Britain's other allies, this turned out to be a big problem. Russia's massive military machine needed logistical support. Germany stood in the way. The best way through was the Turkish controlled Dardanelles. Churchill and the dimwits around him couldn't see through this when all they needed to do was read a map.

Berlin to Baghdad

At the same time Germany was also on a naval building splurge. One of their battleships, the *SMS Goeben*, technically a battlecruiser, but basically a fast steel armored ship with big guns, was on patrol in the Mediterranean. When war broke out between them and England two English battlecruisers tried to intercept. The Germans escaped them at full speed with quite a few boiler-men dying from heat exhaustion. They steamed into Constantinople; an event known as *The Pursuit of the Goeben and Breslau*. At this point in time the Empire was still neutral. But the Young Turks were influenced by German military discipline and also by years of German goodwill to the Empire. That included the attempt to build the famous *Berlin to Baghdad Railroad*; begun in 1903 and finally completed in 1940. When the *Goeben* and *Breslau* steamed into Constantinople, the Young Turks greeted the Germans as heroes. A wise Sultan would have confiscated both ships, placed the German commanders under house arrest and awaited developments. Instead the Young Turks saw the German ships as replacements for the battleships stolen from them by Churchill. By this time, the Turkic rulers decided that Germany offered the best option as an ally if the path to war was chosen; and it was. Of all the belligerents Germany was the only one that didn't want a piece of the Ottoman Empire for themselves; the French eying Syria and Lebanon while the British were getting ready to annex Iraq and Bagdad. Souchon sortied with the consent of War Minister Enver Pasha and Naval Minister Ahmed Pasha. He proceeded to bombard Russian ports in the Black Sea, thus bringing Russia into the war against the Empire. This then dragged Russia's allies, England and France, into war against the Ottomans. They too declared war. Russia and her two allies had been fighting Germany since the beginning of August. But the Ottomans managed to stay neutral until Souchon's sortie on October 29th. Had the Empire remained neutral, the reconquest of the historic homeland might have been possible after revolution threw Russia into disarray. Since Russia had no real historic claim to these lands, and it is evident now that they don't really care too much about them, the history of the world might have taken a very different turn had an intact Ottoman Empire expanded to the borders of China. Instead they went down to ignominious defeat with the Germans.

Natural Alliances

England's other natural alliance was with *The German Empire*, conquered and ruled by the *Kingdom of Prussia* and the Prussian Army. England had the world's greatest navy and Prussia had the world's best army. The ruling elites of both were all Germans; hence it was an alliance made in heaven. When General Washington defeated a Hessian brigade at Trenton in the *New Jersey Campaign* (1776-77) they wore red uniforms and were an integral part of the English Army. Prussian King *Frederick the Great* called it *the greatest strategic campaign of the Age*. That's because the American victory at Trenton and the subsequent Battle of Princeton made the enemy positions on the Delaware River untenable. England had no choice but to surrender New Jersey and retreat to New York. Woe onto any *Loyalists* who had revealed themselves when New Jersey first fell to the British Army. The American Revolutionary War was very dirty albeit strongly sugarcoated. The New Jersey Loyalists lost all their possessions and worse. Later on, England and Prussia allied to defeat Napoleon at Waterloo in 1815. They had nothing to fear from each other until Germany/Prussia stupidly embarked on a battleship building program that directly threatened England's naval superiority. Germany's naval building program was not without reason. England threatened blockade when Germany thought to support South African Boers who had stymied England in a series of wars. But were the Boers, whom the Prussians considered *ethnic Germans*, of a vital national interest to the ruling Prussian Army? No, they were not in the least, and the decision to build fast battleships that endangered England was not in Prussia's interest either. But it was in the interest of bankers and capitalists who now had a voice in what was no longer a feudal agrarian Prussian kingdom in Eastern Europe, but rather a modern German industrialized national state that bordered on France. Soon, France and England found they could not compete with German industrialization either. Both of them ran slave labor empires that relied on cheap natural resources from the periphery of their empires and selling back to the fringe shoddy manufactured goods that the slaves were forced to buy. India, for example, was England's richest slave market right up to Indian independence in 1947. Germany's market was in the industrialized world. To succeed there they needed to produce the high quality goods that neither England nor France could and never would manufacture. Who but a fool buys a British or French automobile? Whosoever buys an English kitchen appliance, tool or automotive part? A French camera or television set? No practical person does. Nobody does. This drove the two slave empires into the welcoming arms of each other. They both found themselves nationally allied for the first time in their history; against the new Germany whose eventual destruction they aimed for.

The Westphalian System

The event that triggered the war was the well known assassination of the heir to the Austrian throne by Serbian nationalists on June 28, 1914. This precipitated the infamous *July Crisis* where the major war powers of Europe tried at first to avoid war while at the same time threatening it with all their might, especially Austria, the offended party. Europeans had been very busy destroying native populations around the globe. But they fought only one major war among themselves since the *Thirty Years War* (1618-1648). *The Thirty Years War* was yet another dynastic war guised as religious conflict to inflame the passions of the ordinary folk into incredible atrocities. Up until *the World War*, the *Thirty Years War* was the most violent and destructive in European history. It is still one of the most brutal in the whole history of humankind. The cause of the war was a schism in Christianity when northern Europe broke from Roman Catholic rule. They would no longer allow Rome to drain their economies of precious metals through the fake *sale of indulgences*. Medieval European agrarian society was a strictly ordered, self sustainable culture that was the highest expression of Christian values. Spirituality had a major influence on all decisions; from everyday life to affairs of state. Its people were extremely devout and truly believed that by making contributions in gold and silver to Rome; they might lessen, or even end, the pain and suffering of their dear departed relatives whose souls were in torment on the edges of Hell in an awful place called Purgatory. But that was invented by the poet *Dante Alighieri* (c. 1300AD) and taken to be real. However it was, there was no question about an afterlife. The eternal nature of the soul and the promise of paradise was unquestionably this culture's social construction of reality and there was hard money to be made from it. Rome's pitchmen would proclaim: *When the coin in the coffer rings, the soul from Purgatory springs!* A number of priests, Martin Luther and John Calvin among them, saw through the scam and demanded that the payments cease. A war ensued that destroyed medieval agrarian Europe, ushering in the Age of Industrialization as the manorial system could not function anymore with millions of dead and displaced people who had nowhere to go. The death toll is unknown but was probably 10 million. The armies that ravaged central Europe *lived off the land* in that every village was fair game; livestock and valuables looted, men killed, women and girls raped, leaving the survivors with nothing to face the winter. The Swedish army destroyed close to 20,000 villages in central Europe alone. Their commander, Gustavus Adolphus, raped so many girls and women in central Europe that he is sometimes cynically referred to as *The Father of Europe*. His multitudinous red-haired descendants were often given, or took, the name Gustavson. This chaos went on for more than 30 years and the devastation was so immense that the European ruling elite decreed that no such war should ever be fought again. They didn't outlaw war, but determined among themselves that they weren't going to allow war to limit their lavish lifestyles. They set rules of behavior that limited war. Henceforth wars should and would only be fought with small professional standing armies that carried their own baggage train with them; civilians, who were the actual creators of European wealth, as confirmed by Adam Smith, were not to be harmed. This was known as the *Peace of Westphalia* after the treaty that ended the war.

The Treaty of Westphalia Today

Most people nowadays have never heard of the *Treaty of Westphalia* as it was signed in 1648. But our ruling elite know about it very well, and they want to finally destroy it, and its legacy, in the name of *Globalization* which is code for the destruction of national ethnic states. This from the NATO Secretary General in 1998:

> *Yet the Westphalian system had its limits. For one, the principle of sovereignty it relied on also produced the basis for rivalry, not community of states; exclusion, not integration. Further, the idea of a strong, sovereign state was later draped with nationalistic fervor that degenerated into a destructive political force. The stability of this system could only be maintained by constantly shifting alliances, cordial and not-so-cordial ententes, and secret agreements.*

This is cipher for entering into the era of *open borders*, the end of nationalism, and the radical eradication of the Caucasian race. We see this now in the massive Islamic infiltration and invasion of Europe and the United States. But in 1648 the ruling elite had other ideas and the Westphalian system introduced the notion of national sovereignty. They stressed the idea that national states should not interfere in the internal affairs of other states. This may seem self-evident today but remember at this point in time, 1648, the idea of a centralized national state was a new one. Yes, there were plenty of kings but often provincial nobles had more power than the king, especially when they presided over provinces rich in natural resources like wine. This was the case when Joan of Arc began her campaign to free '*France*' from the English claimants. Only after Joan's murder in 1431 did the king she crowned gain national power when his armies subjugated the rich province of Normandy from the English. When he finally possessed this populous treasure and the rich provinces around it, the French "*king*" took the first step in ruling the nation we now call France. By the beginnings of the *Thirty Years War*, France was a nation in the modern sense of the word, as was England, Sweden and Spain. They all proceeded apace to loot central Europe; a place referred to as the *Holy Roman Empire* or as one commentator famously pointed out: *It was neither Holy, nor Roman nor an Empire*. It was however a very prosperous land and the major powers looted it until there was no more blood and wealth to be squeezed out of it. *The Peace of Westphalia* ensured that this kind of invasion should not recur. War would be limited by an agreement among the major powers not to allow free-booting brigades to ravage the land. The armies after 1648 would be small national armies with massive attached baggage trains that allowed national states to wage war but in a different kind of way. Henceforth war would be fought with formal non-destructive sieges over provinces like Silesia, rich in coal and iron; that would fuel the German war-machine in the coming World War centuries later. Prussia occupied Silesia from Austria, another German state, in a series of wars in the 18th century. The Austrians have had enmity against the Prussians ever since and the Austrian Empress Maria Theresa sent her daughter Marie Antoinette to marry the French dauphin even though the poor girl was head-over-heels in love with the court piano player Wolfgang Mozart. Maria Theresa thought this marriage would ensure an alliance with France against the Prussians and for a while it did, even though poor Marie would lose her head to the mob. But the Austrians were never able to retake Silesia which is now in Poland after the Germans stupidly lost it through catastrophic defeat. The idea of an Austrian alliance with France would get another Austrian prince killed when Crown Prince Rudolf was assassinated in 1889. He was keen to abandon Prussia and retake Silesia too. Like many political assassinations, Rudolf's death was sold as a *"suicide."* The last Austrian *Empress Zita* was quite adamant that Rudolf was murdered for political reasons. By then though, in 1989, she had lost her crown 70 years before and nobody was listening to her and hardly anybody cared either.

Napoleon goes to Divorce Court

The Westphalian system worked well for 144 years until another French fellow with a genius for war named Napoleon Bonaparte singled-handedly brought this system to a halt. The French armies he commanded conquered most of Europe by living off the land and carelessly impoverishing civilians. This allowed the French to move quickly as they out maneuvered one opponent after another that were still fighting the old way; dragging along baggage trains. Napoleon's star was ascendant until France's enemies caught on to his methods. But he was on top for awhile and crowned himself *Emperor by conquest* in 1805. This didn't go over real well with the old ruling elite who based their political power not only on conquest but also upon exclusive bloodlines that still determine the nature of the ruling elite in Europe and America. When you see some international bigwig getting married always check and see who the ancestors are. They tell you *Prince Harry* is married to an American *"actress."* In reality she is a direct descendant of *John Plantagenet King of England* who conceded the *Magna Charta*. So, in actuality, the American *actress* has a stronger claim to the English throne than any of the current claimants. Napoleon too, tried to marry in by divorcing his beloved wife Josephine to wed Marie Antoinette's royal cousin. But he was a creature of battle, addicted to war and couldn't recognize any limitations on his personal power. Eventually they exiled and killed him. However it is, after Napoleon's final defeat by a coalition of European powers at Waterloo, there was another 100 year period of limited war in Europe. The leaders again stressed the importance of the Westphalian system at home, but with the added attraction of the extermination and exploitation of the rest of the world's population abroad to boot.

Victoria's brood.

Europe in 1914 was ruled by various royal families that grew rich through foreign conquest. Many of them were related to the British royal family named *The House of Saxe-Coburg-Gotha* and its queen *Victoria*. The English are primarily Germans that speak a Germanic dialect called English, which is one reason why *Deputy Fuhrer Rudolf Hess* flew to Scotland in 1941. But that came later. Another example was the German speaking Bulgarian monarchs who began squeezing the life out of their people from the moment they took over from the Sultan. The Russian ruler in 1914, Nicholas II, was Russian for sure, but his mother was related to Victoria. When the English queen parceled out her vast genetic inheritance, *Nicolas II Tsar of all the Russians* got the runts of the litter. Nicky was, unfortunately and for all intents and purposes, quite literally a moron in charge of an enormous Empire. He came to be known as *Bloody Nicolas* after a few thousand peaceful marchers, women and children mostly, all begging for food and work, were gunned down by his Guards. That day is remembered as *Bloody Sunday*. But now, the *Russian Orthodox Church*, desperate for relevancy, tells us that Nicky is a *Saint in Heaven!* Bloody

Sunday precipitated the *Russian Revolution of 1905* which was also murderously suppressed by Nicky's thugs. This was but nothing compared to the slaughter Nicky unleashed in 1914 with his cousin, *German Emperor Wilhelm II*, who was a little smarter than him but not by much. Both decided that a general European war was the answer to a minor diplomatic dispute. The fools ended up losing it all and they had a lot to lose as Nicky, whose family owned Poland, was the richest man in the world.

The Origins of War 1914

Defeated Germany was blamed for the outbreak of war in 1914. That was the verdict of the *Treaty of Versailles*, written by the victors in 1919, and the subject of vigorous debate ever since. Certainly Austria, German speaking, and allied with Germany, fired the first shot from a river gun-boat upon the Serbian capital Belgrade on July 28th. But the Germans told them to go ahead and the Austrians surely would not have, had the Germans remained calm. But they too wanted some sort of war. Germany was a new nation, created in 1871 when an older eastern German nation subjugated a number of free western German states and cites, among them Bavaria, Saxony, Hamburg, Bremen, and 21 others. Prussia forced them to join into confederation with themselves. Many commentators, thoroughly ignorant of history, will often say *Prussia was a part of Germany*. It was the other way around as the *Kingdom of Prussia* ruled the German nation. That kingdom became *The German Empire* and the *King of Prussia* became the *German Emperor*. His capital city and main source of power was no longer *Konigsberg* (now *Kalinagrad*) but further to the west in Berlin; closer to the rich coal and iron fields in western Germany and eastern France. This new nation had superb resources in coal and iron ore they made into the best guns and ammo; with a few notable exceptions like the French 75 mm rapid direct fire field gun, the British *Lee Enfield* rifle and the Russian *Mosin-Nagant M1891* rifle that is still in use. The Germans had the most plentiful weapons anywhere in the world and an old winning military organization centered upon brutal and unquestioned discipline. They also wanted war in 1914 with many of them, both among the ruling elite and the people as well, convinced that war was a *"biological necessity.*" War, they convinced themselves, was part of a cleansing and racially purifying experience; in fact an indispensible means to ensure the triumph of "*natural law in the struggle for existence.*" These are all ideas from Malthus, Darwin and the Eugenics movement: an intellectual approach to life that hasn't gone away. The need for war was stressed by authors like *Friedrich von Berhardi* who had chapter headings like "*The Duty to Make War*" "*The Right to Make War*" and "*Germany's Historic Mission*" in his best-selling *Germany and the Next War* (1912).

The German Austrian corset

In 1914 the German Army was the best in Europe. They were so tough they should have gone it alone. They chose instead to shackle themselves, a metaphor often used to describe this corset, into an alliance with the Austro-Hungarian Empire, the so-called *Dual Monarchy*. There, the *Emperor of Austria* was also the *King of Hungary* and he ruled them both. Austria had a large but completely undependable army made up of 10 subject nationalities each speaking their own language. Only German and Hungarian were the official languages. Within this army, often only the officers spoke German but the men spoke and understood only other languages like Ruthenian, Polish or Italian. The men were then asked to fire upon enemy troops who were sometimes of the same ethnic background as they; all desiring liberation from the Austrian yoke. It didn't work very well and after a few months of war, Austria's army was smashed, incapable of ever again undertaking offensive actions without German help. They eventually tried to quit the war but were afraid of German conquest and thus went down to defeat with them. Austria was then torn asunder by the victors in the *Treaty of Saint-Germain-en-Laye* in 1919 while Hungary was pillaged by *The Treaty of Trianon* (Marie Antoinette's private palace grounds). All were signed near Paris, capital of the victors in 1920.

From whence came the Huns

We might too pity the Hungarians. Like the Turks, no one quite knows where they came from or when. It was somewhere out east, perhaps out in the Ural

Mountains. *German Epic Poetry* suggests that Attila was the original *'Hun'* who occupied the Hungarian Plain and settled there, *c. 700 AD*. Modern scholarship disputes this on little evidence. Fairly recently, in 1700 or so, it was discovered that *Hungarian* is related to the *Ugric* which includes *Finnish* and *Estonian* and well as hundreds of languages in the Siberian Plain. The Hungarians, whose language is the only non-Indo European language in central Europe, settled in the fertile plain that bears their name. They are protected by the Carpathian Mountains to the east and natural alliances with the Germans to the west and north. Both the Germans and Hungarians found each other's friendship in mutual protection against the Slavs and Romanians to the east and south. Rather than resist the Hapsburg Germans, the Hungarians chose to have a privileged position within the Hapsburg monarchy as the largest nation therein. When the Germans went down to defeat in 1918, the Hungarians went down with them and also in 1941-1945 when they went along for the ride once more. Despite it all, they remained steadfast allies with Germany until a feminized and neutered German nation opened its borders to millions of Islamic intruders in the 21st century. Hungary was occupied by Ottoman invaders from 1541 to 1699 and still has the scars. When Angela Merkel's Germany surrendered and lost sovereignty to the invaders, Hungary finally broke ranks with them for self-protection and gave battle without them. Now a new enemy, the globalist European Union, seeks Hungarian destruction and extermination.

The Architect of the Apocalypse

Back in 1914 when the war began, had Germany gone it single-handedly, the history of the 20th century might have been different. Through a series of diplomatic stupidities they found themselves isolated between Russia, a country with the world's largest army, and France, a country with an army just as large and battle worthy as their own. Germany had an expansionist clique that sought colonies abroad in Asia and Africa as well as lands to the east; especially all of Poland that was the private possession of the Romanov family. Poland was undoubtedly a grand prize and German armies did eventually take it early in the war. But the Poles have had the last laugh; swallowing up East

THE PRESENT CALAMITY IN HISTORICAL PERSPECTIVE

Prussia, Silesia and Pomerania in 1945 or about 1/3 of Germany after centuries of being terrorized by both the Germans and the Russians. However in 1914, instead of aiming at Poland and the Ukraine, Germany might have better targeted Austria itself; whose people spoke German and whose ruling family, the Hapsburgs, could have been easily deposed and gladly sent to live in some remote castles and estates with large pensions: a piece of cake they took in 1918 as the victors didn't put a noose around their necks as they should have. The Germans did eventually conquer Austria in 1938, but instead of settling in and defending their *Reich*, both in 1914 and in 1940-41, the Germans chose to take on Russia with all its might and France too with no clear and easily attainable war aims. That led instead to their destruction and dismemberment. To get out of this mess in 1914; caught between two hostile powers, Germany chose to ally with Austria-Hungary and developed a war-plan called *The Schlieffen Plan*. How they figured an independent Austria-Hungary would be an asset is beyond anyone's reason. Austria's commanding General was *Conrad von Hotzendorf*, who would send 500,000 men to their death (dead & missing) and count another 500,000 wounded in the initial campaigns both against Russia to the east and Serbia to the south. They got defeated in both and lost one million men in a few months. Austria's entire professional army was wiped out in probably the single greatest military and social disaster in recorded history. Still Conrad didn't lose his job. In comparison and retrospect, remember The United States suffered national trauma losing 60,000 men over 10 years in Vietnam; while in this war nations were often losing 10,000 men per day! Germany depended upon this mad fellow Hotzendorf to cover its eastern flank all the while he was obsessed with war against anyone within reach (Serbia especially) and a married woman named *Gina von Reininghaus* to whom he wrote over 3,000 letters in the period 1907-1915; which comes out to more than one per day, some of them more than 60 pages in length! This is the man who in a few short months, sent one million men and an Empire into ruin and has been aptly named *The Architect of the Apocalypse*. He should have been hung as a traitor early on. On the contrary, he was instead habitually protected and eventually ennobled despite the blood of a generation on his hands. That might make any rational person wonder, you'd think, what the true object of the war was all about. But it doesn't.

The Schlieffen Plan

The other leg of Germany's strategy was *the Schlieffen Plan*; a war plan that somehow and insanely became a national obsession. Count von Schlieffen was a West Prussian who was Chief of the German General Staff in 1905. He was faced with the dilemma of a two front war; Russia in the east and France in the west. Russia was then also beset with difficulties because it was very large, difficult to govern and like many modern nations that embarked upon industrialization, beset by poverty in the cities. Unfortunately, the ruling elites of industrialized nations have, with a very few exceptions, never been known for compassion and righteousness. *The Nazarene* talked about this in metaphor. But the Russian Army was huge, known as *The Russian Steamroller*; a figure of speech for an advancing mass of troops that may not have the best weapons or leadership but would overwhelm all opponents through sheer mass and weight of shot. In 1904 Russia got the idea that a short victorious war would straighten things out internally. In the same way that American college football teams schedule early season patsies to beef up morale, Russia picked a war with tiny Japan thinking it would be an easy win. They miscalculated and instead got badly beaten as the enemy could fight; something the Americans would find out in 1941-42. In this environment, with the bulk of Russia's army in Asia, their fleet annihilated by Admiral Togo's navy at Tsushima, and beset by revolution at home, Schlieffen proposed a war plan to defeat the French in 6-8 weeks with 90% of the German Army attacking them through Belgium. While this went on, he would give up East Prussia to the Russians. He reckoned that after the inevitable defeat of France, the Russians would be easy meat. Risky business this was, but less so for Count von Schlieffen the West Prussian who had no stake in the rich and beauteous forests and lakes of East Prussia, the ancestral homeland of Germany's ruling class. Perhaps it was the audacity of it all that appealed to the Germans but in fact, when it came time to carry out the plan in 1914, they wavered and weakened the right wing marching though Belgium to protect the fabulous eastern *Heimat*. This ensured victory over the Russians in August-September 1914 but allowed the French to escape the fate envisioned for them. The Russians were forced to retreat from East Prussia but they would return thirty years later and it would be forever.

THE PRESENT CALAMITY IN HISTORICAL PERSPECTIVE

Nothing comes with a guarantee. I don't care if you're the Pope of Rome, President of the United States, or even Man of the Year—something can always go wrong   Loren Visser

Another problem with the *Aufmarsch* through Belgium was British intervention. Great Britain is a country made up of one Anglo-Saxon, or Germanic nation (England). They rule what is left of three Celtic nations, Ireland, Wales and Scotland, not including the annihilated Cornwall after the English killed them all. That's another genocide nobody talks about. While the remaining Celtic nations sent many troops to fight in the war for England, it was England, centered in the world's banking city of London, which called the shots. They had the world's largest fleet and an empire that covered a quarter of the earth and many of those nations, Australia, Canada, India, and New Zealand, amazingly sent over millions of men to fight and die for the English; probably because the English helped them wipe out their own native populations. In the case of India and because poverty was eating the country whole as it is today, army life was better than starving in the streets. With lots of cannon fodder, the English made clear to the Germans that they wouldn't allow them to take over Belgium without a fight. Not that England or London cared about Belgium (they didn't) but because they wouldn't allow the German Fleet anchorages on the English Channel from whence they might sortie freely into the Atlantic Ocean. More importantly they were extremely worried about what Europe would look like with France prostrate and with no allies whatsoever. So while the British Army was initially small, 80,000 men or so, compared to more than a million-man force at the outset for the Germans, they could shoot very well. England's entry and London's gold insured a long war through naval blockade. Since Germany thought the war would be short, they weren't worried about this. Obviously they should have been, considering that, as once observed by Robert Burns; the best laid schemes of mice and men often go askew.

What is an army?

Back in the day of the *Thirty Years War*, a nation had one army. In 1914 they fielded many. A numbered army, or field army, is a military organization that is self sustaining. The largest Roman organization was the *Legion*; of about six thousand men with attached cavalry, artillery and light infantry. At the Battle of Cannae, where Hannibal's troops wiped out eight Roman legions, their losses included 80 Senators and 30 Tribunes. In those days, the ruling elite actually fought for the Republic. That's when Rome was great. The peacetime strength of the German Army in 1914 was 700,000 men expanded to 1 ½ million when the reservists were quickly called up. They moved west against France with seven field armies, numbered 1 through 7 from top to bottom with 1st and 2nd Army allotted the main role in the sweep through Belgium into France. Each army had all the men at arms needed to fight a battle on its own with requisite cavalry, artillery, engineers, signal corps and infantry until help could arrive, a method invented by the Romans and perfected by Napoleon. This is the main argument against a currently fashionable idea that there was no Schlieffen Plan; that the German Army was really fighting a defensive war against the French. In this interpretation, the advance only turned out the way it did because the Germans kept winning a series of battles and just kept advancing like a snowball rolling downhill. Well then, why are 1st and 2nd Armies assigned all the toughest outfits in German Army in a sector where there is only the under-strength and weakly equipped Belgian Army? The plan was to outflank the enemy with an attack that was openly war-gamed in German maneuvers for many years. And if their plan was primarily defensive why leave *Ost Prussen* to be taken like low-hanging fruit?

Plan 17

The Germans moved against France with cavalry the day war was declared on August 1st and it all went awry right away. It is difficult to discern why they thought it was a sure thing. The French meanwhile had their own war plan called *Plan 17* and they allocated four armies to do the job with *V Army* northernmost, defending the Belgian plain. That force was quickly overwhelmed by German 1st & 2nd Army. The main French thrust, was carried out with I & II Armies; (the French numbering their armies with Roman numerals). They were down in the direction of Switzerland and aimed to retake *Mulhouse* (German *Mülhausen*). The French wanted the lost provinces of Alsace and Lorrain that had been snatched from them after their defeat in the Franco-Prussian War. That war was fought because the French wouldn't allow Prussian plans to conquer the rest of the free German states right up to the French border. When the French were defeated at Sedan in 1871 this gave Prussia free reign to do just that. They also annexed German-speaking Alsace as well. Ethnically German, Alsace had been incorporated into France by Louis XIV three centuries before. German nationalists wanted it to be part of a *Gross Deutschland*, or Greater Germany; an empire of all the Germans and not just some of them. This would remain a recurring theme in German history. The German Prime Minister Count Bismarck, casting his eye eastward, didn't want to annex the place at all. He thought, correctly, that it would create permanent enmity with France. But he was overruled by the military who wanted a forward base by which to fight France again just in case there was another war with them, thus insuring that there would be.

The Russian don't go along with the plan

Plan 17 and the *Schlieffen Plan* were exact opposites of each other: one called for the French to assault eastward, ultimately towards Berlin, while the German plan attacked southwestward towards Paris and the French rear. First of all, *Plan 17* gave up France's coal and iron reserves in northeast France. They wouldn't get them back until 1919. This was just too stupid but everyone thought they would win quickly and retrieve any lost territory. And it's not like these plans were secret. On the contrary, both sides knew the other's plan and rejoiced in it. They both felt the enemy's plan unattainable, and they were both right about this. The German plan failed because even though they had more than one million men at arms to do the job, the distances were just too great and the intangibles unforeseeable, like feeding millions of men and horses daily because horses can't pull artillery and feed on grass; they need oats. All of this is termed *friction* and operating on *exterior lines*. Germany would lose 16 million horses in the 1st *War-phase* (1914-18) and the French a like number. The poor creatures can't defend themselves. The one thing predictable was the Russian attack upon East Prussia. It came quicker then Count von Schlieffen thought. His cold calculations gave way to faintheartedness as new German commander von Moltke panicked and diverted 60,000 men and 300 guns eastward to thwart *der Russ*. It was too late to affect outcome out there, but plenty enough to insure defeat on the Marne River before Paris.

Attaque a'outrance

The failure of *French Plan 17* had nothing to do with force and distance and much more to do with hubris and stupidity. The Germans at least recognized the principle of firepower. Their rifles were much better than the unwieldy French *Label*. Their 120-man machine gun companies fired heavy weapons while their 30-man French counterparts fired lighter guns. Finally, the Germans relied on Krupp heavy cannons generally known as the *Big Bertha*, of which the French had few. This gave the Germans a decided firepower advantage. The French didn't care. Their philosophy was *Attaque a'outrance* (*fanatical attack*). After their loss at Sedan, the French war colleges looked for excuses and deduced that their soldiers lacked the requisite élan or fighting spirit. Naturally they didn't consider their decrepit general officers might also shoulder some of the blame. So *Plan 17* envisioned their men, clad in red pantaloons and bright blue shirts, cutting their way through German machine guns with reckless bayonet charges led by officers in white gloves and gold braid. In *praxis* however, German snipers picked off the easily discernible officers and Maxim heavy machine guns did the rest. The French did make some headway because most of the German strength was concentrated on their right wing marching through Belgium. Only a holding force defended Alsace on their left; the French objective. Even so, the holding force was made up of three separate armies each numbering over 200,000 men. Ever since the Thirty Years War, European armies had gotten larger and larger. A typical army in that war numbered 20,000 men. Napoleon's army at Waterloo in 1815 numbered 75,000 men and 250 cannons while the French 120,000-man army at Sedan was outnumbered by 200,000 Prussians and Bavarians. Now, in 1914, the Germans fielded seven armies in the west against France with one and a quarter million men while the French fielded an equal amount in five armies. It was a recipe for a disaster as the French attacked into southern Belgium's Ardennes forest and Alsace thinking the Germans elsewhere.

THE PRESENT CALAMITY IN HISTORICAL PERSPECTIVE

The elite Colonial Corps walks into a trap

They led with their best troops, among them *The Colonial Corps*, 35,000 men in two crack divisions; the *2nd & 3rd Colonials*. These were white guys and not colored men from the French colonies. The *3rd Division* got wiped out on August 22, 1914 which is an unremembered but bloodiest day of the entire war; until the fire-bombing and atomic blasts in 1945. France lost 27,000 men killed on that day on all fronts. The *3rd Division* marched up a narrow road into the heavily wooded *Ardennes Forest* in the morning mist with no recon. The locals told them the Germans were nearby. They had encountered German cavalry as well, but the 3rd went ahead anyway. It's called the *Battle of Rossignol* but it was a massacre. The high command told them the Germans were many miles distant because that is where they wanted and needed the Germans to be. The success of *Plan 17* demanded it! Reality collided with theory as German rifle fire and machine guns slaughtered the *3rd Colonial Division* in a deadly ambush. The victorious Germans then massacred the villagers of Rossignol for no other reason than they could. The other French attacks down into *Mulhouse* fared badly too. In one brief moment of clarity, the French commander-in-chief, Joseph Joffre, cancelled *Plan 17* and shifted his armies northward to blunt the German advance through Belgium and Flanders towards Paris. In the face of catastrophe he did not waver and saved France. His *shift* is named *operating on interior lines* in that as the front shortened for the French, they were better able to move laterally. The Germans, moving forward into enemy territory and *operating on exterior lines*, could only shift forces laterally with much more difficulty. Basically the French supply lines and road network got shorter while the German lines lengthened.

Big Bertha and Schlanke Emma

Meanwhile the Germans were having their own set of problems, the first of which was Belgian resistance. That wasn't supposed to be there. Like most gangster nations, the Germans got plenty upset when the Belgians thought they might defend their own territory. They had erected a series of forts along the border and the Germans attacked them with infantry without waiting for their *Big Berthas*. Gigantic disassembled 16.5 inch barrel width guns that weigh 50 tons are cannons that move slowly. They usually lag far behind the infantry. They had other big guns too, the famous Austrian 12 inch howitzer *Schlanke Emma* (Slender Emma) among them; as Germans like to name big guns after ladies. But they didn't get around quickly either and couldn't be lugged by trains in enemy territory. All these cannons were built when the Russo-Japanese war showed that big guns were needed to reduce modern fortresses. So without waiting for them, the Germans attacked steel reinforced concrete bunkers defended by machine guns and field artillery. They attacked with naked flesh because they were in a hurry. Any time military organizations rush ahead it usually results in disaster as George Custer, and many others, found out to their sorrow. At Liege those poor young fellows got torn apart. The men were asked to advance standing up in what was called a *skirmish line*, shoulder to shoulder and offering no effective fire as a German infantry advance depended upon artillery support. But direct fire field artillery was useless against modern bunkers. German soldiers advanced, uselessly shooting from the hip. Walking into enemy fire was how men advanced at Waterloo one hundred years before, when the foe was shooting single shot muzzle loaded muskets that had an effective range of 50 yards, if that. Even then, 700 well trained men arrayed in line could muster some very heavy firepower. Late in the day at Waterloo, when the Emperor Napoleon ordered his Imperial Guard forward, men that had never been defeated in combat were routed in a close-range fire fight that lasted 3 minutes. The French Guard lost a few hundred men but they were unable to stand up to the concentrated fire of British and Scottish muskets at close range. At Liege, up against machine guns, the German dead were piled so high, the men used their deceased companions for cover as one attack after another failed. Thousands of innocent German boys were murdered and their mothers in sorrow, all killed by commanders who couldn't wait for the big guns; even though the bulk of the German 1st Army simply by-passed the forts and weren't delayed at all. As retribution for resistance the Germans began to murder Belgian civilians by the thousands; old men, women and children mostly. They always seem to be the main targets when military organizations run amok. They also burned down the medieval city of Louvain with its fabulous library, for no military purpose whatsoever just to see it burn. Western civilization's enemy was now clearly defined and German barbarism would serve as a beacon for enemy recruitment throughout the war. Many nations are still afraid of them, which is why their imminent eradication is gladly awaited; even by some of their own people, especially and openly by German women.

The British Expeditionary Force stops 1ˢᵗ Army cold

The Germans were still on schedule. They had to be. They hadn't allowed themselves much time before Russian intervention would threaten *Ost Prussen*. Then they encountered another problem that wasn't supposed to be there: the British Army or, the *BEF*. The *British Expeditionary Force* was in the way! They would be famously evacuated from Dunkirk, 30 odd years later in the next go-round. This time they put up a better fight and the German *1ˢᵗ Army* wasn't expecting it. The BEF was a small army comparatively: 82,000 combat soldiers and 400 field guns and a small air force for recon. But the men were trained to shoot and they were all marksmen. In the BEF if you couldn't shoot you drove a wagon. They fired the light and reliable bolt action Lee-Enfield rifle with a 10 round clip. The average British infantryman could fire 20-30 *aimed shots* per minute. The Germans that attacked them at the Belgian city of *Mons* reported they were up against machine guns. It was just rifle fire. The BEF won the *Battle of Mons* but were forced to retreat when *French V Army* to their right was obligated to withdraw from *Charleroi*, the city Napoleon marched through unopposed on his way to Waterloo one hundred years before. The BEF withdrawal operation came to be known as *The Great Retreat* as the BEF departed under heavy pressure from German 1ˢᵗ and 2ⁿᵈ Army; fighting numerous rearguard actions along the way. The distance between Mons and Paris is about 135 miles and when the BEF got there they were ready to go home and leave the French to their fate. In a series of meetings, Joffre convinced his English counterpart, Sir John French, to stay and fight. Joffre begged and pleaded and brought Sir John to tears. On his knees, he rightly told Sir John that the fate of France and western civilization was in his hands. Sir John came through and turned his army around. Joffre had correctly assessed the situation and saw that German 1ˢᵗ and 2ⁿᵈ Army had not only separated, but also presented to the allied army their widely dispersed flank; leading Joffre to famously exclaim *"Gentlemen, the enemy offers us their flank!"* And indeed they had.

Dueling Scars

German 1ˢᵗ Army was commanded by *Alexander von Kluck* who had large dueling scars across his cheeks. Back then (and there still are German dueling Fraternities), Germans engaged in duels, not to the death but to draw blood. They would stand on small stools, face to face, a few feet apart; their eyes, nose and ears protected, and slash at each other's face with sabers until one or the other fell off his stool wounded. Salt and pepper were then thrown into the wounds and each contestant was then marked for life. There were some men who won every duel and had no scars but most did get one sooner or later, and von Kluck had plenty. Say what you want about those German fellows but they did have guts. The *1ˢᵗ Army* command was the most important one in the campaign because they were their best troops, *II, III, & IV Army Corps*, all Prussian veterans; 225,000 men and 900 guns. The *2ⁿᵈ Army* on their left was of equal strength; beefed up with the *Prussian Guard*, scarred by duels and itching for combat. They didn't know what they were getting into. They envisioned a grand battle where the French would be beaten, a few thousand men killed, and then they would all have stories to tell their grand children. Instead an entire nation and civilization was ruined; scarred emotionally and psychologically from a trauma that knows no end.

The OHL

The German high command was named *Oberste Heeresleitung*, literally *Highest Army Command*, or *OHL*. The Army's overall commander was *Helmuth von Moltke*, called *The Younger* because his uncle *The Elder* was the victor at Sedan in September 1870, celebrated as *Sedantag* (Sedan Day) until 1919 when the Germans didn't want to celebrate war anymore. Like most German officers, von Moltke's face was torn up from dueling, had an inferiority complex *vis-a-vis* his legendary uncle, was in poor health and prone to nervous breakdowns. At first

OHL was in Berlin and von Moltke had his first breakdown there. The Kaiser had an inkling that things might not go so well. He saw a way out of the mess and told von Moltke to halt mobilization. He was right, and the mobilization could have been halted. But von Moltke refused. His Majesty stormed out of HQ and said; *'Well now, you have your war!'* Moltke then collapsed onto his personal psychiatric couch and was *incommunicado* for three days. He had another mental collapse just as the *Battle of the Marne* was shaping up. It's hard to figure because only a few months before he was begging the Kaiser and his Chancellor Bethmann-Hollweg to launch a preventive war against Russia. *Hollweg* was so convinced about the danger posed by Germany's enemies that he decided not to plant any more trees about his estate near Berlin. After all, the Russian Steamroller would soon destroy it all! These fellows not only suffered from delusions of grandeur but were severely paranoid as well.

Friction

The situation was indeed out of control right from the get-go. As the attack progressed OHL was moved westward first to *Koblentz*, and then to *Luxembourg City* which is, even today, quite out in the middle of nowhere. From there OHL could only rapidly communicate with the 3rd, 4th and 5th armies closest to it. Those early radios had limitations. This became a problem because the German Army as a whole had only 35 radios *in toto*. Each army was expected to message OHL first on one wavelength; and then have OHL send another army the message on another wavelength. There was no provision for rapid lateral communication between armies except by courier. So von Kluck, way out there on the right, was pretty much on his own.

The Drive into France

After Mons, German 1st & 2nd Army pursued the *BEF* and *French V Army* relentlessly to the gates of Paris. They wiped out a number of small British units to a man. At the gates of Paris von Kluck faced a dilemma. On his left was *German 2nd Army*, commanded by *Karl von Bulow*. He was 70 years old and would suffer a fatal heart attack two years later. He got one now that disabled him for two days on the approach to the Marne. Both those fellows thought they were the main man in command of the primary thrust. After all von Kluck had the largest and best army in the field. But von Bulow had the *Garde Korps*: *1st & 2nd Divisions* of the *Imperial Guard* the best equipped outfit in the entire world. *The Garde* also had its own splendid heavy cavalry corps. But von Bulow began to lag behind 1st Army's advance that reflected the hard-driving von Kluck. Lateral communication between the two was by messengers on horseback. They had to ride through enemy territory with French cavalry patrols roaming about looking for trouble. Back home, the German newspapers were already calling the war a win; after all, it was only a month old and German armies were approaching Paris! But von Bulow knew something they didn't; he wasn't taking any prisoners, nor capturing enemy guns; things that usually happen when a defeated enemy retreats. Instead, von Bulow was faced with an adversary that was conducting an orderly withdrawal. He thus proceeded more cautiously than did von Kluck. A gap emerged between the two armies. The French could exploit this if they could drive a wedge between the two and then isolate one from the other. Then they could destroy them both piecemeal.

The First Battle of the Marne

By this time Joffre had reassembled the French Army to the north where it now outnumbered the Germans at the decisive point; one of the great feats of general leadership in the whole history of warfare. A new army, the *VI Armee*, under Ferdinand Foch, (who would eventually become Allied Supreme Commander), was beefed up by three crack African divisions. These were tough black African fighters from the desert who really liked a good scrap. Some of these troops were moved to the front in taxi cabs. They kept their meters running as everyone wanted to cash in and did. While the Germans dithered, the French counter-attacked. With the *BEF* they drove the Germans back and threatened the encirclement of von Bulow's army. Having finally gotten the war he was so keen to fight, von Moltke fell into a couch suffering from another severe neurological collapse. The fate of the German Army was then placed in the hands of the hitherto unknown *Lt. Colonel William Hentsch*. He was head of the Foreign Armies Department of the General Staff and became von Moltke's representative. Hentsch had to; since the commander hisself was now an unfortunate and prostrate quivering mass of incoherent flesh. Thus, incredibly, a Lieutenant Colonel assumed command of the German Army at the most decisive moment in its history. The BEF quickly crossed the river Marne. French VI Army also forged the river Petit Morin and both attacked eastward. This threatened the encirclement of both German *1st and 2nd Armies*. Bulow advised retreat and Hentsch agreed. Both von Kluck and von Bulow had simply lost their nerve. This happens all the time at every level of command. Moltke was fired and replaced by *Erich von Falkenhayen* who would run the show for the next two years. But the retreat to a more defensible position ensured the German Army's survival. Both armies tried to outflank each other in a running battle northward called *The Race to the Sea*. They couldn't do it, and 1914 ended with a stalemate in the west. It all evolved into a *European Civil War* that would eventually result in the eradication of the native races in their European homeland. But nobody could see that then.

Home before the leaves fall

The European powers gave way to war quickly because they all thought the war would be short and pretty easy. The general consensus was that the maintenance of million man armies in the field for longer than six months wasn't financially feasible. The *Balkan Wars* had been short and so too would this one. It was just another Balkan war; albeit one that quickly spread to France, Germany and Russia. The fact that the Americans were able to fight four years 1861-1865 slipped past them. The Americans managed to both finance their war and recover too. The Europeans would partially pay for it but never completely recuperate. The predictions of economic collapse in the short term were wrong. The international banking system found a way to pay for it all and still do with paper money. But the cost was the impoverishment the civilian population; the true wealth of nations. Most people were not enthusiastic about the war despite the many photographs showing cheering crowds in Berlin, Paris and other cities upon the declarations of war. For the fellows in the city the war seemed to be a good way to get out of the civilian jobs they subsisted on through long hours at low pay. But they soon saw that those old jobs were better than having their faces torn off. In the first four months of combat 150,000 Frenchmen between the ages of 18-23 would be dead. It was the same everywhere as, and this is also quite astounding: all the belligerents went on the offensive right from the get-go with the exception of Serbia. They wisely stayed on the defensive.

How you gonna keep 'em down on the farm?

People in the countryside weren't celebrating. They knew their young men would be asked to stride into hell and who then would harvest the crops? For the Germans, 3 ½ million Russian prisoners of war would eventually do that. This was the origin of the German reliance upon slave labor camps in wartime. Unlike later on, the Russian prisoners worked mostly on farms and actually lived better than German city-dwellers did. Almost all of those millions of Russians returned home healthy. But agricultural production still fell as the army kept ~~stealing~~ *requisitioning* farm horses to pull the big guns. Not only that, a unique situation arose. When millions of men stand-off shooting at one another for years, none of them are employed at home in any kind of productive capacity. *On the contrary, they themselves needed to be supported.* British coal miners rushed to join the army. Obviously life as a soldier had much more appeal than death in a black hole. In 1915 English coal production fell by 20%. The Germans solved this problem partially with slave labor. But Britain and France had to recall millions of men back to factory and munitions production. By 1918 more than one million foreign workers and slaves worked in German factories under brutal conditions. Women also began to work in war production and all this created social disruption. So how to keep society functioning? One way was to present the nation with *war aims*.

The Septemberprogramm

German social objectives were presented in a paper that clarified its war aims in a breathtaking and practically unimaginable pronouncement: *The Septemberprogramm*:

THE PRESENT CALAMITY IN HISTORICAL PERSPECTIVE

The general aim of the war is security for the German Reich in west and east for all imaginable time.

Issued a month after the war started, the German penchant for hyperbole quickly reached a fever pitch:

For this purpose France must be so weakened as to make her revival as a great power impossible for all time.

This sort of idea, that France, and presumably other countries like Belgium might be wiped off the map, or else crushed into a state of permanent subservience to the German Empire, was not only a direct violation of the *Peace of Westphalia* but lacked common sense. *Septemberprogramm*:

Russia must be thrust back as far as possible from Germany's eastern frontier and her domination over the non-Russian vassal peoples broken.

The Germans wanted to create *Mitteleuropa*, a central European free-trade zone dominated and controlled by them. Nor was the *Septemberprogramm* something that came out of thin air. It was a manifestation of *Pan-Germanism*; the idea that the German people (*das Volk*) were Europe's and the world's superior race. This gave the German Empire the natural right to unite all Germans and place all others beneath them in a hierarchy; with peoples like Hungarians, Romanians, Greeks and Italians near the top on account of their history and physical characteristics. Others, like Slavs, Jews and Poles were near the bottom and slated for deportation. Some of this program would include direct annexation into the Empire while others, like France and Russia, would be kept in permanent subjugation. This was also the major reason why a negotiated settlement to the war, after it had all gone terribly wrong, proved to be impossible. Germany wanted total domination and the supposed security that comes when all foes are conquered either militarily or economically. This is the kind of madness that currently afflicts the USA.

Mitteleuropa

After Germany's catastrophic defeat in 1945 the kern of these ideas remained and served as the foundation for the current *European Union*. Before that it was the *Common Market*. All these unions aimed at the exclusion of Great Britain and the London banking/monetary system. Napoleon's *Continental System* (1806-1812) aimed at the same thing. Thus we see the delayed acceptance of Great Britain into the *Euro System* and *Brexit* as the culmination of a perpetually German organized continental war against the English and their still functioning world-wide empire. This, and French enmity after their betrayal by the English in 1940, always prevented English inclusion into any general European union. Thus too, we see the English maintenance of the *Pound Sterling* rather than acceptance of the *Euro* currency system now dominated by Germany. In 1914-18 Germany actually conquered everything it needed for the creation of Mitteleuropa. If they were smarter they might have held it.

Bavarians can't shoot straight

In the popular imagination the German Army was monolithic. It was rather made up of various German nationalities like Bavarians and Saxons all of whom had been recently conquered by Prussia. They had different attitudes about war and soon grew tired of it. Austria and Hungary also found themselves in death struggle they hadn't counted on and eventually Bulgaria and the Ottomans joined them to their own dismay and sorrow. They were called *The Central Powers*. Italy was first allied with them but chose to switch to *The Allies* as Austria had some ripe prefectures that Italian nationalists wanted. The British, as they usually do, promised them lands that they didn't own. Since those juicy provinces belonged to the enemy, the British and French freely and gratuitously promised them to Italy. But neither block could break through to victory as the destructive power of rapid-fire weaponry was too much for human beings to withstand; something native peoples around the world could have told them about. At first the men dug holes in the ground for protection and this eventually evolved into elaborate systems of trenches. In the years of trench warfare that followed, duty opposite Saxons or Bavarians would present a much more leisurely life style for the adversaries. There were fewer snipers, fewer raids, and fewer bombardments than opposite the more rigorously disciplined Prussians. Whatever comforts the combatants found were few however. The French were determined to retake those areas of France that Germany conquered in the initial phase of the war. Supported by the British, they launched one suicidal attack after another. They all failed against a foe armed with lethal rapid fire weapons and protected by barbed wire. This led to Joffre' replacement in late 1916 as he just couldn't get it; but neither could anyone else. Just getting through the wire was a near impossibility and Winston Churchill once remarked that there had to be a better way of stopping machine gun bullets than with men's chests.

Vodka is banned

In the meantime there was another war waged to the east between Germans and Slavs; an age old conflict renewed in 1914. Since the French knew the Germans were coming they worked out a deal with the Russians. They convinced them to attack *East Prussia* as soon as they could; and the Russians dutifully did. Upsetting Germanic calculations, they surprisingly and quickly invaded *Ost Prussen* from the east with their *1st Army* and northwards from Poland with their *2nd Army*. Like England, the Russians carefully envisioned what the future might look like with France crushed while they stood idly by. They therefore decided to attack. The Russian Army in 1914 was a vast military organization: 1.5 million men that would expand to over 6 million men in a few months. Most of the soldiers were peasant farmers who were illiterate: you don't need literacy to grow wheat and potatoes and distill vodka. Subsistence farmers like these made up 82% of Russia's population. Even so, Russia's economy was the world's 4th largest. Interestingly enough, when the draft call came, 95% of them showed up. That came as a surprise to the ruling elite who were mostly in it for the money. But strangely, this was the moment when the Tsar listened to the voices of the world-wide temperance movement. Alcoholism was a major problem then and now. He felt that with Vodka banned productivity would increase. While that may be true; the sale of Vodka was Russia's largest revenue stream. The timing couldn't have been worse because now troops at the front had to scavenge for Vodka and that wasn't good for morale.

Austria's dilemma

Russia had a lot of territory to defend and still do. Back then Austria was a significant foe and they both had conflicting interests. Russia, a Slavic nation, felt duty bound to protect the interests of the '*South Slavs*' that included the Serbs and Bosnians. The Austrians foolishly sought to expand their interests in the Balkans for wont of anything else to do. They already had ten subject nationalities in a European empire ruled by Germans; albeit Germans who didn't live in Germany. It is anomalies like this that make understanding European political and social history difficult for Americans to understand. In order to stay politically viable, Austria-Hungary shifted its weight south and annexed Bosnia and Herzegovina in 1908. They already administered the place by the Treaty of Berlin in 1878. The provinces were nominally owned by the Ottoman Empire but Austria annexed them into her empire because it made them feel good. That same day Bulgaria declared independence from the Ottomans. These events came as a blow to the Ottomans and also to the kingdom of Serbia since they both regarded Bosnia as their own. Russia didn't like it either because they looked upon Slavic speaking nations to be within their own sphere of influence and not part Germanic Austria's. It almost led to war right then and there but Serbia and Russia backed down. In 1914 they wouldn't.

The Reserve System

When Austrian Archduke Franz Ferdinand was assassinated on June 28, 1914 by a Serbian paramilitary organization called *The Black Hand*, the war mongers in the Austrian government took this as an open invitation to crush Serbia. They wanted another *easy win* just like the Russians thought they would get when they picked a fight with Japan back in 1904. To do this the Austrians needed to '*mobilize*' their army. This is the peculiar procedure that led to a general European war. The reserve system was begun by the

Prussian Army after the disastrous *Treaty of Tilsit* in 1807. They lost ½ their territory and had their army reduced to 45,000 men by the victorious French. To get around this, the Prussians reduced the term of service in their army from 20 years to 3 years; thus the army was no longer strictly professional but rather a civilian one that could be expanded rapidly when the reservists were called up. After they served in the army for 3 years the men were sent home with a rifle and uniform they would don again when called to do so. After a few years of rotating young men in and out of the army, a reserve of many millions could be formed. By 1914 all the European armies except England had adopted this system. So when the Austrians wanted to attack Serbia, their 415,000 man professional army became one of 3 ½ million in a few weeks! The Austrians thought they would walk all over Serbia but instead got 300,000 of their men killed in one disaster after another. After all, the Serbian Army was combat-tested through a series of recent wars against Bulgaria, Greece, Romania and the Ottomans. The Austrian Army was noted only for savagely defeating dirt-poor peasant farmers armed with pitchforks.

Franz Ferdinand is sent to his doom

Few liked the guy except for his wife and kids. He had the knack of annoying anyone and everyone within earshot and more. Some people are like that. But he was not a figurehead. He was *Inspector General of the Army*. He was in Sarajevo to command and observe Austrian military maneuvers. Franz became heir apparent when his cousin Rudolf was murdered by Hohenzollern German agents in 1889. Rudolf was one of four children and the only male from the loveless marriage between Emperor Franz Joseph and the incredibly hot Elizabeth of Wittelsbach (Bavaria). In 1898 she would be stabbed to death by an Anarchist while on a walk in Geneva. What got Rudolf killed was his plan to break free from Germany and ally the Empire with France. Franz Ferdinand had no such desire but instead wanted to incorporate the south Slavs into the Empire on equal footing with the Germans and Hungarians. He talked about a United States of Europe. This didn't go over real well with the Empire's rulers in Vienna and Budapest and they wanted to see him gone. Franz also made the mistake of falling love with

Sophie Chotek, whose title was *Sophie Maria Josephine Albina Gräfin Chotek von Chotkow und Wognin*. You'd think with a title like that she'd be royal enough to be the future Empress. But according to the maticulous blood-reckoning of the Hapsburg clan she wasn't. She was shunned, an awful fate as no one would talk to her nor even turn in her direction. Sophie was forced to enter into a morgantic marraige in which neither she nor her children had any rights to the crown. With all this, and very much like JFK, poor Franz was sent into what was enemy territory in an open car. He had very little escort, although it must be said he requested a light escort to get closer to the people whom he loved and who perhaps admired him too. He got a little too close to them. His driver took a wrong turn in a strange city. He stopped to look around and threw the car into reverse. Gavrilo Princep was an agent of *the Black Hand*, and part of a 7-man hit team sent to kill Franz. Dejected, he was on his way home having, he thought, failed in his mission. He stopped on a street corner to light up. The cigarette hung out of his mouth and he watched the girls go by. Suddenly right before his eyes there they were! The Imperial couple's car stopped right in front of him but two feet away! Open mouthed and shocked, the cigarette fell silently out of his lips and hit the gutter. He looked Franz straight in the eye and like *Johnny Ringo*, fast drew his 38 caliber Browning automatic and shot him and his wife dead. Gavrilo later apologized and said that in the confusion he didn't intend to kill Sophie. It was Govenor Patiorek he was after instead. There are many heroic statues of Gavrilo in Serbia today; with a new one unvieled every few years or so.

The Black Hand

Serbia, like the USA, was born from revolution against foreign occupation. For Serbia, that was the Ottoman Turks. The Ottomans lost Serbia, Bosnia, Herzegovina, Montenegro, Romania, Greece, Albania and Bulgaria as they slowly retreated from Vienna over the centuries. By 1914 Serbia was an independent monarchy but it was actually ruled by a coldblooded military organization named *The Black Hand*, also known as *Unification or Death*. They weren't kidding. Serbian officials either went along with the program to unite all Serbs under their banner or else face painful death by saber; much like what would happen in Imperial Japan in the 1930's. When Serbian King Alexander I and the learned and accomplished Queen Draga sought rapprochement with Austria they were both brutally murdered and mutilated, with their naked bodies thrown upon a dung heap. This didn't stop Austria from annexing Bosnia and Herzegovina in 1908; something that Hungary was against since it did nothing but decrease Hungarian power and influence within the Dual Monarchy. Hungary didn't want war in 1914 either but they were forced into it anyway, as it was German Austria that wanted it. Why they wanted it has more to do with personalities than anything else. They didn't know what else to do with themselves. After Franz Ferdinand was killed by the Black Hand, Austria presented Serbia with a list of demands. Once accepted they would have made Serbia an Austrian colony. Serbia declined and on July 29th the Austrian river monitor *SMS Bodrog* shelled Belgrade in the first act of war. Interesting enough, the *Bodrog*, sunk a few times and raised, is still in service tugging gravel for Serbia on the Danube River.

If your only tool is a hammer, every problem looks like a nail

Mobilization of reserves became the key to understanding European war plans in 1914. Each of the participants was not only ready for war but eager for it. Still though, it was economically impossible to keep a full strength army in the field at all times. To get around that and get an edge on their opponents, they developed elaborate plans to get their armies up to full strength as quickly as possible. As Confederate General Bedford Forrest once remarked, they all wanted to get there first with the most. Germany wanted to get there first with the most against France before the Russians could intervene in *Ost Prussen*. France wanted to get there first on the road to Berlin before the Germans could turn their flank on the road to Paris. The Russians wanted to get there first with the most before the Germans could turn the full weight of their armies against them. The Austrians wanted to mop up Serbia fast before the Russians could get ready for Austria's elaborate and ridiculous two-pronged attack into both Serbia and Russian Galicia. This meant that all the great powers were dependent upon railroad schedules to get men who were civilians with wives, jobs and children into uniform and shooting at the enemy as quickly as possible. The schedule plan became more important than diplomacy, more important than logic and, in the end, more important than national interest. Amazingly, all the continental powers thought the general war was all going to be a piece of sweet cake, easily swallowed and digested.

Mobilization means war!

When Austria presented their demands to Serbia on July 23rd the Russians began mobilization the next day. There was talk about *'partial'* mobilization but in truth the Russians didn't have such a plan; it was full mobilization or nothing. This was stupid. They were faced with a minor and localized problem; war between Serbia and Austria. A partial mobilization in Galicia would have sent any message they wanted to send. The armies slated for the invasion of East Prussia (*1st & 2nd*) were already part of the fully mobilized professional army. There was no logical need to push the envelope. The problem was the imbeciles who ran the country began to believe their own propaganda about *The Russian Steamroller*. They went ahead and ordered full mobilization because they thought they were going to win a general war against the German speaking nations. They imagined too that it was going to be delectable, with *Ost Prussen* the sweetest prize. Only one small army defended it and they knew it. The beauteous province looked so very juicy. Never mind that tiny Japan had whipped them. Ignore the hundreds of mutinies within the army since then, due in part to the brutal conditions of service; low pay, 20-year terms of service and harsh corporal punishments for minor breaches of discipline. To top it off, the lack of proper munitions and general officers with congenital brain defects insured one disaster after another. But never mind all of that; once war was decided upon, mobilization had to proceed apace. Then Austria, Hungary, Germany, France and Serbia needed to mobilize as well and the nightmare began.

Tannenberg 1914-1945

Russia had a lot to gain from war, which is why they gladly rushed into it. They cast envious eyes on the rich and fertile lands of not only East

Prussia, but perhaps Silesia and Pomerania as well, right up to the River Oder. Why not Berlin? With the vast bulk of the German Army in France nothing seemed impossible. When Russia refused to cease its mobilization Germany declared war on August 1, 1914. Two weeks later, *Russian 1st Army* with 258,000 men and 800 guns invaded East Prussia from due east. Dang it, the German plan was unequivocal: those ignorant Russians couldn't do that! German calculations, which were infallible, showed that the Russians couldn't possibly attack for at least 6 weeks! But as Galileo said: *Still it moves*. Russian *2nd Army* couldn't be there either. Nevertheless *2nd Army* simultaneously drove north from Poland. This made the German defensive position theoretically untenable. The German plan, formulated by West Prussians, was to only delay the enemy. *German 8th Army* of 235,000 men and 1100 guns, little of it concentrated, was to fall back to the River Vistula leaving the venerable homeland to the Russians. That was easy to do on a wargaming map munching beer and pretzels. It was much tougher to stomach when your women are getting raped by Cossacks. Hermann von Francois, who was East Prussian, commanded *German I Korps* (20,000 men and 124 guns). This was the toughest outfit in the whole army and he would have none of it. He made a stand at *Stalluponen*, a little provincial town 15 miles from the frontier, now named *Nesterov* which tells you how it all came out in the end. Russian *1st Army* was commanded by *Paul von Rennenkampf* who had the world's largest moustache; big waxed handlebars that protruded a foot or more on either side of his face. He wasn't expecting any trouble as he advanced upon *Stalluponen* because everybody knew everyone else's war plans. The Germans made no secret of the Schlieffen Plan's details as it had become a national obsession; they were going to surrender East Prussia and retake it later. So Rennenkampf was expecting a walk in the sun. His Army was strung out on *the only* east to west dirt road. All the roads were dirt. They were surprised by *German I Korps* who were all East Prussians fighting for their homes and women. Russian *1st Army* lost 3,000 men at *Stalluponen* and had another 7,000 men captured. Rennenkampf was like a confident prize fighter who boldly stepped into the ring only to be promptly hit hard in the face. Mike Tyson once remarked: *Everyone has a plan until they get punched in the mouth*. Rennenkampf had to step back and carefully deploy his army for battle. From this point on he was very cautious because the enemy wasn't supposed to be there! Well they were there, and darn it; he wasn't sure of anything anymore. Little could be gleaned from local recon as the terrain was heavily wooded with lakes, marshes, rivers and streams everywhere. Historically, Rennenkampf is criticized for failing to come to the aid of *2nd Army* commanded by *Alexander Samsonov*. They were supposed to be enemies since they had a dispute in the Japan war when Samsonov accused him, ironically enough, for failing to come to his aid in the *Battle of Mukden*. But Rennenkampf wasn't a fool either. He wasn't going to allow 2nd Army destroyed just to get even with his nemesis. He knew the Germans could, and would, turn on him next. Rennenkampf was a good general and in 1919 the Red Army offered him a post. He declined it out of loyalty to his Tsar. Fearing he would join the Tsar's *White Army* the Reds killed him. Rennenkampf could not have assisted Samsonov at Tannenberg simply because there was no direct route to get there. The roads were not paved super highways. They were dusty trails winding through forests and around hundreds of lakes all in enemy territory. None of them led directly to anywhere where Rennenkampf could have been in assistance to anyone. He had his own battle to fight and he didn't know where the enemy was except that they had just knocked out a few of his teeth.

The Road to Konigsberg

Usually, armies must follow roads as they advance, as the munitions trains must stay on them. The road from Stalluponen led directly to the ancient Teutonic Knights' capital of *Konigsberg*. It wasn't too far away either, only 125 miles; not too far as the crow flies. Its capture would have been a major success for the Russians and a huge lost for the Germans, not to mention a very large feather in General Rennenkampf's cap. But to get there *1st Army* had to fight through the *German 8th Army*, now concentrated just to the west of them. The German theater commander, *Maximilian von Prittwitz*, had gotten courage from the results at Stalluponen and decided to make a serious stand. Russian 1st Army fanned out and met the Germans at *Gumbinnen*, a small and quaint city now named *Gusev*, in the part of East Prussia that presently belongs to Russia by conquest. Gumbinnen was once Lithuanian: *Gumbine* way back when Lithuania was a great eastern European power. The black crossed Teutonic Knights, looking for land, women and booty were defeated by the Lithuanians and Poles in the first Battle of Tannenberg in 1410 AD. They still celebrate it yearly in both Lithuania and Poland as the *Battle of Grunewald.*

General von Prittwitz loses his nerve

As this latest Slav-German battle began, Russian *2nd Army* under Alexander Samsonov advanced north from Poland. They were practically unopposed on the wide-open German southern flank. The drive north headed straight for the Baltic Sea. If they got there the entire *German 8th Army* would be cut off. It looked like the Russian Steamroller plan was working. In fact, both Russian armies were, in American military jargon, all fucked up. They were already low on ammo and transmitted their plans by radio in plain language! Let's face it; devising a code for wireless transmission is not rocket science. But the Tsarist Army couldn't organize it. Even so, with the enemy knowing their locations and direction, *Russian 1st Army* put up a good fight at *Gumbinnen*. They won the battle and took 7,000 prisoners. This panicked von Prittwitz who ordered retreat to the Vistula, which, don't forget, was the original plan all along. He was soon talked out of it by his chief of staff *Max Hoffman*, who would wage war on the eastern front right to the bitter end. Hoffman devised a plan to use the well lubricated German RR net to transport the bulk of *8th Army* westward. He would leave only the *1st Cavalry Division* and some local *Landwehr* (National Guard) to delay Rennenkampf whose army was licking its wounds after their bloody victory at Gumbinnen. The plan would work spectacularly but not before the high command in Berlin sacked von Prittwitz and replaced him with *Paul von Hindenburg* and *Erik von Ludendorf*. They both would become Germany's military dictators when the war eventually went horribly wrong. Poor von Prittwitz died of a broken heart two years later in Berlin; for the victory to come should have been his and his name immortalized in the pantheon of Germanic heroes. Now nobody remembers anything about him.

Lateral movement

Moving troops, and later slaves, by RR was something the German Army is really good at. After successfully withdrawing *8th Army* from Gumbinnen on the same day that French *3rd Colonial Division* was annihilated at Rossignol, they were able to use their elaborate railroad net to transfer the bulk of their force westward. There they would completely destroy the Russian 2nd Army advancing north from Poland. The move west from Gumbinnen is a lateral movement on *interior lines of communication*. An army that does this may move rapidly because the enemy is not in the way. Samsonov's 2nd Army must have, by necessity, advanced much more slowly and carefully. It was made up of five distinct army corps that did not know where they were in relation to each other. They didn't know where the enemy was either. They had good maps, but their advance was separated by a long series of lakes much like the Finger Lakes in upstate New York. This meant the disparate elements of Russian 2nd Army were not in direct communication except by radio which was in its early stages. Samsonov had asked for and received permission to align the axis of his advance further west where the terrain was dryer and less wooded. With nothing much in front of him he envisioned driving right through to the Vistula, threatening Berlin and cutting off German 8th Army. The westward shift in gravity did two things however: it moved him further away from Rennenkampf and also further away from his own *VI Corps* (30,000 men and 100 guns) that protected his right flank. *VI Corps* were forced to continue their march due north on account of the lakes. They became more widely separated from Samsonov with every step they took. The charming little town of *Bischofsburg* lay in front of them. It's in Poland now, called *Biskupiec*, and the Germans are all long gone, victims of History. Like *Publius Quinctilius Varus* who led three Roman legions to their doom in the *Teutoburg Forest*, VI Corps pressed on into disaster unaware the enemy was concentrated before them. Also like Varus, they were strung out on the only road and could do battle solely with their lead elements. They were met by the German *XVII Korps* (28,000 men and 153 guns) fully deployed for battle. The Germans had got there first with the most marching overland from Gumbinnen because the troops were highly motivated. *Russian VI Corps* found themselves overwhelmed as German *I*

Reserve Korps (30,000 men and 75 guns) soon joined the fray. As *Russian VI Corps* began to disintegrate, the rest of *Russian 2nd Army* was itself engaged with both *German I Korps* and *XX Korps*, two very tough, well supplied and equipped outfits that were laterally shifted away from Gumbinnen by rapid RR movement.

They heard a shot ring out

Samsonov was able to deploy his army against Prussian *I Korps* now arrayed for battle against him. As far as he knew, things were going well. He was fighting, holding his ground, and giving as well as he got. On the left he actually outnumbered *German I Korps*. Engaged in an artillery duel with them, his *XIII Corps* on the right took the important RR and road junction at *Allenstein* (now *Olsztyn*). The German position looked weak as it now seemed *Russian 2nd Army* controlled the center! But Samsonov didn't know that his rightwing near *Bischofsburg* had collapsed, and that *XIII Corps'* hold on *Allenstein* was unopposed and fleeting. As the left wing slowly began to run out of ammunition, his centrally located *24th Division* inexplicitly withdrew. Why that happened remains unknown. General Reshchikov commanded the 24th. Perhaps he lost his nerve and misunderstood the situation. We'll never know. He is lost to history but when the 24th withdrew, Samsonov's left fell apart. In the center, *XIII Corps* tried to retreat from Allenstein but was never able to disengage the enemy. VI Corps' destruction on the right ensured the encirclement of the entire *2nd Army*. In essence the Germans were able to isolate and defeat a series of Russian army corps one at a time. They knew where the Russians were, where they were coming from and where they were going; information about the enemy that the Russians lacked. Within a few days Hindenburg and Ludendorf surrounded and destroyed the entire enemy army. This made them both national heroes. As for Samsonov, the poor fellow wandered off into the woods and shot hisself, unable to face the Tsar with news of the disaster. His body was recovered two years later and returned to his widow. As 2nd Army surrendered, von Moltke, who was still dizzy, transferred two full army corps east to help out. Moltke's panic ensured German defeat on the Marne but victory in the east as the beefed up Germans ganged up on *Rennenkampf's*

1st Army. They drove it and the rest of the Russians out of East Prussia and Poland too. Thirty years later they would be back forevermore.

Girl Crazy

Meanwhile the Austrian Army had grandiose schemes of a two-pronged offensive into Poland and Serbia. Obviously they should have looked at any topographical map and seen that the *Carpathian Mountains* serve as a perfect *defensive position* for them anchored around the fortress of *Przemyśl*. However, like many armies before them and since, they didn't bother to do that. In between letters to his girlfriend, Conrad von Hotzendorf simply looked at a road map and saw how easily Russian troops in Poland could be surrounded. Moving swiftly and wanting to impress Gina, his armies made some progress. Unfortunately for him, the only thing the Austrian Army ever does really well is round up innocent civilians, murder the men and gang-rape the women. The Austrian high command labeled this *Vernichtungskrieg*. This was a new term, one the Germans would use in 1941 to define their war with the Soviet Union. It means *War of Annihilation*. It is certainly opposed to any of the tenets of the *Peace of Westphalia* that's for sure. So instead of focusing their efforts against the Russian Army, the Austrians were more concerned with creating a wasteland in Poland. Like the Crusaders on their way to Jerusalem, who took time out to rape and pillage the Christian city of Tyre in 1111, the Austrians began the war by murdering their own citizens; Jews and Ruthenians who were in the Austrian province of Galicia. The Russians also had troops in the area and they successfully counter-attacked. They drove the Austrians back to the Carpathians and they would have captured Budapest had not Russian 1st and 2nd Army been destroyed in East Prussia. Austria lost 500,000 men in this debacle and the Serbian Campaign didn't go any better.

Austria thinks big

Franz Joseph was 84 years old at the time. He was confused about Austria's role on the world stage. He could have stopped the war at the beginning but didn't. He couldn't see any future for Austria without territorial expansion.

The only way to proceed there was south into Serbia and the other Balkan states; eventually conquer it all including Thrace and presumably Istanbul. Fundamentally, the Austrian ruling elite couldn't perceive their own structural weaknesses. Gobbling up more territory from people who were neither Germans nor Hungarians would just add problems that they couldn't deal with. There had been food riots just three years before. Who among them could grasp that in four more years their empire would be dismembered forever? Now they found themselves in a war of their own making not only against Russia and Serbia but also England and France whose blockade of German ports would affect Austria too. France's fleet controlled the Mediterranean and with Austria presently at war with everybody in sight, their imports dwindled. In three years babies would die of starvation in the streets of Vienna. By then Franz Joseph would be dead of old age. He was replaced by *Karl I* who wanted peace at almost any terms but feared German conquest if he gave in. In 1914 and before the first disasters, they rejoiced in German support. They thought their massive combined armies would crush everyone in sight. They never beat anybody.

Serbia's Great Retreat

Somewhat akin to the premature launching of the space shuttle *Challenger*, Austrian General Oskar Potiorek, (who was in the next car when Franz and Sophie were gunned down), began his assault on Serbia before both his armies were ready. Naturally, because he was up against those ignorant Serbs, he thought it would be easy. Gloriously, he wanted the victory to coincide with Emperor Franz Joseph's birthday! So he attacked right into the teeth of the entrenched enemy. Those ignorant Serbs could fire machine guns! The Austrians were repulsed with huge losses. Like Russia, Serbia was short of arms and ammunition. Unlike Russia, Serbia was short of men. In the *1st War-phase*, 450,000 men served in the Serbian Army and 56% of them would die. Serbia would suffer more losses proportionally than any other nation. In 1914 however, every army was fresh, ammo supplies still adequate, enthusiasm still high and when Austria retreated, the Serbs counter-attacked. By the end of the year they maintained complete territorial integrity. Next year though, German troops would enter the fray, Bulgaria would declare war, and Serbia was doomed. Its entire army and a good part of the civilian population trekked to Albania and Greece as the Austrian Army did what it does best: they poisoned wells, cut down orchards, pillaged towns, hanged anyone who looked at them sideways and of course, raped and murdered any woman or little girl they could get their hands on.

The First Final Solution

As 1914 drew to a close *The Three Pashas*, now strangely allied with Austria, were at war with England, France and Russia. This disaster was all their own making as they presented policy as military dictators. They were also isolated. Their newfound allies, Germany and Austria, were not directly linked to them and wouldn't be until Serbia was defeated in 1915. Admiral Souchon was the newly minted commander of the Ottoman Navy, strange navy that it was. He sortied his Germanic/Turkish fleet led by the battleship Goeben and shelled Russian ports. The Tsar's government could only declare war and did so on November 2nd. The Russians, just as foolish as everyone else; fighting Austria, Hungary and Germany and having already lost 1 million men, attacked Turkey like the whole thing was a board game. Nobody knew how to show some restraint. The attack didn't get very far. Enver too looked at a map and saw all those succulent Turkic provinces that were in the Russian Empire. They really weren't too far away he considered, at least not on the map he was looking at. There were mountain ranges to cross, but it didn't matter to him. Nor did it matter that as winter approached, the snow was already falling out there. No need for winter clothing he guessed, thinking that without overcoats the men would be more motivated to attack. Olives are fine food he thought; who needs meat? He cranked up Turkish *3rd Army* and when its commander, the capable *Hasan Izzet*, advised moderation, Enver fired him and took command hisself. Turkish forces were smashed and *3rd Army* lost 90% of its strength; one of the greatest military disasters of all time. Most of the men were dead from frost. The architect of the worst catastrophe in Ottoman history, Enver was looking for somebody to blame. He chose the Armenians who were Christians and an easily identifiable scapegoat.

Armenian Genocide

The Armenians in the Russian Empire did undoubtedly support the Russian troops in every way they could, as they should have. Problems arose when Ottoman Armenians backed Russia up when they invaded Turkey. The truth needs to be told that there were Armenian revolutionary organizations whose aim was an independent Armenian nation. Who could blame them? In 1894-1896 there were a series of sustained massacres of Armenians in the Ottoman Empire where maybe 100,000 to 300,000 Armenians died; mostly women and children. Certainly Russian agents were operating in Ottoman territory among the Armenians stirring up the pot. Turkish agents operating in Russian Armenia did the same. Throw in Christian missionaries advocating a Christian Armenian Republic and the situation was volatile. When war began all the constraints of civilization were discarded. Did the Turkish Army overreact? Certainly they did, but to go on a nationwide killing spree of all Armenian Christians; women and children especially singled out, was a stain on Turkish honor that will never go away. So too was the murder of Syrian and Greek Christians, all of whom had lived in the region thousands of years before the Turks got there. What's interesting is that like the Austrian Army, had the Turks been less interested in revenge against their own population they might have fared better militarily. The historic homeland was theirs as the Russian Empire would soon fall apart. But they were too busy nailing Armenian women to crosses.

Ethnic cleansing

The Armenian Genocide needs to be taken in historical context. The Ottomans weren't the only nation involved in atrocities. The Austrians were doing the same thing to the Serbs, albeit without crucifixions. As the Russians retreated from the Teutonic hordes in 1915, they too rounded up as many Poles, Jews, ethnic Germans and Muslims as they could and tried to kill them all. European nations had come to regard ethnic homogenization as a good thing and the hallmark of a modern state. Nations like Russia and the Ottomans observed that the leading nations of Europe, especially France and Germany, had a single ethnically pure population that spoke the same language (sort of), had the same religion (kind of), had colonies abroad, strong economies and powerful militaries. They wanted to be like them. They thought the way to do it was to kill the unwanted. Malthus and Darwin had shown that this was the modern scientific way of the world. The worldwide *Eugenics* movement proved scientifically that war was one of nature's proven ways toward population reduction and purification. As the unwanted were murdered, the theory said this enhanced the value of the survivors and *survival of the fittest* came to be a popular term. It's still used today. Involved in a war that would have no end and no ethical boundaries either, the intellectual mutants that ruled Europe by assassination and decree took the opportunity that chaos offered to kill anyone they set their sights on with impunity.

Decimation

1914 ended with the French Army killing their own men in suicidal frontal assaults against dug in enemy machine guns. Effete officers then murdered their own men by decimation, as many units refused orders to advance into a hail of lead. It is important to keep in mind that soldiers entering combat in 1914 wore no protective equipment whatsoever. The modern reality sees today's soldiers dressed in black & camouflage, wearing rugged gloves, battle tested armored helmets, goggles, light-weight bullet-proof protective vests that work, secure pelvic protection, as well as optional knee-pads and shin-guards. Soldiers in 1914-15 had nothing but cloth! Roman soldiers 2000 years before had better protection with shields, helmets and shin-guards. Had the French been outfitted like them, they would have stood a better chance. Armed with magazine loaded pistols for close combat, instead of cumbersome rifles, they might have caused some mayhem among the enemy ranks. Later on they considered and tried using body armor but it couldn't stop rifle bullets. The armor that could was too heavy. Also body armor would drag a man down in mud and even drown him. Shields would eventually reappear in the form of armored fighting vehicles but that would come three years later. In the meantime helmets weren't even introduced until late 1915. The Russian Army never wore them at all except for a few imported from the French. Protected only with cloth caps, head wounds took a gruesome toll. The French and British Army chiefs couldn't have cared less, because everybody knew that population reduction, especially among the lower classes, was constructive. Ergo, with a large manpower reserve, a few million dead didn't matter to them at all. Nor did it matter to their masters, who drank sherry from fine crystal glasses as they read the casualty reports. As 1914 ended the French continued to demand bayonet assaults against enemy positions defended by rapid fire weapons. The *38th, 37th and 45th Divisions* just said no. These were crack, veteran troops from Algeria and Tunisia who had defeated the Germans at the Marne. Their valor and commitment were beyond reproach. The French high command ordered the offending regiments decimated anyway. Decimation was a Roman Army practice whereby a unit that retreated without orders had to offer up 10% of its strength to be murdered; the men chosen by lot to be killed by their own. This made the generals feel good but eventually the entire French Army would mutiny in 1917. The French attacks never stopped until then. The Germans were content to stay on the defensive in the west throughout 1915 because it was they who now owned a good part of France. It was up to the enemy to get it back. The Germans would instead concentrate their offensive efforts in the east and win Poland and the Ukraine.

August von Mackensen

At the start of 1915 the Russians still held most of Poland. It was a deep salient, or protrusion, to the west, surrounded on three sides by Germanic armies. Since Nicky owned it all, there would be no retreat to a more defensible position. The danger was a pincer movement: Germans attacking from Prussia in the north and by Austrians in Galicia from the south. The plan was obvious to anyone who could read a map. The German-Austrian offensive to take Poland and hopefully drive Russia out of the war, was commanded by August von Mackensen. It is often possible to see him, in his ornate black and silver trimmed cavalry uniform, sitting in Hitler's box at the 1936 Berlin Olympics. He wasn't there because he was a Nazi but because he was one of the few major players from the war to emerge with his honor intact. He was born in the Kingdom of Prussia, lived through the 2nd Reich under Wilhelm, the Weimar Republic, Hitler's 3rd Reich and finally the Allied occupation; a span of close to a century. He died just before the formal dissolution of Prussia in 1946. He commanded an Army Corps at Gumbinnen and Tannenberg. He was given command of an entire Army Group for this offensive, named *Army Group Mackensen*. Tragically and continually short of ammo, the Russian Army tried to hold but eventually realized that their position was hopeless. Warsaw fell, as did the Baltic States, and only general winter stopped the Germans just short of Minsk on the road to Moscow. A huge swath of territory fell to the Germans and through the Danish government, the Germans made Tsar Nicolas a peace proposal. Nicky rejected it because he had promised his western allies not to seek a separate peace; him thus choosing self-immolation and the destruction of his nation. But the western allies had also promised him Anatolia, Istanbul and the Dardanelles. They do this all the time; give away territory they don't actually own. Here the Germans had a chance to be smart but couldn't manage it. They couldn't promise Turkish Istanbul. But they could make Nicky a proposition he couldn't refuse and offer him India, the grandest prize of all, in return for a *rapprochement*. But they didn't.

Ober Ost

The German Empire now had a vast area in the east under military control and they weren't going to give it up. After Mackensen's stupendous victory, Hindenburg and Ludendorf, who were in overall command out there, created a number of new states. One was *Ober Ost* (upper eastern territory). It was made up of parts of Lithuania, Poland and a place called *Kurland* on the Baltic Sea. There were millions of people there and the only experience the Germans had in colonial administration was in Africa. Accordingly they administered Eastern Europe as they did Southwest Africa. Thus the governance of *Ober Ost* would be brutal. It became a military colony that incorporated new and arbitrary borders that the local population was forbidden to cross without a passport. It included massed forced deportations to German work camps. Ludendorf felt it was his mission to bring the benefits of Germanic civilization to the scum that lived out there, including especially the Poles and Jews who were targeted for forced labor from which few returned in good health. The

Germans wanted *Ober Ost* to have enhanced agriculture as the British fleet's blockade was beginning to have effect. Unfortunately the German Army needed horses and routinely *requisitioned* them from farmers who then, of course, couldn't plant and harvest their crops. Jews and Poles were also expelled from the territories in the hope that their place would be taken by German immigrants. The Germans understood this process as the necessary corollary to the war itself. They defined it in terms like *Raum und Volk* that need to be understood in the context of *Pan-Germanism*.

> *What has been will be again There is nothing new under the sun* Ecclesiastes

Terms like *Raum und Volk*, *Lebensraum*, and *Drang nach Osten* are very much like the American term *Manifest Destiny* and the legendary *wide-open spaces* of the American west. For some Americans it seemed clear that the fate of their nation was entwined with westward expansion to the Pacific Ocean. Woe onto anyone or anything that got in the way. For many Germans, territorial expansion was the reason why the war was fought. It was a biological and spiritual necessity that had to have a higher divine rationale. The word *Volk* in German has a different meaning than its direct English translation: *folk*. *Das Volk* is a tribal term much like *La Raza* (*the Race*), a term used by Mexican irredentists who want to turn the American southwest into the hell-hole that Mexico is. For Germans, the *Drang nach Osten* (the eastward urge) is an inherent sacred *Drang* (compulsion), to expand eastward into Poland and Russia. Entwined in this, is the concept of *Blut und Boden* (Blood and Soil); a primal passion that only the higher consciousness of *Das Volk* as a single organic being can completely comprehend. No ordinary human can truly grasp or manifest it. This is why it all sounds so stupid to the liberal mind. For them the individual is the highest manifestation of self realization in the universe. *Das Volk* is the higher consciousness of the people as a whole; defined as *das Volkskörper* (the racial body), the organic physical body of the Nordic race that encompasses all its members. The term applies to every race. That is why they defined history as a constant struggle for racial supremacy. From this is the origin of the *Führerprinzip*, a term introduced by Baltic German *Hermann Graf von*

Keyserling. It came to mean that once spiritually anointed, *der Führer*, when he appeared, would individually embody the entire consciousness of the Nordic race. Hitler thought he embodied this. These ideas seem both frightening and ridiculous to the modern political mind. Yet modern associations like the American *Democrat Party* as well as NGO's (non-governmental organizations) like *Open Borders* and various *Open Society* groups routinely act upon them. They seek the political and cultural removal of the Caucasian race from their homeland. It doesn't matter that the circumstances are reversed from German racism. On the contrary, the notion that racial differences don't exist is essential to advancement in the modern bureaucratic state. Cultural relativism is the filtering system all employees must pass through on the way up the bureaucratic and political ladder. Governmental and *NGO* staff then implements what is essentially a racist *population replacement program* with no personal ethical qualms. For the modern bureaucrat to whom race doesn't exist, nothing that they themselves do can be racist. The racists are confined to the target population whose resistance to their own extermination is based upon simple ignorance. The ill-mannered *baskets of deplorables* are too uneducated to properly understand the wonderful world of inclusivity and diversity that awaits them. This is why the electorate that supported Trump is defined as uneducated white men. For the ruling elite, *cultural relativism* is perceived as sociologically beneficent, validated as science and *good*. Vicious and ruthless in their urge to purge the old and create a new and better world, they do not and cannot comprehend that their modern ideas are exactly the same as *Raum und Volk* policies. The only difference is that the victim's identities are shifted from one racial group (*Poles and Jews*) to another racial categorization (*White Christians*). As Caucasians are demonized with accusations of *white privilege* and *white supremacy* their removal and replacement becomes sociologically acceptable.

Lebensraum and the Volkish Community

Raum und Volk (Open Range and Racial Identity) is a mystical state of being where *das Volkskörper* can attain its destiny as a supernatural power upon the conquest of the promised Germanic landmass. Both land and people become one entity: *Blut und Boden*, blood and soil. After the Kingdom of Prussia conquered the free German states, the concept of *Pan Germanism* (*Pangermanismus*) promoted the idea that all Germans should be united into one grand country: *Gross Deutschland*. Since there were Germans all over Europe: in France, Hungary, Poland, Russia, Romania, Italy and of course Austria (whose people regarded themselves as German), this process would take a lot of doing. That's why Count Bismarck avoided the problem. But the exigencies of war gave rise to *Ober Ost*. This was an opportunity for the *Pan-Germanic League* (*Alldeutscher Verband*) to manifest their theories of racial determinism into action. The movement was anti-Christian and anti-Semitic as both Judaism and Christianity were seen as religions from afar. They were alien *non-Germanic* doctrines that polluted *das Volk* both physically and spiritually through an intermixing of alien blood and ideas. Spiritually, the Judeo-Christian ethic, and Christianity in particular was debilitating through the worship of a foreign Jewish rabbi as the one God hisself. Hitler didn't devise any of this; he just walked into it.

Kultur and Unkultur

By the end of the 19th century and the start of the 20th, racial determinism became a powerful force all over the western world. It determined not only national political actions, but the way in which many ordinary people viewed society and how they acted interpersonally. Beginning in the 1890's, when the *Eugenics movement* gained traction in the USA, black freedmen became the target of lynching in the USA. Prior to then, it was usually whites who were murdered in this way. Lynching is an American form of justice in a place where roads were few, distances were long, and judicial appointments hard to make and keep. Extra judicial murder of whites was usually gotten over with as quickly as possible. For blacks, it almost always involved torture. By the end of the century the *Darwinian Eugenics* movement presented a *scientific* body of evidence that showed certain races were not only inferior to others but destructive as well. It was a worldview very much akin to Malthusian social policy, except the targets in America were not the poor, but rather black American freedmen and Jews, who were singled out by race and not social strata. In *Ober Ost*, the German social engineers targeted Poles, Jews, Lithuanians, Russians, Latvians and anyone else who lived out there as lower life forms who at best needed help, if not the outright extermination that would come three decades later. The Germans saw themselves as the bearers of *Kultur* which doesn't have quite the same meaning that *culture* does in English. For them, *Kultur* meant a highly complex and spiritually advanced civilization that would include not only the refined arts and sciences but an ethical, moral and physical superiority based on race. Even though they were at war, Ludendorf and his *Volkish* advisors brought in teams of archeologists and historians to piece together an accurate understanding of the history and traditions of the new lands as the elders were deported to make way for German colonists. The Poles, Jews and Russians needed to be gotten rid of because were the bearers of *Unkultur*; a negative, slovenly, ignorant, diseased and destructive force. This is how the Democrat Party now defines their political opponents; *deplorable and uneducated white men in need of reeducation*. In *Ober Ost*, everything about the newly conquered eastern lands was judged to be *schmutzig*, or filthy. The Germans placed a heavy emphasis in communal showers and delousing became a fanatical exercise about cleanliness and physical purification (*Reinigkeit*). What the Germans didn't grasp, but could have, was that when the Russians retreated from von Mackensen's 1915 offensive they practiced a *scorched earth policy* that destroyed everything that might be of use to the enemy, including all farms as well as whole cities and towns. When the Germans got there everything was wrecked. The commander of this retreat was *General Nikolai Yanushkevich*. He had murdered or deported a hundred thousand Jews, Germans and Poles. *Tsar Nicholas*, who is now a saint in heaven, approved of this wholeheartedly as he protected and promoted Yanushkevich until the Reds gratefully killed the General in 1918.

The Government General of Poland

The history of Poland in modern times is a sad one. They have their own unique language and culture maintained through thousands of years. They preserved cultural integrity even after Austria, Prussia and Russia swallowed them up four times; the last partition in 1815. The next would come in 1939 and that would be the most gruesome. When the Germans took Poland in 1915, they could have offered the Poles the opportunity to restore their homeland as a German ally. This would have shored up a good portion of the eastern front and allowed the Germans to concentrate on a single front against England and France. They might have recognized Poland's own imperial ambitions that included the landmass of the erstwhile *Polish-Lithuanian Commonwealth*. Given that Germany was in a death-struggle with two gigantic slave-labor empires with unlimited resources, they might therefore give Poland some of what it wanted. Without a doubt millions of Poles would have enthusiastically formed a government and military units. They already had a number of combat brigades fighting for Germany against the Russians. *The Polish Legions* were led by Jozef Pilsudski, who would become military dictator in Poland after the German surrender. Ludendorf had more grandiose ideas than did Hindenburg. He would become the dominant partner when they were both named supreme commanders of the German Army. He reconstituted the Kingdom of Poland but without a king, and without borders and without a government, except for an administrative title named *The Government General of Warsaw*. The Germans, under the National Socialists in 1939, would give conquered Poland the same name and institute the same policies: slave labor and mass expulsions of civilian populations in favor of German immigrants. But for Ludendorf, an economic union would have provided Germany with at least some of the foodstuffs they needed to break the Royal Navy blockade. Instead Germany did its thing: conquer, loot, pillage and enslave. They needed a vibrant and independent Poland on their side. Instead they chose to exploit them. They were obligated to occupy Poland and maintain large armies in the east until Russia, beset by revolution at home, finally gave up the war in 1918. By then Germany was already beaten and save one last pathetic spasm of violence, they would surrender too. Now in the 21st century, it is Germany herself swallowed up by African invaders while Poland maintains the will to protect its borders and possibly survive.

Weapons of Mass Destruction

1915 was also notable for the introduction of poison gas as a weapon. Chemical irritants have long been a part of war since ancient times. Fires were set laden with sulfur. If the wind was blowing correctly, the smoke would disable the enemy. The French tried a similar tactic with tear gas in 1914 but it dispersed rapidly and the counter-measures were effective. They gave up using it. The Germans, quick to realize that they were in a total war (*Totalenkrieg*), turned to modern chemistry and began using poison gas. *Fritz Haber* was a German Jew and pals with Einstein. He converted to Christianity when he married the chemist *Clara Immerwahr*. He missed the essential message of the Nazarene but instead figured out a way to attack enemy positions with chlorine poison gas. The death toll was horrific as was the method of death; men's lungs and eyes torn apart from the inside. Haber was awarded the Nobel Prize in 1919, ostensibly for chemistry but really for his work in population reduction. By then he had lost his beautiful wife who was in deep despair upon the realization that her husband had become *Doktor Death*. She begged and pleaded with him one last time to give it up and he wouldn't. Dressed in the military kit he now preferred, he left for the front to kill more Russians. In utter despair she stood before him and fatally shot herself in the heart. Before her body got cold, he was out the door, obsessed with chemical murder. Eventually he was forced to flee Germany in 1933 because conversion to Christianity didn't mean he was one, and factions in the new German National Socialist government aimed at the complete annihilation of the Jewish race. His family came to a sorrowful end; both his daughter and son committed suicide and five members of his family died in Nazi labor camps.

> *The superior power of population cannot be checked without producing misery* Malthus

The Allies followed with gas attacks of their own. Both sides' scientists invented ever more lethal gasses. The first attack was in the *2nd Battle of Ypres* in April 1915. The *1st Battle of Ypres* was in late 1914 in the final stages of *The Race to the Sea* and is notable for the destruction of the *German Imperial Guard* who threw themselves upon enemy machine guns to no avail in one last desperate attempt to turn the enemy flank. Wanting revenge, *German 4th Army* tried gas and sure enough, the green cloud killed thousands of men while others ran. But the Germans didn't have any reserves and they themselves were wary of the gas and advanced slowly, allowing the enemy to reform and hold the position. Soon men used make-shift gas masks; cloth and water over the eyes, nose and mouth. Even more effective was urine, once used effectively against *Greek-Fire*, a medieval flame thrower fired by pressurized siphons that water wouldn't extinguish. Soon, gas-masks were invented and while the men hated to wear them, the alternative was too awful. Neither side could break through though, because the gas was unreliable; a shift in the wind meant that the attack aimed at the enemy was actually upon one's own troops! Also, the attack became unwieldy with gas because the attacking troops were themselves forced to wear masks and they couldn't breathe very well either; limiting their effectiveness. In the end gas killed and maimed many thousands of men but didn't kill that many troops relative to total casualties: most of them still fell to artillery and machine guns. Gas just made life for the soldier even more miserable than it could be, in the most ghastly war in the history of the world, one whose horrors would never end.

What about Troy?

Throughout 1915 the western font remained stable and to break the deadlock, the English devised a plan to drive the Ottomans out of the war. The Black Sea is an inland ocean connected to the Mediterranean Sea by the Bosporus Straits controlled by the Ottomans. If that could be opened, Russia might be supplied by sea, as its industry was still unable to meet the demands of modern war. The Royal Navy and the French Navy tried to force the strait with battleships but got outgunned by shore batteries and lost some fine ships. They gave up on that idea and chose to land on the Gallipoli Peninsula to the west. The plan was to take that and from there, drive on to Istanbul and free the straits. They never got off the beach. One of their problems was the lack of maps, or better said, the good maps they didn't have with them because they didn't know that they had them. Like the *Siege of Havana* in 1762, the Brits went in without maps. But they had maps then too. Accurate maps of Havana were captured from the Spanish in *The War of Jenkins' Ear* but they were in the archives of the British Museum and forgotten. The same thing happened in 1915. The Royal Navy had made detailed and very accurate maps of the region in 1840 and still had them. One of those maps was even used by Heinrich Schliemann to locate the historical town of *Novum Ilium* (New Troy) on what appeared to be a mound at a place called *Hissarlik*. The map was used as the frontispiece in his famous book announcing the discovery of *Troy*. Schliemann's discovery of "*Troy*" has often been likened to someone sticking a spade in the ground and finding a forgotten city. But he knew from the 1840 survey map that *Novum Ilium*, a town known in historical times, lay at Hissarlik. Eager to make a name for himself as the discoverer of Troy, he insisted that *Novum Ilium* was Troy. He obliterated the legend *Novum Ilium* off the map and replaced it with the legend *Troy*. Since the village was possibly old enough to be mythical Troy, the name *Novum Ilium* is now forgotten and Schliemann's excavation became *Troy* for every other archeologist since then. However the evidence indicates that the small village he unearthed is not the mythical Troy of *Queen Helen*. The site at Hissarlik encompasses only 5 acres and really can't be the object of a ten year commercial war. And why would the largest and most powerful city in the Greek world be built in lowland marshes? Another site deemed Troy by *Strabo*, the most knowledgeable geographer of the Greek world, is upland, airy, dry and beautiful. The current site at Hissarlik only makes sense as a modern sociological construction that pays no heed to the realities and sensibilities of the Ancient world. In any case, accurate maps of Gallipoli were available, but the Brits didn't know about them. The landing was a disaster and the British Army command found out you didn't need an Oxford education to fire a machine gun. The Turks set up barbed wire obstacles and made their defensive position impregnable. Most of the 300,000 men lost were Commonwealth troops from Australia, New Zealand and Canada, and some French too, as well as many Irish lads. The Irish wondered why their men should die so far away when they were brutally oppressed by the English at home. They rose in rebellion next year but they were slaughtered again by their English masters in the *Easter Rising* of April 1916.

Italia Irredenta

The Italians decided they too had excess population and declared war on Austria in 1915. They had the full support of the nation. That wouldn't last long. Bismarck once remarked *Italy has a hearty appetite but poor teeth*. They were originally allied with Austria-Hungary and Germany when war broke out. As a condition for joining the war on their side, Italy asked Austria for *Trentino /Alto-Adige* and *Südtirol*. These were German provinces in the Alpine foothills that had large Italian minorities. The unredeemed or lost provinces (*Italia Irredenta*) became an Italian *cause célèbre*. Austria wasn't going to give them up on a promise and said no. The Italians then asked England and France for them and they both said sure. Since the provinces didn't belong to them the *accord* was premature. Nevertheless Italy still had to take them and it wasn't going to be easy. They surely weren't very far away on the map that *Generalissimo Luigi Cadorna* looked at. He somehow didn't see the Alpine Mountains into which the Austrians had dug impenetrable positions. The Italian Army showed amazing bravery in attacking these positions to no avail. When the Generalissimo saw the results he knew intuitively the fault didn't lie with him. Instead he began to slaughter his own men; one per day by firing squads and thousands more in unrecorded summary executions. By 1917 the German Army reinforced the Austrians and found a tactical genius named Erwin Rommel all at the same time. He was in command of the *Royal Wurttemberg Mountain Battalion* of about 900 men. Using infiltration tactics, they captured the demoralized *1st Italian Infantry Division* of 10,000 men and all its guns. Then the Germans broke through and almost took *Venice* but were stopped short when the French and British reinforced the Italians. Still though, when Germany surrendered and with Austria dismembered by treaty, the Italians got the Alpine provinces they wanted. Cleverly manipulating their enemies, they managed to hold onto them when they again switched sides in 1944. Like *Arnold Rothstein* at the race track they knew how to pick winners. Millions of Italians were murdered in these affairs but that was the war's object.

Population reduction

Darwinism is an extrapolation and generalization of *Natural Selection*, a process first named and observed by the naturalist *Patrick Matthew* in 1831. He was concerned with increased bounty in foodstuffs and saw this could be gained by selective breeding in animals and plants. Darwin later proposed that these same processes could be a *creative force* in nature. His theory is a generalization because the only truth in it is Matthew's observation. The transformation of one species into another has never been observed nor demonstrated. Essentially, can the small changes that Darwin observed in birds (coloration, beak size, etc.) or in later observed demographic shift (moth and bacteria populations), *create* new organs and species? The answer is no. For example, the massive propaganda machine connected to Darwinist education shills the notion that antibiotic resistance bacteria have *evolved*. This is a deeply thought-out deception and a lie. Those bacteria are not a new species. They have no new organs. They never evolved. They have existed, as bacteria, unaltered since the beginnings of time. What happened was that the drug resistant bacteria (due to slight genetic differences) were *selected for survival* in hospitals. They flourish there, while ordinary bacteria thrive everywhere else. It is not an adaptation, nor creation. Nothing changed except population density. In a place where antibiotics abound, bacteria resistant to them are able to reproduce rapidly and successfully. Those not resistant are killed and unable to reproduce. This is the process observed by Matthew. It's the same with the famous story of the *English Peppered Moth*. No new species was created, not even a new variety. Both the lighter and darker moths were extant in nature. The lighter moths were replaced in English industrial cities by the darker ones since they were better able to camouflage and reproduce. They call this now *survival of the fittest*, a term introduced by the sociologist Herbert Spencer in 1864. But can this sort of *population shift* account for the transmutation of a fully functional land animal like a cow or hippopotamus, into a whale, or for that matter, into anything other than itself? This is not known.

Punctuated equilibrium

Louis Agassiz was one of the great scientific minds of the 19th Century. Among much he established most famously *Ice Age Theory* (1837). He was an early and among the very few academic dissenters from Darwin's new theory. Darwin's *On the Origins of Species* (1859) was *immediately* accepted by the vast majority of academics because it was an atheistic view of life. That's the whole point of it. Darwin's idea gave scientists an opportunity to resolve the history of life through their own research and discoveries. They were no longer hindered or bound by any prerequisite belief that spiritual beings (God) had anything to do with it. This is still the case. Agassiz disagreed primarily due to the lack of evidence. He knew that the fossil record does not indicate a slow transmutation of species from one to another. Species appear and disappear from the fossil record *suddenly* without making any recognizable *directional changes*. This knowledge is as true today as it was then. They may become larger or smaller but they stay what they are. It's called *stasis* or *equilibrium*. Stephen Jay Gould (1941-2002) was the most prolific author in the history of *Evolutionary Biology*. He called the lack of evidence for transmutation "*The trade secret of paleontology.*" Gould was troubled by the *sudden appearance* of new forms as if they were *abruptly created* (like in the Bible). For example, *Bats* suddenly appear in the fossil record 50 million years ago. They do not *evolve*. The oldest forms are the same as modern bats. It's the same with birds. Only birds have feathers; extremely complex organs that are lightweight but sturdy, intricately and finely wrought. There is no evidence for their evolution. The oldest feathers are the same as modern. There is no real evidence for any of it; just complex suppositions based upon genetics. Evolution is sold by an accommodating educational system that just makes it all up as they go along. From a pop science book by (the renowned) George Gamow:

> *Some of the reptiles in the colder regions began to develop a method of keeping their bodies warm. Their heat output increased when it was cold and their heat loss was cut down when scales became smaller and more pointed, and evolved into fur. Sweating was also an adaptation to regulate the body temperature, a device to cool the body when necessary by evaporation of water. But incidentally the young of these reptiles began to lick the sweat of the mother for nourishment. Certain sweat glands began to secrete a richer secretion, which eventually became milk. Thus the young of these early mammals had a better start in life.*

He makes it all seem as easy as buying a new hat. The newly emerged mammals needed fur. They got it when they needed it because they needed it. This isn't an oversimplification of Darwinist thought; but rather the essence of it. It's all fantasy and conjecture. Gould recognized that the fossil evidence for all this was *"virtually nonexistent."* Nothing has changed since then; there have been no great new discoveries. As a way out of this conundrum he proposed (with Niles Eldridge 1972) that evolution by neo-Darwinian means, (natural selection acting upon genetic mutations), would first occur in isolated areas. Then when the successful adaptation did occur and the new species emerged, it would explode outwards leaving no trace in the fossil record. Perhaps it did happen this way but the great question remains; does this, or any kind of evolution, occur through Darwinian means? Are genetic mutations an *imaginative and creative force* capable of accounting for the amazing diversity of life? It doesn't take a genius to figure out why a polar bear's fur is white. Obviously those brown bears that had fur with no pigmentation were able to successfully reproduce in northern climes as clear fur was an advantage for survival in an ice-field. But polar bears can and do mate with brown bears. There is no real difference between the two. Can the processes described by Gamow turn bears into a new species? Well, lop off the legs, twist the pelvis around 90°, put the snout on top of the head, lose the fur and add it all together with about 1,000 other changes and presto you've got a whale. The proposition is absurd. Can fish, slowly and over millions of years, become cows, and all creatures in between, through a series of genetic mutations acted upon by natural selection? The answer to this question is completely unknown and essentially ridiculous. But this evident social construction of reality is mandated in educational systems precisely, and only, because it is atheistic. Darwinism is the foundational belief system for most of modern science. The theory dictates the course of research in fields as diverse as archeology, history, anthropology, biology, paleontology, psychology, and sociology. All results are and must be interpreted according to it. The error in method is obvious. This core belief however negates the Judeo-Christian ethic and all its holy books. It is protected and dissenters weeded out and ostracized because the political drive in western civilization since the French Revolution (1789) has been the eradication of monarchy and the disempowerment of the religious structures that support it.

THE PRESENT CALAMITY IN HISTORICAL PERSPECTIVE

The Human Betterment Foundation

Social Darwinism is now considered *wrong think*. That's interesting because Darwin hisself was the first *Social Darwinist*. From *The Descent of Man* (1871):

> *With savages, the weak in body or mind are soon eliminated; and those that survive commonly exhibit a vigorous state of health. We civilized men, on the other hand, do our utmost to check the process of elimination. We build asylums for the imbecile, the maimed and the sick; we institute poor-laws; and our medical men exert their utmost skill to save the life of every one to the last moment. There is reason to believe that vaccination has preserved thousands, who from a weak constitution would formerly have succumbed to small-pox. Thus the weak members of civilized societies propagate their kind. No one who has attended to the breeding of domestic animals will doubt that this must be highly injurious to the race of man. It is surprising how soon a want of care, or care wrongly directed, leads to the degeneration of a domestic race; but excepting in the case of man himself, hardly anyone is so ignorant as to allow his worst animals to breed.*

Louis Agassiz held similar views. Hence his name is scrubbed from the public square and his statues torn down. But Darwin, whose theory replaced the *God of Abraham*, is sacrosanct, celebrated and adored. Darwin's cousin heeded the call and founded the *Eugenics* (good birth) movement. Their answer was sterilization and *euthanasia* (good death) of the unworthy. Francis Galton:

> *What Nature does blindly, slowly and ruthlessly, man may do providently, quickly and kindly.*

When Nazi doctors were hauled before the Nuremburg Tribunals they said to the Americans: *We got our ideas from you!* And indeed they had. *The Human Betterment Foundation* was established in Pasadena (1923). They led the nation in sterilizations and were in regular communication with National Socialist Germany. American eugenist, C.M. Goethe, in an address to the foundation:

> *You will be interested to know that your work has played a powerful part in shaping the opinions of the group of intellectuals who are behind Hitler in this epoch-making program. Everywhere I sensed that their opinions have been tremendously stimulated by American thought, and particularly by the work of the Human Betterment Foundation. I want you...to carry this thought with you for the rest of your life, that you have really jolted into action a great government of 60 million people.*

They sure did. It hasn't gone away either. California and Sweden continued sterilization of the poor and minorities into the 1980's. Social Darwinism has a new name too: *Sociobiology* attempts to understand human behavior through its evolution from lower animals. It's a scam centered upon dehumanization which is anti-ethical, anti-clerical and contrary to *all* religious thought.

Population Demographics

In the Malthusian-Darwinian worldview, death is a positive growth oriented process. When one group or species dies off it is a natural occurrence and good for the survivors. The weak are weeded out and the strong endure. Malthus:

> *Instead of recommending cleanliness to the poor, we should encourage contrary habits. In our towns we should make the streets narrower, crowd more people into the houses, and court the return of the plague.*

This would clean up the inner city ghettos that Malthus' friends created to house the disempowered serfs in the wondrous *Industrial Revolution*. He'd keep the tarts from breeding and reserve that to a better sort of people. This was natural selection at work! For Darwin (an atheist since 1849) *selection* was the new God. For everyone else who was in a position of power, the survival and propagation of one's own race became the primary urge in a new historical perspective. There was no such thing as limited war anymore. No need for it; there were too many people anyway. In a battle of nations fought by the working class in a struggle for existence the loser *should be* extirpated. In a fight like this, it didn't take a whiz-kid to realize that the most populous nation had an advantage. The *Russian Steamroller* wasn't all it was cracked up to be, but they were still fighting and holding on. They didn't have a lot of ammo but they had lots of men. With France it was the opposite.

Falkenhayen's dilemma

By the end of 1915 Joffre was still in French command. The Allies decided that 1916 would be the year when they would win the war with coordinated offensives in the west, east and south. But the Germans struck first. Erich von Falkenhayen spent the later part of 1915 and early 1916 wondering how Germany might win the war. It seemed practically hopeless. Germany just had too many enemies with huge industrial and manpower advantages. France and England were supplied by the Americans who had unlimited resources. Hindenburg and Ludendorf constantly wanted more troops out east. They figured with one more push they could knock Russia out of the war. That would eventually happen but in early 1916 it wasn't evident. For Falkenhayen there was nothing out there except endless steppe. The Russian Army could retreat as they did in 1812. Napoleon's *Grande Armee* had taken Moscow and it got him nothing but misery. Falkenhayen decided that the only enemy he could decisively defeat was France: they were nearby, couldn't retreat any further and he could outgun them.

Attritional warfare

There is no written evidence that Falkenhayen as Commander in Chief of the German Army ever decided to *bleed France white*. But that's what happened. He picked the fortress city of *Verdun* as the target of his offensive for a number of reasons. Verdun was actually a series of fortified positions that protected the southern route to Paris and Reims, where Joan watched her Dauphin crowned King of France. If it fell there was an open pathway into the heart of France. Falkenhayen knew the French wouldn't give it up. He did some Malthusian population calculations and saw that in a battle with equal losses Germany with 70 million people would eventually prevail against France with 40 million. They call this kind of war *attritional*. It is the last gasp of military thinking; resorted to when there seems to be no other way to defeat the enemy. It's the strategy the United States Army eventually chose in Vietnam and it didn't work there either.

The Suicide of Europe

By November 1st 1915, there were 5 million dead after one year of combat. Pope Benedict issued a plea on *All Saints Day* to stop the killing and predicted '*The Suicide of Europe.*' He couldn't know it but his prophesy would be fulfilled a century later. The problem was too many men had been lost for either side to seek peace. Not only that, but each side wanted more territorial gains than ever before. Since Russia was in so deep, they decided to up the ante. Now they wanted not only free passage through the Dardanelles but to own it and parts of Germany and Austria as well. The English told the Russians *it's yours*. The Germans wanted complete dominion. What everybody wanted was revenge. Every mother who had lost a son wanted it. Every sister who had lost a brother wanted it. The bankers, and the politicians they owned, wanted it because billions in cash and gold was on the line. So it continued, and with Moscow still very far away, Falkenhayen looked west for the elusive victory that would never come. Nevertheless, every war that he ever knew about only ended successfully when France was defeated.

The Battle of Verdun

The German *5th Army* was given the task. It was commanded by the Kaiser's eldest son *Crown Prince Wilhelm*; the last heir to the Hohenzollern throne. He had a good life for himself, riding fast cars and women to the very end in 1951. But he cared about the men under his command and protested loudly when reinforcements were withheld from him every single time he was close to taking Verdun. He didn't know that his Army was there only to kill French and not actually take the place. The French lost 500,000 men defending the ring of fortresses. Philippe Petain commanded *French 2nd Army* that held Verdun. He was a brigade commander in August, 1914, quickly promoted and commanded *French 6th Division* at the Marne in September. Now he was in command of an Army and was one of the few

French military minds that stressed firepower before the war. He was a military genius who was able to see the effects of modern industrialized warfare. He rotated the troops in and out of defensive positions so that the men didn't see their assignments as a death warrant; even though it often was. His men were able to hold Verdun because in the end it was Petain who outgunned the enemy. Later he would be the military dictator of the defeated France in 1940-1944 and be tried for treason. The death sentence was commuted but in 1917 he helped save France from mutiny and the moronic Robert Neville.

The slaughter continues

The German 1916 Verdun Offensive lasted 9 months and permanently ruined the German Army. The 450,000 men killed and wounded doesn't account for the many emotionally scarred, as no one knew about *PTSD*: *post traumatic stress disorder*. They called it *shell shock* but it was the same thing. The losses at Verdun were actually no worse than the losses sustained by both sides in the 1914 August to November war of movement. In those early days the armies were using Napoleonic era tactics against modern weaponry and it couldn't work. Massed formations of troops worked for Napoleon, Wellington and Blucher because the enemy fired single-shot muskets that had neither accurate nor effective fire except at close range; ditto with the round shot cannon. In 1914 everything was different. At least by 1916 the armies had learned to get cover in woods and high ground and to dig in, but the losses were still enormous. Even worse, losses were now coming upon troops that weren't professional soldiers at all; they were drafted men and draft resistance, riots and rebellion would soon break out everywhere. But millions more would die first.

Excess population

Like all the participants, the British Army wanted to win the war. They never managed to figure out a way to do it without murdering millions of men. After a while this should make anyone logically question the nature of the war. The elaborate defensive positions were impossible to break through with massed frontal assaults. But raids got through to the enemy trenches every night when there was no moon. Just a few men with stealth could do it. Plenty of essays were published in military journals early in 1915 outlining tactics to infiltrate the enemy trenches but these were never adopted. The simple reason is massed frontal assaults killed more men. Their jobs at home were now taken by women for lower pay. This process would destroy working class families in the inner cites as outlined by Malthus, Darwin and the Eugenics movement. The planners thought this would purify the nation. Now people might say this is an exaggeration but the whole thrust of European civilization had already moved in this direction. Mass murder became the *modus operandi* of the ruling elite where plenty of sociopaths and psychopaths had already arisen to the top.

The Somme

In 1916 the French asked the Brits to relieve the pressure upon Verdun. England then launched a major offensive at the German position on the Somme River. General Douglas Haig, murderer in chief, planned a week-long 1000 gun preparatory bombardment that would destroy the German wire. But only 200 of those guns were heavy artillery; the rest made a lot of noise but did nothing to disturb the Germans, nor their obstacles. The British didn't have any idea just how complex the German trenches were. Their own were purposefully rudimentary so that they men wouldn't get too comfortable in them. The German trenches had libraries, showers and dining rooms. In addition, they could withstand the heaviest shot the enemy could muster. The British had 60,000 casualties the first day of the Somme Offensive, 40,000 on the second day with whole regiments wiped out. Newfoundland's Memorial Day is on July 1st, first day of the Somme. The *Royal Newfoundland Regiment* of 780 men got murdered by General Douglas Haig. Only 68 Newfoundlanders reported for duty the next day. Events like this were not unusual. Like Conrad, Haig was ennobled for his work in population reduction. The Somme Offensive ground on until November when winter called a halt. The British and French lost 650,000 men for a 10-mile gain. It is important to keep in mind that this state of affairs is the essential nature of Western Civilization in the Darwinian Age of population control and reduction by radical means.

Infiltration tactics

The stalemate based upon the primacy of the defensive continued until a Russian General, Aleksei Brusilov, figured out how to break through. There were some breakthroughs in 1915 but they were done by small units as the men often organized small-scale raids locally. Many men liked to participate in raids. It was something to do at least, and one could always take the opportunity to get back at an enemy that was primarily faceless but nonetheless responsible for dead friends. One such raid was the story of the crucified soldier, a Canadian captured by Bavarians. His unit was operating in the enemy rear area on a night raid. The Bavarians who captured him were really pissed off about something, most likely some recent atrocity by the other side. Saint Joan once told a Scottish brigade attached to her army: *You Scots make good war!* They were known not to take prisoners; just as their eternal English foes did to them. In one instance in 1915 *The Black Watch* slaughtered hundreds of German prisoners. Anyway, some Canadians were operating in German rear areas when the poor fellow, perhaps Sergeant Harry Band, was captured and tortured to death. That's as maybe but it was an effective revenge propaganda ploy. That event, and many others, showed it was possible for small units to avoid enemy wire and machine guns and penetrate the enemy position. Theoreticians began to analyze the ways and means of it and called it *infiltration tactics*. A number of papers were published on how to do it. The problem was translating the small unit tactics into army level operations.

Concentration and centralization of force no longer apply

The reason the massive French and British offensives failed was because the new rapid-fire weaponry, elaborate trenches in depth and fearsome wire negated many of the standard principles of war. If you look at any battle map, and *Waterloo* is a good example, the *French Imperial Guard* is concentrated by Napoleon right smack-dab in the center as an iron reserve. So too are the heavy guns. Lighter and more mobile forces are usually kept on the wings to protect the flanks with lesser forces used in the initial assault. On June 18, 1815 the poor fellows of *French I Corps* got to go in first because they were expendable. Caesar knew these tactics and so did Marlborough and all the great commanders throughout history. That's why they won. But in this *World War*, one that had devolved into attritional trench warfare, General Officers were faced with a situation unknown to them. When General Haig looked at the field on the Somme River he concentrated his force to achieve a breakthrough. That was the only method he, or anyone else, knew. He concentrated his artillery as well, and pounded the enemy position for a week, not understanding the depth and resiliency of the German earthworks. All his troops, both the attacking force and the reserves, were centralized close to the front, including massed cavalry that were supposed to exploit the breakthrough. Unfortunately for the British Army, after a few days of bombardment, the Germans began to figure out something was up and reinforced the position. With 100,000 casualties in the first two days, Haig should have been fired and the offensive halted. If there were social-media in those days more people would have been aware of the disaster and perhaps it could have been stopped. But there were political forces in play that allowed the slaughter to continue for another five months. The Russian Brusilov however, had already figured out a better way.

The Brusilov Offensive

In 1916 the Russians were interested in regaining the massive tracts of land they lost including especially all of Poland. A breakthrough to the *Hungarian Plain* might drive the descendants of Attila out of the war. The Austro-Hungarians were dug in. They used their own Germanic engineering and constructed trenches just as formidable as those on the western front. Unlike Haig, Joffre, and all the other madmen in command on the western front, Brusilov saw that at Verdun, and other offensives orchestrated by the French, concentrated massive bombardments didn't work. So he took another approach, admittedly already outlined and successfully attempted by German, French and Italian theoreticians in small scale operations. Brusilov ordered short bombardments, only a few hours long, conducted by artillery brought to the front by night and camouflaged. Also the bombardments concentrated their short fire not only at the enemy trenches but also upon enemy communication centers. They were always placed on road junctions easily discerned by anyone who could read a map, or by aerial observation, a new thing. Attacking troops were spread out over a front that was 400 miles in width, as opposed to 30 miles at the Somme, or as little as 10 miles at Verdun. Brusilov did not have any use for cavalry as it was clear to him, as one American officer once remarked: *You can't make a cavalry charge until the last enemy machine gun is taken.* Sappers went in by night to cut wire. The attacking force did not have to slog their way across ground that was chewed up by their own artillery either. The Russian attack by-passed enemy strong-points and broke through to the rear-areas in a few hours. They disrupted Austrian communications and captured 200,000 men and took 700 heavy guns in the first two days. They almost reached the *Hungarian Plain* before German counter-attacks put a stop to it. The front was broken, but at the tremendous cost of 500,000 Russian troops. No matter that they took one million Austrians, as they too were doomed; the fate of both Empires sealed and the Tsar overthrown by revolution nine months later.

Romania casts the die

When the war started *King Carol*, who was a Hohenzollern, was inclined to join Germany. But with Germany's ally Hungary holding large tracts of land populated by Romanians, he was dissuaded. *Carol* died in October 1914 and he was replaced by *King Ferdinand I*. But it was his wife, *Queen Marie of Edinburgh*, who wore the pants in the family. Marie eyed those Hungarian lands to the northwest, the famous *Transylvania*, as well as *Bessarabia* that lay to the east. Marie thought that if she were able to pick the winning side she might get both. Related to Victoria she chose the Entente and remarked; *England always wins the last battle.* She overlooked both Yorktown and New Orleans but it didn't matter. Undoubtedly she was only considering Waterloo and with Brusilov's offensive in full gallop it looked like a good bet. Romania declared war on Germany in August 1916 and von Mackensen made short work of them. He was given command of a multinational army in Bulgaria and his attack met little opposition. With former chief of staff von Falkenhayen attacking south, the Romanian Army was doomed: their anticipated Russian help never materialized as Brusilov's offensive ultimately failed to gain its objectives. Mackensen rode into Bucharest on a white horse and took over in December 1916. The smartest German general officer ever, he treated the Romanians fairly and not as a conquered people. Romania emerged from the war somewhat unscathed. Better yet, Queen Marie guessed right. When the Central Powers were defeated she got everything that Romania wanted including Hungarian Transylvania and Bukovina; once ruled by the erratic but often fair-minded *Vlad Dracul* (1430-1476). He's famous now thanks to the many *Count Dracula* books and movies. Also known as *Vlad Tepes* and *Vlad the Impaler*, he was king of Wallachia, and with Moldavia they both became modern Romania in 1866. The Germans would give those lands back to Hungary in 1940. Through the fortunes of war, Romania got it all back and still has it because the Russians finally took Budapest and made Hungary a loser again in 1945.

The Neville Offensive

The French needed to replace Joffre' who just never understood that valor couldn't overcome machine gun nests. They chose Robert Neville. He helped defend Verdun and was a fast talker fluent in English. Like Richard Nixon, he told everyone he had *a secret plan* to win the war. Given the opportunity, he failed to adapt to circumstances. In March 1917 the Germans wanted to shorten their front because, after millions of deaths, they were slowly running out of men. They withdrew from a number of salient positions and the French local commander wanted to immediately attack, as the abandonment of the forward line entailed moving not just men but lots of heavy equipment as well. General d' Esperey purposefully echoed Joan of Arc and said: *Let's get them!* Neville demurred because it wasn't in his game-plan. When Neville's offensive began next month it was just another disaster in the old style. By this time the Germans were ready. They were now in even better defensive positions and the old ones still in use were rock solid. Finally the French Army simply said *no more*.

THE PRESENT CALAMITY IN HISTORICAL PERSPECTIVE

Mutiny

The revolt began on May 3, 1917 with the French 21st Division, one of the toughest outfits in the French Army. They refused Neville's order to attack and were eventually joined by more than half of the army. The men offered that they would defend their positions but wouldn't be sacrificed in anymore insane assaults. An American film *Paths of Glory* (1957) recounts some of this and the mad General Geraud Réveilhac, who was a serial killer in uniform as were many of his compatriots. He got a thrill murdering young men. Like numerous others with similar homicidal tendencies he was habitually promoted, given a place in the *Legion of Honor*, and made rich. He died peacefully in his bed on his vast estate while his men bled to death in the mud, torn apart by enemy lead. These episodes should leave little doubt as to the true nature of the war. How else to explain the extreme reticence to equip the men with any sort of defensive gear? Our civilization can't see it because the concept of *population reduction* is now engrained in our psyche. Gentle, intelligent, religious people see this horror as a good thing, convinced that the world is overpopulated. The French mutiny was eventually subdued, 26 men shot by firing squad and Neville replaced by Petain, the hero of Verdun. There would be no more offensives for the French Army until 1918, or as Petain said; *I am waiting for the Americans and the tanks*. He did. The only French offensive in the final 16 months of the war, reinforced by the American Army and new tanks, won it.

Army life

The Generals did try to make life for the soldiers a bit more reasonable before they killed them, kind of like pigs on the farm. The British managed to stave off revolt by rotating the men in three separate lines of trenches; three weeks in front where bombardments, snipers and raids were frequent, a second line that offered a bit more security and the third line, safe from the enemy. The men were given a shot of rum every day plus plenty of tobacco and tea. They also got a month's leave very year. Every French soldier got a half liter of red wine per day, unlimited dark tobacco cigarettes that would rip your lungs out, as well as coffee and tea. They however, only had two lines of trenches so no French soldier was ever safe from the incessant bombardments, morale damaging raids and snipers who loved to pick off men at dinner time. The Germans got plenty of beer and they never ran out of ammunition either, thanks to their mastery of chemistry. They could always keep shooting and go on killing right to the bitter end, despite any blockade.

The Tsar is overthrown

It wasn't just Brusilov's offensive, where the casualties were quite normal, that broke the Russian Army. The army was made up primarily of peasant farmers most of whom never learned to read and write. What for? With millions of dead soldiers, problems arose because so many officers were killed too. Russian officers were plied with plenty of grain alcohol, were innately fearless and led from the front. Honestly, Russian roulette was a game they played for fun while stone drunk on *Wodka* in the dead of winter. When it came time to replace riflemen the Russian army had a huge manpower pool. But officer replacement was a different story. Those men needed to be literate; hence teachers, mailmen, civil servants, librarians, and others needed to keep a civil society functioning, were now at the front, dying. Munitions were always low and morale sunk with each lost battle. The solders got strong black tea and unlimited Caucasus tobacco but that, and illicit vodka, failed to keep them in line. Workers at home weren't being paid while war profiteers made millions. Starvation and disease were ubiquitous. Finally, on February 23, 1917, *International Women's Day*, 100,000 women workers went on strike in *Petrograd*, once and now *St. Petersburg*, the Tsar's war capital, later renamed *Leningrad*. The next day the men joined them and the police and soldiers didn't resist. This was in contrast to the Revolution of 1905-06 in which the monarchy was almost toppled except for support from loyal officers in St. Petersburg. In 1917 those officers were dead. The Tsar, as was most often the case, was clueless and Russia ceased to function as a national state. A week later he was forced to quit and the Romanov Dynasty came to an inglorious end. It all happened really fast. In Parliament, Prime Minister Lloyd George announced that with the Tsar deposed, and the Russian monarchy overthrown, one of England's war aims was achieved. This sort of hypocrisy and treason results every time Russia allies with the West.

The Provisional Government

When the Tsar abdicated in March 1917 he was replaced with *The Provisional Government*; provisional in that it was supposed to be replaced by a government instituted and agreed upon by a reformed and reconstituted *Duma*, the Russian legislative assembly. That never happened because it became dictatorial under *Alexander Kerensky*. It could have survived had he been wise enough to listen to the voice of the workers and army. They wanted an end to the war. Instead he chose to keep fighting and launched another insane offensive. In retrospect it isn't difficult to discern why. Secret treaties promised a Russian Constantinople upon victory. He also felt it important to protect the war bonds owned by all those banks that fueled the war. Those people put him in power. Lenin wouldn't have it. *Vladimir Lenin* and the Bolshevik party saw the war as the outcome of capital concentration in the hands of the banks that stoked the war machine, or as General Eisenhower called it: *the military industrial complex*. Lenin wrote about it in a short book, sometimes called an essay or pamphlet, entitled *Imperialism, the Highest Stage of Capitalism*. He, like Marx in *Das Kapital*, knew that *Imperialism* had been around for a long time. The Romans carved out a massive empire based upon conquest, plunder and enslavement, as had the Spanish in the Americas and the Dutch in East Asia. What made this war different, argued Lenin, was that plunder was transformed into capital and centralized in European banks. Those banks issued fiat paper money and credit; all given to their other banking friends who made more and more riches the longer the war went on. Lenin said *enough is enough*, and once famously: *We will hang the last capitalist with a rope he sold to us*. Lenin didn't care about war debts and capital obligations to the French and English. He instead promised the people *bread, peace and land*. He delivered on the peace part but the other two were more difficult to manifest as the French, English, Americans and many others began fighting the Russians as soon as they got the Germans to surrender in November 1918. Kerensky was exiled and died in New York City in 1970.

WAR AND MIGRATION 1860-2020

Anastasia

Lenin and the Bolsheviks wanted to be rid of the Tsar and his family right away. They had them packed up and assembled for a trip to Murmansk where a British cruiser would take them to England. Nicky's cousin was King over there so the deal seemed set. With the ship on the way the Brits backed out. There was *5 billion dollars* of Nicky's gold in the Bank of England. They wanted and needed the *moola* that was theirs for the taking provided Nicky didn't show up to claim it. The British government made up some excuse. They said Nicky and his family was the sort of unsavory people that would discredit England's noble and high minded intentions for the future of the Russian people whom they loved so much. With the Imperial family left in the lurch, Lenin sent them to western Siberia. That's when negotiations began with Germany for the girls' release. Nicky's daughters were innocent of his crimes. The Kaiser had Rosa Luxemburg and Karl Liebknecht, the two most famous socialists in the world (including Lenin), in jail. Marxist theory told that world revolution was at hand and it sure seemed that way. Germany was in revolt and Lenin wanted Rosa and Karl out to keep it going. The Germans released them both on the 8th and 9th of November, 1918 in exchange for the girls who were sent to Queen Marie in Romania. For more on this the renowned historian Marc Ferro adds more detail: *Nicholas II Last of the Tsars* (1995). The girls were all in extreme danger, not from the Bolsheviks, but from the many claimants to the massive Romanov fortune who wanted them dead and gone. Anastasia got separated and ended up in America where she died a recluse. She never left any genetic material for examination and the story that she did is a lie. Rosa and Karl remain socialist icons. They were both murdered by German *Freikorps* in January 1919 on a bridge over the *Landwehr Canal* in Berlin. A plaque on the bridge marks the spot. Nicky and his son were probably assassinated as Lenin didn't want them leading the *White Army* that was ravaging central Russia. Stalin said it was Latvians who done the deed on the whole family. It's interesting that the West only believes Stalin when he presents a lie that they like. The Tsar's bones were supposedly recovered (after close to a century) but found to be genetically *'mutated.'* In other words they aren't his. Nobody knows anything. But the legend of the Tsar's cold-blooded and brutal murder, as well as his family, remains central to the demonization of Lenin and Soviet Russia.

The German Empire expands in its death throes.

The Treaty of Brest-Litovsk, a fortress town, was signed in a city historically Polish but later Russian by treaty and now in Belarus; formerly the Soviet Union. It was on the border between Russia and Germany when war broke out again in 1941 and was defended heroically (and to the last man) by Red Army troops. In 1918 the treaty signed there ended the war. Not the whole thing but the one on the eastern front between the German Empire and the Bolsheviks. It went into effect on March 3, 1918, a year to the day after the Tsar's abdication. Negotiations began in the fall of 1917. The Germans and Austrians wanted a treaty quickly signed because they were being starved out by the British blockade. On top of that, the world's leading industrial power just joined the war against them. Lenin and the Bolsheviks sent Trotsky to parley. He took along a team that would represent all the Russians of the Revolution. Hence there was a sailor, a soldier, a worker, and a woman, *Anastassija Alexejewna Bizenko* who had established her credentials by murdering a Tsarist thug. Suddenly the delegation realized they didn't have a peasant aboard! They stopped the car and asked the first one they saw to come along. The fellow was somewhat hesitant so Trotsky asked: *Don't you know who I am?* The bearded farmer admitted he didn't. Miffed, Trotsky asked if he knew his pal Lenin. The fellow showed Trotsky a toothless grin and hopped into the car. The delegation then stalled for time, hoping for world revolution to overtake events. That didn't happen and General Hoffman, victor at *Stalluponen*, seemingly so long ago as to be an eternity, ordered his armies forward again. With the Russian Army disintegrated and the workers on strike, Lenin demanded that Trotsky sign a peace accord now. The Germans imposed harsh terms: they took 1/3 of Russia's population, 1/3 of the land, 50% of its industry and 90% of its coal. The rest of the world saw what a German peace might bring and hardened its resolve. However, Lenin promised and delivered the peace that Kerensky was unwilling to embrace. Lenin quite rightly figured that the cessation of the war was more important than the question of who owned Bessarabia, Poland and the Ukraine. The Germans should have been so smart too, but as always, they weren't. Germany's monarchist and Pangermanic clique saw Russian collapse as a way to expand ever eastward: and so they took Poland, made the Ukraine a puppet state and turned the Baltic States (Estonia, Latvia and Lithuania) into principalities attached to Prussia. This extended the Kingdom of Prussia far to the east, almost to St. Petersburg. That's when Lenin moved the capital from Petrograd/St. Petersburg to Moscow where it still is. These events indicate Lenin's calm geopolitical genius. To keep power, and to hold onto what little territory remained in Russian hands, Lenin surrendered large tracts of territory that were not Russian! They were already occupied by the enemy and all of it, Belorussia, Poland, the Baltic States and the Ukraine, are now independent. The Treaty of Brest-Litovsk established borders that are primarily identical to the present ones. The fact that Lenin surrendered anything at all is the main reason why Russian nationalists, some of whom vainly long for the Romanov's return, still hate his guts.

Racial ideology in action emerge from the war

Brest-Litovsk allowed Lenin and the Bolsheviks to maintain control of the state. They were the solitary political and social force in Russia unwilling to sell out to the West. In this they became the only bulwark against the manifestation of a racial outline of history that began when the first Austrian officer ordered some forgotten and forlorn Serbian maiden hung from a tree simply because she was. Lenin understood the war as the outcome of class struggle and the concentration of wealth in small financial elites (the 1%). This would be the central ideological principle guiding the Soviet state until its dissolution in 1989. The Bolsheviks didn't see it at the time, and wouldn't recognize until it hit them in 1941, that *racial struggle* had already become the central organizing principle of human history for the West. This ideology became the driving force in the *World War*. It was outlined by Darwin in *The Descent of Man*, the *Eugenics* movement founded by his cousin, and later Adolf Hitler and Rudolf Hess in *Mein Kampf*. Every racial or ethnic group that were participants in the combat wanted to express their own identity and this very often meant the expulsion and murder of ethnic groups that had different languages, cultures and religions to their own. This began right away in 1914 as Austria began to ravage Serbia, a nation that lost 25% of its population in the 1914-1918 war. Groups and sub-groups sought the folly and impossibility of racial purity and incidentally, to settle old scores that had accumulated over centuries between Moldavians, Montenegrins, Turks, Armenians, and the literally hundreds of other ethnic groups that had lived in relative peace in *Pax Europa* 1815-1914. These ethnic collections found in the war an outlet for their subdued fury and this was especially true after the German surrender. Large standing armies gave way to smaller, albeit equally vicious, *ad hoc* martial organizations that imposed ethnic cleansing on a massive and frightening scale: pity the Greeks that had lived in Turkey since the time of *Helen of Troy*. The death toll was incalculable and if starvation, starvation-related illnesses, and the 1917-1920 influenza pandemic are calculated in, the war's body count was probably 100-200 million people. The population geneticists rejoiced as they saw population reduction as a positive event.

Ludendorf looks west

The Treaty of Brest-Litovsk that ended the war with Russia gave the Germans one last opportunity to win the war in the west. Foolishly they swallowed up too much of the Russian carcass and, like gluttons at Thanksgiving, couldn't restrain themselves from gobbling up as much territory as possible. This meant that at least 1 million troops were needed to occupy the newly conquered lands in the east. The trickle of Ukrainian grain shipped to Germany wasn't enough to offset the blockade and too bad for any Ukrainians that would starve to death. The Germans were able to transfer 52 divisions westward. It wasn't enough. The million man army that occupied Ukraine could have helped but didn't. Polish and Ukrainian independence along with realistic commercial treaties could have shifted those million men west. But German ideologues were committed to a cultural and sociological conquest of the eastern territories that did not allow for Polish and Ukrainian sovereignty. They never would allow it until crushed by cataclysmic defeat in 1918 and later again in 1945. The fantastic military gains in the east clouded Ludendorf's military mind. The blockade was now the single most important issue Germany faced as Austria, Hungary and the Ottomans could no longer afford the costs of it.

Starvation was now the primary military strategy in a war that had no limits, nor moral constraints.

Institutionalized racism becomes the norm

By this time the USA had entered the war. Born in Virginia, Woodrow Wilson is the only American President who was also a citizen of the *Confederate States of America*. His father was a captain in the Confederate army. Wilson is the most racist President in the history of the USA; with the exception of Barry Obama whose racism was directed against white Christians. Wilson actually felt he wasn't capable of mistakes and never conceived that he might be wrong on any issue. *If there ever was a vacancy in the Holy Trinity*, Mencken wrote; *Wilson thought he was clearly the best and most obvious candidate for it.* Wilson thought black Americans were the scum of the earth and reinstituted segregation back into a hitherto Republican controlled Federal Government that had made strides in establishing equality, at least in the offices of the government. A federal government job was one place where blacks could find a decent profession and not have to take their hats off every time they saw a white man coming. He also held a screening of *The Birth of a Nation* in the White House. The movie glorified the *Ku Klux Klan* and, little known, it was only then, actually taking their cue from a movie, that the night riders adopted white sheets as their uniform. Wilson was keen to make the world safe for democracy but didn't give a hoot about it back home. By now racism was scientifically proven, so they thought, and in 1898 the US Supreme Court ruled (*Plessey vs. Ferguson*) those '*separate but equal*' public facilities were legal. This established an *Apartheid* system of institutionalized racial segregation. Wilson was all for it and made sure that the US Army remained segregated too, with whites doing the fighting and blacks, as lesser men, digging ditches. You'd think that now was an opportunity to emulate the Russian Army that joyfully used Jews in the assault, making sure they were among the first to get shot up. But the idea now was that war was a eugenic purification process, where the bloodletting would be good for the white race, ensuring that only the fittest would survive: like machine gun bullets can pick out the fellows with bad genes? An all black regiment was formed from the *15th New York* and given to the French. Other than that, the combat army was all white except for some Natives to whom the Army generals held in high esteem after losing so many battles to them.

Making the world safe for capital investment

Wilson was under pressure to get into the fight against Germany because American banks had made big loans to France and England. If Germany were to win, billions of dollars would be lost. Wilson's campaign slogan in the 1916 election was '*He kept us out of war*' and it worked. The Republicans, as evident agents for the bankers, were a clearly defined war party. Wilson was a peace candidate and he was re-elected by a large margin, both in popular vote and in the *Electoral College*. But, like almost all politicians, he soon turned his back to the people who elected him and chose war. But the war against the Central Powers had to be sold on another level because who wants to send their kids to die for the bankers? Something else became the battle cry.

Freedom of the seas

The *Lusitania* was sunk by German boat *U-20* in 1915. That sinking was a set-up by the British. The Lusitania was only slightly smaller than the *Titanic*, and she was just as luxurious. Both ships were playgrounds for rich Americans who wanted to get to Europe, take a sauna bath and get in some tennis while they were at it. The Brits wanted *Lusitania* sunk because they needed America in the war and on their side. They figured that since freedom of the seas was an issue that prompted America to declare war on them 103 years before, the trick would work again. In 1812 it was about the *Royal Navy* stopping American vessels and taking American seamen off their ships to serve in the Royal Navy for life as slave laborers. This time it was about *unrestricted submarine warfare* that gave German submarines the right to sink enemy vessels and not be required to adhere to *Cruiser Rules*. According to the *laws of the sea* a raider like *U-20* was obligated to stop a merchant vessel with a shot across her bow, search the ship, and if it carried contraband, capture it and then care for the crew. After all that, and only then, could they finally sink it. This was impossible for a tiny submarine and the Royal Navy began to arm merchant vessels too, thus making them auxiliary cruisers. This made *cruiser rules* irrelevant. *Unrestricted submarine warfare* gave German boats the right to fight the enemy on even terms. Try explaining that to Aunt Millie out in Topeka.

The Lusitania is sunk

There is no question that *Lusitania* was carrying hundreds of tons of war material. The stuff is still down there and salvage crews have been warned off on account of the danger. The German government knew what was going on and warned Secretary of State William Jennings Bryant. He went to Wilson and asked that the President warn Americans not to travel aboard the ship. Wilson, who wanted war, refused. When the ship was sunk Bryant resigned. The Germans then went public. They knew exactly when she sailed and posted a warning about the danger of entering a war-zone in American newspapers. It wasn't a secret either when she would enter the narrow straits of the English Channel where *U-20* would be lying in *ambuscade*. Restricted waters are where submarines congregate because they are too slow to catch big fast ships like *Lusitania* in open waters. It isn't a pleasure to find one's self in the icy waters of the North Atlantic and have little chance of rescue. It's a big lonely ocean even in a life-boat. But at a time when millions of men were being gassed and shot to death it was ludicrous, even treasonous, Senator La Follette would say, to allow 123 drowned Americans, who chose their own fate, to dictate war or peace for an entire nation.

The zigzag maneuver

There are a few general misconceptions about how submarines operated in 1915. Nowadays, nuclear attack submarines zoom about underwater at 60 miles per hour. Back in 1915, the boats maneuvered mostly on the surface where their diesel motors propelled them at c. 15 mph, much slower than *Lusitania's* top speed of 25 mph. Submarines submerge only to avoid detection. There they are propelled by battery at an even slower 5 mph. But with a very low and tiny silhouette, U-20 on the surface would have spotted *Lusitania* well before she herself was spotted. Treacherously, *Lusitania* was unescorted even though many destroyers were in the area. A single destroyer, a high-speed vessel that is the bane of slow and weakly armed submarines, would have protected her. But she was denied because the Brits wanted the big ship sunk. To make matters worse, *Lusitania* wasn't zigzagging: a maneuver not to dodge torpedoes, but to prevent tiny boats like *U-20* from plotting an intercept course. This is the only way a boat like *U-20* can sink a big fast ship. Why Captain Turner did not zigzag is unknown and he wasn't asked about it. Like the Titanic that arrogantly sailed with a massive fire in her coal bunker and plowed straight ahead at full speed through an ice-field, Lusitania sped straight-ahead to her doom in submarine infested waters. *U-20's* Captain Schweiger, who would be killed in action two years later, was able to plot an exact intercept that placed his boat in position to sink a ship he would otherwise never have been able to get close to. With one torpedo shot he hit the Lusitania in her munitions laden hold and tons of ammo blew up, sinking the mighty ship in 18 minutes.

Armed Neutrality

To London's lament, this event wasn't enough to bring the USA into the war because Wilson needed reelection the next year. The US government, run by Anglo-Saxons, was not *neutral* but favored the English, not only because of a common language, laws and heritage: but because powerful American banking interests lent billions to English and French banks to fuel the perpetual war. The exception was many Jewish banks that refused to have anything to do with England's ally Tsarist Russia. By this time American money was no longer printed and distributed by the American government but by a private conglomerate called the *Federal Reserve System*. The title is a misnomer: it is a banking cartel; a confidential and very secret corporation. They were closely allied with the London based Rothschild Bank and the United States congress essentially handed over the country to them in 1913, one year before the sorrows began. At the same time Americans were forced, by a constitutional amendment, to pay a tax on their income. Individual Americans thus became indentured servants forced to finance the banks by their own work. In the 100 years since its creation, the USA dollar has lost

99% of its value as banking interests stole the wealth of the nation. This made wily England, America's oldest enemy, now her closest ally. This also shifted America's economy away from private industrial competition, with the wealth accumulating in individual families whose loyalties were American, to international bankers whose only loyalty is gold. Thus we see in the 21st Century American wealth and industry shifted onto international platforms and the American nation impoverished.

The blockade affects everybody

Right from the get-go in 1914, the Royal and French navies blockaded the Central Powers and also cut the trans-Atlantic cables from Germany to the USA. This meant that news in America came mostly from England. Luxuries like coffee, tea, tobacco and chocolate became scarce in Germany. Food stuffs too, since they were declared contraband. A massive German military infrastructure needed supply; thus grain and meat became paltry. German people, which include Austria, began to die from starvation related illnesses. The German Navy tried to break the blockade in 1916 and the Kaiser's beloved fleet finally sortied. The resultant *Battle of Jutland* in the North Sea was one of the few instances where these fantastically expensive and elaborate big-gunned ships that could fire and hit moving targets 20 miles away, actually fought. The battle was a draw and both navies limped back to port. But the outnumbered and out-gunned German Navy was never to foray again. Germany's only hope was a reverse blockade against England with submarines. They eventually sank 11 million tons of Allied merchant shipping which is a lot, but not adequate to starve Great Britain out. They also tried strategic bombing with rigid airships (Zeppelins) and the twin-engine Gotha bomber but that wasn't enough either. Eventually the convoy system defeated the submarines and the Americans were able to ship millions of men to France without losing a single one of them. But some American merchant ships were lost in the German U-boat (*Unterseeboot*) campaign and Wilson presented this, and a silly German proposal to Mexico that they wage war together. Well, the folks in Texas, New Mexico, Arizona, California, Colorado and Utah, states that Germany proposed to give back to Mexico, voted for war. So did the politicians from most of the other states that are often in the pockets of the bankers. It is worth repeating Wilson's rationale for war, presented in his *Grand Finale* to Congress:

> *We shall fight for the things which we have always carried nearest our hearts,—for democracy, for the right of those who submit to authority to have a voice in their own Governments, for the fights and liberties of small nations, for a universal dominion of right by such a concert of free peoples as shall bring peace and safety to all nations and make the world itself at last free. To such a task we can dedicate our lives and our fortunes, everything that we are and everything that we have, with the pride of those who know that the day has come when America is privileged to spend her blood and her might for the principles that gave her birth and happiness and the peace which she has treasured. God helping her, she can do no other.*

Wilson didn't dedicate his own fortune, or his own blood, to be sure. That would be donated by the little people. But this template; that America might bestow its moral, material and spiritual treasures upon the whole world and every nation in it, became the essence of United States foreign policy from there on in, right to the present day. The only exception was the period 1923-1933 when three Republican Presidents (Harding, Coolidge and Hoover) returned America to *Armed Neutrality*. With that exception, there was a massive transfer of American wealth, and the blood of millions, to fund a policy of perpetual war. This is always presented as a noble American sacrifice for the greater good of humanity, now and forever. Wilson asked Americans to forego their own families, communities, associations, wealth and happiness (national characteristics that have all since broken down), as well as their lives, for the benefit of the entire world's evolution and betterment. It is a policy of complete madness that didn't work then and doesn't work now. It's an easier sell today because Americans these days aren't as savvy as they were back then. In 1917 not everybody at home was enthralled to go fight in a war that was murdering men by the millions. The problem was not just getting a declaration of war, which they got, but also how to get men to enlist and go fight in a toxic gas, high explosion, machine gunned, barbed-wire *no-man's land* battlefield? It wasn't an attractive proposition at a time when the song *I didn't raise my boy to be a soldier* was the nation's biggest hit.

Patriotism is the last refuge of a scoundrel

Samuel Johnson said that and he might have said it's their first refuge. The low-life in suits always wants to eliminate debate and dissent. Wilson and the war-mongers named it *the war-effort*. It isn't uniquely American. The Kaiser said: *We are all Germans now*. Socialists Karl Liebknecht and Rosa Luxemburg didn't agree and they, among many others, were thrown into German jails for treason when they resisted. Wilson pushed both the *Espionage Act* and then the *Sedition Act* that made dissent a thought crime. Eugene Debs was a Socialist who ran for President in 1912 and drew a million votes out of 15 million cast. Wilson only got 6 million votes and was never very popular anyway. When Debs spoke against making the bankers richer by war he was jailed and in 1920 drew another million votes for President while in lock-up. The vindictive Wilson kept him in jail. He was not released until three years later. Pardoned by the next President, Debs died soon afterwards. It was the same for Emma Goldman who was deported. Goldman sued to stop the draft by arguing it violated the 13th Amendment to the US Constitution that prohibited involuntary servitude. She lost. Socialist Senator Robert La Follette wasn't buying the *freedom of the seas* argument either:

> *I say this, that the comparatively small privilege—the right of an American citizen to ride on a munitions loaded ship flying a foreign flag—is too small to involve this government in the loss of millions and millions of lives!!*

What La Follette didn't understand was that Wilson was intent to wage an ideological war against monarchy. He was especially keen to destroy the Hapsburgs and recognized, essentially correctly, that the Austro-Hungarian Empire was their personal possession. Wilson aimed to destroy it; ignoring the old adage: *don't take down a fence if you don't know why it's there*. That monarchy held central Europe together in relative peace for 1000 years. Wilson replaced it with states that would embark on the most destructive war in human history within 20 years. No matter. The Hapsburgs were deposed along with the Hohenzollerns and Romanovs. This marks the moment when monarchial rule is replaced by liberal democratic rule worldwide. This is supposed to be not only a good thing, but the natural evolution of human government to its highest stage. However, as we observe the following century (1919-2020) this is not evident. The notion that liberal democratic rule is the premier form of government that humans can ever realize led us to believe that the destruction of whole nations and cultures is justified to insure it. *We had to destroy the village in order to save it* said an American officer after napalming a Vietnamese village into oblivion. Neither he nor Wilson had any other war aim except the vague notion that democracy American style, as a replacement to monarchy, would surely make the world a paradise. Most Americans believe this absurdity wholeheartedly and is the reason why they are perpetually content to wage maniacal wars just so long as it doesn't interfere with a delicious *Egg McMuffin*® breakfast and football in the afternoon. Wilson was like God on the 6th day of creation: he would breathe a valiant and vibrant humanity into existence, and it would be in his own image.

The wealth of nations is now war

Since the object of the international banking system was, and still is, Germany's destruction, American banks lent France and England huge sums to fight them. *J.P. Morgan Jr.* controlled more than 2000 banks both in the USA and London. With this money, France and England then bought not only munitions from the USA but every sort of weapon; even trench fighting knives and brass-knuckles. Morgan became the sole weapons supplier to England and France and got a cut on everything. He was *Big Daddy Warbucks* in the then famous *Little Orphan Annie* cartoons. It is important to know that in the year 1900, American industry accounted for 50% of the world's production. Americans had invented mass production and interchangeable parts, known as *the American system of manufacturing*. With this boon, the American war industry raked in the dough and thus began the *Military Industrial Complex*. War industries now run the United States government in concert with the

Federal Reserve that prints money and sells it as *federal government debt*. All of Morgan's loans were assumed by the United States under the pretext of the *Federal Reserve* and paid for by *Liberty Bonds*. Thus every-day ordinary Americans began to assume and pay for the debt of international bankers. The Federal Reserve was only a few years old and already ripped off America's wealth to compensate foreign adventurers. Henceforth they would always need more war to maintain this perpetual protection racket. The scam works under a number of guises. The sale of weapons to small nations that have no real military use for them is disguised as *foreign aid*. It goes to military dictatorships that use the money to support their lavish lifestyles. The military gear mows down the ordinary people who are kept in slavery. Prior American wars weren't fought to support the banking elite. The American Civil War was, for both sides, about slavery and the rights of the states as sovereign nations. That war was financed by the states themselves. The limited 1898 war with Spain came when some Americans saw that the decrepit Spanish Empire was easy pickings, especially the Philippines as a coaling station for trade with China. But now, in 1915, with international bankers in control of America's money supply, war became industrialized and men became commodities whose lives were to be spent at will.

The Great Migration

When the war began, 90% of black Americans still lived in the former slave empire; the *Confederate States of America* (1861-65). The slave-traders were defeated but the black freedmen stayed put. It was a life they knew and freedom was better than slavery, despite constant harassment and oppression. The Democrat Party ran the southern states and the *KKK* as well, also known as *night riders*. They murdered black freedmen and their families indiscriminately. One of the reasons for the founding of the *National Rifle Association* (NRA) was to prevent southern states from passing laws that prohibited the freedmen from owning guns. The blacks were armed but outnumbered. They were law abiding but governed by a ruling political class that only used the law to protect themselves; just as it is today. When the war began in 1914, American industry quickly expanded to produce war material for England and France.

THE PRESENT CALAMITY IN HISTORICAL PERSPECTIVE

The problem was the central European labor pool was denied emigration to the USA as Germany, Austria, Hungary, Italy and Russia needed their young men for the meat grinder. Since most of the industrial output of the USA was in the north, just like in 1860, the factory owners sent their Pinkerton goons down south to recruit blacks. It began as a trickle but increased in intensity as young white Americans were now employed to be killed in the sacrifice of combat. The white inhabitants of Boston, Chicago, New York and the other large industrialized cites in the north began to resent and resist the new arrivals. These were the sons and relatives of the 500,000 white northerners who had given their lives to free the slaves. But now their livelihoods were threatened by blacks who would work for lower wages in their desperation. The factory owners embraced it and the *Industrial Workers of the World*, the largest and most diverse labor union in the world, tried to organize the blacks into their organization. But faced with poverty or death, the blacks accepted the lower wage. Wilson's war would be a vehicle to destroy organized labor as union leaders were attacked, imprisoned and murdered for their impassioned and implacable resistance to the *war effort*. The same process is at work today. The individualized capitalist system in America evolved into a collectivist system that no longer obeyed or adhered to the dictates of supply and demand. The need for commodities was set by a national government that constantly seeks cheap labor and markets defined and delineated by a perpetual war machine. This is the nature of the international communism that is now centered in the United States.

Dissent declared a war crime

By 1917 Germany and Austria-Hungary were desperate. The Central Powers felt they were running out of time; and they were. The blockade was terrible for their people and starvation was widespread. Germany was willing to risk American intervention and declared unrestricted submarine warfare on February 1st, 1917. The American Navy was sensible enough to keep out of the declared war-zone that surrounded England & France. Not a single American warship was lost but merchantmen, private contractors in it for the money, were sunk. It still wasn't enough to convince Americans to make war. It was the *Zimmerman telegram* that did. Diplomatic stupidity seems to be a German national trait. Seeing that Russia was about to surrender, German foreign minister Arthur Zimmerman sent a note to the Mexican government to make common war against the USA. In return Mexico would get back their lost territory in the Texan Rebellion (1836) and Mexican War (1845). The absurdity of it is beyond comprehension. The Brits intercepted the message because they had broken the German diplomatic codes. The Germans only needed to deny the note's authenticity but they didn't. This gave Wilson the excuse he needed to ask for a declaration of war at a time when American Presidents still felt obligated to do that. He got it on April 2nd 1917 and he truly expected American men to rush to the colors and join up. They didn't. In truth, the population of the USA has been in rebellion not only in the southern states, but in northern and western industrial cities as well, almost since the nation's inception. After the Civil War, the revolt was in full swing. Since the 1870's over 35,000 men each year were killed in industrial mishaps. That's 3 ½ million men every ten years. It was industrial murder incorporated. But now, with the war, strikes by workers were declared *unpatriotic* by the controlled press. The repression would effectively neuter the *Industrial Workers of the World* that had invented sit-down strikes and revolving picket-lines. The *IWW* was open to any worker, any race or gender. Thus they were the particular target of Wilson's Pinkerton goons and police thugs. The more restrictive *American Federation of Labor*, the *AFL*, changed its anti-war stance in 1916 and its leader, Samuel Gompers, assisted Wilson in suppressing the *IWW* and all socialists generally. In the heartland of America, farming communities barely survived. Now Wilson wanted their young men for the massacre. Neither they nor their families wanted them to go. Oklahoma revolted but the *Green Corn Rebellion* was viciously repressed. Still in rebellion a century later, every county in Oklahoma would vote for American nationalist Donald Trump in 2016. But in 1917, with their young men taken away from them, millions of American share-croppers, who were farmers that rented their farms, lost their land and were forced to migrate to the cites in poverty. This was reminiscent of the forced English migration from farms to cities resultant to the passage of the *Enclosure Acts* and all its subsequent human misery. Wilson and his cronies couldn't have cared less.

THE PRESENT CALAMITY IN HISTORICAL PERSPECTIVE

All they ever want is excess population in poverty where men and women can be easily manipulated.

Hell no we won't go

Wilson and the banking war party tried their best to sway public opinion but couldn't do it except through repression. They created the *Committee of Public Information (CPI)* and it emerged as America's very own *1984* style *Ministry of Truth*. The head of it was George Creel, born in Missouri; a slave state just 52 years before. He was Wilson's kindred spirit. The *CPI* maintained strict censorship. Germany and anything German was portrayed as bestial. The central committee created poster art works to promote the war and wrote speeches for the 75,000 volunteer '*4-minue men*' who gave prepared pro-war talks to movie goers between reels. They also created the phenomena of news creation, now called *fake news*. Thousands were jailed for opposition to the war, mostly *Wobblies*, as members of the world's largest union were called. Long prison terms and murders would break the *IWW*. A climate of fear emerged as newspapers encouraged neighbors to inform on their friends and even upon their own family members if they thought they acted *unpatriotic*. Later on, anyone with a German name was forced to register as a foreign agent and a list of *enemy agents* was created. Four thousand innocents were jailed by a young *J. Edgar Hoover*, a fellow good at keeping lists. Still, it wasn't working: very few wanted to go *over there*. Six weeks into Wilson's war, only 78,000 men had enlisted. These were the same sort of fellows that joined up for the Mexican War; young men looking for some adventure, wine and women and maybe some booty as well. Back then, the US Army measured 8,500 men, but when 50,000 young men swelled its ranks, all of whom could shoot, the Mexican Army was defeated. Interestingly, most European *experts* predicted the opposite. But now they wanted and needed 2-3 million more men under arms to fight the Germans. And it wasn't 1845 anymore either; the enemy was now the toughest army in the world. Wilson was forced to declare a draft. The last time an American President tried that, there were bloody riots in 1863. The whole scheme of forced conscription is contrary to the American spirit, not to mention the Constitution that nowhere gives rise to the notion that a central government may pull people out of their homes and force them into uniform to fight in some foreign war far away. Yet here it was, and Creel, a genius at propaganda, proposed naming the draft *Selective Service* while at the same time fashioning an anti-German hysteria that swept the nation. German-American culture was the 2nd oldest, largest and most patriotic ethnic group in America; for in truth there were German cities and towns in America where the main language was still German. This would never return. With no more volunteers coming, and under the threat of imprisonment, men were forced to line up and register to fight. It sure sounded better to be *selected* and thanked for their *service*. Suddenly the most popular music was a war song: *Over There*. It sang *Jonny get your gun* and it all worked like a charm. When war was declared in April 1917 the US Army numbered 85,000 men. By the spring of 1918 a million man American army was across the ocean in the field against the Germans, with another million men in reserve. When the Japanese planned war on America 25 years later, they might have taken note of this but didn't.

Blackjack Pershing

John J. Pershing was given the highest rank there is; *General of the Army*. This put him up there with Washington, who defeated Cornwallis, and Grant, who beat Lee. It didn't matter that Pershing had never actually beaten anybody. He had only chased Poncho Villa out of Texas and Poncho was going that way anyhow. But Pershing looked the part and that was good for sales. He also had a good military mind, was supremely confident and wanted to keep casualties low. Wilson liked that because unlike the Kaiser, he needed votes to stay in power. He also stressed to Pershing the importance of maintaining the integrity of the American Army. They both wanted a victorious American Army in the field for the subsequent peace negotiations. When he arrived in France, his Aide, lieutenant colonel Charles Stanton, said '*Lafayette we are here!*' General Lafayette commanded the French troops without whom Washington couldn't have defeated Cornwallis at Yorktown. When Stanton's remark was attributed to him, Pershing didn't argue. The French loved it and every American they saw as well. Later on when Pershing met with Field Marshall Foch, the Allied

THE PRESENT CALAMITY IN HISTORICAL PERSPECTIVE

Supreme Commander wanted American soldiers to be dispersed among British and French units. Pershing told him to go to hell. He told Foch: *General, we will fight where and when you command, but we will fight as an American Army!* Wilson was in accord. Now it is true that Pershing sent two intact American divisions to fight with the Brits when they needed some help, and he gave the all-black 15th Regiment to the French to do with as they liked; but he kept the rest of the million men under his command together as an intact American army in the field. They met the enemy in their own sector that was south of the primary field, at a place called the *Meuse-Argonne*.

Sturmtruppen

The German spring 1918 offensive was code-named *Michael* and is often referred to as *The Ludendorf Offensive* after the crazed military dictator who had usurped power from the Kaiser. Wilhelm himself was quite a courageous fellow. He once had Annie Oakley shoot a cigarette out of his mouth from 30 paces. But he completely caved in to people like Ludendorf. The General could only calculate divisional strength and not national well-being which was irrelevant to him. He was now completely in charge of Germany's fate and the circumstances that led to this madness is what happens when national power rests in the hands of a single individual. Ludendorf lived his life as a Prussian officer. He saw history in terms of military offensive actions. There was no need to bring the Americans into the war with either unrestricted submarine warfare or the crazy plan to wage war against the Americans with Mexico and Japan. There was no need to waste the German Army in one last vain attempt to gain Paris and swiftly end the war as in 1914. In fact that should have been a lesson learned. The war could have been won with the maintenance of *Mitteleuropa*, a rich and fertile land that was now theirs. But his single-minded obsession with the attack, one that paid no heed to geo-political realities, doomed Germany. Unleashed on March 21, 1918, the initial barrage lasted just five hours, as opposed to the old style week-long bombardment. Then the shock troops went in. The Germans called them *Stoßtruppen* or *Sturmtruppen*, a reference that was to take on a far more sinister tone when similarly dressed thugs beat up, robbed and murdered defenseless Jews in a massive racial purge twenty years later. These troops in 1918 were real soldiers however; heavily armed with submachine guns, portable heavy machine guns and light artillery, reliable hand grenades and flame throwers along with the new helmets; the *Stahlhelm* (steel helmet) that afforded good protection and is now universally in use among armed forces. They attacked the hinge between the British and French and broke through. Luckily for the French, the German *master of war* had no real strategic aim in mind for his offensive. The object was to break through and after that, come what may, he'd figure it out. Unfortunately for the German Army, supplies were slim. The French found themselves in the same position they were in 1914; in retreat before a better armed enemy in open terrain. But this time the new army that saved the day was American. General Foch was in command of the hastily formed *French VI Army* that had helped turn the tide in 1914. This time he was a Field Marshall in command of all the Allied armies. His southern flank was protected by Pershing and the Americans. With no need to shift forces north, Foch's armies were able fall back in good order. When the Germans were finally slowed due to supply problems, he then ordered a *counter-offensive in echelon* with the American Army striking first in the south, followed two days later by the French to the north and after that the British Army in the far north. In this way the enemy couldn't be sure where the main focus of the attack was and also could not shift troops to the north as the south was under assault. Now Pershing's army would find out just how tough the conditions were. They would lose more men in the coming counter-offensive than any American Army ever. Their plan was to attack northeast to Sedan and cut off the German armies facing the French and English.

Blackjack loses his way

The counter-attack began on September 26 with fifteen divisions of the *American 1ˢᵗ Army*; their toughest outfit. Pershing had hoped to conduct a war of movement and avoid the massive casualties typical of this war. He couldn't. The Germans had four years to dig into this forest and while they were tired and demoralized after so much blood-letting, they still knew how to conduct defensive operations. The Americans got bogged down and began to lose 6,000 men a day, which makes the 10 years of Vietnam seem like a cakewalk. Pershing's hair quickly turned grey, a known phenomenon: when

Marie Antoinette saw the head of her best friend, the Princess Lamballe, paraded through the streets of Paris atop a pike, her hair turned instantly white. Still though, Pershing and his army pressed onward, backed up by massive artillery support. The American way of war is always centered upon the massive concentration of firepower from whatever the source. Unfortunately for them however, they had not yet figured out infiltration tactics and attacked German machine gun positions with frontal assaults. It was murder. But the American Army was akin to the *Russian Steamroller*. They hadn't yet seen four years of carnage and were still enthusiastic. What's more, the Americans suddenly grasped the combined arms concept that would be the way of the next war. Their air force was not just for recon, but for ground attack in support of the advancing infantry as well. They had the ideal aircraft for it too; the rugged French built *Spad XIII* that someone said had the gliding angle of a brick. Lots of rookie pilots were lost trying to land the beast under power. But it was fast, could climb better than any other airplane out there and was armed with two reliable heavy machine guns that didn't jam. It was this war's ideal ground attack aircraft. Since American pilots were purposefully not given parachutes, they stayed with the ship to the bitter end. Pershing too had seen what tanks could do and formed up the *1st Tank Brigade* armed with the *Renault FT*, the first modern tank with a rotating turret, engine in the rear and crew in front. George Patton often commanded on foot in front of his tanks. He also often elected to stand aloft in an open turret without helmet so his men could see him and rally behind him, somewhat akin to Joan who never wore a helmet for the same reason. Despite massive casualties, the American Army did in one month what the French had been trying to do for four years; they cleared the Argonne forest. They lost 100,000 men doing it.

The Trench System is Broken

The German Army got worn down. There just wasn't enough force with one million men still holding down the Ukrainians. Those people should have been allies and not conquered peoples. But the Germans would never figure this out. French counter-attacks once again repelled the invader before Paris.

The problem for the French was that they misinterpreted the results. Since the defense had ultimately prevailed they didn't recognize the significance of the German penetration. In fact the Germans had broken through a static defense. *The defense no longer had primacy!* This had tragic results for the French Army, and for western civilization as a whole, as the revitalized German Army would break through again two decades later.

Starvation as a means in war

All through the war starting in 1914 and only ending with the Treaty of Versailles in 1919, Germany was blockaded by the British fleet and supplies were short. Many times in the 1918 Ludendorf Offensive, German units stopped to loot French delicatessens as the troops and officers were amazed at the variety of fresh meats, cheeses and fruits ordinarily available to the French. These goods were simply not there anymore in Germany as the Kaiser threw lavish parties for the upper-crust while people starved in the slums of Berlin. The Kaiser's social contract was broken. His monarchial system no longer protected the nation. Millions of men were dead and maimed. Every small village had its medieval church bell melted down for bullets. Electric cables were torn up for shells in the now lightless streets. Finally, in one last act of folly, Admiral Hipper ordered the Kaiser's fleet out for a concluding suicidal mission to go down with their magnificent ships in a blaze of glory. The Germans call this a *Todesritt*; a death ride. With this, the sailors revolted, and like in Russia, the revolt of the fleet spread to the cities. With the nation in chaos the Kaiser fled to Holland and the rule of his family, the Hohenzollerns, came to an end; as did the Romanovs in Russia and the Hapsburgs in Austria.

The Blockade Ends

With the treaties signed in 1919 and the blockade lifted, some measure of normalcy returned to the west. In a somewhat analogous situation to what the United States found itself in 1945; in possession of a massive military machine without any enemies and not wishing to disarm, the victors and defeated powers joined forces to attack Bolshevik Russia. This was something Patton and Churchill fantasized about in 1945. It didn't last. The war so devastated the people it was impossible to get them lined up for more. The exception was hardened veteran soldiers who couldn't or wouldn't assimilate back into civilian society. In 1945 the United States was untouched by war with relatively few casualties and had a booming war economy when it embarked on world conquest. In 1919 Europe was broke and in revolution. The American Army, for the most part, went home victorious because in those days democratic action still worked in the USA. Americans were very isolationist and didn't want anything to do with foreign wars. Still don't, but it gets shoved down their throats like it or not. Back then, participation in the war had to be sold to them using a massive propaganda machine developed by Creel and his protégé Edward Bernays. He was a student of psychology, innovator in crowd psychology, and Sigmund Freud's nephew. Bernays once remarked that in 1917 he was hired to sell the war, then in 1919 hired again to sell the peace. He came to the conclusion he could use psychology to sell anything. The American Congress wasn't sold on the *Treaty of Versailles* and refused to ratify it. Bernays went on to vend whatever he was paid for, including cigarettes to women, advertised as *women's liberation*.

Self Determination

There were a number of reasons why the treaty was never ratified by the US Congress; foremost among them American's unwillingness to join any international legislative body like *The League of Nations*. American President Woodrow Wilson authored *The 14 Points,* an outline for world peace that included *The League* and other really good ideas like disarmament, freedom of the seas and something called *self determination*. Almost everyone in Europe had heard of Wilson's *14 Points*, especially the one about self determination; even in small villages in the hinterlands of *Ober Ost*. The problem with *self determination* was that only the defeated nations were forced to concede it. Just in that respect, the treaty was a fraud to begin with, and it didn't hold up for too long. Even today there are areas in Italy (*Bolzano, Alto Adige*) that are *autonomous* where the people speak German, are ethnic Germans, and have German public schools. There are areas in Romania where large German and

Hungarian minorities in the province of Transylvania still live. They were even more populous back in 1919. Wilson had a PhD in political science and even he couldn't figure it out. Austria-Hungary, for example, had 10 distinct subject minorities that had to be divvied up. The victors arbitrarily decided who got what. Germany lost some territory and the victors took whatever they could from Russia including Poland which belonged to Russia by treaty. So the German province of Pomerania was broken in two, a part given to the new Polish State to create the *Polish Corridor* to the sea. The brains who wrote the treaty never figured that the Germans might want it back, which they did. But the treaty reduced the size of the German Army to 100,000 men so there wouldn't and couldn't be another war, right? But that 100,000 man group, which would include some conscripts later on in the early 1930's, would become experienced officers in an army that quickly swelled to 3 million men ready for revenge in 1939. And it's not like no-one ever saw it coming either: Field Marshal Foch, the Allied Supreme Commander, said: *This isn't a peace accord but just a twenty year armistice*. He was exactly right but for the wrong reasons; he wanted even harsher terms imposed upon the Germans. The war was awful and every nation involved in the outbreak did their share to cause it and make it ghastly. The Germans got blamed because they lost.

Fanny Kaplan; mystery woman

Another reason the treaty failed was because Russia, the largest nation in Europe, and the one that suffered the most casualties, didn't participate in the process. Instead, every nation that thought it could grab a piece of Russia went in and tried to gobble up a chunk. It looked like easy pickings. The victors also wanted a return of the Romanovs; something they call *Regime Change* nowadays. The Romanovs may have been congenital imbeciles but at least they paid off their debts, or promised to. That was infinitely better than what Godfather Lenin offered; which was nothing at all. Lenin was a man of the people who lived in small apartment near the Kremlin with his wife Krupskaya. They usually walked to work or else took the streetcar to the Kremlin. He never used his position of power to accumulate wealth, nor did Trotsky who commanded the *ad hoc* Red Army, nor Stalin who, before he was imprisoned in Siberia, was primarily a heavily armed activist who robbed banks to finance the revolution. They, and all the people around them, were committed revolutionaries keen to dismantle the capitalist monarchial system. Lenin is demonized in the west as the author of the *Red Terror* but it was the *White Terror* that struck first. Tsarists and disgruntled socialists assassinated Bolshevik leader *Moisei Uritsky*, a *Cheka* (secret political police) leader in Petrograd. Then they went after Lenin himself. The *Social Revolutionaries* (SR) had won the election of Nov-Dec 1917 when 75% of Russia voted socialist in one form or another. With 37% of the vote, the SR Party won the most seats in the *Constituent Assembly*. Lenin's seizure of power wasn't from Kerensky but from them. That's why they were out to get him. Lenin was shot twice in the chest and neck by *Fanny 'Dora' Kaplan*, in August 1918. But was it her? Maybe it was Lydia Konopleva, who was a crack shot and involved in other plots? What of Grigory Ivanovich Semyonov? He was the ring-leader of the so-called *Central Battle Unit*; a Petrograd death squad that killed a number of Bolshevik politicians. Seems like he knew everybody; did he know Stalin too? He certainly knew both Lydia and Fanny. Lydia gets away and disappears from history, perhaps lost in one of the endless purges. Semyonov got away too, was welcomed into Stalin's Communist Party, and testified against his former comrades in the SR. It was Semyonov who armed Kaplan. The story is Fanny was born in the Ukraine but some say maybe Brooklyn. They say Fanny's eyesight was too poor to have been chosen to be the shooter. But did she already know Lenin very well enough to easily recognize him? She was friends (lovers?) with Lenin's brother, so why wouldn't she know him too? The day she shot him, Lenin was among the crowd as he always was, unarmed and unprotected because he was fearless. He stopped to talk with a worker about bread shortages and then turned for Fanny who called out to him. In the end, you don't need the eyes of an eagle to shoot someone you already know point-blank with a Browning 45. After Kaplan gunned him down, Lenin began riding to work in an armored car and who could blame him? They killed Kaplan right away, urged on by Lenin's wife Krupskaya, who wanted Fanny dead. You might say they were all pretty cozy.

The Red Terror

Red revolutions in the past usually fell apart internally; Europe in 1848 for example. Reds are political theoreticians. They want to govern. Historically they usually collapse when the forces of reaction attack them with trained military units. Now though, they had the Army on their side. The Bolsheviks wanted to re-organize Russian society from the top and not from below as in 1848 or 1905. According to Marxist ideology, that meant the disintegration of centralized monarchial control in Russia and subsequently the destruction of capitalism throughout the world. They felt that even the most illiterate peasant could understand their program. They were right about that as *Bread Peace and Land* isn't a difficult concept to grasp. But the *Whites* and *SR* already managed assassination cells early in 1918 against all the Bolshevik leaders. Either the Reds would fight back or be destroyed. Thus, they began to murder their internal political opponents because both the *Whites* and the *SR* had no interest in compromise and, somewhat akin to the modern *Color Revolutions*; they had the backing of the capitalist west. Nor did the *Whites* and *SR* have any interest in negotiation, as they had the support from the *fifteen separate nations* that invaded Russia in 1919: including Britain, France, Italy, Japan, the USA, Poland, Greece, Romania, Serbia, German freebooters (the *Freikorps*) and the Czech *White Legion*. This Czechoslovak outfit, numbering 65,000 men as well as 2,500 wives and children, had fought against Austria for the Tsar. They kept fighting now against the Reds and battled across Russia on the *Trans Siberian railway* stealing as much gold, silver and jewels as they could. They rolled ever eastward and were finally evacuated by the Japanese and Americans from Vladivostok. From there they returned to Europe and formed the core of the new Czechoslovak Army. They were finally betrayed by the western powers and handed over to the Germans in 1939.

Lenin and the Revolution demonized

As the years went by, it became important for the West's political managers, and the media they control, to demonize Lenin as the instigator of the *Red Terror*. They always need an enemy. Academicians at all the finest schools are used to legitimize the hate even though the Tsar's terror killed 20 million Russians in the wars and urban misery he condoned and promoted while he lived in splendor. Lenin was 48 years old, vigorous in the prime of life when Kaplan gunned him down. He died 6 years later; pale and shrunken, emaciated from strokes. The greatest scholars of our time wonder why Lenin was in such poor health. There is little or no mention of his assassination in typical encyclopedic entries or scholarly articles and books. Some go so far as to say the shooting was good for him. Modern historians lament that Lenin was in such poor health when he made Stalin *General Secretary of the Communist Party* in 1922. If Lenin weren't so sickly they say, he may have made a more astute decision! Stalin must have somehow tricked the poor old guy. The actual explanation is pretty simple: Lenin was too weak to do the job anymore. So he appointed the one thoroughly committed communist who could. Professors of Russian history can't talk about Lenin's assassination because they are forced to adhere to the ridiculous standards of the utterly corrupt academic machines that employ them. They must support the notion that Communism under Stalin and Lenin was doomed from the start and not in accord with the natural arc of history that inevitably leads to liberal democracy. If they don't present facts to support this, the door to success in the academic system is closed to them, permanently. The truth is, Lenin suffered from lead poisoning literally and figuratively from the day Kaplan shot him. He was forced to cling precariously to life, in pain, every moment for the rest of his days. The ensuing strokes killed him not because he was generally in poor health, but because the two 45 caliber slugs that Kaplan pumped into his neck and chest ruined his life, as it would any man. The bullets were not removed until Lenin was on his death bed.

A lie told often enough becomes the truth   Lenin

The Bolshevik revolution succeeded not just because of Lenin or Stalin, but because socialism in general was supported by the vast majority of Russian people. How could it not? The Bolsheviks controlled Petrograd and Moscow and all points in between. They had majority support in the *Russian Heartland*; that area that makes up the land mass that is historically Russian. *The Whites,* who fought for the return of a crooked, decrepit and murderous monarchy, lost because they did not. Today, Russia has discarded those regions that supported the *Whites* and Putin's overwhelming internal support comes from the historical Russia that also supported the Bolsheviks.

The Turks Keep Fighting

Ottoman Prime Minister Talaat Pasha visited Berlin in September 1918 and was informed that Berlin would soon seek a separate peace and might give up the fight. The Ottomans kept their war going until 1922. Ethno-centric thinking allows westerners to think the war ended in 1918 even though the Turks kept fighting four more years. In addition to the victory at Gallipoli, they also defeated and captured an entire British army at *Kut al-Armara* in 1916. The Brits lost 40,000 men there. Despite their victories, the Turks couldn't hold out forever once all their continental allies were defeated. They eventually conceded parts of their Empire to the British and French who themselves couldn't hold it after the carnage of round two (1936-45). The continued warfare not only stripped England and France of their gold reserves but psychologically ruined them as well. Like Japan in 1945, the Turks wanted to surrender: but at the same time hold on to at least a slice of their empire. But the Allies wanted revenge, not peace. Consequently the Ottomans signed the *Armistice of Mudros* on October 30, 1918 and ended four years of vicious warfare the next day. The document gave the Allies the right to occupy any place they wanted including the Dardanelles. The Ottoman Empire was then dismembered at the *Treaty of Sévres* signed outside Paris on August 10, 1920. They were treated even worse than the Austrians and Hungarians who at least were left with an historic homeland. The British, French, Italians and Greeks took big chunks of territory. The Turks were left with only a small nation confined to the Black Sea coast *and without Istanbul*. Like all the treaties that ended the war, Sévres was based upon payback and had nothing to do with self-determination or any of Wilson's other grand ideas. The Turks rebelled and were led by the victor of Gallipoli; *Mustafa Kemal Atatürk*. The extremely bloody *Turkish War of Independence* followed. The Greeks were driven off mainland Turkey but managed to retain the

Aegean Islands that were theirs historically. The British, French and Italians were also beaten back and Atatürk became Turkey's first President following the Treaty of Lausanne in 1923. He created a secular state and strong relations with Germany. Now the situation is different as Turkey is devolved into tribalism. But when Germany lay prostrate in 1945, it was Turkey that sent workers to help them because so many millions of German men were dead or missing. These Turks were assimilated into German society without violence and the current German breakdown only occurred with the massive African and Middle Eastern invasions in the 21th century.

Lord Balfour makes a Declaration.

Another reason for the not especially inevitable Ottoman defeat was the *Arab Revolt*, tales of which are usually centered about *T.E. Lawrence* also known as *Lawrence of Arabia*. It was among the Arabs that inhabited vast swaths of Ottoman territory that Lawrence, who went native, and the British Army, found their best allies among the myriad races of the Empire. They both promised the Arabs freedom from Turkish rule and the mastery of their own countries. They vowed that an Arab state would surely be formed as soon as the Ottomans were dismembered. They lied of course. The Ottomans were running out of resources and saw their future to the east; back towards the historic homeland. They continued to fight out there until the Reds stopped them. Arabia certainly wasn't worth the effort anymore and who could know there was oil out there? Jerusalem fell in December 1917 as the Turks abandoned the Arabs; whom the Brits would soon betray. Even before the *Fall of Jerusalem*, London issued a declaration that supported the creation of a '*national home*' for Jews in response to the well-funded Zionist movement. Never mind that they had already made secret agreements with France to carve up the whole Levant among themselves. The Arabs didn't like the Jewish homeland idea either and still don't. But Britain needed money because with America in the war, those loans from American banks now went to Wilson in Washington. Wilson's racket needed the money to finance his three million man army. Lord Rothschild and Jewish banks were ready to fork over more gold to England given a promise that Palestine would be a Jewish nation. Up until then Jewish banking houses supported Germany. The Germans found out about this betrayal as they had to when the money dried up. When they later said they were stabbed in the back, it was about this duplicity.

Germany a haven for Jews

When Count Bismarck and the Prussian Army created the German *Reich*, one of the first things they did was grant citizenship to all the Jews. They were the first European nation to do this. Jews weren't asked to convert. Their freedom of association in Germany was unlimited. By 1914, Germany's Jews were completely assimilated and had become German. They supported the war and the only Jews who didn't were in the communist minority. The situation was the opposite for Germany's enemies, especially in Russia. Historically there were few Jews in Russia. When Russia, with Germany and Austria, annexed and demolished the Polish-Lithuanian Commonwealth in 1795, Russia suddenly had millions of Jews. The passed the *May Laws* that severely limited Jewish participation in Russian life. Jews had no rights and could, quite literally, be freely killed. Jews could only live in the western Russian Empire in a place called the *Pale of Settlement*. It was in this area where millions of Jews were killed in the 2nd *Phase* of the war. When Germany and Russia began combat in 1914 Jewish bankers refused to loan money to Tsarist Russia. Instead they helped Germany. Jacob Schiff, for example, who had financed fully half of Japan's war against Russia in 1904-05, refused to assist Russia in any way. Balfour, slippery as an eel, gave the Zionists a country that wasn't his to give. The Jews fell for it. They hoped gold might resist the treachery that abounded. Lord Balfour consequently gave them the famous *Balfour Declaration* on November 2, 1917. In return, England got the loans it needed to keep fighting the war. For the Rothschild family and their banking friends, a Jewish nation would be a good place to fall back on in case Europe got too hot for them, which it soon would. Wealthy Jewish bankers already weren't welcome in Russia and were barely tolerated elsewhere.

THE PRESENT CALAMITY IN HISTORICAL PERSPECTIVE

Exodus

Moses was undoubtedly an historical figure, the primary evidence being the books he wrote and the chronology of Jewish history from Egyptian enslavement to the conquest of Israel *c. 1500 B.C.* The sad truth is that during this 3,500 year era the Jews had their own nation for only 400 years, including the last seven decades since independence in 1947. For the most part they were either enslaved or survived as a subject minority in larger nations. As Europe evolved into a modern, progressive entity, the millions of Jews therein were given the opportunity to *'assimilate.'* In the case of Germany/Austria, France and England, that meant citizenry with all the rights that everyone else had. A Jew arose to be Prime Minister of England. This worked for a while but it seemed for many Jews that they were better tolerated than actually assimilated. With this understanding, the *First Zionist Congress* met in 1897. In an extraordinary twist of fate, the *World War* transformed *Zionism* from an idea into reality in the span of one generation. Ideological problems arose because not all Jews are Zionist and not all Zionists are Jews. There was, and is, a Christian Zionist movement that preceded it by 250 years in England and Scotland. These Christians believe that the re-establishment of Israel is an essential fulfillment of Biblical prophecy: a prerequisite for the re-emergence of the Christ. Thus, in 2017 American President Trump, himself of Scottish-Christian heritage, recognized Jerusalem as the Capitol of Israel in spite of international outrage and internal condemnation from the Democrat Party. However, American Evangelical Christians are all for it. The Zionist movement also created a schism among Jews, one that still exists between Orthodox and Reformed Jews. *The Orthodox* didn't believe that the creation of the Jewish state was necessary for the advent of the *Redeemer*, and that overt political moves might hinder it. It would be the Messiah hisself who would create the paradise where death would be no more. The *Reformed Jews*, like the Zionists, all later funded by the Rothschilds, thought the re-creation of Israel was at hand; and it was. But in those early years, the Brits would renege on their promises to the Jews and eventually hinder Jewish settlement in Palestine. They saw Arab oil, already discovered in Iraq, as more important than Rothschild gold which was limited and came with strings attached. The Rothschilds continued to fund Zionist movements worldwide but always for their own ends. Arabs and Muslims generally, came to see Germany as their only friend in the continued *War of the Ottoman Succession*. While they didn't agree on everything, especially Jewish emigration to Palestine, the Germans did strive for Arab independence. Historically Germans never had any claims on Syria, Iraq and Egypt, all of which were conquered by France and England. They still don't, as the globalist and communist Merkel betrayed her own nation and opened Germany's borders to Middle Eastern and African invaders in 2015. Her aim is to finish the job the Nazis started: a *Judenfrei* Central Europe as part of a racially mixed *Eurafrican* continent. Her constituents are so historically dumbfounded they can't grasp it.

Wilson beats a hasty retreat

With the various treaties signed by the belligerents but not yet ratified by the United States, Wilson booked out of town. Like Germany in November 1918, his army was needed at home. The war not only disrupted American farm work but race riots and strikes became the norm. The United States was in revolt again, as it often is. Massive strikes, massacres and race-riots ensued that the Pinkertons and US Army both put down with mass incarcerations, assassinations and machine guns. Wilson left Europe in a shambles too. He was under the impression that western liberal democracy was the cure-all for social problems world-wide. It wasn't. What worked in the English and Nordic world couldn't solve problems in Romania and Italy. In 930 AD the oldest legislative body in the western world (the *Althing*) was founded in Iceland. *Magna Carta* was signed in 1215. The American constitutional republic dated from 1777. But in 1919, Hungary went from a 1000 year old kingdom, to soviet republic and then into military dictatorship all in one year alone. Democracy didn't enter into it. Italy became a fascist dictatorship, as did Romania; both in a very short time. Bulgaria remained a kingdom with supreme autocrat Tsar Boris III calling all the shots. Poland quickly turned to military dictatorship in 1926. Spain tried a republican government that was overthrown by a German and Italian invasion in 1936. Greece became a military dictatorship in 1936 as well. The United States adopted communism as an economic system for a way out of the Great Depression in 1933. New President Franklin Roosevelt used massive borrowing and gold confiscation to fund a centrally planned economic expansion that became the fundamental organizing principle of the American economy. Both Fascist Italy and Communist Russia served as a model. That same year Hitler and the National Socialists took over Germany. Lenin had died of his wounds and Russia became a soviet dictatorship under Stalin and the Communist Politburo. Democratic republics were not the wave of the future for Europe as envisioned by Wilson. Rather, radical fascist, communist and military dictatorships became the norm; ones that would overturn and forever destroy the 19th century vision of a modern gentrified and progressive European social order.

PART II

THE TRANSFORMATION OF THE WEST INTO A PERMANENT WAR ECONOMY

THE KAISER ABDICATED on November 9th, 1918. This was after Admiral Hipper, the new German *High Seas Fleet* commander, ordered his men off on a *Todesritt*; a suicidal *death-ride* attack upon the British fleet. His idea was to go down in a blaze of glory. The sailors thought otherwise and revolted. Over the next few years they tried to kill him. The only one they got was Admiral Sheer's wife, whom the assassins shot dead in the heart while the unsuspecting Sheer's were out for a stroll. They purposefully let him live to bear witness in sorrow. When the workers in coastal cities heard about the navy's mutiny, they did the same and the rebellion spread, just like events in Russia. It really looked like the worldwide proletariat uprising predicted by Marx and Lenin was on. This scared the monarchist/banking elite. The only thing that could help them restore civil order was the Army; otherwise engaged in a death grip with the western allies. Therefore, the Army needed to be recalled and they begged for a ceasefire. The western Allies were all for it as there was some doubt among them that they could ever actually beat the enemy. It was signed in a fancy railroad car in the little forest where Joan of Arc led her last sortie. The terms were harsh and stripped the German Army of its ability to wage war. All they were left with was their rifles and they began to walk home leaving their heavy weapons, rolling stock, horses and vehicles behind. The lead elements arrived in Berlin a few days later and were greeted by Friedrich Ebert, Provisional President of the Provisional Government of the new German Republic. Standing beneath the Brandenburg Gate he greeted the soldiers as returning heroes who were undefeated (*unbesiegt*). Heroic they were but Ebert forgot about Verdun, both battles of the Marne, the Argonne and four years of slaughter with nothing to show for it. This was the birth of *The Stab in the Back* legend. Ludendorf was the chief architect of the German Army's destruction. He picked up on the theme when a London columnist suggested it. The warlord leapt from his chair and looked for an alibi; 'Yes, that's it!' he cried. "We were *stabbed in the back* by the goddamn Jews and Communists!" Hindenburg, another mass-murderer, joined the chorus. A young non-commissioned officer who had been shot-up, decorated six times and seen his regiment lose 80% of its strength in one senseless battle after another, heard the news of the *Dolchstoß von hinten* and resolved to enter politics. In 15 years he would be Chancellor of the *Third German Reich*. This was Adolf Hitler; the most significant man of the 20th Century. The guy's power is so profound that he influences politics to this very day; even the term *hate-speech* was invented on account of him. It is fundamentally impossible to find a rational conversation about him. Quite literally, no one may say a good word about him. Many references to him will state that he is the most evil man in the history of the world; including Caligula, Genghis Kahn, Tamerlane the Conqueror, and Frank Nitti. Everything about him is demonized as a symbolic evil that represents Germany in the public mind. Anybody who wants to talk about the war and Hitler's role in it has to see the conflict in pathological terms. Not only was Hitler insane, he was a homicidal and genocidal maniac, often visibly frothing from the mouth, the spittle dribbling down his chin onto his disheveled old food-stained tunic. This vision makes all the destruction seem worthwhile: the enemy was not only mad but the single most despicable character in the history of the world; the epitome of evil.

Demonization

Benito Mussolini clarified the fascist state. His movement confuses people because it is now defined in absolutist moral terms rather than political and economic. It cannot exist because it is evil. It is so malevolent the liberal mind won't comprehend it as it entirely negates the power and rights of the sacred personality. Fascism turns all this upside down. Mussolini:

> *Liberalism denied the State in the name of the individual. Fascism reasserts the rights of the State as expressing the real essence of the individual.*

Mussolini was an Italian socialist around at the beginnings of the 20th Century. A good film about that era is *1900* (1976). He became the editor of the foremost Italian socialist journal *Avanti!* He spoke nine languages and, with Giovanni Gentile, would define Fascist political theory. Mussolini, like millions of other Italians, was wounded in the war. He formed a political action front with a few thousand like-minded fellows who called themselves *Fascisti*, a Roman symbol for strength and unity. They wore black-shirt uniforms and were tough guys hardened by war. Mostly out of work too as Italy in 1922 was a failed state. Mussolini was the smartest among them and they heeded his call; 30,000 *Blackshirts* marched on Rome. Benito hisself drove in a really nice car to Milan. Thousands of war veterans joined up as they went along, because all you had to do was don a black shirt and you were in. They demanded a new regime as the series of corrupt governments in power were fragmented and useless. Since Mussolini wanted to work within the capitalist-banking system he wasn't regarded as a threat to the established social order. That meant he wasn't a communist outlaw like Lenin, and so the King made him Prime Minister. He established a one-party system through force and the assassination of political opponents. His and Gentile's scheme of the state contradicted 18th & 19th century ideas about reason, intellectualism, and progressive democratic principles based upon *individualism* and the gratification of the senses. In this way Fascism is opposite in structure to the prevailing western notions of liberalism: that the *self-worth* and the attainments of the individual personality are the objects of life. *Humanism*, the study and glorification of the accomplishments of humankind, represents the scientific accumulation of knowledge for the enhancement of human well-being: *I think therefore I am*. For the Fascist mind this is contrived egalitarian rubbish. The individual's only worth in Fascism is in relation to the well-being of the State. Mussolini and Gentile saw that whatever the political inclinations of the workers were, they all rallied to the flag when war broke out. Thus it was easy to reason that nationalism transcended class values as outlined by Marx. Both of them abhorred the notion that an obviously corrupt western liberal democracy was the wave of the future. It had done nothing but bring upon the catastrophe of the war that betrayed Italy: for while England, France, Japan and even Romania fattened up on the carcasses of the German and Hungarian states, Italy had gotten only one small province. It surely wasn't enough for Italian nationalists who had pushed for war in the first place. They saw the richest provinces of Italy devastated by war as well as millions killed and maimed. They wanted what was promised to them and were angry that they didn't get it. *The Blackshirts* that now ruled Italy claimed vast swathes of European territory as rightfully and legally theirs; including Nice & Corsica (both French), Dalmatia (Yugoslav), Albania and indeed the whole Adriatic coast as well as Malta (British), and lots of Greek islands. They were only going to get those places through war, and Italy wasn't ready for that. Nobody was. But in the meantime Mussolini used executive action to get Italy out of the economic depression they were in. Strikes were declared illegal and corporate owners were obligated by threats to their well-being to improve working conditions. Borrow and spend was the way to institute a massive public works program that put millions of people back to work and improve the quality of life.

The New Deal is the same old deal

Franklin Roosevelt would use Mussolini's method as the model for his *New Deal* in 1933-36. This would feature finally giving workers the right to strike and then violently suppressing them when they did. In 1934 the nation was again in revolt. This was especially true when 12 Democrat governors called out the National Guard to break up the *Textile Strike* with bayonets, shotguns and machine guns. In spite of the atrocities, there were general strikes across the country. Huey Long of Louisiana emerged as a popular alternative to Roosevelt's phony *New Deal* but there were some big payoffs and Huey died in a hail of bullets from his '*bodyguards*' while a *patsy* took the rap. Roosevelt was then enabled to lead the country into a war the vast majority didn't want. It took some social engineering but he managed it.

Ll Duce

In this period, 1922-35, Mussolini was the most admired and celebrated statesman in the world. The august *New York Times* wrote regular and numerous articles praising him and his government. Indeed, the authoritarian, totalitarian model is one that the American liberal elite crave and admire because it protects their interests. The *Saturday Evening Post*, the largest circulating magazine in America, published his biography in serial form. The *Veterans of Foreign Wars* reckoned the *Fascisti* to be patriotic nationalists whom American veterans might emulate. Like all socialists, Mussolini wanted to change Italian attitudes about their own self-esteem. He sought to shape how they thought about *their nation* and not their racial composition. The well-being of the individual was important only that healthy, vibrant people create the same in a nation. Mussolini was a nationalist, and he wanted Italians to be proud of their country. It worked. Although many of them were not Fascist, they liked and admired Mussolini because he was among them; he walked the streets, ate pasta at local eateries and drove about town in an open car. He became the most popular Italian leader since Julius Caesar, who alas and alack, also came to a bad end.

Edda charms London

International adoration changed in 1935. Mussolini began to act upon the idea that combat hardened a nation spiritually and made its peoples great. The *Duce* (leader) used the old Roman Empire as an historical model and went after Ethiopia to expand the Italian Empire. He did this with the consent of England and France. Prime Minister Pierre Laval gave *accord*. Mussolini then sent his gorgeous daughter *Edda* to England with instructions to tell everyone she met that Italy planned to invade the African kingdom. Edda, who was 25 at the time, was the most renowned woman in Italy. She went to the finest schools and got juiced in all of them. When she married *Count Gian Galeazzo Ciano*, it was the most fabulous social event in fascist Italy. She became a Countess and looked like one. Ciano saw the marriage as a ticket to bigger and better things and he was right; he soon became foreign minister. After quite literally telling every taxi driver in London that Italy was on the warpath, Edda informed Britain's Prime Minister Ramsay McDonald. He offered no objections. Apparently it was open season on Ethiopia, a nation both independent and Christian, and one of only two African nations still free from western colonialism. None of that mattered. Both the British and French regarded Italy's presence on the horn of East Africa as a threat to their commerce. But Italy had already acquired those lands by treaty. For France and England, Ethiopia was inland and not worth a European war. Italy invaded without a declaration of war because by this time, war was legally criminal behavior.

War is outlawed

Legal problems regarding war arose earlier when the French tried to get their hands on Wilhelm II. He is another famous victim of demonization. All the French propaganda outlets blamed him for the war. Willy had absconded to Holland and was set up in a nice castle as his family, once the rulers of a vast empire, still had lots of *moola* in jewels, land and other ill-gotten gain. The victors wanted to put him on trial as a war-criminal but the Dutch wouldn't hand him over. Wilhelm had, in fact, broken no laws. War was not an illegal act, nor was conspiring to wage war. They did it all the time. This was when the French Prime Minister got the idea that war should be made illegal. *Aristide Briand* was lucky enough, and old enough, to have missed the shooting war but served as a minister in various functions, mostly in Greece where the Allies had opened a southern front in 1915. He was pals with Jules Verne and Briand's girl friend was, undoubtedly, the most interesting woman in the world. She was *Princess Marie Bonaparte*, a direct descendant of Emperor

Napoleon I and there is a statue of her in the *Philadelphia Museum of Art*. It's called *Princess X* and is shaped like a very large phallus; in tribute to her as one of the first psychoanalysts and sex researchers. Briand had connections all over the place and tried to get her crowned Queen of Greece; even then a nation in permanent chaos. She would have been a worthy successor to *Helen of Troy* but alas it was not to be. Later on she would ransom Sigmund Freud from the *Gestapo* (a German acronym for *Geheime Staatspolitzei; secret state police*) as well as all his private papers and rigamarole. She set him up nicely in London because she had the dough. She was part of that circle of Royalists and Imperialists still waiting around for the French Republic to fail, an event that might, even now, be just right around the corner.

It seemed like a good idea at the time

In between trysts with Princess Marie, Briand outlawed war. What a fine fellow he was! The *Kellogg-Briand Pact* was presented to the world in 1928 and was originally signed by 15 nations with many more to follow. Briand got American Secretary of State Frank B. Kellogg to lend some weight to the treaty although Kellogg never lifted a finger. Needless to say the treaty didn't work very well. One can still encounter articles heaping derision upon it. Little discussed is that the treaty turned upside-down our understanding of the legality of war and what acts constitute war. According to international law at the time, neither Wilhelm II, nor any of the other actors involved in the outbreak of the war, did anything unlawful. In fact, that was why nations *declared* war. Now, thanks to Kellogg-Briand, nations don't declare war anymore. The USA hasn't declared war on anybody since 1942 even though they are involved in an endless series of conflicts ever since. But the treaty took another profound step in that it made *boycotts legal*. Prior to 1928, if a nation tried to interfere with another nation's trade economy, it was considered an act of war. Blockades of any kind were deemed to be *de facto* declarations of war. But now, the situation was, and is, turned completely upside-down. Briand thought that an embargo would be a way to dissuade nations from aggression *short of war*, but it didn't work out that way. Given the devious nature of the thugs that run western civilization, and all the others for that matter, boycotts became a favorite way of waging war without actually declaring it. The USA and their *European Union* lackeys now use boycotts to starve and bankrupt target nations into submission; all by imperial decree.

Ethiopia

In this environment, Italy chose war as the path towards national well-being. Noting the illegality of it all they did not declare it. Nevertheless war it was and in the long-run it didn't work and never does: but try explaining that to a fellow in uniform addressing 200,000 fanatics from a balcony in the center of Rome. Henry Kissinger once said *power is an aphrodisiac* when he was romantically engaged with movie stars. In 1935 Mussolini was on top of the world and it would have been impossible to enlighten him that everything would all fall apart in a few short years. Sensibly, there was no need for Italy to invade the *Kingdom of Ethiopia* except for blind imperial ambition; and that was the root cause. Italy already controlled, by accord, a large swath of land on the southern edge of the African horn, and also *Italian Eretria* on the north shore. Eretria, now an independent nation, still retains whole districts of intact early 20th Century Italian architecture in its capital city *Assab*. From both these places Italy controlled the Red Sea and its commerce lanes. Investment in, rather than invasion of Ethiopia would have led to the creation of an Italian *sphere of influence* and a favorable balance of trade for Italy. They wouldn't have needed to station 250,000 troops there to enslave and massacre a hostile population.

The Battle of Adwa

Italy already tried to conquer Ethiopia in 1896 but was defeated. The Italian Army, much like Custer at *Little Bighorn*, advanced three separated brigades against a larger enemy force, a military strategy akin to suicide. Each Italian column was isolated from the others by poor maps, rugged terrain, and like Custer, they held the enemy in low esteem. They were wrong and each column was defeated in turn by a resourceful enemy that knew the lay of the land. Interestingly enough, Italian prisoners were treated decently but Italy's African allies, mostly Muslims who would wage war against Christian Ethiopia, had their right hand and left foot cut off. Forty years later Mussolini wanted revenge for Italy's humiliation. Italy's stated justification was, ostensibly, to eliminate slavery in Ethiopia. Of course there was slavery all over East Africa run by Arabs. Very few know that the center for the African slave trade was and still is Zanzibar on the east coast of Africa. At its height, the Arab Zanzibar slave traffic was four times larger than the Atlantic slave commerce to the Americas. The *League of Nations* declared Italy an aggressor and tepidly tested the waters with an oil embargo which was ignored by anybody that had oil for sale. Suddenly, in the western imagination at least, Mussolini's Italy began to lose some of it allure when their military looked like it might evolve into a real threat to English and French world hegemony. Mussolini himself, who was the object of adulation only months before, now began to be portrayed as a silly buffoon. The invasion proceeded apace anyway.

The Rape of Ethiopia

The Italian Army was eventually led by *Pietro Badoglio*, one of the most despicable characters in the whole of human history. When Mussolini became Prime Minister in 1922 he initiated a 10-year genocidal war against native Libyans with the aim of *population replacement* by Italian settlers. Badoglio was in command and his aim was the eradication of the Libyan people. He came close. He was thus the first governor of *Italian Libya* and in his whole time there established concentration camps where thousands died in wicked conditions. He poisoned wells, destroyed orchards and murdered thousands of innocent women and children hostages. He soon took command in Ethiopia. Like in Libya he was up against a militia army that brought their own rifles into battle; some of them armed with spears and arrows. This is militia defense and it is very effective when backed by a regular army: like the *Viet Cong* militia supported by the *North Vietnamese Army*. Ethiopia's army wasn't anywhere near as good. Even though the whole Ethiopian nation responded to the call to arms, they had few rapid fire or heavy weapons. They put up a good fight but were in an awkward strategic position. Much like the Russians defending the Polish salient in 1915 with Germans to the north and south of them, the

Ethiopians had large enemy contingents to the north in *Italian Eretria* and lesser forces to the south in *Italian Somaliland*. They fought a delaying action hoping for help from the *League of Nations*, to which both Italy and Ethiopia were signatories. Aside from a few small 50-man independent brigades made up of anti-fascist (*i.e.* communist) fighters, nobody else came. England and France boycotted some Italian exports but they didn't want Italy on the side of a National Socialist Germany that was already rearming. In truth too, the invasion of Ethiopia was very popular in Italy. Both France and England already had vast colonial empires in Africa and the hypocrisy was evident. Italians, in a barbershop, or in the halls of state, were fond of saying; *Why not us?* Indeed, why not them? The conquest was over in seven months with less than 2000 Italian dead. But Badoglio's use of poison mustard gas sprayed over an under-armed enemy, as well as civilians and livestock, turned the tide of an international opinion manufactured by the liberal democracies' controlled press. For in truth, the conquest of this very large and populous nation was so easy for Italy, they began to worry about Italian claims upon their own territory and vaguely acknowledged Ethiopia's deposed king, Haile Selassie who said: *It is us today. It will be you tomorrow.*

The League of Nations crumbles

A few years earlier in 1931, Japan invaded Manchuria, a very large and desolate province that was administered by the Chinese but not Chinese. Therefore, Japan argued, we have as much right to the place as anybody else. The native peoples there spoke *Tungusic* and are related to the *Turkic*, also not ethnic Chinese as noted earlier. When all those peoples first migrated out of western China some 1000 years ago, many went west and established the Ottoman Empire. Others settled in Siberia and Manchuria. Since their women are among the world's most beautiful, they have a tendency to reproduce rapidly wherever they go. But, like the Ethiopians, the residents of Manchuria didn't stand a chance against a determined invader armed with rapid fire weapons. There are not many left as the Japanese set about to exterminate them. Of course, the *League* failed to act. The whole purpose of the *League of Nations* was to prevent armed aggression. But Manchuria was far away and Japan was helpful in the world war against Germany. They escorted British troop movements from Australia, India and New Zealand all the way to Europe. Japan also drove the German *East Asia Squadron* out of Asian waters to where it was eventually destroyed by a British fleet off South America. For this, Japan was rewarded with the numerous Pacific islands that belonged to Germany, as well as *Tsingtao* (*Qingdao*), the German sphere of influence in China. Most people are familiar with Tsingtao rice beer as the Germans, naturally, established a brewery after they invaded and took the place from China in 1891. In 1919 it was given to Japan in direct violation of the letter and spirit of the *Treaty of Versailles*; especially since China had been an ally in the war against the Central Powers. This was an embarrassment to Wilson, rectified when sovereignty was returned to China a few years later. But it was too late. Chinese nationalists (*Mao Zedong, Zhou Enlai*) rejected the west and turned to Soviet Russia for support. By this time, Japan began to conquer a vast Pacific empire that included Korea, Formosa (Taiwan) and then Manchuria. Soon they would wage war against the liberal democracies as the peace promised at Versailles proved wholly illusionary. A good film about this era is *The Last Emperor* (1987).

The Cabinet of Dr. Kalergi

Count Richard von Coudenhove-Kalergi was a prolific author and perhaps the most important man that most ordinary people have never heard of. His father was an Austro-Hungarian count with Greek, Polish and Bohemian heritage. His mother was from landed nobility in Japan and Richard himself had married a 13-year old Jewess at a time when that wasn't anything particularly out of the ordinary. She was a real beauty and became an actress under the stage name Ida Roland. Richard, like many, was dismayed by the war and the dissolution of the *Dual-Monarchy*, the successor state to the *Holy Roman Empire*. From its creation in 800 until its termination in 1918, the Empire offered its citizens a safe haven with some notable exceptions like the *Thirty Years War* which was an invasion from afar, or the *Rhineland Massacres* (1096) that convinced many Jews it might be safer to migrate east to Poland. They settled there and became Poland's entrepreneurial class. By then tribal pogroms were a thing of the past in the Dual-Monarchy. Even when racially motivated bloodbaths erupted in the Balkan Wars (1912-13) that may be regarded as the beginnings of *the World War,* Austria kept tranquil. But with the outbreak of a general European war in 1914 these events spread to the Austrian Army. They took it upon themselves the mission to rid the world of Serbs and Jews. With Austria-Hungary's dissolution in 1918 and the creation of small independent successor states in accord with the Treaty of Versailles' policy of *self-determination,* these problems were not lessened but, on the contrary, increased. For example, Germans in the new nation of Czechoslovak faced the same kind of discrimination that Jews faced in Tsarist Russia. Europe was mired not only in political crisis but tragically became emotionally and intellectually destitute after the war. Nothing seemed to make sense anymore. All the old ideas that held Europe together throughout the Christian era were now discredited: not only by war but by the materialization of the godless Darwinian ethos and its deadly Eugenics movement. What emerged was essentially not only anti-Christian but anti-human. We can see this in today's science oriented educational systems. They present atheistic intolerance of any ideas that are not centered upon empirical materialist and behaviorist notions that humans and human history have no intrinsic value. Modern Sociobiology teaches that an ant colony has as much inherent significance as the whole of human society. Environmentalism stresses the notion that the world would be better off if humans could be completely wiped-out: ecocentrism gone mad. This is certainly the case in the 21st Century as Germans and Swedes, for example, are 40 years away from extermination. This extinction of an entire race and culture is seen as a good thing, even by many of the people facing oblivion. This is all part of a structured assault upon the norms and mores of western civilization.

Nothing outside the state

Coudenhove-Kalergi got an inkling of all this first hand as Mussolini's Blackshirts marched on Rome in 1922. For Mussolini the emergence of a well-structured and efficient national state was the final quest. The well being of the individual, including spiritual enlightenment, was only important to preserve the advent and success of the nation-state. Each human, in the fascist scheme of things, is like the cell inside an animal. Healthy reproductive cells would constitute a vigorous body-politic. Mussolini and Gentile wrote: *All within the state, nothing outside the state, and nothing against the state.* Count Kalergi saw things differently and concluded correctly that Mussolini's ideas might only lead to more war. He then resolved to change the nature of European civilization in two ways; first by eliminating national states. He would replace them with regional locales that would concern themselves with restricted issues centered upon provincial problems. This would end national wars and he drew inspiration from the *Holy Roman Empire* and its successor *Austria-Hungary*. In its thousand year history, the only horrific war it experienced, with the exception of the world war they started, was imposed upon it by rival national states. The Empire, despite its flaws, had protected western civilization and its spiritual Christian core from all comers including Turkic invaders that were halted at the gates of Vienna. Kalergi's second solution was the eradication of the white race. He saw them as intolerant and warlike despite astounding achievements in art and science. But of course, gentleman and pacifist that he was, he had no plan to murder anyone in this endeavor. Rather, in accordance with Eugenic principles, European Caucasians would be bred out of existence. He was not only the creator and forerunner of the *European Union* but also the euphemistically named process of *replacement migration* that is driving white Europeans into disappearance. As an admirer of Egyptian civilization, Kalergi envisioned an intermixing of North Africans with Europeans to breed the aggressiveness out of the race. How this would happen was anybody's guess. Muslims had been in Europe for centuries and there was little to show for it except for some magnificent architecture in Spain. Algeria was a part of France for close to a century and while there was some modest mixed-race interaction, there was nothing that would change the essential nature of France or of Algeria and Algerians. Anybody who looked into it and read his books might easily discern that *forced mass migration* from Africa into Europe was the proposed plan. This was delayed by the rise of nationalist movements throughout Europe but is being implemented now in the 21st Century. This is why the concept and mere mention of nationalism is anathema in the *European Union* and the *Democrat Party* in America.

Kalergi also proposed that Jews and Christians mix and become one religion with Jews in leadership positions. Kalergi felt Jews have the highest intellect and spirituality on the planet. That may be true, but only a despotic authoritarian state could enforce such a process. Kalergi envisioned this happening naturally and peacefully through eugenics. Since the whole of the European ethical foundation is based upon the books of Moses, Christians would accept this he thought; if only they could be educated properly. And they would be. One might have asked the Count what all those fancy ethics amounted to at the Siege of Jericho. It should all work itself out in the end he said, and he proposed a conference to find a solution to the perpetual warfare paradigm. The war-weary ruling elite went for it as the contrived nature of modern war and its incomprehensible horrors had made them mad.

The Pan European Congress

The first one was held in Vienna in 1926, the proposed capital of the new race and new nation of *Eurafrica*. They even had maps drawn up. Otto von Hapsburg was there; he being heir to the Austrian throne and all keyed up to assume another. Two thousand other deposed and entitled snobs showed up for the conference, all of them out of a job and looking for work. As a Tennessean might say: there were more Dukes and Duchesses, Counts and Countesses than you could shake a stick at. See, the European nobility still had lots of *scratch* because the bourgeois liberal democracies hadn't stripped them of their wealth, like that nasty Lenin and his brutish Bolsheviks did. Nope, they still retained their royal titles, heritage and wealth. But they didn't have anyone down on their knees to kick around anymore. In the new *Eurafrica* they would. What's more, they reckoned the new replacements would be shorter, browner, and weaker, both physically and intellectually. Most importantly, with neither a heritage nor common culture to bind them into a cohesive race of peoples, they would be ideal slaves. There were a number of immediate issues resolved like an anthem; and the current EU hymn, Beethoven's *Ode to Joy*, was chosen. There would be common markets and a common currency too: *the Euro*. Kalergi designed a flag with 12 stars representing the *Twelve Tribes of Israel*.

same as the current EU flag. Since there was something in it for them, lots of wealthy bourgeois Jews showed up at the conference too.

I'd rather barbecue

There were all sorts of Jews in Europe at this time, just like there were all sorts of Germans. The Prussians still ran the country and they admired hard work, some dueling, nettle and vinegar salads, black bread and butter, more military training and a cold beer at the end of the day. Bavarians liked the cold beer part along with fresh barbecue any time of the day. They were like the *Helots* in Sparta who tended the fields and went to war with the Spartans whenever the Laconia was threatened, which was often. After the Kingdom of Bavaria was conquered by Prussia, Bavarians were forced to go to war whenever Prussia did, whether they liked it or not. They didn't, but the alternative was to get shot down like the innumerable hostages the Prussian Army would take and murder on their way to Paris or wherever else the enemy might be. But the victims' identity wasn't based upon race. Later on it would be, and the German Jews at the *Paneuropa* conference were keen to find some alternative to rule by the Prussian Army.

The problematic nature of Zionism

The Jews are very much like the Germans and it's a shame how things turned out. Both races were spread out all over Europe and not just within the boundaries of the German national state. Russian Jews were in a poor situation under *Saint Nicolas II*. Under his rule, it was open season on them. In Tsarist Russia, the military or police could kill a Jew anytime they wanted to, and not suffer any repercussions, sort of like American cops who, until the national revolt in 2020, could shoot down anyone with impunity. In Imperial Russia, if some bureaucrat took a liking to a lovely Jewess, well then, her husband might be easily disposed of. It was practically impossible for a Jew to advance anywhere in the Tsarist civil service. They were the lowest of the low. Needless to say, when Lenin showed up, Jews became enthusiastic leaders in the communist revolt because there was no place to go but up. Also, and most significantly, it takes intelligence to be a Marxist and that's why Lenin initiated a nation-wide literacy program in 1919. It's also why most American Marxists hang out in universities and government. Stature as a communist revolutionary requires an actual principled command of both *Das Kapital* and *Imperialism*, Lenin's comprehensive analysis of the modern war machine. Most Bavarians and their American counterparts, colloquially known as *Joe Six-Pak*, don't care to comprehend it at all. Basically they just want to mind their own business and barbeque. As a result, cultural Marxism has to be beaten into their heads in a systematically enforced grade-school thru university education and media propaganda system. Sadly, if that doesn't work, then ridicule, banishment, loss of income, lawsuits and finally, if necessary, a beat-down by thugs usually does the trick. It is now called *The Cancel Culture*: conform or disappear. German Jews were in an altogether different situation, and that included Jews in Austria, which was, and is, a German nation. German Jews had risen to the top in Imperial Germany and Austria. They were influential politicians, academics, doctors, artisans, writers, industrialists, and capitalists, most of whom had real assets. These were the kind of Jews that the Zionists wanted in Palestine. But alas, and it doesn't take a whole lot of genius to figure why not, German Jews didn't want to go there. Germany is a really nice place, not the least of which is really fine wine and food. Germany represented *high civilization*, and why would any sensible Jew surrender that life, where they were doing very well, for one in the desert among a hostile Arab population that wanted to kill them dead? They wouldn't and didn't. This was a problem for the Zionists who shared a dream that German Jews didn't want any part of. The solution was Adolf Hitler.

The NSDAP

Hitler quickly became head of the *National German Workers Party* right after the war because he was the smartest guy in the room. And be sure, there were other smart guys in the room too; fellows like Anton Drexler, Gregor and Otto Strasser, and Dietrich Eckart. Hitler added *Socialist* to the party's name because he was one, as they all were. They were not *Alt-Right*. They were left-wing radicals and they were all *Pangermanists*. They were German nationalist in a way that cannot be completely understood by modern liberal democrats. National Socialists viewed nationalism *mystically*. The differences they had in party ideology were about how far to the left they wanted to go. The party consisted of many types; academics, bourgeois patriots and many war veterans who'd been to hell and back. Hitler promised to reverse the Treaty of Versailles and restore Germany to the stature it had before the war. He also wanted to collectively transform German society into a homogeneous one; which was the aim of the Russian Empire, the Balkan States and Ottoman Empire when the war began. To get there they all murdered subject minorities in the chaos of world war. Nothing that happened in the 2nd phase of the war (1936-46) was any different from the events that preceded it in the 1st phase (1912-23), except that the 2nd phase was ten times worse. In 1915 the Russian Army wiped out the Jewish population in eastern Poland and Belorussia, including any Muslims, Germans and Poles that got in the way. That was the start of the Jewish Holocaust but it isn't remembered anymore because the perpetrator, Tsar Nicholas II, is now a saint residing in heaven close to the gentle right hand of Jesus who weeps for him. Saint Nicholas got what was coming to him from a Latvian death squad and by the 1930's the actors had changed.

The Holocaust in Historical Perspective

On almost every international issue, the United States and Israel stand alone and united against the rest of the world. The dire complexity in this situation should be evident but it isn't. We in the west are unable to place the *World War* in historical perspective because the true motives and actions of the participants remain mysteriously hidden. In the liberal democracies, any rational attempt to understand the history of the 2nd *War-phase* is always modified by that. The true history is concealed and replaced by a series of legends that support the notion of a righteous and victorious war against a profound and evident evil. The American historiography that emerged from the *2rd War-phase* placed the United States as saviors of the world from unmistakable iniquity. The German nation, led by the most malevolent man in the history of the world, was an enemy that needed to be utterly crushed for all time. All events in this narrative are therefore viewed monolithically.

There could not have been any factions, or dissent, or moderates, or any possible alternative path from the pathologically insane wickedness of the one evil man who destroyed European Jewry with gas and incineration. Hitler's aim had to have *always been* the complete destruction of the Jewish race, and all his plans and actions, and that of his political party, is viewed, *and must be viewed*, in that context. The outcome is predetermined and inevitable. It doesn't matter that everything is seen through the lens of hindsight, working backwards from the present to 1945 and then further back to 1933. All preceding acts must therefore relate *only* to the outcome, and the outcome is absolutely known and never in doubt. The result is the death of the six-million, and that must and does explain everything, now and forever. Who knows or cares that 98% of all the Jews killed in the Holocaust didn't speak German. Never mind that for most of them, the only German they ever met was the soldier or policeman who killed them. Ignore the Latvians, Lithuanians and Ukrainians that gleefully participated. Disregard that all Jewish deaths pale in comparison to the 27 million (minimum) Soviet dead. Everything Hitler ever did must have the Jewish Holocaust as a motive, from the get go, planned and executed with typical German competence and ferocity. Any historian not in accord with this interpretation is ostracized, ridiculed, driven to despair and sometimes jailed.

Der Machtergreifung

Hitler was named Chancellor, (the German equivalent to Prime Minister), in January 1933 by Paul von Hindenburg who was the smiley-face front man to the mad military dictatorship under Ludendorf. The primary reason Hitler was chosen Chancellor was his fierce anti-communism. Hitler was a racist but in those days, who wasn't? In 1543 Martin Luther wrote *The Jews and their Lies (Von den Jüden und iren Lügen)*. It wasn't pretty. Luther thought it a good idea to set fire to Jewish synagogues, schools and villages and send them all on a journey to the infernal reaches. It took 400 years, but the National Socialist Party would do just that on his birthday in 1938. It wasn't just Luther but many others as well. *Joseph Arthur de Gobineau* invented the scientific study of races when he wrote *The Inequality of Human Races* (1856). Darwin too contributed to this understanding of races with *The Decent of Man* (1875) where he introduced the term *'sub-species'* (*Untermensch*) to categorize some races. No one doubted the existence of racial differences as they are evident. Why are 90% of the players in the *National Basketball Association* (NBA) of African descent? Why are 90% of Olympic sprinters of West African heritage? Why are 90% of Olympic swimmers Caucasian/white? The question only was, and still is; how and why do racial differences exist? In today's world we are told they don't exist. Bushmen created wondrous art 10,000 years ago. They obviously had the same artistic capabilities as the men who designed the Taj Mahal and Chrysler Building. In what way then did their civilization evolve? It didn't. Why did they remain hunter-gathers? Why did people of European descent walk on the moon? To recognize this practically unbridgeable cultural gap invites the charge of racism. *Diversity is our strength* is proclaimed but we may not ask the question; where is the proof for the assertion? Israel's razor-wire, concrete and titanium steel reinforced border wall belies the idea that Jews see diversity and inclusion as strength. They don't, never did, and never will.

Die Volksgemeinschaft

Hitler and the National Socialist Party wanted a racially homogenous society. So did the Zionists. In 1933, Hitler's primary enemy was the Communist Party, whose strength was in cities, especially in Berlin and among the workers. The Jews, who also lived mostly in cities, were an integral part of the Communist movement. When street battles broke out between the National Socialists and Communists, Jews were often among the casualties. But once Hitler assumed power, an event named *der Machtergreifung* (the seizure of power) there were no attacks upon Jewish culture in Germany. There were no home invasions where Nazi thugs raped Jewish girls before their horrified parents; made up events told and re-told to inflame international outrage. The rule of law still prevailed in Germany and would until the terror bombings in 1944-45 destroyed the fabric of German society. In fact it was *The American Jewish Congress*, *The American Jewish Committee* and the *B'nai B'rith* that struck first. They organized an international boycott of German goods in early March 1933; not on the basis of anything that Hitler and the National Socialists *had done*, but solely based upon things that Hitler *had said* before he became Chancellor. Three weeks later, in response, the National Socialists began to organize a counter-boycott of Jewish businesses. They didn't bash in windows or murder shopkeepers, but painted a yellow star on them and asked people not to shop there. Their boycott lasted one day. There was some intimidation but no broken glass. Berliners just ignored the Nazis, as they had done in the polling booth. The violence in the street was between political factions. The Nazis set up a prison for their political enemies in Dachau but no one was sent there on account of their race. It is important to note that not even one single German Zionist organization joined in, or advocated for, the anti-German boycott. In fact, they were against it. *The Zionist Federation of Germany*, the largest Zionist organization in Germany, wrote to the National Socialist government in early 1933:

> *In Boycott propaganda – such as is currently being carried on against Germany in many ways – is in essence un-Zionist, because Zionism wants not to do battle but to convince and to build…*

Indeed the Zionists and the National Socialists had similar goals: they both wanted Jews out of Germany.

Therefore by their fruits you will know them

What Hitler and the National Socialists wanted in Germany was a situation like in the USA at the time between African-Americans and the Anglo-Saxon ruling elite: separate but equal facilities as confirmed by the United States Supreme Court (*Plessy vs. Ferguson* 1898). Of course the separate but equal facilities weren't so, but the law provided legal justification for the segregation of races. In addition, the *Democrat Party* was in control of all the legislatures and governorships of the former *Confederate States of America*. They prohibited, *by law*, any social intermixing of the two races. They defined it as *miscegenation* and it included marriage, co-habitation, sex and procreation, or even eating in the same store. The National Socialists wanted something like this in Germany but not as harsh. They wanted an agreement (*Abkommen*) between them and the Jews, and *behold*, so did the Zionists. They were both especially keen to prevent inter-racial marriages, something that had become quite prevalent in Germany because there is nothing in the world more beautiful than a Jewish woman. The *Zionist Federation* wrote to the German government:

> *Our acknowledgment of Jewish nationality provides for a clear and sincere relationship to the German people and its national and racial realities. Precisely because we do not wish to falsify these fundamentals, because we, too, are against mixed marriage and are for maintaining the purity of the Jewish group and reject any trespasses in the cultural domain…*

In what was a *win-win* situation, both sides agreed to cooperate. What happened was that during the 1930's, the German government did more to support the establishment of a Jewish homeland in Palestine than any other government in the world; so much so that the *Grand Mufti of Jerusalem* thought Hitler was a Jew, or if not that; then surely a Zionist. And by his acts, he was. Nobody is allowed to talk about this anymore.

The Haavara Agreement

In the meantime, everyone else, especially Great Britain, was doing all they could to prevent the Zionist state. Now this is heresy in the world of the liberal democracies. A good example is Ken Livingstone, the former mayor of London and member of the Labor Party. In 2018 he had the temerity to mention the cooperation between the Germans and Zionists in the *Haavara* agreement. A howl went up about him speaking the truth and he was forced to resign from the party. Anyone even vaguely remembering *das Abkommen* (the agreement) will immediately be attacked under the all-encompassing banner of *anti-Semitism*. The lens through which the Holocaust is viewed absolutely prohibits and defiles even a discussion of any benign motives by Hitler whatsoever. But it is the truth. The full support of Israel and the protection of the Judeo-Christian ethic require that this sort of madness needs to stop. If not, it will eventually bring about the abandonment and destruction of the Jewish state. When Germany and the other Nordic nations fall, as they soon will, Israel's isolation will be absolute.

Das Abkommen

The *Haavara* (transfer) *Agreement* was signed August 25th, 1933. Most discussions on the transfer agreement, and there aren't many, focus on economics. Basically, it was difficult and costly *for anyone* to leave Germany and take their wealth with them. The transfer agreement allowed Jews to sell whatever possessions they wanted to, and deposit the proceeds into a German holding company. The money would then be used to buy tools, tractors, piping, drills; whatever equipment Jews would need in Palestine. These would be German made as a promotion to German industry. The goods would then be shipped to Palestine, on German ships, and sold by a Jewish holding company. The profits were then returned to the original Jewish provider. This allowed 60,000 German Jews to leave Germany for Palestine with their wealth intact. A Jewish official in Palestine wrote:

> *The economic activity made possible by the influx of German capital and the Haavara transfers to the private and public sectors were of greatest importance for the country's development. Many new industries and commercial enterprises were established in Jewish Palestine, and numerous companies that are enormously important even today in the economy of the State of Israel owe their existence to the Haavara.*

The monetary aspect of the *Abkommen* is usually the only one considered, and *Edwin Black*, who first wrote about it in *The Transfer Agreement* (1984), stressed that without it, the modern state of Israel might not exist. Black, who is Jewish-American, was disowned by his mother for publishing the truth. This is always the case in Holocaust studies; the narrative must adhere to the strict guideline that there never was any deviation from the path to the death camps. And yet, the facts show that there were divisions and factions within the National Socialist Party. At the time of the *Haavara*, the moderate faction was in control of the National Socialist party. Hitler was the leader of this pragmatic faction, and only later did the radicals led by Heydrich, Goering, Rosenberg and Eichmann gain control of the party's Jewish policy. This happened when Hitler became obsessed with his role as Commander in Chief of the German Army in Russia (1941-45). The mass-murder programs began only then. This understanding is anathema to *Holocaust Jewry* that demands a *single malevolent force* bear the complete burden of responsibility for the Holocaust.

Separate but equal, Nazi style

There was much more to the *Abkommen* than is generally noted. Once the Germans and the Zionists saw that cooperation was not only possible but profitable, they established more trade agreements. Jaffa oranges were now shipped exclusively to Germany in exchange for timber and cars. That is why one still sees mostly German autos on Israeli roads. The 2nd *War-phase* was a temporary interruption for the German-Israeli mutual aid and mutual admiration society that continues extensively to this day. This will soon end as communist Chancellor Angela Merkel's Islamization of Germany aims, again, to drive the Jews out of Europe. Now a newly navigated *Paneuropa* project will finish the Jews off. This time the killers will be imported. The invaders themselves are a homogenous whole centered upon a religion that sees Jews as a deadly enemy, something the *Paneuropa* planners saw coming.

Kalergi's Paneuropa is banned

In one of his first acts as Chancellor, Hitler banned the *Paneuropa* movement in Germany. Today's German globalists who rule the nation, know that only the barbarian invaders have both the will and central organization to modify the Nordic race through demographic change. If this means the expulsion of Jews so be it. But in fact, during the time of the *Abkommen*, German policy was far more forgiving of Jews than can be presently admitted. The *Nuremburg Race Laws* of 1935 (based entirely on American race laws passed by the Democrat controlled southern states) only reinforced this. Zionists greeted them with satisfaction. The Zionist paper *Judische Rundschau* wrote on September 17th, 1935:

> *Germany ... is meeting the demands of the World Zionist Congress when it declares the Jews now living in Germany to be a national minority. Once the Jews have been stamped a national minority it is again possible to establish normal relations between the German nation and Jewry. The new laws give the Jewish minority in Germany its own cultural life, its own national life. In future it will be able to shape its own schools, its own theatre, and its own sports associations. In short, it can create its own future in all aspects of national life.*

The new race laws prohibited Jews from displaying the German flag but rather encouraged them to fly their own flag; the blue and white banner of Israel. They could fly this over their own schools, sports clubs and the more than 40 *kibbutzim* German Jews established in Germany at the time. The last remaining Kibbutz, in Neuendorf Germany (near Berlin), closed down in April 1943.

The Nazis were all for it and wrote in *Das Schwarze Korps*, May 1935:

> *The recognition of Jewry as a racial community based on blood and not on religion leads the German government to guarantee without reservation the racial separateness of this community. The government finds itself in complete agreement with the great spiritual movement within Jewry, the so-called Zionism, with its recognition of the solidarity of Jewry around the world and its rejection of all assimilation notions. On this basis, Germany undertakes measures that will surely play a significant role in the future in the handling of the Jewish problem around the world.*

American Jews were also in complete accord. Stephen S. Wise, President of the *American Jewish Congress* on June 13th, 1938:

> *I am not an American citizen of the Jewish faith, I am a Jew... Hitler was right in one thing. He calls the Jewish people a race and we are a race.*

This is why American Jews need to recognize today's enemy. American Jews, who are contributors to the Democrat Party, want open borders for America but closed borders for Israel. Population replacement in America and Europe is promoted as '*inevitable*' but race exclusivity for Israel is strictly enforced. The hypocrisy and duplicity are remarkable. Undoubtedly there are presently many Jews who would like to see their former oppressors destroyed. They might consider that once the Caucasian races (Israel's only friends) are bred out of existence or exterminated in camps, Jews will not be on top in the *New World Order*. They would be wise to again heed the words of Haile Selassie: *It is us today. It will be you tomorrow.*

The end of liberal democracy in Central Europe

Hitler's seizure of power was indeed that. He was no friend of the Jews but liberal democracy was the primary enemy. We in the west suffer under the delusion that the end of all political action must and should be the creation and maintenance of the liberal democratic order including all the phony elections. Like Mussolini's *Fascisti*, the *National Socialists* rejected all aspects of the liberal order and recognized that it would be madness to hand back power to corrupt politicians who are bought and sold to the highest bidder. In a short time the *Reichstag* lay in smoldering ruin. Communists were blamed, imprisoned and their party banned, as were all others. The *Enabling Act* was quickly passed and signed by the chief enabler himself, Paul von Hindenburg. Hitler now had dictatorial powers. Ernst Rohm was head of the *Brownshirts* or *Sturmabteilung*; a four and one half million strong private army. Hitler personally murdered him in the *Night of the Long Knives*. This was done on behest of the Prussian Army. General Kurt von Schleicher, Hitler's predecessor as Chancellor, was shot down like a dog along with his wife in their own home. *NSDAP* founder Gregor Strasser died too, gruesomely killed by the spineless Heydrich. Strasser was too radical for the Nazis who were aghast at his plan to abolish all private property. The German General Staff, yellow sniffling cowards all of them, shrugged it off and forced the Army to swear allegiance to Hitler, who was now *Fuhrer* for life. Hitler had banking friends, some of them Jewish, and all of them anti-communists. Dr. Heinrich Brűning, German Chancellor 1930-1932, in a letter to Churchill in 1947:

> *I didn't, and do not even today, for understandable reasons, wish to reveal that from October 1928, the two largest regular contributors to the Nazi party were the general managers of the two largest Berlin banks, both of the Jewish faith, and one the leader of Zionism in Germany.*

One of the first things the world's most evil man did was nationalize the German banking system. For some, that might be the epitome of iniquity. German banks then made very low interest loans available for public works. That invigorated the economy and helped create full employment in three years. It wasn't just banks either. Major American firms like Standard Oil, Ford, General Motors and IBM all poured investment money into National Socialist Germany.

The German economic miracle

The German economy from 1933, until it was overwhelmed by war in 1944, was collectivist: but not in an intellectual sense as in Soviet Russia: rather as a nationalist communal endeavor; *die Volksgemeinshaft* (Racial community). When Hitler took power the German economy was in shambles. The Treaty had drained all its gold. So many were killed or emotionally destroyed by the war that the birthrate was in steep decline. About *fourteen thousand* firms filed for bankruptcy every year. More than 100,000 people lost their livelihood every year too, and 35% of the population was on public assistance. Germany still owed 19 billion *Reichsmarks* to foreign creditors on account of the Treaty. That was a lot of money. The Treaty not only blamed Germany for the war but was designed to keep the nation permanently impoverished with complete destruction of the German race the ultimate goal. This will soon be achieved by replacement migration. But in the 1930's Germany temporarily halted the Paneuropa extermination process with an immediate assault on unemployment. Hitler quickly appointed West Prussian *Hjalmar Horace Greeley Schacht* as head of the *Reichsbank*. He helped put National Socialist economic plans into action. Full employment was achieved in five years. Germany was then out of the worldwide depression that began in 1929. America wasn't out of it until the 1950's despite massive government borrowing for public works and war industries. Critics say that the German economic revival was due to war spending and the elimination of Jews and women from the work force. War spending by itself will never end a financial depression as the products are mostly single use items. Instead, the National Socialist state was a *German* government and not an *internationalist* one. It sought the *Pangermanic* goal of national self sufficiency. Speculation and profits by small banking elites were ended. Interest rates were low and the money invested in Germany, not *offshore*. Jews made up less than 1% of the population and they were not discriminated in the blue-collar workforce unless they were communists. Women's participation actually increased even though couples that raised a family, especially large ones, were given subsidies and tax incentives. In fact, labor participation among German women in 1939 was higher than was that of the USA and Britain in 1945. Workers were respected and the beer was good. Everything the National Socialists did was aimed at the making of a vibrant national economy and identity; *die Volksgemeinshaft* and the re-creation of *Pan Germania*.

Re-militarization

There was once an Irish fellow who proposed that time ran backwards; that as every second passed, we were all moving towards to our birth, and away from our death; the apparent forward movement of time being only an illusion. He offered a number of elaborate and sometimes amusing proofs; but the idea didn't catch on, even though one of his drinking buddies was James Joyce. So too is our view of German rearmament. *Der Machtergreifung* was in 1933. Seven years after that the German Army stood triumphant from the Atlantic in the west to the Vistula border with Russia in the east, from the

Mediterranean Sea in the south to the *Nordkapp* at the edges of the Arctic Ocean in the north. Less than 5 years later they would be crushed in catastrophic defeat. The establishment view is that only the pathologically evil and sinister mastermind, Adolf Hitler, could have created this vast military machine; all at odds with the peace loving liberal democracies England and France. Yet German rearmament didn't occur with Hitler in 1933. It began long before that. In 1921 they formed up *Arbeits-Kommandos* (work squads) as a way to train troops. The *Black Reichswehr* (Secret Army) organized death squads for political opponents. They were led by *Kurt von Schleicher* who got was coming to him on the *Night of the Long Knives*. *Carl von Ossietzky*, from an ennobled family, was a courageous journal publisher (Die Weltbühne) who revealed secret Luftwaffe training in the 1920's with the *Soviet Red Air Force*. He died of disease in a Nazi concentration camp. A very interesting graphic novel about this era is *Berlin* by Jason Lutes 488 pp. (2018). Modern commentators fail to recognize that Prussia ruled Germany and that the German Army ruled Prussia. In 1933 they were still limited to 100,000 men in ten divisions with no air force and no tanks. Why didn't France seek real peace? Why didn't they reduce their army from the 600,000 active soldiers with 5 million men in reserve? Why didn't they stop sucking gold out of Germany? Now admittedly, about half that army was needed to control France's vast slave empire that ran from South America, to Africa and Southeast Asia. And yes Virginia, the liberal democracies did have slave empires. They still do. England's slave empire included South Africa's gold mines and the whole Indian sub-continent. India had the world's richest economy in 1805, or until the Brits conquered the place and turned it into a human cesspool of misery. But that's what England does.

Das Rhineland.

Observing the peace negotiations at Versailles, Field Marshall Foch predicted the next European war. He wanted to annex for France a place called the *Rhineland*, a German province rich in coal, iron and the best white wine. It lay to the west of the river that has its name. Most importantly for France, it was a staging area for the Germans to attack France without having to fight across the river to get there. But President Wilson wanted *self-determination* and because Americans are important in the French scheme of things, they gave in to him. They should have ignored him and just taken the place as spoils of war. Since 90% of the inhabitants of the Rhineland spoke German, it remained German; with the provision that the German Army wasn't allowed in. Ergo the Rhineland was famously *demilitarized*. Ultimately the French Army had to keep the enemy out of there. With the Germans reduced to a 100,000 man army that would be easy, right? But Germany wasn't helpless. True the army was small but there were still 4 ½ million *Brownshirt Sturmabteilung* street fighters ready and willing to mix it up. It would take a while to prepare them for army life but it's not like Germany didn't have any reserves. As always, the German Army had more than enough artillery. Their banker friends began to immediately figure out ways to evade the treaty and rearm. The treaty prohibited a German Air Force. Many German armament firms like Junkers, opened plants in Sweden where they designed and produced aircraft for the future *Luftwaffe*. Pilots were trained in gliders, or flying for *Lufthansa*, the national airline. Versailles said the German Army couldn't rotate men in and out of service as did the Prussians when they circumvented the *Treaty of Tilsit*. But men get sick, and they get old and new men get mustered into service. By 1935 another fifty thousand men, sitting at home enjoying the fruits of the 10,000 breweries that sprawled over the countryside, were fully trained officers prepared for the renewal of war.

The Franco-Soviet Pact

In 1934 when Germany and its sinister government concentrated on the well-being of the German people, the nations that defeated Germany in the *1ˢᵗ War-phase* continued to prepare for more war. Russia, with its *one million, three hundred thousand man standing army, ten thousand tanks* and another <u>*10 million men in reserve*</u> still had factions, centered on Trotsky, who demanded world revolution and the conquest of the west. Stalin was able to resist them but for how long? In 1935 France and Soviet Russia negotiated a pact to yet again surround Germany as they did in 1914. What were they afraid of? In fact it was Germany afraid of them. With Poland as a buffer and potential ally, the German Army decided that in the face of the soon to be signed *Franco-Soviet Pact*, they would strike first. They would occupy the Rhineland and let the chips fall as they may. Most of the references to this event promote the idea that it was Hitler who ordered the operation. '*Hitler re-militarized the Rhineland*' all the books and articles say. Later, it would be '*Hitler invaded Poland*' as if the fellow was alone with a six-shooter like John Wayne at *Fort Apache*. Hitler wasn't doing anything on his own and certainly nothing that the German Army didn't want or agree to. He may have been a *Dictator* in the western sense in that he didn't need any parliamentary majority to implement social policy. But he had less power than Mussolini at this stage. Hitler's foreign minister was *Konstantin Hermann Karl Freiherr von Neurath*, who was Hitler's link to the noble ruling elite. They supported Hitler because he guaranteed the perpetuation of their assets and status. Mussolini's foreign minister was his son in law who did as he was told. The Chief of the German General Staff was *Ludwig August Theodor Beck*, who was 100% behind the *Dictator* because Hitler did everything that Beck and the rest of the Prussian officer corps told him to do; which was rearmament and the preservation of their status as the *de facto* rulers of the German nation. In the end, when it fell apart and needing someone to blame, they all pointed their bony fingers at the man with the moustache.

Alea iacta est

The die is cast spoke Caesar at the head of his army when he crossed the Rubicon. Hitler acceded to the wishes of the German ruling elite and gave the order to cross the Rhine. The 32,000 man force included 19 battalions of infantry and one police battalion. If the French counter-attacked, the Germans were prepared to conduct a fighting withdrawal back across the Rhine and stop the French there. They had strong defensive positions backed up with plenty of big guns and ammo, something they never ran short of. They were also now officially in violation of the Treaty of Versailles. It was up to France to enforce the Treaty but they did nothing; primarily because the nation's government was broke and couldn't afford the mobilization of the full 6 million man army. They could have fought back with the 260,000 men they had in the field but they figured the Rhineland wasn't worth it. The standard story is that had the French fought back, the Germans would have been easily beaten and *'Hitler would have been stopped.'* The histories and documentaries always use the word *stopped*. If only he could have been *stopped* they say, then all those poor people wouldn't have died. *But stopped by whom*? Ten years later, after the wheels came off, the Prussian officer corps tried to present themselves as paragons of moral and civic virtue. They certainly would have *stopped* Hitler, if only they could have. Regrettably, they were handcuffed: those miserable French had let them down. Had those weak, ineffectual and effete French done anything at all, Hitler would have been propelled into inglorious oblivion and *stopped*. The only thing is there were very few people on the German side who wanted him *stopped*. They liked the guy and everything about him. So did the other side. For them, Hitler was a politician who was a bit out of the ordinary. However that might be, he didn't like Jews and communists. The French and British elite didn't like those fellows either. At this time, all the governments in Europe decided that they'd rather work with Hitler than anything else. They didn't view Hitler as the manifestation of pure evil as we do today. They wanted a return to the *status quo ante bellum*; a stable situation where France and England were on top but confined by a *balance of power*. That remedy had worked for the entirety of *Pax Europa* (1815-1914). They were willing to share power with Germany for awhile to get there again and stay there. Britain didn't want a strict enforcement of the Versailles Treaty. They were willing to concede to a revision. Above all else they demanded the preservation of their colonial slave labor empire. Germany was good with that provided she could have *Pangermania*. Hitler misjudged the situation and, in the end, he was played for a sucker. The west would never agree to, or allow, *Pangermania*. They would delay war until the economic situation allowed the massive re-armament they wanted. They knew Germany would never be able to defeat the west in a long war; that the result would be the same as the *1st War-phase*, with Germany blockaded and starved to death. But this time they would make sure Germany was annihilated. That is how it turned out, but getting there destroyed the liberal order too, and in a most incomprehensible way.

The Masters of War

The standard histories say the war began anew on September 1, 1939 when Germany attacked Poland. One can also say the war started in 1936 when the Rhineland was incorporated by military action. That was followed up a few months later when both Germany and Italy invaded Spain. Then, as now, Spain was an impoverished nation. Four hundred years ago they were the richest country in the world with a vast slave empire. Many of their colonies rebelled and in the end, the USA took what was left of it. The Spanish people themselves lived for hundreds of years under the ruthless oppression of the Catholic Church and an autocracy that kept laborers in a state of feudal serfdom. The military, police and judiciary backed them up. In 1934 the people revolted. Soviet Russia helped the rebellion with their best military equipment that they sold for Spanish Empire gold. A few thousand Americans formed *The Abraham Lincoln Brigade*. All told about 40,000 volunteers helped the Republican Army. It wasn't enough. The German Army invaded with a full division of 13,500 men with tanks and guns. The Italians sent even more: the *Corpo Truppe Volontarie*, a 50,000-man force of four divisions, four independent brigades, a tank battalion and support units. Both the Germans and Italians sent their air forces for some indiscriminate bombing of civilians and city destruction. *Francisco Franco* was the *Generalissimo* and killer in charge of murdering a million Spanish in combat, firing squads, death squads and concentration murder camps. He stayed on as military dictator until he died in 1975. The *Spanish Civil War* still tears the country apart and *Catalan independence* is a part of this. Spain as we see it today is an artificial construction held together by force. The Republicans lost because Soviet Russia was the only nation willing to help them. But supply was difficult when the Italian navy and air force intervened in the Mediterranean. The Italians made a huge contribution and Franco couldn't have won without them. They wanted to re-create the Roman Empire and make the whole Mediterranean their lake as did Caesar. A friendly government in Spain was a part of that imperial vision. But they lost a lot of equipment: thousands of guns and troops, and close to 10,000 vehicles that Italian industry couldn't quickly replace. The German participation was much more measured. For them, Spain was just a place for the Army to test their military equipment on live targets. Their sights were set instead, as always, on *Mitteleuropa and Pangermania*.

Deutsch-Österreich

When the western truce was declared in 1918, Austrian *Emperor Karl I* tried to preserve his throne as a constitutional monarchy. He was no longer king of Hungary as they wanted to go their own way. So did the Serbs. *Karl* and *Empress Zita* found themselves out of a job. Hungary and Serbia lopped off huge tracts of territory, some of which rightfully belonged to them, and Austria was left hanging. They had a huge capital city, Vienna, that didn't have a purpose anymore. It was once the center of a massive continental empire. Now it was the capital of its own small Germanic province. With two million people, including hundreds of thousands of bureaucrats, the city made up 1/3 of the new Austrian nation's population. The rest of the country was mostly mountainous. Innsbruck is certainly a great ski-vacation destination, but what was the rest of Austria supposed to do besides yodel in the hills to the sound of music? Admittedly they still haven't figured that out. In 1919 the logical solution was union with Germany. They named their new nation *Deutsch-Österreich* because historically there never was any such thing as an *Austrian*. People who lived there considered themselves German and their ethnicity was listed as such; *Deutsch*. After 1945, when being German became synonomous with death camps, they all decided they didn't want to be German anymore. Thay have a right to do that. However, in 1919, the framers of the Treaty of Versailles had no intention to make Germany more populous and powerful. On the contrary, they wanted to destroy Germany. It was only because their own armies were too exausted that they agreed to the armistice that led to Versailles. *Ergo*: union between the two was prohibited even though that was what they both wanted. Self determination was for winers. It just wasn't appropriate for losers. The Treaty hit Austria hard. They lost the *Sudetenland* that was awarded to the new nation of Czechoslovakia. *Bozen* (Bolzano) and the very large *South Tyrol*, was given to Italy even though it still has a German majority. From the get-go Austria was a failed state. It still is.

Anschluss

Count Bismarck, who was prime minister of Prussia, organized a series of wars by which Prussia conquered states like Bavaria and created the German union. The schoolbook texts call this process *German unification*. The question he and all subsequent German leaders faced, even today, was what kind of German union did they want? In 1990 the *Bundesrepublik* (West Germany) annexed the *Deutsche Demokratische Republik* (East Germany). Oh happy day! Now the East Germans want to go their own way again, and the question still remains: what is Germany? Was it one that encompassed all Germans: the greater Germany solution; *die Großdeutsche Lösung*? Bismarck elected on the pragmatic or limited (*Kleindeutsch*) solution. This decision made quite a few people unhappy. Germans that lived elsewhere in Europe, (and they were all over the place), would not be the object of German foreign policy under Bismarck. Hitler, who was also a pragmatist once he became Chancellor, opted for all the marbles. This was, not coincidentally, the aim of *Pan Germania*. Hitler's foreign policy pleased all the nationalist factions in Germany, especially those in the Army. It was something most ordinary Germans wanted as well. In the end, it was what they were all fighting for when the war broke out in 1914.

Willkommen ins Reich

The German Army welcomed Austria into *das Reich* on March 12, 1938. The invasion met no opposition. The Austrian Army's eight divisions were also greeted warmly but those fellows were a bit disappointed. They thought they could start killing Jews again, just like old times, the sooner the better. Hitler wouldn't allow it. Germany had reached an accommodation and they weren't going to change it just because the Austrians wanted to do what they do best. The Austrian Nazis, now in power and emboldened, did pull the Jews out of their homes to scrub the streets for one day. But by 1938, five years after worldwide headlines read *Judea declares war on Germany*, not a single Jew in Germany had been killed on account of either race or religion. That is not to say that there wasn't any religious discrimination in Germany. There was. The *Jehovah's Witnesses*, a Christian sect, were violently suppressed. Eventually 5,000 of them would be guillotined for refusal to cooperate with Hitler's government in any way, including military service. But the Jews were safe in Germany. Many of them still wanted to leave and did, but there was a large group too poor to pick up and go. The Zionists didn't want them and neither did the National Socialists. It was this group of German Jews that were in trouble. With *der Anschluss*, another 200,000 Jews were added to the German population. The wealthy got out, the poor didn't.

Sudetenland

The annexation of Austria was the successful culmination of 100 years of German aspirations and foreign policy. If Hitler had died just then, he would now be remembered as the most famous and beloved German leader there ever was. Six months later he wanted more. The Sudetenland is a mountainous and forested province that brews the best beer in the world. All the ingredients for beer are indigenous to the region and the water there is naturally soft. One of the monumental events in the whole history of western civilization took place in the (then) German city of *Pilsen* with the invention of blond *Pilsener* beer in 1842. The brew is smooth as silk. Germans had brewed beer and lived there for thousands of years, but they were all driven off or murdered by Edward Benes and his police in 1945-46. Benes was the peace-loving President of Czechoslovakia who caved in when the German Army and the *Blut und Boden, Pangermanic* crowd wanted to welcome the *Sudeten Germans* into the *Reich*. If Hitler was ever to be *stopped* short of world war, it was here; but Benes lacked guts. John Wayne once said to an antagonist: *You have a yellow streak down your back a mile wide.* The same could be said of Benes. He was a real man when it came time for his thugs to machine gun German women and children into ditches, but when real courage was needed he ducked for cover. There was one other thing (never mentioned) that the Sudetenland had a lot of, and still does: one of the world's richest deposits of uranium ore.

Appeasement

For a long time the Sudetenland was synonymous with the policy of *Appeasement*. When viewed through hindsight, the surrender of the Sudetenland in September 1938 is seen not only as a sign of the abject capitulation by France and England to the depredations of an insane and malevolent bandit, but also as a policy failure of monumental proportions; one that influences American foreign policy to this day. If there is any wonder why the USA always seems to be mired in unwinnable but expensive wars, it is not just the brutal economics of it. It is also the philosophical notion that any step back away from war will lead to future catastrophe. This overlooks the fact that British foreign policy throughout the 1920's and 1930's was about revising the Treaty of Versailles to which both Germany and Russia were excluded. There is a presumption that the Treaty was realistic but violated by Hitler. The notion that either France or Britain might enforce its provisions is based upon the ultra-shortsighted supposition is that neither Germany nor Russia would ever again re-emerge as great powers. By the time of the *Remilitarization* and *Anschluss*, they both had.

Go home and get a nice quiet sleep Neville Chamberlain

Neville Chamberlain was a decent sort of fellow who represented the interests of the Anglo-Saxon British ruling elite. That's why they made him Prime Minister. He was a businessman and came from a political family. He missed the war and sincerely didn't want another one. When the *Pangermanists* demanded the incorporation of the *Sudeten Germans* into the *Reich*, the politician in Chamberlain wanted to make a deal with Germany; and why not? After all, that is what politics is all about. He made what was then a radical decision and decided to board an aeroplane and see Hitler personally without his Foreign Secretary Lord Halifax. It was just going to be him and Hitler. This was one of the first face-to-face international summits. In 1934 Hitler and Mussolini met in Venice to discuss the fate of Austria. Afterwards *Il Duce* proclaimed Hitler *"a mad little clown."* Maybe, but Hitler got his way four years later. These sorts of meetings, now commonplace, were unusual back then. Normally, it was diplomats stationed in the opponent's capital city that would conduct diplomacy by cables to and from the home office. This was exactly how the war began in the *July Crisis* in 1914. Heads of state would usually only meet at funerals or at major international conferences like *The Congress of Vienna* (1815) or *Berlin* (1878), all planned months in advance. But in the summer of 1938 there was no international conference scheduled, and another war seemed inevitable. Small central and eastern European states were vital to France. She hoped they would hem-in and limit the power of both Germany and Russia. But the Czech ruling elite weren't smart enough to let the German majority in Sudetenland live in peace. Germans had dominated the whole region of Bohemia when they were a part of the Austrian Empire. Now the Czechs couldn't resist kicking them around a little bit. Benes thought he was secure with France beside him but the French weren't so sure without England.

The state is only a means to an end.   Mein Kampf

What Chamberlain couldn't comprehend was the utter distain and contempt that Hitler and Mussolini held him. The feelings were mutual. Chamberlain referred to Hitler as a *"half-mad dog"* and a *"common housepainter."* There wasn't a whole lot of difference between Hitler and Mussolini, and yet even as early as 1938, we see the first references to Hitler as *"mad."* Why wasn't *Il Duce* that way too? To the western liberal mind, his showboating theatrics were just as silly as Hitler's. Both he and Hitler were products of the war and their political parties were perceived as street-rabble even though that was never completely true. Simply put, the liberal democrats couldn't figure Hitler out. They thought he was an ignorant housepainter when he had a mind like a steel trap. They thought he was driven by nationalistic impulses like Mussolini but he wasn't. For Mussolini, nationalism and patriotism meant allegiance to *Italy* as a nation-state. The liberals could understand this. For Hitler, the nation-state was not an end itself. Germany as a nation-state was rather a means to an end; and that end was the creation of a racially homogonous *Volksgemeinshaft*. The liberal mind cannot grasp this. Hitler didn't create this movement, or this idea. It was there before he was born. He represented *Pangermanic interests* that were intrinsic to German nationalism. He knew very well that he might ignore them to his peril. Hitler was demonized as a street fighter, or as Churchill would later say, *a gutter snipe*. But that was only how he gained political power in a nation torn apart by war. Now he was *Reichskanzler*. For both he and Mussolini, their opponents represented the utterly corrupt and contemptible political marketplace of commonality that routinely bought and sold votes, nations, and people, to the highest bidder. For the British and French, Hitler and Mussolini were street thugs and gangsters who had gained power illegitimately. Neither side understood the other.

Summitry

Hitler and Chamberlin met twice in hastily arranged meetings that we now call *summits*. Hitler came out on top because he was willing to risk war for the *Pangermanic* ideal while the west wasn't. How could the west go to war against something they didn't quite rightly comprehend? Even so, in August 1938 they were all close to war. England put the fleet to sea while France called up reservists and mobilized for war. Germany had men at the Czech border ready to attack. All of them, without Benes, met and held a meeting in Bavaria's capital to decide the fate of the *Sudetenland*, and by implication, Czechoslovakia itself. Hitler lied and told Chamberlain what he wanted to hear: that the *Sudetenland* would be Germany's last territorial demand in Europe. The only thing was; *Danzig* and a large portion of *Ost Prussen* were given to Poland in 1919. So who could believe him? One could, but only by ignoring *Pangermania*. That is what the west wanted to do because, as it still does, the west only recognized *Stateism*. The Czechs were about to be sold down river because the west couldn't understand Pangermanic ideals and motivations. What the Czechs didn't grasp and should have, was that the peace faction in England didn't care about them or Danzig. They wanted a stable border on the Rhine and the Germans moved east towards the Soviet Union through Poland if necessary. The British war party, centered on Winston Churchill, was in the minority. Chamberlain and the peace faction were willing to concede Sudetenland and wait out developments because they all had an ace in the hole: three newly engineered 4-engined heavy bombers, the *Sterling, Lancaster* and *Halifax*. All three could carry 6 ½ to 7 tons of bombs and reach Berlin. So part of Chamberlain's play was a waiting game. He also fell under Hitler's spell. Hitler could be charming. He understood how to placate Chamberlain when he learned that the English fellow wouldn't back down on every issue. Chamberlain insisted that the territorial integrity of the Czech rump state be respected. Hitler assured him it would. Finally, they both signed an agreement to avoid war with each other. That should have been Hitler's aim at all costs: it was the *Royal Navy* embargo had insured Germany's defeat in 1918. Hitler thought he had it all figured out but he didn't.

Peace in our time

When the *Munich Agreement* was finally signed in September 1938, Neville Chamberlain was the most popular and revered politician in the western world. Cheering throngs adored him all over Germany. It was the same when he returned to England. He emerged from his aircraft he waved the paper that he and Hitler had signed. He proclaimed *peace in our time*. Everybody cheered. Two years later he would die in sorrow when all his dreams and accomplishments were shattered. Now he is presented as pathetic and forlorn, standing on a wet dreary runway waving a soggy piece of paper signed by "*Herr Hitler*" that promised *nothing at all*. The larger tragedy was the mistaken assumption that any conciliatory diplomacy like this would inevitably and automatically lead to Armageddon.

English fascism

England had a large fascist movement among the English working class who saw that socialism and communism didn't protect them from the rapacious capitalist elite. The communists didn't give a fig about the atrocious working conditions all over Britain. What they cared about was the intellectual indoctrination of the working class and the subsequent world revolution they thought would inevitably follow. The fascists didn't care about that and still don't. They wanted better living conditions for the oppressed workers immediately. England was the birthplace of the horrific industrial revolution that supposedly made everyone's life better but didn't. This was, and is, the appeal of fascism; the movement aims for an enhanced community, not as an idea in some future social utopia where everybody gets free stuff, but as an immediate present reality. The leader of the English Fascists was *Oswald Mosley, Baronet* and his fabulous well-connected wife, *Lady Diana Mitford* who was pals with all the top Nazis in Berlin.

Unity Mitford and der Fuhrer

Lady Diana's sister *Unity* was also a looker, although some say not quite as hot as her older sister. *Unity Mitford* became Hitler's girlfriend in 1934. The circumstances of their meeting say quite a bit about life in National Socialist Germany before the war, and Hitler's place in it. When he was in Munich, which was often, he would dine out because the city has hundreds of cozy little places to eat and relax. Unlike today's politicians, Hitler didn't ride about in an armed and armored motor convoy defended by burly thugs in tinted aviator glasses. He cruised around in an open car with his pal Hoffman and a few friends. Hitler and his buddies weren't that far removed from the old street-fighting days and they packed their own heat. The Browning semi-automatic fits quite snugly under that leather overcoat you always see Hitler wearing. He had some favorite spots and anybody who wanted to know, knew where they were. One such place was the *Osteria Bavaria* (it's still there) that had Hitler's favorite snack; sweet apple strudel and black tea with crème. It was the guy's one vice and he could eat it all day. People would come in to have a few drinks and chat. Since *der Fuhrer* was the boss, he did most of the talking. In *The Maltese Falcon* (1941) *the Fat Man* told Sam Spade: *I'm a man who likes talking to a man who likes to talk.* The Fat Man would have liked Hitler. Unity set out to meet him and hung out at a corner table in the *Osteria*. After a few months of making eyes at him, der Fuhrer was finally moved to ask: *Who's the babe?* It was love at first discourse and they became inseparable. *The Fat Man* also confided to Spade: *Talking isn't something you can do judiciously unless you keep in practice.* Hitler was in complete accord. In Unity he found his ideological soulmate. Eva Braun was put on the back-burner and tried, halfheartedly, to commit suicide; something one of Hitler's earlier girlfriends, the delightful Geli Raubal, had sadly accomplished in utter despair. Geli just wanted to have fun and Hitler, fearing her laugh, infectious personality and beauty was too attractive for life, kept her isolated in a Munich apartment. He drove the poor girl crazy. Eva was more subdued, but she too just wanted to do girly things. Quite differently, *Unity* knew all the ins and outs of National Socialist dogma. Since that often depended on who last spoke; she frequently knew what Hitler was thinking before he did. She became his constant companion for the next five years and when Hitler addressed a 250,000 strong throng at the *Heldenplatz* in Vienna right after *Anschluss*, it was *Unity Valkyrie Mitford* right up there on the balcony with him (among others).

Hitler the homo

Back in the day when homosexuality was a crime punishable by prison, Hitler was often accused of being queer, or at best, *latent homosexual*. He just couldn't ever do anything right. He only had one testicle they wrote, and the one that he did have was shrunken and deformed. Who would know? Nevertheless and in truth, he chased every skirt between Landshut and Berlin. In the 1936 Olympics he tried to pick up American sprint champion Helen Stephens who never lost a race in her life:

> *He comes in and gives me the Nazi salute. I gave him a good, old-fashioned Missouri handshake. Once more Hitler goes for the jugular vein. He gets hold of my fanny and begins to squeeze and pinch, and hug me up. And he says: 'You're a true Aryan type. You should be running for Germany.' So after he gave me the once over and a full massage, he asked me if I'd like to spend the weekend in Berchtesgaden.*

Helen stayed in the Olympic village but he still couldn't escape homophobic slurs from the western liberals. However, the actuality of repeated sexscapades caught up to him. In 1939 Unity was pregnant and wanted to marry. Hitler wasn't interested for political reasons. Much of his support came from women. There were no elections that mattered anymore but Hitler's hold on power was constantly on a razor's edge. There were always revolutions in German history and, as a precaution; Hitler liked it that women liked him. He was late 40's, still healthy, big baby blue eyes and eligible. Plus he was ruthless. Modern feminists say that women don't and shouldn't like that sort of man, but they do. Not wanted and unwed, Unity shot herself. Or so the story goes; it varies according to who tells it. The scandal was kept out of the press and she was rushed back to England, still bleeding, but she didn't lose the child. She went straight into a clinic for unwed mothers. Shrouded in mystery and official denial, what became of the child is unknown. Even though she was inside Hitler's inner circle and in his bed for five years, Unity was never, ever, debriefed in any way by British intelligence. Hitler welcomed Eva back with open arms.

The Czechoslovakian corpse is devoured

Six months after Austria was annexed, the German Army welcomed the *Sudetenland* into the *Reich*. The wolves were waiting. Poland annexed *Teschen*, a beautiful little city, and the coal-rich area around it, called *Zaolzie*, meaning *the lands beyond the Olza River*. No wonder Wilson was confused. Hungary wanted a piece of the prize and grabbed a big chunk of the lovely *Carpathian Ruthenia*. Germany took the biggest and tastiest hunk by naming the rest of the Czech nation a protectorate. Germany also created the new nation of Slovakia from the Czech rump state and it became a steadfast German ally. Naturally, the *Bank of England* handed over all 227 tons of Czechoslovakia's gold to Germany. Whose side was England on, did you say? The annexation of Czechoslovakia as a protectorate was Hitler's first big mistake. There was no need for it. The tiny nation was completely surrounded, landlocked and dependent upon Germany. But then again, there was all that gold.

Poland dips in

Poland then took the opportunity presented by the now open season on small states. In 1919 the Baltic States and Czechoslovakia were safe under the French umbrella. Now they were all easy pickings. Poland wanted a piece of Lithuania and took Vilnius, known also as Wilno, Wilna, or Vilna depending on who you talked to. Italy saw what was going on and presented demands upon France asking for Nice, one of the nicest places in the whole world. They also demanded Corsica (the birthplace of Napoleon), and Savoy. The French told them to go to hell. France had a big army to back them up. Lithuania didn't. In 1919 they had been given Memel, now *Klaipeda*; a nice seaport and resort once a part of *Ost Prussen*. Germany wanted it back and got it. In exchange, they signed a treaty that gave Lithuania free access to the port for 99 years. Lithuania at least was smart enough to see the writing on the wall. Poland was not.

Restructuring central Europe

It was twenty years after Versailles and by Germen reckoning, it was time to fix up some of the obvious oversights and misapplications of history that went into the self-determination process. It was reasonable for Hitler and the German foreign office to assume that these relatively minor territorial alterations would and could be done without war. And they were. Lithuania proved reasonable as Memel was after all German and not Lithuanian. With the Germans who once lived there all dead and gone, it is pure Lithuanian now. Hitler solidified his control over foreign affairs because he seemed to be right all the time. Those that opposed him and advocated caution were wrong. Joachim von Ribbentrop was in as Foreign Minister and von Neurath out. The commander in chief of the Army, Werner von Bloomberg was out, replaced by Wilhelm Keitel, a fellow who liked listening to a man who liked to talk. What Hitler talked about now was getting back Danzig from Poland. Hitler assured everyone it was going to be just like Memel. He made Poland a similar offer and the Poles would have been wise to take it. Instead they turned to England and it was their last mistake. Poland would soon be obliterated with 6 million dead. Because we view the *2nd War-phase* only in retrospect, there seems to be an aura of inevitability about the destruction of Poland. But what if Poland's leadership accepted the loss of Danzig and chose instead a closer relationship Germany as did Lithuania? Back in 1916 when the German military created *Ober Ost*, it also tried to recreate a Polish state as an ally. Unfortunately the crazed Ludendorf ran the show. This alliance could have worked in 1939 except that England and France decided to intervene. This is now viewed as a good thing even though it made the annihilation of Poland certain.

Winter for Poland and France

On Saturday November 11, 1939 the *Third French Republic* held its last military assembly. It was a grand parade through the *Arch d' Triumph*. Every unit in the French Army that defeated the *Hun* was represented. Six months later they would be utterly crushed, disarmed, and prostrate. France would be dismembered with 2 million prisoners taken by the hereditary enemy. The French found themselves in this situation because they believed their own distorted propaganda. Germany started the war in 1914; wasn't that evident? The Treaty of Versailles said so. *The Hun* was to blame for everything and them alone. Never mind that Germany was the last continental power to mobilize when the operational plans called for war at the instance of mobilization. Russia was first to mobilize, then Austria, then Serbia and then France and Germany on the same day. They were all at war while Germany dithered. French cavalry was already across the border in *Alsace* when Germany mobilized and declared war. Yet Germany was affirmed the culprit and had to pay for all the subsequent misery in gold. And who got all that gold but for the fellows who *wanted more war*; endless very profitable war? The people of France certainly didn't see any of it. For them it was the same as it ever was. The Treaty of Versailles was a French creation designed to place France atop the European food chain. It weakened everybody but them. What they couldn't perceive was that all the small states the treaty created would be swallowed up by the German nation that was adjacent to them. Those states; Austria, Czechoslovakia, Poland, Lithuania and later the engorged Romania: all needed the protection offered by France. But none of them were anywhere near France. How could France protect them short of war? In 1919 France had a 10 million man victorious army. Twenty years later they didn't. Slowly the French creations slipped away into the German orbit. When the French found themselves again at war with Germany it came as a shock. It was they who were now isolated; their only ally being loathsome England, the ancient enemy who would soon attack the French fleet and betray them.

The Polish Corridor

When the German Army marched into Prague on the *Ides of March, 1939* the English Prime Minister, Neville Chamberlain, was deeply offended. This was something no one on the German side could understand. They thought he was a useless shopkeeper of no account who somehow became Prime Minister. But *Hitler had broken his word*. For Chamberlain, this was an insult and in the old days the gauntlet would have been thrown. What's more, Hitler had violated the *Treaty of Westphalia. Nations were not to be completely destroyed.* There had to be some integrity and stability in European affairs, or else there would be no place for gentlemen like Chamberlain. For Hitler, the Westphalian system was unknown and it's probable he'd never heard of it. It isn't mentioned in either of his two books. Yet there it was; Czechoslovakia was wiped off the map, completely extirpated. But so was the Ottoman Empire; and where was the Westphalian system then? In truth the Westphalian system only applied to the great western powers and only when they emerged victorious. Hitler could see through all this as well as anybody.

The Focus

The British war party was led by Churchill, who saw war as his only way back into political power. His backers were the *Focus for the Defense of Freedom and Peace*, a group of bankers known originally as the *British Non-Sectarian Anti-Nazi Council to Champion Human Rights*. They kept pushing Chamberlain to confront Germany. Finally he gave in. With Germany demanding Danzig, England gave the Poles a guarantee: they would protect them with the sword. Never mind that England was a naval power and not a continental one. Never mind that even Chamberlin himself didn't think the concept was viable. The French unquestionably knew they weren't going on the offensive to protect Poland. It was a bluff and Hitler always called on bluffs. The problem was the sham pushed Poland into war with Germany, one they could never win. The *Anglo-Polish Agreement* pledged British and French military support to defend Poland. The Poles signed it as a drowning man grasps at straws. They then arrogantly rebuffed the

Germans. Danzig was their only route to the sea and that they wouldn't give it up under any circumstances. What about something like the *Memel* deal? Nope. There would be no negotiations. Poland was fooled by the liberal democracies and then dumbfounded when Germany and Soviet Russia suddenly signed a *10-year non-aggression pact*. Russia went aboard because they felt the French and English were not negotiating with them in good faith. And they weren't. The English ruling elite would have much rather seen Bolshevik Russia destroyed than come to any accommodation with them. However, the first duty of any nation is to protect itself. Russia was mauled by Germany in the *1ˢᵗ War-phase* and a pact with them seemed like a good idea. And it was. Joachim von Ribbentrop was only on the job a few months when he arranged arguably the greatest diplomatic *coup* of all time. The world was literally astounded and the accord gave Germany a free hand to deal with Poland. Later on, when Germany turned the tables and invaded Russia, von Ribbentrop was asked if he would resign; because after all, the German invasion was a complete repudiation of his supreme ambassadorial accomplishment. He looked at the fellow like he had two heads. For von Ribbentrop, the treaty was but a scrap of paper. He was like his boss: innumerable lies, deceptions, cheating; any means to justify all ends were but a part of the deadly game they both played. For von Ribbentrop, had he then resigned he may have lived long enough to write his memoirs and retire gracefully to Monte Carlo. Instead, he hung onto power until the Fall of Berlin and was hanged by the neck until dead at Nuremburg.

Polish cavalry

Ethnic jokes often have a small kernel of truth. For example: how many Indians does it take to screw in a light bulb? Answer: *all one billion of them praying for the old light to go back on*. Hitler made some jokes about Polish leadership after Poland was vanquished in a month-long war: *They were, after all, Polish* he quipped. One of the legends that emerged was that Polish cavalry attacked German tanks. See, those dang Poles were so stupid they didn't even know what a tank was! The image of idiotic Polish horsemen that charged, *Don Quixote* like, with lances against steel vehicles was presented as fact for decades. It still is. But it never happened. There were occasions when Polish cavalry drew enemy fire to allow friendly infantry and guns to withdraw. The Poles knew very well what a tank was and had some of their own. Their problem was a strategic one. Like Ethiopia, they were surrounded on three sides and had no chance. The French Army advanced 5 miles into Germany, broke a few windows and then withdrew to safety. They had a strategic plan and it didn't include Poland. They knew that when they guaranteed Polish independence a few weeks before.

The secret protocols

There was no *"secret agreement"* between Russia and Germany to divide Poland in the *Nazi-Soviet Pact*. It did define *spheres of influence*. However, there was no agreement to jointly invade and divide Poland. This interpretation of events was invented to demonize Soviet Russia and Stalin after 1945 when a new enemy was needed to keep the war machine funded. Since Germany and Soviet Russia did, *in fact*, divide Poland between them; ergo Soviet Russia can be labeled just as much an aggressor as Hitler's Germany. What's more, Stalin can be labeled a war criminal as well. It was all sold to the ever gullible masses by compliant historians smooth as silk. In truth, Russia feared all the western powers, including Poland. They were worried about a German-Polish pact, with them both allied with Japan to attack and dismember Russia: just like they tried to do twenty years before. There were many on the German side that saw this as a strategic goal. Just give us Danzig and let's make a deal they said to the Poles. Poland foolishly wouldn't consider it. When the nation was quickly defeated, only then did the Soviets act. Presently, the Soviet incursion in Poland is offered as just another act of Russian-Soviet imperialism ordered by Stalin in conjunction with Hitler; both of whom were homicidal and genocidal maniacs. But for Stalin, and the Soviet Union, the Polish intervention was based upon long-standing ideological concerns. This explains the massacre of 20,000 Polish Army officers and intelligentsia in the *Katyn Forest*. This is always blamed on Stalin. It was actually proposed by *Lavrentiy Pavlovich Beria* head of the secret police (*NKVD*) and one of the most dangerous men who ever lived. It was voted on by the full Politburo. They feared a German-Polish alliance, and in the spring of 1940 it wasn't already clear what Germany wanted to do with Poland. It was only after Germany invaded Soviet Russia in 1941 that the Germans themselves decided upon the complete eradication of the Polish nation and its people.

War is the continuation of politics by different means   Clausewitz

When the Red Army entered eastern Poland on September 17th 1939, the Poles were already evidently defeated. Their government had abandoned Warsaw and fled to Romania. Stalin would not allow Germany to take all of Poland. This would give the German Army a very advanced outpost from which to launch a better offensive into Russia than either Napoleon or Hindenburg ever had. Russia held no illusions. If they were going to have a common border with Germany it was to be as far to the west and as far away from the heart of *Mother Russia* as possible. The Soviets centered their geopolitical strategies upon the notion that the western imperial powers: France, Germany, England, the USA, and now Japan, must be prohibited, as much as possible, from forming an alliance against them. The obliteration of Poland was, for Russia, never a part of this ideological goal; but it quickly did so upon Poland's utter ruin. Stalin outlined in *Socialism in One Country* (1924) that it wasn't just class struggle as envisioned by Marx that caused revolution. Rather it was *internecine world war* among the imperialist powers that would radicalize workers to revolt. Therefore, if the Soviet Union could get the imperialist powers to wage war against each other, they would be unable to form an anti-soviet, or anti-Russian, coalition. Historically this is the only sort of war the west was ever able to wage upon them. Stalin and the ruling Politburo hoped for a long capitalist civil war where a workers insurrection, brewed by that war, might overcome and destroy the capitalist imperialist powers one by one and forevermore, just as it did Russia in 1917. This almost happened, and would have, had the Americans not been there to throw money at it after German defeat in 1945. However, in the short term; if the imperialist powers were going to allow Poland's annihilation, (and they were), then Soviet Russia had a right to protect its own existence. It was obvious and unmistakable that France and England, cowering in the west, were of no account to them.

THE TRANSFORMATION OF THE WEST INTO A PERMANENT WAR ECONOMY

Air Power

Back in 1912 an Italian officer named *Giulio Douhet* dropped a bomb from an airplane on a crowd of civilians gathered for a market. The Libyan women and children scattered bleeding and maimed. It was the first time anybody was ever bombed from a flying machine. A light went on for Douhet. This was the way to win wars he thought. Armies and navies weren't needed. Bomb the enemy civilian population and the war would be won. He didn't know it then, but he advocated the principle of *total war* in which a nation's civilian population was the primary target and not its military. This would play itself out in the 2nd *War-phase* when civilian casualties far outnumbered military ones. In the 1st *War-phase*, primitive airplanes were used for scouting. Then, fighting aircraft were built to shoot down the scouts. Every year the French play a tennis tournament at *Roland Garros* court. In 1915 Garros forever changed the nature of air warfare when he affixed steel protectors onto his wooden propellers. This allowed him to fire machine guns through them. He became a national hero when he shot down a few German scouts. It was risky business though, as a deflected bullet could kill him or else down his own *aeroplane*. Anthony Fokker then invented synchronized firing through the propellers for the *Deutsche Luftstreitkräfte* (*German air combat force*) and the modern fighter was born. Tony's designs (with *Reinhold Platz*) were so good that his *Fokker D-VII* fighter was specifically banned by the Treaty of Versailles. But it was the Americans and French in 1918 that developed ground attack tactics that wrought havoc among the German Army. Italian ace *Amedeo Mecozzi* wrote about this in a series of essays (still mostly in Italian) in the 1920's. He advocated air power in conjunction with ground forces. Douhet countered and stressed strategic bombing as a method for victory, independent of armies. The bomber would always get through he wrote; and when it did, *en masse,* the cowed enemy would cry uncle. It never worked out that way but no one knew it at the time. So all through the 1930's every nation's air forces had to reckon with the problems thus: fighters or bombers, and if both then how many of each, tactical bombers or big strategic bombers and what sort of strategy to use with all of them? Interestingly, every nation involved in the 2nd phase of the war took a different approach and nobody got it completely right. The French however, managed to get it utterly wrong.

The Fall of France

The German Army's destruction of the French and British armies in the spring of 1940 is the most astounding feat of military arms in all of history including Alexander's overthrow of the Persian Empire with a relatively small Macedonian army. They both did this by outmaneuvering their foes. In 1914 when German 1st and 2nd Armies drove through Belgium the French weren't ready for them. They fell back to Paris and the next four years of war were fought on French soil. Some areas, called the Red Zone (*Zone Rouge*) are *still uninhabitable!* In 1940, the French weren't going to allow this to happen again. Instead, they drove into Belgium to meet the enemy there; and in fact stopped the Germans cold. However, the German attack through Belgium was a feint, a ruse of war. Their main thrust came through the Ardennes Forest, in an area the French high command thought to be impenetrable. They were right; it is impossible provided that the place is adequately defended. It wasn't. With the bulk of the French Army's best troops, as well as the British Army headed northeast into Belgium, the Germans took Sedan, far to the southwest and deep in the French rear. Two weeks later the British Army would be fleeing on boats and two weeks after that, German 6th Army would march into Paris.

Armee de l'Air sits this one out

Back in 1914, a *Royal Flying Corps* scout spotted von Kluck's advancing German 1st Army and reported in person back to Army HQ. He was met with disbelief. Sir John told him; *Look here old chap, the Germans aren't anywhere near us.* Sir John's staff was amused by the sprightly pilot whom they didn't take seriously. Finally, Sir John asked *I say old boy; how does that contraption ever get off the ground?* Luckily for Sir John and his army, they were already in a good position at Mons, protected by deep canals and surrounded by ubiquitous slag heaps. In 1940, the French Army wouldn't be so lucky. In a simple twist of fate, just as the Germans were prepared to commence their main offensive into the impenetrable Ardennes forest, they were spotted by a French *Armee de l'Air* aviator. He just happened to be in the right spot at the right time because scouting was no longer a priority mission for the *Armee de l'Air*. They had become an independent military branch in 1933. All the things that worked in 1914-18; scouting and ground support, were relegated to secondary missions behind the new theories of Douhet. The now autonomous *Armee de l'Air* would concentrate on strategic bombing and protecting French cities from air attack. The French Army would fend for itself and was, in fact, caught up in an inter-service rivalry with its own air force. So the French Army high command disregarded the scout's observation. They knew very well the Germans could not be in the Ardennes. They accused the *Armee de l'Air* of using scare tactics to throw the Army off its mission. The French had a plan and reality wasn't going to interfere with it. *Sacrebleu! The Hun was in Belgium!*

The Ardennes

Erich von Manstein was a Prussian General Staff officer who had a mind for chess and military strategy. Chess is a wargame where the terrain is mutually known. There are no hidden features. Both sides begin the game with equal force. But there can be hidden attacks even though all the forces are there to see. This was the military situation in May 1940. The path into France through Belgium was evident and everybody had been there before. The Germans were ready to give it another try because they felt they had additional new weaponry. But so did the French. The German advantage lay in the fact that over the past few years they had conducted a number of military operations while the French had none. There was Spain, and while the invasions of Austria and Czechoslovakia were unopposed they were still large scale military operations that needed to be coordinated and supplied. In Poland the German Army was able to synchronize the use of mechanized armored divisions and *Luftwaffe* ground support. It didn't work perfectly all the time but they were getting the hang of it. Luftwaffe chief Hermann Goering was a larger than life figure in many ways. Aside from his impressive girth he oversaw the construction of the German Air Force, *der Luftwaffe*, (literally *air weapon*) as an adjunct to the Army, and not a rival to it, as in

France. German twin and single-engined bombers were tactical weapons designed to support friendly infantry in the attack; as outlined by *Amedeo Mecozzi* in his essays: *The Attack Air Force*. The Germans never would utilize big strategic 4-engined bombers; but in the attack upon France in 1940 they would execute Mecozzi's tactical theories perfectly.

Manstein's Gambit

Control of the center is one of the general principles in chess. The player who controls the four squares in the center of the board will usually go on to win the game, or at least gain strategic advantage. When von Manstein looked at the French position in 1940 he saw that the Ardennes forest was *directly in the center*. To the French right lay the Maginot line; a series of fortifications that began just south of the Ardennes and ran all the way to the Swiss border, 150 miles away. That part of the front was safe from attack. On the French left, north of the Ardennes, was the Belgian plain; flatland with few good defensive positions. This was the path the Germans took in 1914 and the French were sure they would again. But if the Germans could take the Ardennes, they would occupy the center, far inside the French rear. From there they could take Sedan, cross the Meuse River, and then drive across the plains of central France to the English Channel. This would isolate the French and British in Belgium and cut them off from their supply sources: they would have no food for men, no fodder for horses, no gas, no ammo and no place to fall back on. They would be doomed. But the *German General Staff* wanted to attack through Belgium again, where the terrain was known. However, this could result in stalemate once more and another lost war. Manstein presented his plan to Hitler who then convinced the General Staff to go for broke. There was some resistance but in the end, like gamblers in Las Vegas, they went all in.

Sedan is taken

It took the Germans two days to fight their way through the forest that was defended by two divisions of elite French and Belgian light infantry and cavalry of about 30,000 men. The French and Belgian troops had very few heavy weapons and were up against an entire enemy army group of 200,000 men, 3,700 guns and 2,250 tanks. Even so, given the terrain, they put up a tough fight and caused massive traffic jams for the Germans; often backed up 10 miles or more on narrow single lane roads with dense trees alongside. They had no exit and no path of retreat. Had *Armee de l'Air* showed up at any time on May 10th, 11th or 12th they could have shot up the defenseless Hun columns. But they didn't. That wasn't their mission anymore. French wargames in 1938 predicted it would take the Germans just 3 days to penetrate the Ardennes. Like the American 1932 wargame *(Fleet Problem XIII)* that showed the Japanese could successfully attack Pearl Harbor from the north, the French wargame was discarded and ignored. As the German Army cut its way through the forest, nobody on the French side could understand the situation. They were fighting the Germans in Belgium, up against another army group of 100,000 men, 2000 guns and 1000 tanks. It looked like the real attack and the French were beating the hell out of them. But on the 12th, Sedan, defended by reservists, fell. Two days later, German tanks were across the Meuse into the heart of France. For anybody who could read a map the battle was lost. It was only on this day that *Armee de l'Air* tried to bomb the bridges across the Meuse. They didn't score even one hit because this wasn't something they practiced. French bombers were slow and *der Luftwaffe* shot them out of the sky.

Guderian grasps the situation

Panzer means armor in German; any kind of armor; like what the Teutonic Knights wore when they conquered *East Prussia* from those nasty pagan *Old Prussians* whose language and people are now extinct. They come and they go. Heinz Guderian was born in Kulm, Prussia, now Chelmno in Poland. You can visit the place on a death camp tour since all those camps are in Poland, or the infamous *Government General*, which wasn't Poland. Ordinary people can get very confused by it all. This is why Poland is very sensitive about saying the death camps were Polish, or even in Poland; which they weren't, since Poland didn't exist then. But then the Poles also don't like to admit there ever was a time when Poland didn't exist, like when they were a part of Russia, or Prussia, against their will. For someone like American President Harry Truman, who was from Missouri, it was all downright impossible to figure out.

What is a tank?

Heinz Guderian, a cavalryman, was an early advocate for armored forces and wrote a book about panzer tactics: the famous *Achtung Panzer!* (1937). He got most of his ideas from the Austrian *Ludwig Ritter von Eimannsberger* (*Der Kampfwagenkrieg* [*The Tank War*] 1934). A tank isn't any kind of wonder-weapon; those would come later. It is an armored self-propelled gun with machine guns to prevent enemy infantry armed with Molotov cocktails from turning them into blazing infernos. The main gun can fire high-explosive (HE) shells against infantry, armor piercing (AP) rounds against hardened targets and smoke shells too when the situation becomes uncomfortable. French tanks were much better than anything in the field for the Germans. Capt. Pierre Billotte's *Char B1* tank singlehandedly destroyed 13 enemy panzers at the *Battle of Stonne*. The problem for the French was that their tanks didn't have two-way radios and German tanks did. While the enemy communicated by wireless, and FM radio, the French high command used motorcycle messengers and carrier pigeons. Even so, when the German panzer forces broke through at Sedan, German generals wanted the panzers to stop and wait for the infantry to catch up. There was only one person in the world who grasped the position and he happened to be in just the right place, in the right time, with the correct instrument of war to win it. General Guderian disregarded the command to wait and drove off in the direction of Abbeville on the Channel coast. He had not only panzers but also attached mechanized infantry that could keep up. For heavy artillery he had the *Luftwaffe*.

Maps

In the 1914-18 war, the German Army fought the French four solid years and couldn't beat them. Twenty-five years later they obliterated the French Army in two weeks. The breakthrough at Sedan was important but the single most significant edge the Germans had in 1940 was accurate *Michelin maps* of France (1938 version), courtesy of the tire company. *There was no treason in this.* Both Germany and France were open societies. Anyone could buy the maps at a gas station. The French had accurate maps of Germany as well, but didn't need them since they stayed on the defensive. After the breakthrough, when Guderian began his drive north, the French often put up fierce resistance. But with accurate maps, the Germans always knew where they were and where the enemy was; even though they were in French territory. Every element of the *Wehrmacht* (the armed forces) had *the same maps* including the *Luftwaffe*. That knowledge meant they could swiftly contact friendly air forces (with wireless) and tell them *exactly* where they were. Since the Luftwaffe had *the very same maps*, they were often there in 20 minutes, bombing the enemy position. The French had no answer as *Armee de l'Air* was most often not in the area. This situation quickly demoralized the French Army. They would have a defensive position set up, hold it, and then suddenly squadrons of *Ju-87 Stuka* dive-bombers and *He-111* medium bombers would show up raining death from above. The attacks were low level and extremely accurate. It was a slaughter. Guderian drove to the coast until he ran out of gas.

Dunkirk

The French call the place *Dunkerque* and one of the great mysteries of the war is how and why *Hitler* let the British Army escape their fate. That is how the question is most often posed: Why did *Hitler* let them flee? He didn't. There are quite a few movies about the situation and the get-away itself is so riveting, the question is seldom addressed. There is the silly story that Hitler allowed the Brits to evacuate so as to curry favor with them. However, the best way to knock England, or any opponent, out of a war is to capture its army. Hitler knew that but again, this comes from the notion that Hitler was the supreme commander. He wasn't. Domestically he was in charge, but the German Army was its own machine. Hitler had input but the Germans halted to reorganize because *the Army* felt they needed to. They were out of gas, both literally and figuratively. Their soldiers were amped up on over-the-counter amphetamines (*Pervitin*). They crashed. You can see pictures of them conked out in full uniform, helmets on, lying on the side of the road fast asleep. The panzers were out of gas. Tankers were siphoning gas out of destroyed or abandoned enemy vehicles. Guderian's breakthrough at Sedan was 150 miles from Abbeville. The Panzers made it in a few days but the rest of the army (except for the few motorized infantry units) had to walk it. That included the vast majority of horse-drawn artillery. The Luftwaffe too was unable to set up new air bases in the short time available. They had to operate far (200 miles) from the Dunkirk pocket. The battlefield itself was very large. Watching a movie it is easy to get the impression that the Germans were just outside the Dunkirk city gates. Actually the perimeter was vast; 150 miles long, 100 miles deep at some points, and it included not only the BEF but the 1st French Army and the Belgian Army as well. They put up a good fight for some time. Within the perimeter was the city of Lille, where elements of 1st French Army fought off seven Germans divisions. Their resistance was so ferocious the Germans permitted them to surrender with the full honors of war: the crack *2nd* and *5th North African Divisions* marched into internment with fixed bayonets and flags flying, an honor General Washington denied Cornwallis at Yorktown. In truth, the Germans didn't permit 330,000 enemy troops to escape the trap for political reasons or anything else. The just didn't think the enemy could conceivably pull it off. The BEF arrived on ferries and the Germans knew they weren't going to get out the same way. Evacuation seemed impossible and the Germans felt they had all the time in the world. They didn't. It took almost 900 vessels, of which 250 were sunk, to execute the mass departure. Leaving all their vehicles and guns behind, the BEF, and parts of French 1st Army, escaped to fight another day. They still blame Hitler of course, who became a convenient target after the war along with fat-boy Goering. But it was the German Army that screwed this operation up and no one else.

A new kind of war

The German method of war became known as *Blitzkrieg* (lightning war). They never named it that though. For them it was *Bewegungskrieg* (mobile warfare). Often a losing football team will make changes in tactics and strategy at halftime and emerge from the clubhouse to win the game. The

THE TRANSFORMATION OF THE WEST INTO A PERMANENT WAR ECONOMY

team that was winning at the half didn't need to make any corrections because they were doing fine. It happens all the time. It was the same for the resurrected German Army. They figured they needed to do something different and there was no question in their mind that there would be a next time; there always had been. The first thing they decided was no digging in: they weren't going to construct the trenches that led to static positions. They were also going to avoid the rigid command structure that had emerged under Hindenburg and Ludendorf; who wanted to control *everything*. They re-emphasized *Auftragstaktik* (mission tactics), or the term they most often used; *selbstständigkeit* (independent command). Once the orders for an operation were given, subordinate commanders had the leeway to interpret them as they wished. If they needed to disobey superior orders they could, provided that the mission succeeded. Thus Guderian did what he wanted to, and not what high command ordered him to do. No one would ever be disciplined for disobeying orders, but would instead suffer reprimand for *failure to carry out the mission*. Since armored vehicles and ground attack air forces had beaten them up in 1918, the Germans were keen to develop both. When they renewed the war against France they had ten panzer divisions and the world's best air force. The French fell behind because they didn't understand the nature of their victory in 1918.

Becoming English

In July 1917, the *English Royal Family* changed their name and became the *House of Windsor*; it sounded English even if they really weren't. They used to be the *House of Saxe-Coburg and Gotha*, some German places that are actually still in Germany and not in Poland. Before that, English kings were Hanoverians, and before that Dutch-German, and before that Welsh, and before that, they were Norman French. The last King of England who was actually English was Harold, famously shot through the eye with an unlucky arrow at Hastings in 1066. In 1917, with the war against Germany raging, the royal family wanted to be English, even though they were actually German. Being masters of disguise, they easily pulled it off. Then, in 1940, they found themselves at war with Germany again and wanted out of it. The last go-round had broken the bank and put them in hock to the Rothschilds and their conspirators. When Chamberlain returned from Munich in 1938 with the *peace in our time* paper in hand, he immediately appeared on the royal balcony with the king and queen. That was their way of saying; *we approve*. The general consensus was: *We don't want to fight those people again*. Nevertheless they found themselves at war with them thanks to Chamberlain's vanity and the stupid guarantee to Poland. Now they were about to lose the army. The situation was bleak.

Churchill

The fellow is so dynamic it isn't even necessary to use his full name. He is one of those larger than life fellows, like Hitler and Stalin, who dominated events in the *2nd phase* of the war. His full name was Winston Spencer Churchill of the Duke of Marlborough clan. That's Spencer as in Lady Diana Spencer who married heir apparent Prince Charles in 1981. The Royals and their press lackeys always present the idea they are just like the rest of us. They aren't. Many people still think Lady Diana was a commoner and an ordinary, albeit gorgeous, schoolmarm. In fact, she did work with children; right after *finishing school*, and right after she was brought up by her *governess* in the magnificent *castled estate* she was born on. The truth is only reluctantly admitted because these people have jealously guarded bloodlines and family trees that date back thousands of years. There aren't any Jews in those genealogy charts either. *Ivanhoe* loved the raven-haired Jewess Rebecca but didn't and couldn't marry her. It was the voluptuous blue-eyed blond and devout Rowena that got his hand.

The King abdicates

Churchill was a brave and adventurous fellow in his youth. His bloodlines made him *First Lord of the Admiralty* where he conceived the Gallipoli disaster in 1915. By 1929 he was out of power and trying, with some measure of success, to make some easy money as an art forger. One must be a good artist to be a successful forger and Churchill's brush strokes were like that of *Charles Maurin*, a little known impressionist whose paintings sold well in Paris. Still, it wasn't enough to maintain his magnificent country estate staffed by dozens. That's where *The Focus* came in. Like the American *Council on Foreign Relations* (CFR), *The Focus* published a small journal for insiders whose aim was the destruction of Germany. They funded Churchill at a time when he was essentially destitute. He thusly and dutifully stopped attacking labor unions and shifted his focus, so to speak, onto Hitler and Germany. It wasn't easy as Hitler was liked and respected by many; including *King Edward VIII* who was himself very popular and pro-labor. Unfortunately Edward shirked his duty to the English speaking peoples when he chose to marry a slovenly bred and twice divorced American socialite. Choosing a life of leisure and debauchery with his harlot, Edward betrayed England and abdicated for his half-witted brother *"Bertie"* who lacked the intellect and intestinal fortitude to resist the machinations of the war party.

Peace feelers

When the war began to go badly in May 1940, Churchill was named Prime Minister and formed a war cabinet. That was on May 10, the day the Germans launched their offensive that would defeat France. With the BEF trapped ten days later, Churchill's government looked for a way out of the mess. But that would have been the end of Churchill's political career; as another military disaster was at hand. Lord Halifax tried to broker a peace with Mussolini as mediator but the *Duce* wanted Gibraltar, Malta and Suez. This was impossible and the *Duce* then declared war on a defeated France; only to have his army badly beaten by the French as the Italians tried to rip off Nice and Savoy. An entertaining movie about these days is *Darkest Hour* (2017). At this point the stories started that Hitler let the BEF take flight. That's nonsense. But with the army successfully extricated Churchill could continue the war, and did, right to the bitter end. The French tried to establish a new main line of resistance near the old 1916 front lines on the Somme. But they couldn't hold it with their best troops and mobile forces in captivity. They surrendered on June 22 in the very same railroad car, in the very same little forest outside Compiègne in which they took the German capitulation in 1918. The place is called the Glade of the Armistice (*Clairière de l'Armistice*).

Strategic bombing

Hermann Goering is everybody's whipping boy in the backwards lens by which we view the *2nd War-phase*. He gets blamed for the catastrophe at Stalingrad even though he had little to do with it. He takes the heat for the loss of the air war over Germany even though the Luftwaffe won that war until overwhelmed by American material superiority in 1944. He was a fighter pilot in the *1st War-phase* and flew with von Richthofen's *1st Fighter Squadron* (*Jagdgeschwader 1*), the famous *Flying Circus*. With those fellows he shot down 19 enemy aircraft and was obviously very athletic with superior eye and limb coordination. Later on in life when things began to go badly, he put on the pounds overeating and snorting cocaine. He was a Jew-hater *par excellence* not because he had anything against them, but saw it as a way to legally rob rich ones of their art and other treasures. In *Fort Apache* (1948), Lieutenant Colonel Owen Thursday told a corrupt Indian agent: *You are a blackguard, a liar, a hypocrite and a stench in the nostrils of honest men*. Hermann Goering was all that and worse; but, it might be said, a good father who didn't beat his wife. He cheated the hangman's noose at Nuremburg by biting into a cyanide capsule. However, he did design and organize the *Luftwaffe* into the most formidable instrument of war for its time, however brief that was. He didn't do this alone but was the driving force. There were divisions in the Luftwaffe, just like all the other air forces, that were divided over whether or not Douhet's theories were correct. In Spain, they tried terror bombing and concluded that it was ineffective and counter-productive. Yet they used it anyway in Poland, bombing Warsaw with incendiaries. The Luftwaffe's *primary mission* became ground support for the Army but it was difficult for Luftwaffe command to get terror bombing out of their heads. They had a command structure independent of the Army but they operated according to their *mission* when they could. They didn't see the need for long-range bombers as all their enemies were close by; but wasted resources trying to bomb Moscow with tactical bombers that got badly shot up. Initially they developed fast bombers (*Schnellbombers*) that could, hopefully, outrun pursuit. They couldn't, and they needed both defensive armament and close fighter support. In the end, the He-111, and twin-engined medium bombers like it, served as their most reliable offensive weapon throughout the war. Like many military organizations at the time, nobody really knew what they were doing but they acted like they did. Interestingly, many aircraft which the Germans began the war, they also finished it with. That isn't because they weren't innovative; they were. The Luftwaffe had, by 1944, a small fleet of heavy bombers, the first operational jet bomber (the *Ar-234*), and the first operational jet fighter, (the *Me-262*), and the jet powered *Ho-229* the world's first flying wing (never operational). When it came time to blame Hitler for everything that went wrong, the story emerged that he delayed the production of the *Me-262* jet fighter to further its design as a fighter-bomber. Actually both the Army, and the Luftwaffe themselves, wanted the fighter-bomber concept. This was perhaps the biggest mistake the Germans made as even a few jet fighters in 1942 would have decimated the Allied heavy bombers raiding Germany. The thing that held back German advanced aeronautics was the lack of specialty metals that forced them to use cheaper designs: a *V-2* ballistic missile cost the same as a torpedo, didn't need a pilot, nor complicated metallurgy; just set the gyroscope, aim and shoot. V-1 cruise missiles were even cheaper. *Projekt Amerika*, the *A10* missile that could hit New York, was ready to test-fire when they surrendered. The Luftwaffe had target maps of New York City with nuclear bomb-blast damage radii delineated. Either in prototype form or operational, the Luftwaffe had anti-gravity projects and flying disk aircraft that were called *foo-fighters* by Allied pilots. They developed all the modern weapon systems of today's warfare; including operational mobile ballistic missiles, phased array radar (functional over the horizon), 2nd generational digital computers, infrared night vision optics, miniaturized television cameras, semiconductor chips, miniature vacuum tubes, transistors, air to surface guided missiles (smart-bombs), photon cascades (lasers), and fiber optics. So how'd they lose?

There are known unknowns   Donald Rumsfeld

To begin with, all the things we now know about air warfare were not known in 1940. Everybody was just figuring it out, as nothing like this war had ever been fought. When the *Battle of France* ended, Luftwaffe losses were 1,428 aircraft of which 1,129 were lost due to enemy action, mostly ground fire.

That happens when fanatical ace pilots go in at zero altitude and low speed. More significantly, 3000 air crew were killed, and 1400 wounded. One of the new facts to emerge was that unlike land warfare, air losses resulted in far more dead than wounded; when one of those airplanes went down it usually took everybody with it. The Luftwaffe had gotten chewed up, as did the French, whose air force was almost completely destroyed. Not knowing the future and rebuffed by the British war cabinet, the Luftwaffe was given a strategic bombing mission; the task of preparing and gaining air superiority over England in groundwork for invasion. They weren't built for this mission: their bombers were too slow, carried a relatively diminutive bomb load and their fighters had very limited range. They got shot up again, with 3,500 killed and the loss of another 2,000 planes in a 3-month air war. Those losses were never made good and the pilots were irreplaceable.

World War

When all these events came to pass, no one anywhere felt they were part of a world war. Nobody looked at September 1, 1939, as we do now, as the start of *World War*. This was a localized European event in which borders were continually modified, nations extirpated and new ones created. France was made, by catastrophic defeat, a much smaller nation. Paris was occupied and a new capital established at *Vichy* in the south. Their army was disbanded and, contrary to the rules of war, their soldiers were confined and kept in work camps. France kept its colonies and navy but had to obey any and all decrees from Berlin. They began to round up Jews and ship them to labor camps in Germany. The French police were enthusiastic about this. They'd wanted to get rid of those people for a long time and this was an opportunity not to be missed. Since France was eventually among the victors, it is not well known that 90% of all French Jews disappeared without a trace. Now in the 21st century, the French have the North African invaders kill the remaining Jews with impunity, as do the liberal and so very progressive new Germans. One way or another, the French and Germans eradicate Jews with the best of them as *"Mama" Merkel* and an ultra-sophisticated beta-male French President grin for the cameras.

THE TRANSFORMATION OF THE WEST INTO A PERMANENT WAR ECONOMY

Oil

When Poland surrendered nobody on the German side thought the French and English were really going to fight a war over it. Then again, who would have thought anybody would fight a world war over Serbia? The Germans took Norway in April 1940 and it was the loss of Norway that forced Chamberlain to resign, and made Churchill Prime Minister. Norway was vital for Germany to protect the deliveries of Swedish coal; and that coal was required to produce synthetic fuel and rubber since the Royal Navy's blockade stopped the import of it. Germany didn't have any oil and most of the world's oil (70%) was produced by the USA. That supply was now cut off. There was just enough oil in Germany, which they got from Romania and Russia, for a few months of mechanized combat. Thinking ahead, *I.G. Farben* was commissioned in April 1940 to build a massive synthetic fuel and rubber plant at a place called *Auschwitz* in the new *Government General*, as Poland was now named, just as in 1916. The location was chosen due to the close proximity of plentiful water and when the plant was operational it used more electricity than all of Berlin. The *Auschwitz-Birkenau* conglomerate would produce not just gas and rubber, but also high-octane aviation fuel, plastics, synthetic fibers, stabilizing agents, resins, methanol, nitrogen, and uranium enrichment. It would be the largest and most important factory in the *Reich* because it kept the *Wehrmacht* rolling. *I.G. Farben* would make huge profits too, because they wouldn't have to pay the 35,000 workers who would be slave laborers. This was where those French Jews were sent. England remained as a nuisance but not a threat. Without consulting Germany, Mussolini invaded Greece and the Italian Army was unable to get very far across the border before being flung back into Albania. Almost as an afterthought, the German Army easily overran Yugoslavia and Greece in the spring of 1941 which made the Soviet Politburo think Germany might be on their way to Iraq and its oil. That would have been a good idea; to make war against England in conjunction with their old Turkish allies and take both Iraq and Suez. But good ideas were something the Germans were running out of. Germany had the war won. *Mitteleuropa* with all its resources was theirs. But they wanted more.

War with Russia

Franz Halder was Bavarian and *Chief of the German General Staff* in 1938 when he was a conspirator in the *Oster Plot* to kill Hitler. The plan was aborted when the Sudetenland was successfully incorporated into the *Reich*. From that point on, when Hitler seemingly made one correct decision after another, Halder concentrated on what he did best; military planning and logistics. The next year he, and his staff, began to map for the invasion of the Soviet Union. The plan, code-named *Operation Barbarossa*, was solely the brain-child of the German Army and made serious strategic misevaluations. The primary one was its emphasis on the capture of capital cities, in this case Leningrad and Moscow. Recent events indicated that after the capture of an enemy capital city, the nation would soon, if not immediately surrender: Brussels in 1914 and 1940, Bucharest in 1916, Warsaw in 1939, Oslo and Paris in 1940, Belgrade and Athens in 1941. But these were small countries. Even a large western European nation like France would be only a tiny province in a Soviet Union that encompassed 12 time-zones. Population wise, Germany had 90 million people in 1941, the Soviet Union 200 million with 41% of the population under 21 years of age. Russia had the world's largest army, the world's largest air force, the world's largest tank park (over 30,000 vehicles) and more resources than any nation except the USA.

Hitler suggests a southern strategy

Hitler's relationship with the Army was like that of General Pershing and Marshall Foch. Pershing's army would fight when and where the French Field Marshall commanded. But it would be Pershing who determined how those commands were carried out. Hitler suggested a southern thrust towards the oil of the Caucasus and the grain of the Ukraine. This was especially true when Eduard Wagner, the Army Quarter-Master General, warned Halder that supply resources (oil), as well as transport difficulties, would halt the offensive 500 miles in, or 250 miles short of Moscow. Halder ignored him because he was the smartest guy in the room. His plan would defeat the Red Army in two months. The Army wanted to drive on Moscow in the center and defeat the enemy in the same way France was destroyed; with rapid armored thrusts into the enemy rear. It would be Hitler as Chancellor who would decide upon war, but it would be the Army (Halder) that decided how the commands would be carried out. Since Halder's plan was obviously perfect there would be no problems.

Rudolf Hess takes flight

Hess was Hitler's oldest and closest friend whom he admired and held in the highest esteem. It was he who transcribed, wrote and edited *Mein Kampf* when they were both political prisoners in 1923. Therefore Hitler entrusted Hess with the most important task of all: his final peace proposal to the English ruling elite. This would stabilize and pacify the western front. He worked this out with Hess and Goering, the two people closest to him. They all knew that normal diplomatic channels wouldn't work; Churchill would see the proposal and squash it. The offer also stabbed Italy in the back; them now fighting the British Army in Africa. Like the *Godfather*, Hitler wanted to make England an offer they couldn't refuse: therefore it had to be secret and delivered *incognito*. What Hitler didn't know was that the peace proposal was already in English hands when Hess took flight; leaked by Goering. The problem was, the British ruling elite didn't want to negotiate with Hitler. He had already betrayed them when the Czechoslovakian rump state was annexed after Munich. Hitler had broken his word. Who could trust him? Hess and Goering both thought *Barbarossa* was a deadly mistake with the British Empire still arrayed against them. They were ready to throw Hitler to the wolves if they could get peace with England. They presented themselves as a reasonable alternative to Hitler. Hess knew the *14th Duke of Hamilton* very well. What's more, his mentor *Karl Haushofer*, one of the inventors of *Geopolitics*, was also close to Hamilton and the British resistance that included Lord Halifax, Chamberlain and the Royal Family. Haushofer assured them that Hess could be trusted. In a remarkable feat of navigation, Hess flew solo, at night, to within 10 miles of Hamilton's estate in Scotland. In an astonishing coincidence the duke just happened to be at home too. The standard story now is that there was no internal British resistance to the war and that Hess was a fool to think there was. There was no such thing and there never could have been any such thing, as the Nazis were so evidently evil. Clearly it was all a product of Hess's deranged mind. But in fact the war had thus far devolved into terror bombing and got England nothing except more dead, debt and sorrow. They wanted out of it and even more so when Germany's plan was not to invade them, but Russia instead. Penultimately, England would get nothing out of the war except the dissolution of its empire and subjugation to the newly minted American way of endless war and military entitlements. England's ultimate result would be what we see today; the pending destruction of the English speaking peoples. They failed to gain peace as Churchill foiled them through a bit of luck. Unfortunately for Hess, he was captured by local police and, instead of meeting the duke, he was taken to Churchill who had Hess locked up in isolation for the rest of his life. Hess and Goering were ready to offer complete withdrawal from France (except Alsace), Norway, Netherlands, Denmark and Belgium, the restoration of Poland (except Danzig) with a member of the British Royal Family installed as King of Poland. Also, the preservation of the British Empire, including especially Suez and Gibraltar, and the full-strength maintenance of the Royal Navy and Air Force was guaranteed. Ceding Denmark and Norway were significant. They were willing to give away the store to make war with Russia. But peace would have meant Churchill's fall from power and grace just as it did in 1945. Churchill therefore kept Hess *incommunicado* and never allowed him to reveal his mission. The secret lay hidden from public view to this day. As for Hess, Hitler didn't realize that his friend would be forever kept in a small room. *Der Fuhrer* didn't comprehend that Churchill was just as ruthless, despicable and wicked as he was. Goering backed off and said he knew nothing.

Barbarossa

Halder and his deputy *Friedrich Paulus* planned the operation. Hitler wanted to go south. Halder and Paulus scoffed at him. They certainly knew more about war than the *Bohemian Corporal*. Never mind that the logistics section told the planners specifically that there was only enough oil for two months of mechanized operations; just like in France. That didn't dissuade Halder in the least; he thought the whole thing was going to be easy as rhubarb pie. Nobody was ever more wrong. *Operation Barbarossa* began on June 22, 1941. Coincidentally, Napoleon led his *Grand Armee* of 600,000 men into Russia on the very same day in 1812. Napoleon actually made better progress than the *Wehrmacht* but he wasn't up against an army fighting fanatically, tooth and nail, for every inch of ground. *Barbarossa* was the largest military action of all time: three million combat soldiers, 600,000 horses, ten thousand vehicles, five thousand planes (including transports) and close to 30,000 guns of all sorts; all launched simultaneously on a front that was 1000 miles long, from the Black Sea to the Baltic. In three army groups, there were 142 divisions but only 32 of them were mechanized. That's why they needed so many horses. Like in the *1st War-phase*, German farmers suffered: grain production fell by 50% the next year. It must be said that Hitler too thought it would be easy: *Just kick in the door*, he said, *and the whole rotten structure will come tumbling down*. Most foreign observers felt the same way. They all thought the Soviet system was corrupt, but it wasn't. It was Russian but without the Tsar and his rotten minions. This was revolutionary Russia and while many Russians didn't like it all that much, it was still better than anything the Tsar ever offered. The war was about their homeland and not a referendum on Joe Stalin. They weren't going to quit until either they or the last German invader was dead.

The Red Army is strategically misplaced

The Wehrmacht made rapid progress initially, because the Red Army was not in defensive positions! It was deployed forward. They were supplied with maps of Poland, Romania and Germany, all seemingly in preparation for attack. After the war and before he was hung by the victors, Field Marshall Wilhelm Keitel said *Barbarossa* was launched as preventive war, in anticipation of a Russian assault. Anyhow, looking at the noose, that was his story. How then to explain Russian dispositions? If they were on the defensive, then their massive losses in the first few months; 5 million casualties, might have been lessened. Most likely, the Red Army still hadn't digested the lessons from the French Campaign. They were simply unable to grasp just how quickly German armored formations could penetrate into the operational depths and exploit any breakthrough. But Russia, with its huge population could withstand the sorts of losses they took. Not so for Germany. When the campaign began, Germany had 80% of its 20-30 year old population already in uniform. By the end of August, only *two months* into the campaign, the German Army lost an astonishing 700,000 men! This was far worse than any two-month period in the *1st War-phase*. They had no more reserves and, like the year before, they were extremely low on gas too.

Steel and Coal

Army Group North had the easiest of goals. They were to drive along the Baltic coast and take Leningrad less than 600 miles away. Supply would not be an issue. They took Riga in July and the port served as a supply hub deep inside Soviet territory. Unlike the rest of Russia and Ukraine, there were paved roads. German planners determined that one single track railroad line was worth 1000 trucks. Russia's narrow gauge RR lines needed to be converted and this wasn't easy. Embankments, ties and tracks all needed to be replaced and rebuilt. But this is the sort of thing that Germans are good at and it was done. They knew very well they were short of oil and rubber, so much so that German trucks drove around with steel wheels. They had lots of steel and coal; perfect for building the most massive railroad system the world ever saw. Since the Germans had air supremacy their trains could move about freely. This is why Halder and Paulus chose the central thrust rather than the southern route to the oil fields: the railroad lines led directly to Leningrad and Moscow. They never took either city. If German military planning and execution was all that it's made up to be, then Leningrad, *at least*, should have fallen easily. There were no supply problems on that front and they had paved roads. But they were stopped anyway. Rather than look inside themselves, German generals blamed the weather and the roads. To confirm their own brilliance, they sold the lie as a believable alternative to their own incompetence. Incredibly, the myth of a superior German Army, defeated only by bad luck and bad weather, is still generally presented and believed.

The Luftwaffe gets shot up again

The Luftwaffe had a good first few weeks in the Barbarossa Campaign. By the end of June they had shot down 1,438 *Red Air Force* planes and destroyed another 3,176 on the ground. According to German reckoning that was over half their total strength. As was *always* the case, German military intelligence underestimated Soviet strength. The Reds actually had 15,599 aircraft at the start. The Luftwaffe began the campaign with 2,250 combat ready planes. Three weeks later they had lost 550 with 336 more damaged for 40% losses. The long-term problem for Germany was that Soviet construction already outstripped them. The Reds produced 5,173 fighters in the last half of 1941 but Luftwaffe replacements only numbered 1,619. The Luftwaffe was also fighting in North Africa, the Mediterranean and England so not all the replacements could go east. As the German Army penetrated deeper into Russia they faced the same predicament as at Dunkirk; they had difficulty building new air bases to keep up with the rapid advance into enemy territory. This meant the Luftwaffe only had air supremacy in Russia for the first three weeks of the campaign. They never had it again.

Memoirs

After the war, many German soldiers wrote their recollections. Guderian was one and *Panzer Leader* tells the story of a bungling and ignorant Hitler who frustrated the brilliance of professional soldiers Halder, Manstein, Rommel and, of course, Guderian hisself. Halder got himself a cushy job working for the US Army's historical section selling the same story. They even gave him a medal. Halder's legendary presentation was the tale of the *Noble Cause*: the valiant but losing struggle against the profound evils of Soviet Communism that might have been, ought to, and certainly should have been won; had not the amateur and criminally insane Hitler continually got in the way. Oh, yes, admittedly there were atrocities Halder conceded; some of them inhuman and wicked beyond belief. But the Army didn't do that either! It was the evil Hitler and his *SS Sonderkommandos* who done the deed. We soldiers fought a righteous war all the German generals insisted and agreed. They didn't, but they might have planned a few things better; like calculating the effects of Russian weather.

Rasputitsa

Considering that the German Army fought in Russia only 25 years before, they might have remembered that the four seasons in Russia are not the same as in the west. Somehow they didn't recall. There are six seasons out there. Two of them are named *Rasputitsa*, or the muddy season and they come in April and October. There was only one paved highway in Russia in 1941; the one through the Baltic States to Leningrad. Everything else was dirt and twice a year they become impassable. The mud is so deep it can suck your boots off. The great planner and military genius Halder didn't take this into account. After Smolensk was taken on the dirt road to Moscow, Guderian, who commanded *Army Group Center's* panzer forces, wanted to drive straight to Moscow which was c. 300 miles away, due east. The problem was a Russian army group of five armies numbering *one million men* was to the south, in Ukraine. Guderian wanted to take Moscow and leave this enemy force on his flank. It was at this point that Hitler just said no. It was impossible, he said, to push onward upon a single narrow supply bridge when *one million enemy troops* lay to the south of it. This was the first time Hitler interfered with the campaign, either in the planning or execution phase. He did so as *Oberkommando der Wehrmacht* (Commander in Chief of the Armed Forces). This was a position much like that of the *President of the United States* who is nominally commander in chief of the military. Hitler had named himself commander in 1938. However he was not commander of the German Army. That title, and not a ceremonial one, was held by *Field Marshall Walther von Brauchitsch* who was *Oberbefehlshaber des Heeres*. They ran their own show until now. Hitler had cajoled them into accepting Manstein's Ardennes plan. Now the situation was precarious and they obeyed Hitler for the first time. They did so because he was correct. The panzer forces, over Guderian's strenuous objections, drove south and helped encircle the Red Army's concentration near Kiev where 750,000 enemy troops were captured. Most of them would soon die in captivity, as the German Army did not make adequate provisions even for its own troops. It worked both ways: in 1941-42, 95% of captured Germans did not survive either, usually shot on the spot. The death rate for Soviet Red Army prisoners of war in German hands was 58% overall, and close to 100% in the 1941 Barbarossa Campaign. The murders and maltreatment only lessened in 1942 after Hitler intervened upon Albert Speer's realization that Red Army prisoners would make useful slave laborers. For comparison, the death rate among German prisoners in Russia was less than 15% as they were kept alive upon orders from the *Politburo* and put to work as slaves in 1943 and afterwards. Both sides were committed to total war (*Der totale Krieg*) a phrase invented by Ludendorf and resurrected by Goebbels in a famous speech at the Berlin *Sportpalast*.

For want of an air-filter

With Kiev taken, Guderian again directed his Panzers towards Moscow. But the rains came in October and made the roads impassable; like they do every year. Who could have seen this coming? Neither Halder, nor Guderian did. It is impossible to comprehend that both those fellows later complained about, and blamed their defeat upon, the lack of paved roads in Russia. The lack of preparation is astounding. When the German Army invaded, they didn't even know who was on the Red Army General Staff. The only name they knew was Semyon Timoshenko, the commander in chief. They had no idea whom they were fighting and they didn't care, because it was going to be easy. They didn't have accurate maps either. This would make the Russian campaign different from France when they *always* knew where they were. In Russia they seldom did. No more quick response from Luftwaffe fast-movers in a nation that was incomprehensibly vast. All they could do was drive generally east and hope for the best. It worked very well for a few months but as they penetrated deeper, men and horses began to die. The vehicles broke down as the ever-present red dust from the unpaved roads just ate up motor lubricants. Where are those *gottverdammte* air filters, the men wanted to know. Well, they were on the trains that didn't come, and when they did, they had something else. You can shake out an air filter a dozen times but eventually it stops protecting the motor. Supply trucks were loaded up with food and ammo; that was the first priority. No room for winter clothing either. Very few on the German side foresaw the consequences. They thought this was just another local war for territorial adjustment when it was a battle of annihilation. The decision to make war on Russia was the most historic decision that any German government ever made. The blame for this momentous and catastrophic choice lay squarely upon Adolf Hitler as Chancellor of the German Reich, and the German Army General Staff itself. It is their fault alone for creating the situation that now exists: with the German race facing physical eradication and extinction; a fate they once envisioned for the peoples of the east.

The golden spires of the Kremlin

The mud did force a slow-down that allowed German forces to concentrate again. They used the time to get resupplied. When the November frost hardened the roads, they began the central advance upon Moscow anew. They got to the suburbs. There is a persistent legend that a recon battalion reached *Khimki* (or *Himki*) and from there, about 12 miles from the city center, saw the golden spires of the Kremlin. A monument there commemorates the spot. But maybe it was the village of *Nefedyevo*, where some Germans possibly saw the same thing. Then again, it might have been *Krasnaya Polyana*, taken on November 30 where, with binoculars, the Moscow skyline can be seen. Or perhaps the morning sun presented a golden glow glinting off the frozen snow, a well known phenomenon out there in the boondocks. Nobody can say for sure since there were no survivors.

The Red Army strikes back

Richard Sorge was a Soviet spy in Tokyo who was tortured and killed by Japanese military intelligence in 1944. From his post in the German embassy he was able to inform the Politburo that Japan was unlikely to invade Siberia and would instead soon, and amazingly, attack the United States. In fact, in late November, the Japanese *1ˢᵗ Air Fleet* had already set sail for Pearl Harbor. This allowed the Red Army to transfer five crack divisions to Moscow. In the retreat the Reds were also able to dismantle heavy-industry factories and move them to the Ural Mountains, far from enemy reach. The Russian people, in their profound selflessness, burned everything in the path of the invader. The weakened Wehrmacht was unable to resist the influx of fresh Siberian troops and their own poor planning. On December 5th, the Red Army counter-attacked and drove the Germans off. They would never return to Moscow. For the German Army the battle was lost. By then German losses were one million men, all their horses and most of their tanks and vehicles. This was a military disaster of the first order. *Army Group Center* began to withdraw and disintegrate. It was 40 degrees below zero, wind-chill even colder and they were in danger of complete annihilation. Tired of being bullied by what was, *in effect*, the Prussian Army High Command, Hitler fired one half-dozen general officers and named himself *Oberbefehlshaber des Heeres* on December 19th, 1941. From here on in, he would direct the war, and it would consume him. With *Army Group Center* on the verge of dissolution, Hitler gave his famous *Stand Fast Order* because he sought a static front-line position, similar to the only war he ever knew: the western front in 1914-18. He rightly reckoned that holding a prepared position, even a woodshed, was better than marching into oblivion at -40°F. The *Stand Fast* order is an oversimplification of what remained a fluid situation. It meant; *we are not retreating to Berlin. Hold!* They did and *Army Group Center* wrested victory from defeat: when the *Battle of Moscow* was over six weeks later, the Reds lost 1,600,000 men to 257,000 for Germany. The losses are staggering for the rational mind to comprehend. *Army Group Center* would maintain its integrity but now, as Chancellor, Hitler would make his greatest error when, as predicted by Sorge, Japan attacked the USA.

Japan

In 1854, Japan was a medieval kingdom (*shogunate*) under an agricultural manorial system. It was a strictly ordered society with few laws, little crime, and no prisons: there was no need for them as death was penalty for all crimes. The Japanese Archipelago was self sufficient and there was plenty for all with no real poverty, at least not in the western sense. The rice wine and beer were good as was the salted fish and plums. All that changed when Commodore Perry sailed into Tokyo harbor and demanded to land. There was only one point of entry for foreigners and Tokyo wasn't it. Perry demonstrated the power of his exploding shells on some empty buildings and the Japanese said, in effect; *Okay, welcome to Japan*. Perry was there to open up international trade and not conquest. The inhabitants were wise enough to add up the proposition and chose trade rather than resistance. Being extremely wise, they were able make the adjustments on a national level. Unfortunately for the Japanese people, this meant the destruction of their life in the bountiful countryside for one of wage-slavery in the industrial mills in cities that now grew like weeds. Silk production changed from a cottage industry that provided local needs to one where Japan controlled 80% of the world's international production in just a few years. Like in medieval Europe, the silk farmers and other agricultural workers were driven off the land into cities. There they found poverty, shanty towns, rampant crime and prostitution. Police and prisons were invented, and for the men, forced military service and the privilege to die for the emperor. This is presented in the textbooks as wonderful for everybody.

Conquest

Perry made another voyage and this time he took along a small-sized steam locomotive and tracks. The Japanese figured out how to make a big one. They imported experts in naval construction, weaponry and mass production. Forty years after Perry visited, they conquered Formosa (now Taiwan) and ten years after that, their navy sank the Imperial Russian Fleet at the battle of Tsushima. Korea became theirs, as did Manchukuo, and then when France fell, Indochina. They chose war with China in 1937 as a military clique that ruled by bloody assassination with sword took control of the nation. They drove the Chinese inland with the ultimate aim of exterminating them biologically with bacteriological weapons. By mid-1942 they owned all of Southeast Asia and large swaths of the Pacific Ocean as well. All this, so it seemed, necessitated war with the United States. But by 1945, just three years after the apex of imperial mastery, American heavy bombers let loose the maelstrom of nuclear war upon them. Like Germany's verdict to war with Russia, Japan's choice to wage war with America was the single most significant decision any nation ever made, but it was done with relatively little concern for possible negative outcomes.

THE TRANSFORMATION OF THE WEST INTO A PERMANENT WAR ECONOMY

At least Germany's judgment was based upon long-standing philosophical trends and historical events. Just as importantly, Germany was able to wage war directly upon Russia as they shared a common border. German conquest of Russia was a reasonable conclusion in 1941. Japan, conversely, was not able to attack the United States in any meaningful way except on the periphery. Yes, Japan could easily take American naval and air stations on Guam and Wake Island but how could Japan attack the American means of production in Detroit or Pittsburgh? That was impossible. Invasion was completely out of the question. All Japan had to do was study the American way of war to see that the end result could only be the extermination of one or the other; and that could only be Japan. Yet they chose war with America almost as an afterthought. *Whom the gods will destroy they first make mad* said the Greeks. Japan's military leadership held, quite literally, the rest of the world in contempt as they did their own people.

The Samurai Spirit

Shogunate Japan in 1854 was like Medieval Europe c. 1500. It was a completely sustainable and ecologically sound agricultural society. The difference was; the collapse of the European medieval agrarian social order into industrial nationalism took centuries. In Japan, the shift took just a few years. Japan was not completely closed off to foreigners in 1854. Traders, usually Dutch with whom they had a treaty, could enter at Nagasaki and trade specie and weapons (mostly) for tea and silk. Japan was ruled (loosely) by the Shogun who was a medieval warlord. His retainers (*Daimyo*) in the countryside maintained order with a strict hereditary societal structure. Everybody knew their place and obeyed the precepts of *Shinto* that saw the world as one living organism with everything, very evidently, in its own place working and living in harmony with everything else. The wind and rain fed the land, the rivers and the sea fed all else. Spring came and the grass grew by itself. What more do you need to know? The system worked for 650 years and the *Code of Bushido* was the moral system that made it work on a human level. Like the *Chivalric Code* that defined the morality of armored knights, Bushido characterized the duties of the Samurai warrior that were, above all else, the protection of women and their children. How else could society survive? When the Shogun proved unable to resist the incursions of Americans and other *Barbarians*, power shifted back to the Emperor who alone was able to afford the maintenance of a full-time army in the field. The armored Samurai warriors resisted but the world's best swordsmen (supported by *some* guns) were defeated in a final series of battles in 1868 by the Emperor's troops armed with muskets and round shot cannon. The Samurai's final subjugation and humiliation came in 1876 when they were prohibited from wearing their swords in public. The Emperor's Army became the most powerful institution in Japan. They observed the complete breakdown of Shinto and Bushido in everyday life. Young women were now openly bought and sold into slave-like conditions in the silk mills and prostitution. They, as warriors, were no longer able to protect Japanese women who were now commodities. On the contrary, they were made protectors of the slave masters that trafficked in the women who, only a short time before, were revered. To maintain their honor, *the Army internalized the Code of Bushido* so that it protected and enhanced solely the power of the Army and no one else. Never mind the poor and destitute. Japan now manufactured that as a way life. The Army viewed Japanese society with contempt as it was now unmistakably inhuman. Hence they respected only themselves and honor came to be defined simply as obedience and the willingness to die in battle for the Army in the name of the Emperor. They began to formulate national policy as it was they who would have to be the caretakers of Japanese society, or what was left of it. The civilian leadership had fallen into the trap of international corruption and *dishonor* on a massive scale. The Emperor would be obeyed only if he went along with the schemes of the Army leadership. Luckily for him, the Emperor Hirohito was in full accord. If not, he would be murdered and replaced; as would, of course, any civilian politician or newspaper editor who got in the way.

More oil

The 19th century was the age of coal. The 20th became one of oil. Any nation that wanted to increase its means of production and international trade needed it. Germany, Italy, and Japan didn't have any. Their enemies, the USA, USSR and England (from the USA) were awash in it. The Italian navy stayed in port on account of it. All the Axis Powers were eventually strangled from lack of it. Needing it, Japan occupied southern Indochina from whence they might take the oil rich Dutch Indonesian colonies. War was coming and America forced Japan's hand. They were dependent upon the USA for oil but on August 1st, 1941 the USA established a commodities embargo upon Japan. This was in reaction to Japan's occupation of southern Indochina. Their occupation of northern Indochina was tolerated by the Americans because it was evidently a part of Japan's war with China, The southern thrust could only mean war against the west. The Americans decided they could no longer fuel Japan's military with iron ore, steel, scrap metal, machine tools and oil. This erstwhile *act of war* was made legal by The *Kellogg-Briand Pact*. At the same time, the US Navy moved its base of operations from San Diego in California to Pearl Harbor, 2,500 miles closer to Japan and the Philippines. Just to be sure that Japan got the message; the US State Department sent them a note demanding that they withdraw from China. The problem for the Japanese was that the Americans didn't differentiate between China and Manchukuo. There were people on the Japanese side who wanted to get out of China as the war seemed endless and to no avail. They knew this right away. In 1938 Japan had 800,000 troops in China and couldn't supply them. Japan's industry only produced 30 tanks a month. What had begun as a limited war to gain resources from northern China had become total war when the Chinese Communists and Nationalists agreed to stop fighting each other and wage war together against the Japanese invaders. China now had a really good army. The Japanese Army wanted to withdraw to the north but China wouldn't let them easily do that. It's been said many times that it is easier to begin a war than to end one. Sure it was, especially since this one didn't begin as the result of any rational decision but rather as a military adventure gone awry.

The path to war

When Germany beat everybody up in 1940, Japan was able to use those victories to its own advantage. Their war with China was a race war of annihilation. There were no prisoners taken. Atrocities abounded. Defeated and prostrate, England, France and the Netherlands weren't able to supply China from Burma and Indochina anymore through the famous *Burma Road*. With that supply line now cut off, the war in China suddenly looked like it might be winnable for Japan. When they then occupied the southern half of Indochina and Saigon, the USA felt that war was close. Why else would Japan use scarce resources to do that except to move south into Dutch Indonesia and its oil? It was at this point that America chose war with Japan but they were clever enough to allow Japan to make the opening attack. Ergo, they decided to stop giving the Imperial Japanese Navy the means to wage war, thereby presenting Japan with a conundrum. But the problem for the Japanese peace factions, both within the Army, the Emperor's circle, and in the *Diet*, was that while withdrawal from China was reasonable, even desirable, leaving Manchukuo was not. They could withdraw from China and hope that some sort of international alliance might protect Japan's position as a great power. Or, they could wage total war against both Asia and the West despite the apparent insurmountable odds against them. Japan chose total war in the belief that its spiritual power could overcome the West's decadent material superiority.

Ethnic bioweapons

Japan hoped for victory in China with the human experiment and death factory, *Unit 731* and others like it, where they wanted to isolate germs or viruses specific to Chinese people and wipe them all out. This is not farfetched. Chinese germ warfare labs in the 21st century expect to, or already have, isolated bacteriological agents that will only attack people with blue, green, and hazel eyes, leaving their own population intact. One of their centers for this operation is in *Wuhan*. These are called *ethnic bioweapons*. When America's oil embargo was expanded into a full trade embargo that included frozen assets, acts that are *de facto* declarations of war, the Japanese war party had its way. The only question that remained was the strategic approach. Unfortunately for Japan, they chose an attack upon the USA as the first act of war against western imperialism. It should have been the last option and avoided at all costs as America alone produced 50% of the whole world's gross domestic product. Japanese leadership knew this but didn't think it mattered.

The IJN needs something to do

In the 1904-05 war against Russia, the Army and Navy both played important roles. But the Army's move south into the Dutch East Indies (now Indonesia) left the Navy with little to do except escort the troop ships that would carry the Army into the oil rich Indies. The Navy had a massive budget and needed to justify its own existence. In a situation difficult to comprehend, Japan in 1941 didn't have a government. This could be said of all the Axis powers. Mussolini governed without any input from the *Fascist Grand Council*. It was he who decided to war upon America even though the vast majority of ordinary Italians knew it wasn't a good idea. Germany came closest to have a rational administration; Hitler's navy pushed him towards war with America, the Luftwaffe and Army being ambivalent. Japan had a government that only affected little people; the powerless workers, housewives and farmers that tried to survive everyday life in what had become a brutal police state. Japan made the transition from medieval fiefdom to centralized military industrial state too quickly for all organs of the national state to adapt to any sort of federal control. The Army didn't submit to any sort of civilian advice and never would. Even worse, factions within the Army now decided national policy. Japan had a parliament (*Diet*) but it could only pass ordinances that didn't affect the Army. In a death struggle with Germany, Russia's influence in neighboring Manchukuo was limited. Ergo both Manchukuo and Korea were safe and the Army could confidently move south. It would be the Army that would secure the oil for Japan's empire and maintain its colossal budget and prestige. The Navy was out in the cold and incredibly, war with America was chosen as a way to give the Navy something to do.

The national defense state

Japan's war against the United States was fought, amazingly, mostly by the Imperial Japanese Navy (*IJN*). Like the Army, Japan's Navy was answerable only to the Emperor. They would fight America and the Army would fight on the Asian mainland. For the small minds that made up the Japanese military elite this was a reasonable plan. They never could imagine that the USA would literally march an army, island by island, across half the globe and occupy Tokyo in four years time. Who could see that coming? It seems, even today, like an absolute physical impossibility. However, Japan's leadership might have looked at the campaigns of Genghis Khan to see that such colossal conquests were not only reasonable but actual. Even their own proposed and genuine expansion would rival what the Americans did to them. But, like all the Axis powers, Japan never imagined that what they were dishing out, they might soon have to eat.

War plans

The original Japanese war plan against the USA was defensive. They knew the American operation, the somewhat famous *War Plan Orange*, called for a fleet sortie across the Pacific and a final *decisive battle* to be fought somewhere near the Japanese home islands. That fleet action would be fought in home waters just like *Tsushima*. They would hopefully whittle down the enemy force with submarines and aircraft, including nighttime zero altitude torpedo attacks from their fleet of twin-engined long range medium bombers. This was a good plan. Both fleets sought the *Decisive Battle* that was the strategic centerpiece of Mahan's famous *The Influence of Sea Power upon History: 1660–1783* (1890). The problem for Japan was that by 1940 American naval planning had given up on the idea that one grand strategic naval battle could win a war. Nelson whipped the French fleet at *Trafalgar* in 1805 but Napoleon didn't surrender until ten years later and it took the British, Austrian, Prussian and Russian armies to do it. Even before the relatively minor disaster at Pearl Harbor, the Americans shifted their planning in a new direction that involved *island hopping* all the way to Japan and that's what happened. This is the kind of plan that appeals to the American way of war. It evolved from their conflict against the Confederate States: war that emphasized a mechanically engineered massive concentration of firepower against an enemy weakened by naval blockade. The Japanese didn't think this way. They saw war mostly as a struggle of morale;

where sailors, troops and airmen with superior ethical determination and fanaticism could conquer against all odds. They proposed that an entire nation with no fear of death, and one that was spiritually directed toward a *national self defense* would be invulnerable. Thus, Americans softened by the world's highest standard of living would be easy foes. Laughably, the Japanese didn't comprehend that the machinery which gave some Americans their perceived luxuries could be swiftly re-tooled for war.

A medieval army

Joan of Arc was appointed by her king to lead a relief mission to the city of Orleans that was besieged by the English. In fact, *she accompanied* the expedition. The *Duke of Alençon* and the other sub-commanders went along because they thought a relief mission was a good idea, not because they were going to allow Joan any actual authority. A medieval army did what it wanted to do, depending on how the men, and their commanders, felt about it. It wasn't Roman with their strict adherence to draconian centralized discipline. When Caesar gave an order it was carried out. The *Duke of Alençon* could only hope that a general consensus for action might arise after prolonged discussion. When they arrived at Orleans, Joan got fed up with too much dawdling reluctance to face the English. She donned her armor and gathered a few hundred men for a sortie. The senior commanders reluctantly mounted up. When she quickly took a lightly held bastion, it was her first step in assuming overall command of the king's army. Joan won over the men with her courage and personality. She did the same with her captains because she knew how to deploy troops and artillery for battle better than they did. Finally, the *Code of Chivalry* directed the moral integrity of all the commanders. There were some noteworthy contra instances like when Henry V ordered thousands of prisoners murdered at Agincourt, but he was English. Japan's military *in action* was structured in much the same way. The wars in China and Manchuria all began when local commanders chose aggression. Tokyo's civilian leadership then went along with it rather than offend the Army: they knew there were elements within the Army like the *Imperial Way Faction* that would have liked to cut the lot of them to pieces. There were plenty of men available for grisly operations because the *Code of Bushido* meant that Japanese troops always obeyed orders and never surrendered. They held enemy prisoners in contempt for doing so. Hence the *Bataan Death March* and the *Rape of Nanking* where local commanders let things get out of hand. Japan's armed forces were modern in their weaponry but medieval in their attitudes. There was no government directing the Army and Navy. The ruling military was composed of groups that promoted policy and various sorts of strategic plans by threats of dismemberment to anyone opposed. These people made the *Blackshirts* seem like girl scouts. Decisions were not the result of a rational discussion that weighed pros and cons. Their empire, when it included Korea, Manchukuo and Formosa was large enough to have economically dominated Asia, and quite possibly the world, for the rest of the century. America had indeed excluded their nationals and goods through restrictive immigration and tariffs, but there was no bigger market than China. Japan's military leadership never gave peace a chance because there were no civilian control mechanisms in place. They didn't know any other way besides war. But their method of war was flawed. They relied upon the notion that qualitative and spiritual superiority could overcome quantitative disadvantage. This was probably true when combat was fought by Samurai warriors with fine steel swords. Against the Americans it was folly.

The American way of war

The Americans operated under a completely different mindset. They invested important resources into air-sea rescue and were able to save thousands of sailors and airmen from a watery death. The Japanese didn't bother with it. If you failed in your mission, death was both honorable and preferable. Their aircrews were all issued parachutes but most of the men didn't wear them and used them as seat-cushions. It's not that Japan's military didn't care about the men. They did. But Japanese airmen and sailors were imbued with the belief that direct combat with the enemy was the way of the warrior. The rescue of men who had failed in their duty wasn't a part of this set of laws. The *Code of Bushido* that dictated no surrender also directed policy away from other roles that were not combat oriented. The Navy, for example, was very reluctant to escort merchant ships and tankers. The destroyer captains didn't want this sort of duty. They wanted to face the enemy and not shepherd commercial vessels. According to the *Code of Bushido* they had to be given this opportunity. As a result, Japan never developed a convoy system that brought the resources of the Indies to Japan. American submarines wrought havoc among the unescorted and helpless merchantmen. Americans invented the attack submarine so they knew how to use those boats better than anybody. What's more, American submariners couldn't care less what the target was. They saw quite well that a tanker loaded with oil was a ripe target. Japanese submarine captains, on the contrary, didn't want commercial raiding missions. They wanted to attack enemy warships and did sink some American carriers and cruisers. But they could have wreaked chaos on the undefended American west coast and at the Panama Canal bottleneck. If Japan actually had a government it could have directed a successful commercial war against the United States. They never did.

Advancement to the level of mediocrity

Nor could they ever find the right men for the job. The Navy promoted men solely on the basis of seniority and therefore chose *Chūichi Nagumo* to command the *First Air Fleet* that comprised their only six *fleet carriers*. These were large aircraft carriers that could each launch between 75-90 single-engined aircraft. It was them, and a few escorts, that would attack Pearl Harbor. Nagumo was getting old, had arthritis from too much sword play, and didn't know the first thing about naval aviation. He made a mess of the attack but once on the post he couldn't be fired. That would result in *loss of face* (*mentsu wo ushinau*) and quite possibly ritual suicide. Yamamoto should have taken command himself but didn't. This was the single most important military operation in the whole 3,000 year history of the Japanese Empire and they completely blew it. Yamamoto stood in port and maintained radio silence; deaf, blind and dumb. Japanese naval aviators sank four battleships, damaged four more and shot up the whole of Hawaii's air defense. When the fliers returned, they found Nagumo on the bridge of the *Akagi* muttering: *Four battleships…four battleships.* He thought it was 1905. The Admiral figured the battle was already won. When *Minoru Genda*, who helped plan the attack, pleaded for another attack to shoot up American oil storage, dry docks and machine shop facilities (locations that were all <u>exactly</u> known)

Nagumo said: *Even a thief does not return for more.* For him and Yamamoto the operation was *a raid*. They turned tail and fled. They could have rendered the Pearl Harbor base inoperable and forced the Pacific Fleet back to San Diego. This would have created real problems for the American navy because operations out of Pearl Harbor threatened the Japanese from a *central position*. San Diego is 2,500 miles to the rear and a place from whence it would be more difficult to carry out offensive operations.

What did Roosevelt know?

Through the backwards lens by which we now view events in the 2nd War-phase, aircraft carriers were, undoubtedly, the premier naval weapon in 1941. However nobody knew that at the time. The big-gunned battleship formed the core of every fleet. This is why it is difficult to assume that American leadership, specifically President Roosevelt, knew of the Japanese attack on the battleship fleet at Pearl Harbor. Nobody on the American side wanted to lose those ships. Aircraft carriers were regarded as scouts. It is true that all the American battleships were lined up together on *Battleship Row* and that was good for administrative purposes. It made a swell target. In the event of attack the enemy could and did easily identify and attack them. But the American's didn't think the Japanese could pull off an operation like that. They actually thought that the Japanese, as a race, didn't have the necessary hand-eye coordination to be successful dive and torpedo bomber pilots. USN battleships could have been dispersed in the confines of the harbor but that just wasn't as pretty and awe inspiring as having the fleet lined up for review. Those were after all, very beautiful ships. However, their own wargame in 1932 showed that Pearl Harbor was vulnerable to attack from the north. All Army Air Force planes were lined up in neat rows too. They too should have been dispersed. This is why the stories of advance knowledge won't go away.

Japanese codes

In *The Scarlet Pimpernel* (1934) Leslie Howard remarked to Raymond Massey: *Devilishly clever race the French, how they speak that unspeakable language of theirs defeats me.* Perhaps this is why the Japanese never figured out that since 1923 the Americans were reading their diplomatic codes. Japanese is a difficult language to begin with and the idea that a *gaijin* might be able to understand it in code seems quite impossible. Those Americans were quite devilishly clever. On the evening of December 6th 1941 the code-breakers presented President Roosevelt with a 14-point Japanese declaration. It was to be delivered in whole, at exactly 1 PM Washington time the next day. Keep in mind that Roosevelt was not a recipient of *PURPLE*, the Japanese diplomatic code. When he was entrusted with de-coded transcripts they'd been found in his wastepaper basket. It was withheld from him until 1942 because fellows like Simpson and Marshall felt that Roosevelt and the people around him were Communists. They were. So the declaration was brought to him, he was allowed to read it and then taken from him. What Roosevelt read was not a declaration of war *per se* but a notification that negotiations were at an end. The frightening part was the instruction to deliver it exactly on time. Well, that should have been alarming but it wasn't. Roosevelt reads it and says to Harry Hopkins: *This means war!* He then walks out the door and goes to work on his stamp collection. The Chief of Naval Operations goes to the theater. Army Chief of Staff Marshall can't remember what he did that night but the next morning he goes horse-back riding. Refreshed by his morning gallop he arrives at his office at 11:30 AM and it dawns on him that 1 PM Washington time is sunrise in Hawaii. They say the phones didn't work that morning. He then informs General Short by commercial telegram that war might very well be declared by Japan that day. *Western Union* doesn't deliver it until Hawaii's air force is reduced to burning hulks. Admiral Kimmel, who had a hunch to crank up the fleet the night before, but decided against it, is not informed at all until he sees Japanese bombers sink the bulk of his battleship divisions.

What is it about 'war warning' that you don't understand?

JN-25, the Japanese Naval code, was not yet completely decoded and Kimmel wasn't on the list of recipients anyway. Two weeks before Pearl Harbor, both Admiral Kimmel and General Short received a *War Warning* from the *Chief of Naval Operations*. Three were sent, dated November 24, 27, and 28, 1941.

It read: *This dispatch is to be considered a war warning.* Yet, on December 7th, neither General Short nor Admiral Kimmel were in any way prepared for a Japanese attack that could only come from one direction; north by northwest. Neither did either of them ever consult with the other about the *war warning*. General Short's only job was to protect Hawaii from invasion and the fleet. None of his planes were in the air that morning, nor had he been conducting any search upon possible avenues of approach. He later said that wasn't his job. Since when is reconnaissance not a military mission? Admiral Kimmel had 71 *PBY Catalinas* that had an effective range of 1,250 miles. These flying boats are still in use as aerial firefighters. They are probably the best recon aircraft ever invented until the *SR-71 Blackbird*. On December 7th none of them were in the air nor had they been. The *United States Pacific Fleet* conducted no aerial recon whatsoever. One explanation was that there weren't enough aircraft for a full 360° sweep! That's so ridiculous. The only possible enemy was Japan and the only possible approach was north by northwest. That's a 45° arc. There were certainly enough aircraft for that. But instead the commander chose to make no searches whatsoever. They had 96 warships in Pearl Harbor. None of them were on picket duty. None of the vulnerable battleships had their torpedo nets down. Everybody was asleep at the wheel. Admiral Kimmel and General Short were both relieved of command and charged with dereliction of duty. When the moment came to defend their men and ships they both failed. General Short died of a broken heart in 1949 as did Admiral Kimmel in 1968.

A date which will live in infamy

Short and Kimmel got blamed and Roosevelt just kept smiling. He gave a speech in self righteous indignation about a dastardly and *unprovoked* attack but it was all lies. In a series of communiqués to Churchill (declassified in 1972) Roosevelt reiterated again and again his desire to provoke war. "*Everything was to be done to force an incident*" he wrote. The British too had an interest in provoking war between the USA and Japan. Very few Americans can grasp that Great Britain is America's oldest enemy and still is. It was they who orchestrated the delivery of the German Pacific Ocean colonies to Japan at Versailles. Wilson, not as smart as he looked, let them get away with it. The

THE TRANSFORMATION OF THE WEST INTO A PERMANENT WAR ECONOMY

Mariana, Caroline and Marshall Islands were all astride the American sea-lanes to Guam and the Philippines. The British felt that a clash between America and Japan would come sooner or later. They would do whatever they could to weaken two potential adversaries. It was obvious to any rational observer that Japan could never win a war against the United States. For England the best possible outcome would be some sort of devastating initial success that would, hopefully, sink the American fleet. They had broken JN-25, had a vocabulary and knew *1ˢᵗ Air Fleet* was at sea. The Americans shared everything they had with them but didn't get anything in return. Churchill reckoned correctly that once the shooting started out there, it wouldn't take the politically devious Roosevelt long to start shooting at the Germans too. One must also wonder, what happened in the Philippines? Generalissimo Doug MacArthur had a fleet of B-17 bombers out there. The next day after Pearl Harbor they were all lined up on the runway in tidy rows. Japanese bombers destroyed them all. Those fellows had 9 hours warning that the war was on and still got caught napping. It all looks like a set-up.

What didn't Yamamoto know and when didn't he know it?

Even after the tactical victory at Pearl Harbor, where four battleships were sunk, the Japanese naval commander, Isoroku Yamamoto, continued to use carriers as lightly escorted scouts and raiders. They were the core of his fleet but he didn't know it. Yamamoto was, without a doubt, the single worst military commander of all time; including *Xerxes* who had the waves lashed at the *Hellespont* when they done him wrong. Yamamoto had the grandest fleet in the world in 1941 and four years later it would be, in its entirety, at the bottom of the sea. He was elevated to heroic status by the Japanese who needed some sort of valiant figure to emerge from the nightmare, and also by the American Navy whose own reputation was enhanced because they beat a naval genius comparable to Nelson. He wasn't. In December 1941 nobody knew anything about how to use naval aviation. Yamamoto and Nagumo sure didn't. The Italian Navy never built an aircraft carrier: not because they didn't believe in air power but because nobody quite understood what a carrier was good for. That seems silly now but the Italians thought that Italy itself; thrusting southward into and dominating the Mediterranean was an unsinkable carrier. They studded the coasts of Italy with airbases. What they didn't understand was that an aircraft carrier provides *instantaneous* local tactical air support. No need to radio in for air support 100 miles away that might, or might not, arrive in time. The Royal Navy didn't know too much either. They allowed their best aircraft carrier, *HMS Glorious*, to be captained by a submariner. He didn't believe in the need for aerial reconnaissance. Sailing blind with its aircraft stowed away, *Glorious* got gunned down by two German battleships. The logs and inquiry for this mishap, where 1500 young men drowned in freezing waters, are sealed for 100 years and can't be viewed until 2041. It seems Churchill let those fellows drown because the ship closest to *Glorious*, a cruiser that could have rescued the men, was transporting the Norwegian king to England. His safety was deemed paramount. Let them drown said the Prime Minister, and Vice Admiral Cunningham, who sailed away from the drowning men, got a medal.

Force Z

Three days after Pearl Harbor, the British Empire suffered an appalling blow when *Force Z*, the battleships *Prince of Wales* and *Repulse*, were sunk by *Betty* and *Nell* land-based Japanese naval air of the *22nd Koku Sentai* (Air Flotilla) based in Saigon (now *Ho Chi Minh City*). The battleships went out alone with only four destroyers as escort. They sought to intercept and destroy the Japanese invasion force that would eventually take Singapore and the oil of the East Indies. This was the first time that battleships under power and maneuvering at sea were ever sunk. Until this time, nobody knew that aircraft could actually do this as all the battleships sunk at Pearl Harbor (and at *Taranto* in 1940) were at their moorings. With Force Z destroyed, Japan landed an army on the north coast of Malaya and Singapore was now doomed. The British Army never imagined that an enemy could advance through the jungle to attack Singapore from the rear. If they themselves couldn't press forward through the jungle, then certainly no one else could either, they reasoned. The Japanese were just more resourceful. When their soldiers were out of rations and got hungry, they observed what the monkeys ate, knowing they could eat that too. They were tough, ruthless

THE TRANSFORMATION OF THE WEST INTO A PERMANENT WAR ECONOMY

fighters in remarkable physical condition. They attacked Singapore from the rear and captured 80,000 men, all their guns and vehicles. When Singapore fell the Japanese attained all the geo-political objectives they had set out for themselves in the decision to wage war with the United States and England: all of Southeast Asia and its oil resources were now under their control. Their empire became one of the largest in the history of the world. Incredibly, a very minor event unraveled the whole thing. American ingenuity being legendary, they loaded 16 twin-engined B-25 medium bombers onto an aircraft carrier and bombed Japan. This was, in effect, very close to a one way suicide mission as the planes could not return to the carrier but had to instead land in China. Japan launched *The Zhejiang-Jiangxi Campaign* the next month to capture the air bases the *Doolittle Raiders* landed on. They used bubonic plague bombs and indiscriminate massacres. The story goes that 250,000 Chinese civilians were murdered by the Japanese Army in revenge. That might be exaggerated but will never be known. The B-25 raid upon Japan revealed Japan's limitations to wage modern war. Since Tokyo was bombed, and the Emperor threatened, the *Code of Bushido* then dictated policy. The *IJN* had *lost face* in allowing the enemy to approach the *Imperial Palace*. It was then their responsibility to assure that such events never recur: hence the Midway operation designed to prevent the future approach of American warships through the North Pacific. Any brief history of the American way of war might have shown them how utterly stupid it was to harbor the idea that they might escape a war with the United States unscathed. Strategically, this minor raid should have been shrugged off. Instead, the incursion dictated Japanese naval strategy. It is important to note that throughout, the Americans had broken the Imperial Japanese Navy codes. The Japanese never got wind of this, which seems impossible. The Pacific Ocean is a huge expanse of water. The only way to grasp the size of it is to hold up a globe with the mid-point of the ocean before you. There, the Earth looks like a water planet as the Pacific Ocean covers half the globe. In April 1942 the *IJN* divided the *First Air Fleet* and sent fleet carriers *Shokaku* and *Zuikaku* and the light carrier *Shoho* into the Coral Sea. They found the American Navy laying in wait for them in *ambuscade*. Warning bells should have rung. The resultant carrier battle seemingly went in their favor; they lost light carrier *Shoho*, with *Shokaku* damaged, while the Americans lost fleet carrier *Lexington* with her sister ship *Yorktown* badly damaged. They remained too confident. *Shokaku* was then laid up for three months and *Zuikaku* was kept out of the planned Midway operation, ostensibly to train new aircrews. The American carrier *Yorktown*, as badly damaged as *Shokaku*, was repaired in 48 hours and fought at Midway: thus another difference between the *IJN* and the *USN*. To be on the safe side, the Japanese changed their encryption system, as they often did in a routine manner, but not the *code family*. What this means is that American cryptanalysts were not completely baffled by the changes and were able to crack the new codes again by 1943. However, enough radio traffic already revealed Japanese intentions in the North Pacific. At Midway, the Americans would waylay them again in another far more devastating trap.

Carrier tactics

Admiral Yamamoto was not an advanced naval thinker and *carrier admiral*. His dispositions for the Midway operation show that. The principle of concentration was beyond his domain. Yamamoto sent one light carrier and *Junyo* (heavy but slow) on a fool's mission to the Aleutian Islands. Those two carriers would have helped the main force; first-rate aircrews flying excellent machines manned them. Along with them were the only two ships in the Japanese fleet equipped with radar. What a waste. Once Midway fell, the Japanese would have been free to take any Aleutian island they wished. The star-crossed Admiral Nagumo, who should have been eased out of *Akagi's* bridge and into an armchair, or at best, command of a battleship division, still commanded the reduced *First Air Fleet*. It was impossible to demote him. Three hundred miles behind them were the battleships of the *IJN*. Japanese nomenclature for the operation reveals the mindset: the vast armada of battleships, cruisers and escorts to the rear were termed *The Main Body*. The precious but very vulnerable carriers were named *The Advanced Striking Force*. Advanced forces are, by their nature, expendable. Had Admiral Yamamoto truly recognized the value of his carriers, they would have been surrounded by all the battleships and cruisers of the entire fleet. Instead, the carriers were sent out practically alone to meet the enemy on even terms. Those big-gunned battleships of the *IJN* should have been in the van, shelling Midway in preparation for the invasion by the *Imperial Marines* who were, by the way, outnumbered. Instead, the dear pilots of the *First Air Fleet*, who took two years to train, were sent in to do the job that battleship guns should have. Super-battleship *Yamato* would have pulverized the small sand islands that offered no natural protection for the defenders. This would have left *1st Air Fleet* free to conduct naval operation against the American fleet. Neither Yamamoto nor Nagumo could see through this.

> *Any seasoned trapper will tell you; if you don't know what it is you're after, you're better off staying home*   Ned Buntline

The Battle of Midway is a classic naval encounter. The opposing fleets were evenly matched thanks to Yamamoto's decision to divide his carriers and to keep his battleships in the rear, out of harm's way. The *First Air Fleet* struck Midway and the pilots returned fearing that another attack was needed before the invasion might commence. Incidentally, that first strike got chewed up. Midway was loaded with antiaircraft guns. Shooting is an American *forté*. How could the Japanese not know this? Out of 108 aircraft, 38% were lost or damaged! *The Charge of the Light Brigade* suffered fewer casualties. Military organizations can't take hits like this and continue to function. In truth, the *IJN* was confused about its mission. Was it to destroy the American fleet or take Midway? Yamamoto gave both as objectives. But if the *IJN* were to concentrate upon Midway, what would be the consequences of a *United States Pacific Fleet* intervention? This is a simple, *what if scenario*. But sadly, it was just another deep concept beyond Yamamoto's field of imagination. There were indications that the Americans were about: increased radio traffic from Hawaii and American submarines were spotted. Normally submarines don't concentrate in the middle of a vast ocean unless there is a friendly fleet about. Yamamoto, this time out with the fleet in command of the *Main Body* (300 miles to the rear), declined to inform Nagumo and maintained radio silence. The only word for this is more stupidity. Fly a float plane over there and give Nagumo the data. Yamamoto forgot the lessons of Coral Sea and assured himself the Americans were not around. He was wrong, and they got in the first strike. With the Japanese rearming for a second hit on Midway, one of Nagumo's reconnaissance aircraft reported that there *'seems to be'* an American carrier at sea. At this point Nagumo made two grave tactical errors. Since he was a battleship admiral he turned towards the American carrier. That's what battleship admirals do: close and engage. Nagumo couldn't grasp that his attack airplanes had a range advantage over the Americans of 150 miles. This was known data and should have been a decisive edge. When he turned closer to the enemy he gave them the benefit with their shorter range. It was now easier for the Americans to find him and loiter over the target. Nagumo should have turned away and fought the battle at long range. From there he could hit the enemy and not allow them to hit back. But he fought the battle like a Samurai warrior. He couldn't comprehend the nature of naval air tactics that were completely foreign to his soul. Nagumo closed the range and with perfect poor timing decided to land the Midway strike. He wanted to rearm with torpedoes for a full-strength air attack against the enemy carrier. He should have instead attacked *immediately* with the 63 aircraft ready to launch from *2nd Carrier Division* commanded by *Admiral Tamon Yamaguchi*. He begged Nagumo to launch. The attack could have been airborne in less than 45 minutes; such was the efficiency of Japanese maintenance crews. The greatly reduced Midway strike could have safely landed on *Akagi* and *Kaga* with the damaged airframes jettisoned. But Nagumo was the wrong man for the job. Commanders like him and Yamamoto always imagine that the enemy will do just what they want them to do. They won't admit that on occasion the enemy might be one step ahead of them. *Field Marshall Montgomery* said in the *Battle of the Bulge* that he wanted to *'tidy up the battlefield'* before he would commit his reserve. That's all well and good if the enemy will let you. Undoubtedly Nagumo wanted to tidy things up too. However an enemy aircraft carrier was spotted! The situation was urgent! *How can one not imagine that a strike is, or at least might be, on the way?* Land-based bombers from Midway had already attacked. The enemy knew where they were! Nagumo decided to get his flight decks spick and span and only then launch a full attack. One half hour later, with gasoline and bombs all over the flight decks and hangers, a group of American dive-bombers appeared overhead.

> *The situation was a carrier pilot's dream. No anti-aircraft, all three carriers heading straight into the wind. Earl Gallaher's 500 pound bomb hit squarely on a plane starting its take-off. Immediately the whole pack of planes at the stern was in flames 50 feet high. My bombs*

landed exactly on the big red circle forward of the bridge. Seconds later the flames were 100 feet high. Ten minutes after the attack I saw a large explosion amidships on the Kaga. Rockets of flame, pieces of steel bolted upward to about three or four thousand feet high Lt. Norman "Dusty" Kleiss.

With the Japanese *combat air patrol* at sea level destroying the attack of *Enterprise Torpedo 6 squadron (60%* lost), *Hornet Torpedo 8 squadron* (100% lost) and *Yorktown Torpedo 3 squadron* (90% lost) the nimble *Zero* fighters that protected the Japanese carriers were out of position. The American dive-bombers had an unopposed attack. Incredibly, in what is the most foolishly arrogant act in the history of naval warfare, Japanese aircraft carriers were not camouflaged. Their flight decks were painted a lovely tan in perfect contrast to the wine dark sea. If that were not enough, and in case the Americans needed an even better target, each carrier's flight desk had a big fat orange meatball painted on top. American pilots have always been good, having invented the airplane. Within three minutes, fleet carriers *Akagi*, *Kaga*, and *Soryu* were hit, on fire and sinking. Only *Hiryu* was saved, being out of position. She got in a strike, which eventually sank *Yorktown*, but *Hiryu* didn't last long; sunk later in the day by an American strike. *Admiral Yamaguchi* calmly went down with *Hiryu*, contemplating the moon with *Tomeo Kaku*, the ship's captain. There is no rule of the sea that a captain must go down with his ship. That is the case only when there are still men or passengers aboard. The Admiral would have been a supreme successor to the incompetent and pathetic Nagumo; but he chose suicide.

The vulnerable aircraft carrier

Aircraft carriers today are just as much at risk as were Japan's carriers in 1942. They are quite possibly still as defenseless as they ever were against a determined enemy attack; especially in confined waters like the Sea of Japan and the Straits of Hormuz where the American navy, amazingly, likes to bandy them about. Small nations like Korea and Iran don't have the resources to build large fleets but they do have the wherewithal to launch *thousands of missiles and self-propelled mines* that either home in at 2,000 miles per hour, or rise up from below. Newly invented hypersonic missiles come in at *fifteen thousand miles per hour!* Any one of them can blow up a carrier whose electric counter-measures can be easily disabled. Yes, Koreans and Iranians know how to do that too. Take a look at your digital TV; it's probably made in Korea.

To be, or not to be: that is the question

With the loss of the four fleet carriers Yamamoto must have suddenly realized just how important they were. It is practically impossible in the age of steam to force a fleet action upon an enemy. Jutland happened because both fleets were at sea looking for trouble. With his carriers lost, Yamamoto might advance his battlewagons, but the Americans could simply avoid them. Yamamoto then felt there was no other recourse except withdrawal. However, the Aleutian force still had 80 aircraft available. In addition, *Zuikaku* and light carrier *Zuihō* were coming. Fuel was not a factor. Within a few days, the *IJN* could have concentrated four fresh carriers, and continued the operation. With Yorktown sunk and the torpedo air-wings of *Enterprise* and *Hornet* completely destroyed, victory was still at hand. Is prudence the better part of valor? Napoleon was often able to turn what seemed to be an irrepressible tide, as did Nelson. At this point it was still possible to press home the attack and wrest victory from defeat. But it would have called for a complete grasp of the new situation and a reordering of the commander's priorities. This was the one thing not immediately possible. Alas, like Hamlet contemplating poor *Yorick*, Yamamoto sadly retreated. In the end nobody in the Japanese chain of command was ever demoted or reprimanded for the debacle. Nagumo would remain in command until reassigned in November 1942. By then, 60% of the elite naval aviators that attacked Pearl Harbor were dead. What's even worse, Yamamoto allowed his rare and rigorously trained naval pilots to operate from land bases where they continued to get shot up and killed. The only thing he really cared about were the battleships that he didn't know how to use. Finally, there were three American prisoners taken in the battle. They were interrogated and then weighted down with jerry cans, thrown overboard and drowned.

THE TRANSFORMATION OF THE WEST INTO A PERMANENT WAR ECONOMY

The long goodbye

The American-Japanese naval war of 1941-1945 was the most vicious and savagely sustained naval and amphibious campaign in the whole history of the world. American college students, who seek *safe-spaces* because *words do hurt*, can't comprehend what 18-19 year old boys and girls experienced in that war just a few years ago. There was no mercy. There were very few prisoners taken. Those that were taken were often routinely mutilated and killed. There were mass-murders and mass-suicides of whole populations. Yamamoto didn't live to see the awful end. He was notoriously punctual and with the Japanese naval codes broken again, an American squadron of P-38s ambushed him on a flight into *Rabaul* in 1943. For the Americans, they went directly onto the offensive just two months after Midway. They drove inexorably ever westward towards the Japanese home islands. It took two more years before Yamamoto's grand fleet was destroyed in its entirety. How could it have been any other way? The Japanese built 17 aircraft carriers during the war but only one from the keel up. The rest were hybrids and conversions. The Americans built 142 carriers. They constructed over 800 destroyers and used 304 against Japan. Japan was able to build only 63. The USA built 34 million tons of merchant shipping to Japan's 4 million tons. Japan was simply overwhelmed. When the USA took the Mariana Islands in late 1944 their new heavy bomber, the B-29, was within range of Tokyo. The USA spent more money building the B-29 than they did on the Manhattan atomic bomb project. The pressurized and heavily armored bomber, the most advanced weapon system ever constructed, laid waste to Japanese cities with fire-bombs. You can still see this seared into the Japanese consciousness in their post-war films. Fire-breathing monsters like *Godzilla*, or gigantic winged creatures like *Rodan* and *Mothra*, all born from nuclear bomb tests, awakened Japanese memories of death from above. The fire-bombs were but a prelude to the atomic attacks in August 1945. But still, Japan wouldn't surrender. They had a few aces they might play, were it not too late.

Legends of war

Most people think the history of the war is settled today. It was *The Good War* fought by *A Band of Brothers,* and part of the larger *Greatest Generation.* The enemy's infamy contributes to the notion that the war was righteous. But why are so many documents still secret? Why are the records from Japanese germ warfare stations *Unit731* and *Unit100* still undisclosed? The medical doctors that worked there, by their savagery and callous indifference to human suffering, make Joseph Mengele look like Florence Nightingale. Why were these murderous thugs given immunity and promoted to important positions in the Japanese medical establishment? The legend has it that Japan surrendered not only because of the atomic fires over Hiroshima and Nagasaki but because the Soviets invaded Manchukuo three days after the first bomb fell. Why should Japan care so much about Manchukuo when Okinawa, one of the home islands, had already fallen? In truth Japan wanted to surrender after Okinawa fell but the Americans ignored them. Japan then saw they needed to fight it out. Why should they suddenly cave in when Manchukuo was simply attacked and not yet taken? Were *Unit731* and *Unit100*, both located in Manchukuo, far more important to the Japanese war effort than anyone now wishes to admit? What about the Japanese atomic bomb? The legend has it there was no such thing. That information, and there is plenty of it, is still denied, never discussed and denigrated as impossible stuff. The legends and myths surrounding the bomb are maintained because the atomic world order that emerged out of the most brutal and destructive war in all of human history is still central to the American way of life. That world order is dominated by their nuclear might. It was they who emerged from the war not only as victors but as the shining lights of morality, righteousness and wisdom. It was they, and only they, who had the scientific wherewithal and resources to build the bomb; and what better target than *Imperial Japan* whose ultimate aim was the complete eradication of 500 million Chinese? One might then very well understand why the US Navy destroyed five Japanese atomic fuel cyclotrons just after the surrender. They were used for uranium enrichment but tossed to the bottom of Tokyo Bay. They don't exist. They never existed. The standard history is that Japan's bomb never got beyond the theoretical laboratory phase. Japan's physicists were *'too primitive'* to produce a bomb, wrote the *New York Times* in 1979. Even so, as we now know, it's not that difficult to build a bomb. The only things needed are uranium, ordinary water, large centrifuges and the massive amounts of electricity needed to run them. Once the idea is imagined that uranium can explode (Leo Szilard, 1933, Otto Hahn, 1938) the actual physics part of it isn't that complicated. There are physical and mechanical engineering problems that need to be overcome; but like all endeavors, once the path is known, human ingenuity can attain the desired result.

Unterseeboot-234

On March 25th, 1945, the German boat *U-234* set course for Japan. The boat was a big transport submarine that had an interesting cargo and passengers. There was a disassembled Me-262 jet fighter aboard and an Hs-293 glide-bomb as well. On board too, was *1200 pounds of uranium oxide and 50 gold-lined cylinders filled with U-235 bomb-grade uranium and fuses for nuclear bomb detonation*. Luftwaffe officers were aboard as well as two Imperial Japanese Navy officers. Before the boat got to Japan, Germany capitulated. The Japanese officers committed *Hari-Kari* and the captain struck his flag to the American Navy. All the captured uranium was immediately sent to *Oak Ridge Tennessee* and used to arm the Hiroshima bomb. We are repeatedly told that neither the Japanese nor the Germans had any use for this sort of material. One of the legends presented in film is that *Kirk Douglas* and the *Heroes of Telemark* (1965) blew up the German heavy-water plant in Norway. That stopped the German atomic bomb project cold, no need for further discussion. This is a factual but inconsequential event. In truth, the Norwegian / German heavy-water program was a ruse. They had no intention to build the huge and terribly expensive nuclear reactor that needs heavy-water to produce plutonium for a bomb. Germany didn't need plutonium for a bomb. They had plenty of uranium; Japan less so: hence the voyage of *U-234*. The whole of atomic bomb building was theoretical at this time. No one knew for sure if any of it would actually work at all. The Americans, wealthy and safe from attack, built the reactor that needs heavy-water for plutonium and also the centrifuges for uranium enrichment. They built both types of bombs thinking that at least one of them might really work. The Germans and Japanese were interested in the easier to construct uranium-235 bomb and had no need for heavy-water and plutonium. The American plutonium bomb was tested in New Mexico in the famous *Trinity* experiment. It was dropped on Nagasaki. Their untested uranium bomb, quickly armed with uranium-235 and triggers from Germany, was used first and it destroyed Hiroshima. You can watch the dozens of documentaries about these events and none of them will ever explain or even mention that the bomb tested was not the one used first; that the Hiroshima bomb was experimental and different from the New Mexico Trinity bomb. Obviously there is something very wrong about this deception but nobody ever wants to talk about it.

In Xanadu did Kublai Khan A stately pleasure-dome decree

When we read Coleridge's poem it is easy to imagine the *Kublai Kahn* as some fat old boy surrounded by drug-fueled concubines. In reality, he was grandson of Genghis Kahn and was the Mongol Emperor of China by conquest. Wise beyond his years and buried in the unspoilt secret Kahn tomb deep in the Mongolian wilderness; he once set his gaze upon the fertile gardens of Japan. Two fleets were assembled in Korea and each was destroyed by the legendary *Kamikaze Divine Wind*, one in 1274, the other in 1281. Then and now, Korea is a natural invasion route into Japan; which is why the Americans won't get out of there. As a defensive measure Japan invaded (1905) and then annexed Korea in 1910. In 1923 a Japanese firm that produced nitrogen fertilizer and explosives (Japan Nitrogen Fertilizer Company: *Nitchitsu*) began construction of the largest military-industrial complex in the Japanese Empire. They chose the little Korean village of *Konan* (now *Hungnam*), because it had a good harbor. They used Korean slave labor for the construction of a huge hydro-electrical system fed by three rivers diverted from their natural course north to the *Yalu*. When the dams were completed, *Nitchitsu* produced and used 1/3 of all the electrical power in the entire Japanese Empire, akin to the Auschwitz complex that produced an energy output greater than Berlin. The plant also produced many of the same sorts of things the *I.G. Farben* plant at Auschwitz did: aviation fuel, oil and rubber, primarily from Korea's abundant anthracite coal deposits. But most of the electrical energy drove the huge centrifuges to produce weapons grade Uranium-235. *Konan*, present day *Hungnam*, is still a central location for North Korea's atomic and hydrogen bomb production.

Japan's atomic bomb

Yoshio Nishina, who worked with Niels Bohr in Denmark, was one of the Japanese physicists '*too primitive*' to have envisioned and built an atomic bomb. It was his small centrifuges that the US Navy jettisoned into Tokyo Bay. They were located in the *Riken Institute* in the Tokyo suburbs. The laboratory was run by the Japanese Army and when it was bombed in April 1945 the story goes that Japanese atomic bomb research ended there. But the main Japanese nuclear effort was in Korea and run by the Navy. The lack of cooperation between the Japanese Army and Navy was famous. For example, each had its own separate fleet of transports. When an army transport was half full, it sailed that way, even if navy supplies were on the same dock going to the same place. The atomic bomb project was administered the same way: separately and secretly. By August 1945 the Navy conducted their first successful test. Journalist David Snell, back in the day when newspapermen had some ethics, interviewed Japanese counter-intelligence officer *Captain Tsetusuo Wakabayashi* (pseudonym) who was an eyewitness. This was published in the *Atlanta Constitution* in 1946. Whether this story is true, is as maybe. But the Russian Army took Konan ten days after Japan's test. The Reds wanted the place so badly they couldn't wait for ordinary infantry to get there and took it with airborne paratroops. They disassembled the entire factory (as they knew very well how to do) and took everything back to Russia. They let the 700 workers go but kidnapped the scientists as booty. Those fellows were never seen nor heard from again. Four years later, the USSR *announced* that they exploded their first atomic bomb. This event was delayed until 1949 as they undoubtedly stockpiled weapons in the event that the planned American pre-emptive nuclear attack was actually carried out (*Operation Dropshot, Operation Bushwhacker,* for example).

Secrets

The Americans had their own reasons for keeping Japan's bomb undisclosed and so did the Japanese. After all, Japan didn't have a lot of moral high-ground to cling to in 1945. They killed 20 million people in China, most of them women and children, along with any and all military age men and boys they encountered who were specifically targeted for death. Not wanting to waste ammunition, Japanese officers ordered their men to use bayonets on the children. However, with the atomic attacks, Japan was suddenly a victim! *This was all too good to pass up.* So the germ warfare and atomic bomb projects were excluded from the Japanese memory stick. Japan is still occupied by the Americans. They threw a lot of money into the place. Interestingly, the nations that Japan invaded: China, North Korea and Vietnam became the new enemies and Japan an American ally. Unfortunately for Japan, they chose to invest in nuclear electrical power. One of their largest nuclear power plants recently melted down and Japan's water is already radioactive. There is no fix and it's never going to get better. Japan is now in clandestine negotiations with China to transport their entire population to the western Chinese wilderness. The Japanese home islands, including especially the big island of *Honshu*, will be uninhabitable within 50 years, if not sooner. It's difficult to imagine what the 100 million people on *Honshu* plan to do as the worst news is being kept from them by the government of Japan. Most people over 50 will probably choose to die there. Once China gets the possibly 50 million young to middle-aged Japanese that want to emigrate, there will undoubtedly be factions within China who will plan to enslave and kill them all. The Sicilians and Corsicans say: *Revenge is a dish best served cold.*

World War

Within a few days upon Japan's Pearl Harbor attack; Germany, Italy, Hungary, Romania and Bulgaria all declared war on the United States. The Americans greeted the German and Italian declarations with glee. They wanted to fight those people for a long time and now there was no need to engage in a propaganda push to convince ordinary Americans that Germans and Italians were vicious enemies and existential threats. It was the Hungarian, Romanian and Bulgarian declarations that caused real consternation in the American State Department. They wondered; why in the world do those people want to fight us? Through back-channels the Americans asked all three nations to please reconsider their declarations of war and rescind them. Hungary is Germany's oldest ally and when the eastern European borders were recently rearranged (1938-40), Hungary got a good piece of Czechoslovakia and later, the tasty and mouth-watering addition of northern Transylvania from Romania: lands Romania had taken from Hungary when she was on the winning side in 1918 and Hungary wasn't. In compensation, Romania got Bessarabia when Army Group South (which Romanian armies were a part of) overran the place in 1941 on their way to Odessa, Kiev and points east. Bulgaria wanted Macedonia from Greece and the erstwhile Serbia. So she supported Germany and they got what they wanted. But Bulgaria was wise enough never to declare war on the USSR. All three nations declared war on the USA because it was far away while Germany was close and had something to offer. The Americans waited until June 1942 to declare war on them and the declarations of war on Hungary, Romania and Bulgaria are the last time the USA has ever declared war on anybody. In the ensuing *Cold War*, Bulgaria would join Mongolia as the USSR's firmest ally and she still waits, like a forlorn bride at the altar, for the reluctant Macedonia to fall submissively into her lap.

Hitler's hubris

Germany had its reasons to declare war on the USA but it was a strategic mistake of the first order. It came from their *stab in the back* legend. The Germans didn't recognize the tremendous military achievement it was, both naval and logistical, for the Americans to send a million-man army across a submarine infested ocean without losing a man. They then entered the field and beat the German Army. But the German Army came to blame all this on Jews and communists who were for them interchangeable enemies. Neither the Germans, nor any of the Axis fascist powers, were able recognize the American ability to very rapidly project force across vast distances. They are still the best at this and it represents the *American Way of War*. Germany declared war on America because it was impossible for them to grasp that in less than a year, an American army would be in North Africa and defeat Rommel's *Afrika Korps*. American bombers would be in action against them in less time than that. But Hitler heard few dissenting voices when, as head of state, he embarked upon war with America. He was told about Pearl Harbor two days after the Red Army counter-attacked in front of Moscow. He was way out east in *Rostov* where *Army Group South* had advanced an amazing 1000 miles into Russia but had stalled. Had Halder and Paulus listened to him and committed the bulk of German forces to the south and captured the oil fields there the war might be already won. But they didn't. Now, after foolishly sacking *Army Group South* commander *Gerd von Rundstedt* who hadn't achieved the impossible with limited force, Hitler rushed back to Berlin to present his declaration of war to the Reichstag. They would rubber stamp it and cheer *Sieg Heil* because, like the Americans in Iraq and Afghanistan, they couldn't correctly imagine the consequences.

Where is Pearl Harbor?

Distant at first, Hitler didn't rightly know where Pearl Harbor was. For the past year he had been pressured by *Kriegsmarine* Admiral Raeder and submarine commander Karl Donitz to declare war on the Americans. After all, they were engaged with them in an undeclared naval war. Ships were lost, submarines sunk. They wanted to take the gloves off. The Americans had already declared war on them by giving the Royal Navy 50 vintage destroyers. This was a *de facto* act of war. It was Roosevelt and his party that wanted war and up until Pearl Harbor, the Germans had resisted. The day after, Hitler immediately gave his navy permission to start shooting. His reasoning was: now that America was engaged with Japan, the *Imperial Japanese Navy* would, *in effect*, immediately become the fleet the Germans needed to wage war against England: for indeed Singapore and Hong Kong were prime Japanese targets. Japan's war thus became an *indirect way* to defeat England. Who knew; India might fall next and soon. With Singapore, Burma and India in Japanese hands, Hitler's peace offer might seem very sweet. The *IJN* was now the surface navy Germany needed to fight a *global war against the British Empire*, an enemy that remained stubbornly undefeated and thus the *strategic reason* for Germany's declaration of war on the United States. It's amazing that an army of professional historians and pundits can't figure this out. That's because Hitler must remain an object of scorn. As an irrational genocidal maniac, deeply thought out strategic decisions cannot and must never be attributed to him.

Let's try submarine warfare (again)

Unrestricted submarine warfare had almost strangled England in 1917 and it seemed like Germany's perfected boats and improved tactics might do the trick this time around. The German Navy never did get a fleet capable of combat versus the Royal Navy. Raeder's navy got funded for some large super-battleships like *Bismarck* and *Tirpitz*, and that gave a lot of construction work to the north of Germany; which is why Hitler was in accord. But those battleships were for the most part useless. *Bismarck*, for wont of anything better to do, was sent on a fool's mission commerce raiding in the North Atlantic. Unescorted, she was tracked down, damaged by naval air and sunk by naval gunnery. This was an enormous waste of German resources. Instead of *Bismarck*, they could have built *thirty thousand 88mm flak guns* that were effective against both tanks and aircraft. By this time, after the loss of fast battleship *Graf Spee* in similar circumstances, Hitler had it figured out. No more resources would be wasted on surface ships. But Germany still had a navy of submarines that Raeder and Karl Donitz were both keen to let loose on the undefended American east coast. Hitler gave them the get go as soon as he could, as his mind was made up for war. The Army, preoccupied with Russia, went along with it because Prussian leadership did not and could not imagine the consequences of a *World War* against the United States. The American Army in 1918 was a headache to be sure. But their advance was only one sector in a German general retreat. Their own excuse, held dear by their former commanders, was that Jews and commies actually beat them. Now they were embarked upon a war of annihilation against Russia as a part of a massive German colonial project. They lacked the imagination and foresight to see that such a war could be directed back at them by an American enemy they could not effectively counter-attack. Indeed the Japanese faced a similar quandary. Even if they won a *decisive naval battle* against them, and then ravaged the entire American west coast, they would still be 3,000 miles away from Washington. Most of America's shipbuilding facilities were on the east coast. What would prevent the Americans from building a new navy? They Japanese had no answers to these questions and nor did the Germans. Both of them now faced foes arrayed against them that became a coalition of mighty world powers. Their enemies had practically unlimited resources in manpower, scientific expertise, construction, and manufacturing. They also owned 90% of the world's motor lubricants. But somebody, somewhere, should have asked Hitler, Keitel, von Ribbentrop, Halder and all the rest of them, how they planned to wage war against an American nation that they couldn't attack? All they had were a dozen U-boats operational in the North Atlantic Ocean. Only later on, when all seemed lost, would there be the frantic rush to build the *Amerika Bomber*; the one that could carry a heavy nuclear weapon across the ocean to vaporize New York's financial center and Washington's governmental conglomerate. They almost pulled it off.

Don't miss the bus

There were more reasons why Hitler, as head-of-state, felt drawn into a war against the United States. When peace-loving American President Roosevelt had his army, navy and air forces occupy Iceland in June 1941, it was clear that the Americans were ready to keep the commercial life-line to England open with war. Iceland is still occupied and is an American protectorate as is Greenland. Truman tried to buy Greenland and so did Trump in 2019. The Americans just might take it from Denmark the nominal owners. Germany too wanted to expand in the Atlantic and was in negotiations with Spain for bases in the Canary Islands from whence Columbus set forth in 1492. Spain was warned off an alliance when Admiral *Wilhelm Canaris*, chief of German military intelligence (*der Abwehr*), warned Franco that Germany would soon lose the war. Canaris was a German traitor working for the bourgeois west as were many other officers like Halder and Gehlen. Franco disregarded Canaris because the very rich *French Morocco* was there for the taking. With France relatively powerless, Spain only needed permission from Germany.

But Germany wanted sovereignty over any Canary Island bases and Franco was unwilling because his position was as precarious as Hitler's. Even more enticing for Spain was the very real possibility of regaining Gibraltar, ceded to England in the *War of the Spanish Succession* (1713). Spain still wants it, but in 1940 Germany was leery about having another porous ally like Italy. Spain wanted an alliance with Germany for the same reason many others did: it looked like the *Axis Powers*, primarily Germany and Japan, were going to win the war. Japan had an expression for this mood: *Don't miss the bus* they said. That's the reason why so many authoritarian military dictatorships all chose war with the United States within a few days of each other. They felt the tide of history was with them; that the western liberal democracies were not only corrupt but its people weak and soft from unbridled consumerism. They should see us now.

America enters the fray

In 1940 America was quite different than it is today. Back then, *Greco-Roman* and *Judeo-Christian* values held the USA and Great Britain together in an iron grip of public morality and virtue. Americans and Britons were law-abiding. Roman values of hard work and personal integrity were paramount in the lives of ordinary people. They were ready to sacrifice their lives fighting an enemy that was presented as evidently evil. The Japanese may now deny it ever happened but the *Rape of Nanking* left an indelible stain on the American consciousness, as did the destruction of Rotterdam and Warsaw by fire. Sure the films that promoted these events were produced by internationalist factions that wanted war. But these, and many other acts of *total war* designed to eradicate whole nations, were made even more unpalatable by the fact that the perpetrators went and declared war on the United States by sneak attack. *You wanna' fight, let's fight* was the prevailing national mood. Churchill came over, addressed the US Congress and asked: *What kind of people do they think we are?* It was a good question presented to very friendly yet warlike peoples with a common language and heritage. Thus, in a stroke of political and public relations wizardry, Churchill turned England's war into America's war. What's more he made America's oldest enemy into its closest ally. It was a war the

American people didn't want. Until Pearl harbor eighty percent were against it. They had no clue that Roosevelt had been provoking German and Japan with acts of war for the past two years. Now Roosevelt told them that that December 7th was a date that would live in infamy. Perhaps, but he lied when he said Japan's attack was *unprovoked*. Since most Americans are usually asleep when it comes to international affairs, they believed him. Now in 1941, and unlike in 1917, the American people didn't bat an eye when their President asked for total war. They only wanted to know: *Where do I sign up?*

Terror bombing

Are a factory worker's family legitimate military targets? Is it acceptable military policy to kill his wife and children and burn down his home? According to aviation theorist *Giulio Douhet* in *The Command of the Air* (1921, 1927) it is not only acceptable, but those *innocent people* should be, and must be, *primary targets* if the war is to be efficiently won. There was a great debate about this. Unfortunately, this is what the war degenerated into. Of the approximately 75 million people murdered in this war, 75% of them never had a gun in their hands. Sir Arthur "Bomber" Harris, 1st Baronet:

> *The Nazis entered this war under the rather childish delusion that they were going to bomb everyone else, and nobody was going to bomb them. At Rotterdam, London, Warsaw and half a hundred other places, they put their rather naive theory into operation. They sowed the wind, and now they are going to reap the whirlwind.*

Harris could have said that about the Japanese and Italians as well. They were all eager and ready to ladle it out but remarkably unprepared to take it. They all knew very well that the Americans and British had big, 4-engined, long-range heavy bombers. Did they think the enemy wouldn't use them? It's not a difficult process to figure out. The only thing holding anyone back in Europe was Christian morality. Certainly the Germans didn't give that too much consideration in Spain, nor in Poland. Masters of improvisation, they tossed incendiaries out by hand from Ju-52 transport planes down on an undefended Warsaw. Did they never consider that they might not always be in command of every situation? Apparently not and they weren't prepared for the first Allied terror bombings that took place in July 1943. The aptly named *Operation Gomorrah* targeted Hamburg. The Americans did some daylight damage. The British then used incendiaries from their heavy bombers at night and the fire-storm killed 42,000 people. Incredibly, this was not what the *United States Army Air Force (USAAF)* had in mind when they entered the war. In fact, their plan was to avoid civilian casualties.

High altitude precision bombing

In a practice run somewhere back in Texas during the inter-war period, an American bomber managed, presumably on a windless day with unlimited visibility, to drop a stick of bombs directly onto a target from 20,000 feet. The legend grew that with the *Norden bombsight*, a B-17 could drop a bomb into a pickle barrel from high altitude. The bombsight was a complicated computer that allowed a bombardier to pilot the plane over the target and calculate wind, altitude and speed all at once. The inventor, Carl Norden, was a devout Christian who wanted to shorten wars. He knew about Douhet's theories and felt that precision bombing would eliminate, or at least reduce, civilian casualties. We still hear about *smart-bombs*, and selective targeting, but the bombs are just as dumb now as they ever were. That's because in the end, humans still have to guide them. However, in 1941 nobody had anything figured out at all. The Americans spent 1/3 of the money they would invest in the atomic bomb, *one billion US 1940 dollars*, on the Norden bombsight. They felt they could win the war with it. The *USAAF* adopted the notion of *pin-point precision bombing* as their primary mission. This was typically American as they felt British methods to be cowardly. Americans aviators wanted real military missions; ones with meticulous planning and exact execution. Bombing women and children at night wasn't it. Of course the *Royal Air Force* had tried daylight bombing and got badly shot up. They <u>resorted </u>to night missions, as did the Luftwaffe over England. The Americans were going to do it their own way; deep daylight penetration into enemy airspace without escorts. The *8th Air Force* went and assembled their machines in England on 130 airfields in East Anglia. They began by bombing German military targets in France, short-hop stuff, in the spring of 1942. Before that even started, USAAF training casualties and losses, way back in Texas and California, were as follows: *14,903 men killed, 14,873 aircraft lost in 52,651 accidents.* The United States invested 25% of its military budget into aviation and it was one of the single most dangerous jobs in the history of warfare, with the possible exception of *Kamikaze* suicide pilots over Okinawa; and they lost far fewer men. *In addition to the astonishing preparation losses*; the *Luftwaffe* and enemy *flak* shot down *a further* 18,418 planes with over 40,000 men killed, 12,000 men missing (presumed dead) and another 1000 aircraft that just disappeared without a trace. Typical missions lost, on average, 10% of their strength on every operation. The men were told that after 25 missions they could go home. These fellows were mostly young guys (as were their Luftwaffe counterparts), aged 17-25 years, and simple math told even the most uneducated Oklahoma farm-boy that not only wasn't he going to make 25 missions, but that it wasn't even going to be close.

Don't sit under the apple tree with anyone else but me

Post war films like *12 O'Clock High* covered up the severity of losses. *Gregory Peck* as the dynamic General Savage did restore morale to his demoralized bomb-group. In a feel good attempt to promote popcorn sales, his revamped missions were often successfully completed with zero casualties and maybe a crash landing where everybody walked out remarkably unharmed, no problem. In reality, the farther the assignments penetrated into Germany the greater the losses. On missions deep into Germany in 1943, American fighters didn't have the operational range to fly escort. The Germans had the world's best radar and knew by which direction the bombers would come. Luftwaffe fighters would intercept the moment the escorts peeled off and keep attacking until the enemy bombers entered the *flak box* where *88mm flak guns* would shoot them up all the way into the target, and then again on their way back out (*flak*: a German acronym for *Fliegerabwehrkanone* or air-defense-cannons). During this time the fighters would land, refuel and attack again as soon as the enemy bombers left the *flak box* on their way home. Luftwaffe fighters, usually the Me-109 and Fw-190, would attack the bombers head-on as they determined the Plexiglas nose to be the enemy's weakest point; hence the term *12 o'clock high* as a directional indicator: the fighters would come in out of the sun from straight ahead. The B-17 was heavily armored and amazingly offered protection against 20mm cannon shots. It could deflect machine gun bullets and stray *flak* as well. But the weak point was the Plexiglas nose that allowed the crew to see. It was indispensible and couldn't stop anything.

American Air Power

Every event in this war is forever understood from 1945 looking backwards, the pundits always supreme in the wisdom of hindsight. Thus all events are easily predictable. The 8th Air Force, and by implication the newly minted *United States Air Force* (the *USAF* founded 1947), was a big winner. Postwar television programming, with weekly shows like *Air Power*, hosted by Walter Cronkite (the most trusted man in America), only confirmed this basic fact: the *American Air Force* certainly deserved not only far-reaching accolades for its big win, but also stupendous funding from America's now massive military budget. Therefore, the Luftwaffe never stood a chance and nor would those goddamn *Russkies* either. It was evident: the Luftwaffe was beaten by American technical knowhow and strategic genius. The B-17 was an engineering marvel and its ten 50 caliber heavy machine guns would, with dozens of bombers flying in close support of one another, put out massive defensive firepower. In the end they and their escorts (almost entirely), would destroy 15,000 German fighters in the air and another 18,000 on the ground. This air campaign, the only one like it in the history of the world, was named *The Defense of the Reich* and in the end it demolished the Luftwaffe. Nevertheless, the truth is that by the end of 1943, the Luftwaffe had won the air war over Germany and the 8th Air Force driven from the sky.

A slower heavily armed plane, able to clear its way with its own armament, can always get the best of a faster pursuit plane   Douhet

The Germans tried to get around the problems posed by enemy interceptors with *Schnellbombers* that were faster than enemy pursuit. As their unexpectedly massive losses in France and England attest to, it didn't work. Additionally, their bombers weren't armored and nor did they have much in the way of defensive armament. The B-17 had it all and the USAAF theoreticians thought the bombers could take care of themselves. Hence they didn't build *air superiority fighters*. It was after all, the <u>United States</u> <u>Army</u> <u>Air Force</u>. The fighters they did make were ground attack aircraft like the P-47 and P-38 that would support American troop movements; and they were good at it. But they weren't suited to fly escort. The fellows in charge of strategic bombing didn't care. They felt they didn't need escorts and the light losses they incurred on short missions into France confirmed this. All this would change when they began bombing Germany.

Good luck, good hunting, and good bye

As the bombers approached, the Luftwaffe fighters would gather above them like wolves stalking a herd of moose in the wilderness. The bomber squadrons would try to keep a tight formation in what they called a *combat box* to maximize defensive firepower. The squadron commander would be constantly radioing wayward pilots to tighten formation. These were young fellows who were very athletic with keen eyesight; but maneuvering 30 tons of metal at 20,000 feet isn't easy and mid-air collisions were common. Your car weighs about a ton and is on *terra firma*. Imagine moving a thirty-ton bomber around at 300 miles per hour, in a non-pressurized cockpit, in a -20° F temperature environment, 2,500 feet higher than *Mt. Everest* base camp. All this with lots of people determined to kill you. The Luftwaffe pilots hid in the sun and would pick out the squadron with the loosest formation. Then they would dive in at 450 miles per hour, close to what a jet can do in level flight. At first, in the early missions, they would attack from behind but, heavily armored, the B-17 was so well constructed it could fly on one engine! But a few crash landed and Luftwaffe tactical experts determined that the best way to attack was head-on. This murderous fire would kill the pilots and wreak the B-17s instrumentation. Losses began to mount. After *Blitz Week*, a series of raids on northern Germany that lost 88 bombers with just as many heavily damaged, the USAAF decided to go after Luftwaffe production. The attack on

Regensburg was personally led by commanding *General Curtis LeMay* who often volunteered to lead the most dangerous missions and this was one. The resultant raids on Regensburg and Schweinfurt in August 1943 were catastrophic. Hundred of bombers were shot down and damaged beyond repair. Thousands were dead and wounded. Like German *Stukas* over England, the *8th Air Force* was withdrawn from battle. Unescorted high altitude precision bombing against resolute opposition was proven impossible. That is when the P-51 appeared and allowed the Americans to continue bombing in 1944. But the Luftwaffe fellows weren't fools either; they moved their production facilities underground.

Alliances in name only

The Axis powers, primarily Germany, Italy and Japan were never able to collaborate in any meaningful way. Often they were at odds with one another. In 1936 Japan and Germany (later joined by Italy and many other minor fascist powers)) signed the *Anti-Comintern Pact* in an alliance against the *communist international movement*. Russia had few allies. The *Mongolian People's Republic* was the Soviet Union's oldest one. Mongolia, with no natural defenses against Japan and China, sought refuge with the Russian bear because they were the only nation that had no territorial ambitions in Mongolia. In 1931 Manchuria was reestablished as a *Manchu* empire and renamed *Manchukuo* with the last Chinese Emperor *Puyi* as its nominal ruler. It was however a phantasm. Manchukuo was a Japanese possession ruled not actually by Japan, but by the *Kwantung Army* that governed the place according to its own dictates. Staffed and manned by the best divisions in the *Imperial Japanese Army* (IJA) it was them that conquered Manchuria completely on their own. It was this army that began the war with China too, again of their own volition. In 1939 the very same *Kwantung Army* wanted to expand westward into Mongolia and northward into Siberia. They were defeated by the *Soviet Red Army* and Mongolian cavalry in a series of battles. Right at this time, von Ribbentrop signed, sealed and delivered his peace pact with Soviet Russia; thus stabbing the erstwhile Japanese *anticomintern* ally in the back. Two years later, with *Army Group Center* in its near-death experience before Moscow, Japan would begin to execute its own attack upon the USA thus freeing up five Red Army Siberian divisions to counter-attack their supposed German ally. Italy would often do its own thing to the consternation of Germany and in 1939 Hitler sat in bemused indifference as Hungary attacked Slovakia for a succulent slice of Ruthenia. It was every man for hisself. The Axis powers were also unable to cooperate industrially. Mussolini, a socialist, governed Italy in support of Italian workers. It was their jobs and work that manned the Italian armaments industry. If Italian planes, tanks and guns weren't as good as the German ones, so be it. Plus, Germany didn't have the resources to assist Italy in armaments production either; they had enough problems on their own. Japan was too far away to materially support anybody. Romanian, Bulgarian and Hungarian pilots flew German warplanes and did a good job defending Romanian oil production at *Ploesti*. The American 15th Air Force (re-organized from the 12th and 9th Air Forces), based in North Africa and later Italy, lost 5,000 bombers over there. They hindered Romanian oil production but didn't stop it, and wouldn't, until the Red Army overran the place in September 1944. By this time the German Wehrmacht was running on synthetics. Fuel supply was a problem that never went away for Italy either.

Veni, vidi, vici

Italy was always out-manned and out-gunned. No one there understood that the conflict they eagerly entered wasn't an ordinary boundary war that would end with the exchange of a few provinces. The list of fools included especially Mussolini. What he got Italy into was a battle of nations that would result in whole empires vanquished, just like in the *1st War-phase*. When Italy declared war on France and England in June 1940, the King and his ministers were all for it. *Malta, Nice*, and even the grand prizes of *Egypt* and *Gibraltar* all seemed like they might be easy pickings. They weren't and after Italy was driven out of Libya, they needed German help. Rommel then came, saw and conquered. This was the one area in the world where the Axis Powers could and did successfully cooperate. When General, and later Field Marshall Rommel landed with two mechanized divisions he immediately went on the offensive with the Italian Army. Despite being held back by *OKW* they drove the British out of Libya and all the way back into Egypt. Like before at the Kremlin, legend says a German recon battalion got within sight of the Suez Canal. But the Axis armies were undermanned, under supplied and driven off. Aside from fuel, water was a problem as well. The Germans didn't need much water as their rations were canned. The Italians needed more. They ate pasta which is easy to pack, store and transport because it is very lightweight. It is also very nutritious and fulfilling. Unfortunately, pasta needs water to cook, and in a delicate environment this was a problem when feeding half a million men. If Italian industry had managed to produce a few thousand more tanks and trucks, Suez might have been theirs. But they lost 10,000 trucks in Spain, and instead it was they and the Germans driven back to Tunisia. There they were all surrounded and captured by the British driving west from Egypt and the newly landed Americans in French North Africa. For the Italian prisoners it was great, as their war was over. They were all shipped to California to work on avocado farms in the nicest climate in the whole world. The Germans were sent to bust rocks in west Texas hell-holes. Hitler, now commander in chief, made the mistake of reinforcing Rommel when it was too late; thus throwing away an additional 300,000 men that didn't need to be lost, as well as hundreds of Ju-52 transports (and their irreplaceable very skilled pilots) that were better used in Russia. Soon afterwards Mussolini was deposed.

Impero Italiano

By July 1943 the war had become a catastrophe for Italy. The empire that Mussolini and King Victor Emmanuel declared only seven years before was gone with the wind. The British and American armies invaded Sicily on July 9th and the Italian Army quickly disintegrated. On July 19th five hundred American bombers dropped 1000 tons of explosive on Rome. Of course they bombed the working class sectors of the city that were Mussolini's base of support. The Italian 8th Army in Russia (*Armata Italiana in Russia*) of 235,000 men was already destroyed at Stalingrad in 1942. Only ten thousand of those fellows ever got home alive. Italian women would march alone through city streets with a picture of their boy that asked: *Where is my son?* Even in the Italian fascist police state, no one would dare arrest them. *Il Duce* had become eminently unpopular.

Gran Consiglio del Fascismo

Mussolini was much more a dictator than was Hitler who had to deal with old and well established institutions. Prussia was a great power since the time of the *Teutonic Order* back in the 16th century. Hitler made decisions that were in accord with the wishes of Prussian organizations like academia, church, police, judiciary and the Prussian Army. Elements within all those parties, for example, wanted the Jews out of Germany. It was Luther who told them it was not only permissible to burn down Jewish synagogues, schools and villages with them inside, but that it was a good thing. Like Prussia's conquest of Germany in 1870, the *Kingdom of Sardinia* conquered Italy at the same time. But Sardinia was not a great power and when its army conquered the rest of Italy and Rome, the opposition was armed mostly with crucifixes. The hypocrisy of *the Great War* and Italy's role in it further weakened whatever power remained in the hands of the monarchy. When the *Black Shirt* march on Rome met little resistance, Mussolini was wise enough to keep the king as a figurehead. Mussolini's organization was centered upon the *Fascist Grand Council* that ruled by decree. Now it was all falling apart and on July 24th 1943 the *Grand Council*, by a vote of 19-8, gave Mussolini a vote of no-confidence. Count Ciano voted affirmative. This all took Mussolini by surprise and it shouldn't have.

Beware the Ides of March

When *Calpurnia* awoke on the morning of March 15th, 44 BC she had a dream, or vision, of her husband, Julius Caesar, profusely wounded and bleeding to death. She begged him not to attend the Roman Senate that day. At first he decided to stay home but was convinced by a conspirator to go. On his way there, someone approached Caesar and handed him a letter. He didn't read it and nobody knows what it said. Perhaps Shakespeare's soothsayer gave him a vague warning. The Forum was crowded like always with jugglers looking for handouts and women of all ages shopping. Plenty of people knew about the plot, and they had to, because 27 senators all stuck a knife in him. There were rumors that Caesar was to name himself king and that made a lot of them spitting angry. He was acting like one and after all, it must be true or why else would he be in consort with that Egyptian slut Cleopatra? She would eventually be murdered by *Gaius Octavius* who was the last person to see her alive. He would also kill her son by Caesar and would then be proclaimed Emperor Augustus Caesar to Rome's eternal sorrow.

25 Luglio

On the 25th of July, 1943 Mussolini got up to go the work like he normally did. In a scene eerily reminiscent of the *Ides of March*, his wife *Donna Rachele* begged him not to go. *You won't come back*, she cried, again and again; *you won't come back!* He ignored her and she never saw him again. When he arrived, the King advised *Il Duce* that he was no longer Prime Minister and had him arrested and imprisoned. He was replaced by the loathsome Pietro Badoglio who had to somehow get Italy out of its alliance with Germany without surrendering sovereignty to them. He couldn't do it. There were already German troops in Italy and when Mussolini was toppled they invaded from bordering Austria and took over. While they were at it, Germany also administered and, *de facto* if not *de jure*, annexed the wondrous and mostly German speaking (still is) province of *Südtirol* (*Trentino-Alto Adige*). That was how they did things. But Hitler held back on annexation because of the real affection and admiration he had for Mussolini. He was after all a fluent German speaker and Hitler's erstwhile political idol. But *Südtirol* was the province that Italy fought for in 1915-18 and its loss deeply disturbed all Italian patriots. Italy soon switched sides. Like a cat falling out of a tree they landed on their feet and got the place back when it was all over. But with Südtirol theirs (albeit temporarily), Germany again increased the size and wealth of *the Reich* even though the war wasn't going very well anymore. It hadn't since the calamity at Stalingrad.

Fremde Heere Ost

By the time *Operation Barbarossa* and the subsequent *Red Army* counter-attack petered out in the winter of 1942, the German Army that had conquered Poland and France didn't exist anymore. More than one million men were dead or missing. They were able to make good the losses by drafting younger boys, now 17 years old. If you want to envision what the German Army in 1942 looked like, take a peek at your local high school and junior college football teams. *The Red Army* that tried to destroy *Army Group Center* by encirclement in the *Battle of Moscow* 1941-42 also suffered debilitating losses. They allowed the German Army to set up defensive positions that they assaulted frontally. It didn't work and never does. This allowed the Germans to stabilize the military position in the center and plan their next move. Hitler was commander in chief for the first time and he gave the orders now. They would move south and capture not only the Ukraine and all its riches, but the oil fields of the Caucasus regions far to the southeast on the way to the Caspian Sea. That's a long, long way from Berlin. Alexander tried a maneuver of that scope and it didn't turn out very well. The Americans would later airlift *National Guard* troops from Vermont and Wyoming and other states out that way too. That didn't work for them either. But the German Army almost pulled it off. They probably would have, had they not been rife with traitors at the highest levels. Halder was still *Chief of Staff* and he appointed another charlatan, *Reinhard Gehlen*, to command *Foreign Armies East* that was the German Army's intelligence branch for the eastern front. Like his mentor, Gehlen would sell out to the Americans. In the meantime they both fed Adolf Hitler completely false information about the strength and composition of the Red Army.

Fall Blau

Operation Blue was the code name for the German 1942 summer offensive that would get them to the *Volga River* and the oil region of *Maikop*. This was as far as they would ever get. Gehlen's *Fremde Heere Ost* estimated Red Army tank strength at 6,000. In reality they had 24,000 tanks: all those factories that had been relocated to the Ural Mountains were now on line. Gehlen informed Hitler that the Reds had only 6,000 military aircraft. They actually had 21,000. Gehlen and Halder both estimated the Red Army to be at the breaking point. They weren't. But on the basis of the information they provided, Hitler set the wheels in motion because Germany desperately needed oil. Synthetic production was only beginning and Romania could only supply

Germany with 5 million tons of oil annually. They needed twice that amount. An ominous moment came in early 1942 when German motorcycle recon battalions were re-equipped with bicycles. That should have scared everybody but there was no turning back. The Germans needed oil and there was only one place to get it. Had the true strength of the Red Army been known, the offensive would have been strengthened if not cancelled. The useless continual siege of Leningrad that killed mostly women and children could have been lifted to shorten the lines. The center could not be weakened as the 15 month *Battle of Rzhev* ground on at the cost of two million, three hundred thousand Soviet casualties. But it didn't need to be constantly strengthened either. Instead, obsessed with capital cities, Halder and the General Staff continuously reinforced it. Paulus was given command of 6th *Army* that was to spearhead the operation. Finally promoted to his level of incompetence, he couldn't handle it. The Reds retreated out of the Ukraine, trading space for time. This was costly as Soviet grain production was reduced from 96 million tons in 1940 to 30 million tons in 1942. Meat production fell from 5 million tons to 2 million tons. Milk production was halved. With the people starved, the Red Army had to stand and fight. *Stalingrad*, now *Volgograd*, and formerly *Tsaritsyn*, was as good a place as any.

The worst policy of all is to besiege walled cities: Sun Tzu

Stalingrad was never an objective of the 1942 summer campaign. Even before the drive towards the Volga began, the German Army did some *mopping up* in the rear. In North Africa, Rommel captured *Tobruk* and with it, 38,000 British troops and thousands of trucks. In the Crimea, von Manstein destroyed three Soviet armies and took 175,000 prisoners with another 240,000 captured at Kharkov. The Red Army shrugged it off and continued to fall back upon the Volga and the oil fields. When German 6th Army approached Stalingrad they looked down from the hills above the city and saw the gleaming Volga; the longest river in Europe and the route the Vikings took when they sailed into the Caspian Sea for trade. Below them too was the erstwhile city of *Tsaritsyn* once named after the *Tsardom of Muscovy*, now named after Stalin who defended it in the *Revolution*. Its shining white architecture glowed in the summer sun and it was one of the world's most modern and beautiful metropolises. Naturally 6th Army called upon the Luftwaffe to bomb it into rubble. They did and 75,000 inhabitants were killed. This was how the German Army did things. It always worked in the past: bomb them and they give up. Now though, 200,000 civilians didn't flee the explosives. They would not leave their homes and their city to the invaders. They dug in. Eventually they would be joined more than two million Red Army troops of whom one million would die there. But they would drive the enemy away and protect the city, the Volga River transport and the Caucasus oil. The German Army would lose a like amount and never recover.

Romania fattens up again

Romania was one of the big winners in the *1st War-phase*. Queen Marie counted on England winning the last battle and they did. Romania was rewarded with three very sweet and succulent provinces that engorged her: Northern Transylvania from defeated Hungary as well as Northern Bukovina and Bessarabia from the prostrate Russia. Romania had achieved all her territorial ambitions and when Queen Marie died in 1938 she didn't live to see it fall apart. There were some new kids on the block now, thugs dressed in black with swastika armbands who wanted to rectify all the results of Versailles. Hungary, always close to Germany, got back Transylvania. When von Ribbentrop signed his infamous agreement with the USSR in 1939, Romania was stripped of Bukovina (returned to Russia) and Bessarabia, (now the present day *Republic of Moldavia*) was also returned to Russia. Out in the cold when Germany invaded Russia, Romania leapt at the chance to regain the lands she lost to the USSR. The Germans then gave Romania more conquered lands from the USSR and created the *Transnistria Governorate* that included territory east of the Dnieper River. Presently there is a breakaway province from *Moldavia* called *Transnistria* or the *Pridnestrovian Moldavian Republic*. It is the last country on earth that still sports the hammer & sickle on its flag and national shield. In 1941 it was all given to Romania as well as the Russian port city of Odessa on the Black Sea. The *4th Romanian Army* took the place after a two month siege that cost them 86,000 killed and wounded. These are really big losses for a small nation, or any nation. The Red Army finally withdrew from Odessa in October 1941 and on the way out booby-trapped their massive and luxurious HQ. There were some nasty explosions. Naturally the Romanians blamed the Jews for everything. Jews were all communists anyway so might as well kill them all, even that old grandma over there with her children. They killed 30,000 Jews in retaliation and the Germans stood around and watched them do it. The fellows who had cameras took pictures. That was how things went out there.

The manpower shortage

When 1942 rolled around, the Germans needed the Romanians more than ever because they were now short of everything. The losses in *Operation Barbarossa* couldn't be made up. This was the biggest problem for the German Army in 1942 aside from oil. The year before, with their army at full strength, they didn't really need the Romanians. Now they did. They wanted some help from the Hungarians too and got it because Germany had been good to them. The Italians sent an army because Mussolini had gotten really dim-witted. On top of the world in early 1942 the *Duce* couldn't imagine that the magnificent army he sent into Russia would be annihilated. All three nations became an integral part of the offensive to take the Caucasus oil. By their own assessment the German predicament was: they were short 740,000 men, 36,000 trucks, 44,000 motorcycles (that they didn't have gas for anyway) and 2,100 tanks. The only way they could make up this deficiency was with the use of auxiliary allied troops. This doesn't mean the Hungarians, Romanians and Italians were slovenly cowards as so often portrayed. They weren't at all. But they did lack heavy tanks, effective anti-tank weaponry and heavy guns. It was this deficiency in heavy weapons that made them 2nd line military organizations. The Duke of Wellington once famously appraised the 2nd rate troops under his command: *They need to be positioned in places where the enemy is unlikely to attack.* The Germans did that. Hence, they placed the allied armies on their flanks because it was unimaginable that the Red Army had the strength and wherewithal to counter-attack. Gehlen told them so.

Babi Yar

The distance between Berlin and Stalingrad is about 1,500 miles. Some of the men who got all the way out there walked it. The 6th Army, assigned to *Army Group South*, was involved in the encirclement battles around Kiev in the first summer of the war. As always seems to be the case, they over-reacted to minor skirmishes in the rear, most of which almost always turn out to be *friendly fire* incidents. The famous American football player, Pat Tillman, was done in by *friendly fire* in Afghanistan. It comes about when units in the same army fire upon one another in the heat and confusion of battle. The Germans always like to blame others for their own misdeeds and errors. After Kiev was taken in September 1941, 6th Army wanted to *mop up*. There were a few friendly fire incidents and in retaliation, they rounded up every Jew they could find. After all, it was well known that while not every communist was a Jew; every Jew was a communist; including all women and children no matter what the age. They were collected with the help of Ukrainian militia and murdered in a small ravine outside the city called *Babi Yar*. What was particularly awful was that the 6th Army soldiers made the women disrobe. It wasn't enough to just kill these poor ladies. They wouldn't allow these women, huddled in fear, to be murdered with even the slightest modicum of decency: they needed them to be mortified first in disgrace and shame. Nowadays Jewish historians blame this massacre on German auxiliary police; the infamous *Einsatzgruppen* who were German Army death squads. This is, first and foremost, to keep the money flowing into Israel from German banks. The *Abkommen* is still in play and Germany is one of Israel's protectors while Ukraine and Russia are not. Ergo, Jewish organizations like the *Jewish Virtual Library* and various Holocaust memorials ignore 6th Army's participation in the *Babi Yar Massacre*. Primarily this protects the reputation of the German Army and the legend of the *Noble Cause*. Today's Jews don't even mention 6th Army. They blame Hitler and his minions for *Babi Yar*. This view of history is fundamental to German-Israeli relations. *The Legend of the Noble Cause* is, aside from a few paragons of virtue like Sophie Scholl, pretty much all Germany has from the war. The Jews are willing to throw Germany a bone because they are, as always, Israel's largest euro trading partner at 2.3 billion dollars annually. But in truth, it was 6th

THE TRANSFORMATION OF THE WEST INTO A PERMANENT WAR ECONOMY

Army that perpetrated this mass murder. It was their men who shot 35,000 innocents into an empty gulch. Their men took the pictures of those poor exposed ladies holding their naked babies to their breasts before machine gunned into a mass-grave. But the war's true history is manipulated and kept secret to protect present realities. This depends upon complete acquiescence to an agreed upon certainty that Hitler and his *Sonderkommandos* did the deed, and all the deeds. In fact, 90% of all atrocities and massacres were done by the German Army. All dissenting voices to this view are mercilessly weeded out, disempowered and imprisoned. So 6th Army must emerge from all this with its chivalric reputation intact; and it has. Those men are the object of pity and admiration when in fact their actions are a disgrace upon humanity. It would take a year and a half but 6th Army would finally get what was coming to it and be eradicated to the last man.

6th Army lives of the land

Napoleon's *Grand Armee*, a conglomerate of more than a dozen nation's armed forces, invaded Russia in 1812. They lived off the land and took the direct route to Moscow as did Guderian. But at least they got there. On the way, woe onto all the small farms that the *Grand Armee* looted of every head of livestock and every bushel of grain they could find; and too bad for the farm villages that would suffer mass starvation from it. Once in Moscow, the Russians wouldn't surrender to Napoleon. Guderian would have suffered the same result had he taken the place. When Napoleon got word of a *coup* in Paris against his rule, he made off *post haste* and left his army in the lurch; not the first time he ever did that either (see Egypt). On the way back home, the *Grande Armee* trudged through all those lands stripped bare on the advance. In what was one of the mildest winters in Russian history, the men died of starvation. In 1942 with a supply line more than 1000 miles long, German 6th Army lived off the land on their advance to the Volga. They took everything not nailed down. The Ukrainians were scheduled for extinction anyway so it didn't matter what happened to them. Thousands of Ukrainians, perhaps millions, died trying to survive on grass and shoe-leather when winter closed in. Modern day Ukrainians don't care about this atrocity very well as they too, like the Jews, find the legend of the *Noble Cause* to their benefit. *The Noble Cause* is anti-Russian, and necessarily, pro-German. This is significant today because Ukraine is ruled by pro-Nazi thugs. They celebrate the Nazi occupation because it validates their present anti-Semitic and anti-Russian policies.

The economy of force

Fall Blau was Hitler's first major operation as military commander and he screwed it up. There is no denying it, even for the most strident Hitler apologist (there aren't many). Yes, Halder's military intelligence operation, *Fremde Heere Ost*, did provide Hitler with superbly erroneous information. But a military commander needs *some common sense* and Hitler's decision making in this operation didn't have any. The objectives were far flung with deficient attacking force. There is a story that Hitler had a photographic memory. It is true he was able to remember minute details of military deployments. The most famous anecdote is that he knew how many anti-aircraft guns were stationed on a tiny island in the English Channel. But in this campaign he forgot what the objectives were, even though he set them! Why in the world would he transfer Manstein's victorious 11th Army north to the static Leningrad front when Maikop, Grozny and Baku had the oil and were in the opposite direction? This redeployment was from Halder, still consumed with capital cities. Hitler gave in to him and ignored the principle of *economy of force*. If Hitler were a military historian he might have understood this but he was social historian; that is what his books were all about. He never wrote about military matters because he didn't understand them. In the Crimea, a rested and refit 11th Army was right where he needed them for *Blau*. Instead he dissolved a victorious army and threw it to the wind.

> *The battle of Waterloo was won on the playing fields of Eton* Wellington.

The Battle of Waterloo is a good example of a military operation even though it was fought in a single day on a field 10 miles wide. *The Stalingrad Campaign* (as it came to be known) was fought over a period of 6 months on a field thousands of miles wide. Yet the same principles of war apply to both. All units in the French Army at Waterloo finished the battle right near to where they began it. Napoleon wasn't moving troops and military organizations about *willy-nilly*. The same can be said of all his battles, even 3-day affairs like the *Battle of Arcole* (1796). In baseball they say: *take what the game gives you*. In early July 1942, the 11th Army finally reduced the fortress and siege of Sevastopol. Although mauled, the dictate of *economy* indicated that 11th Army should stay in the center of Army Group South. In a few months it would be refitted and reinforced. Kept in the center it could have saved the day when 6th Army was encircled. Instead it was dissolved with the troops and guns sent 1000 miles away! In truth Hitler had no experience on the operational level except in the vaguest sense. He wasn't helped by his staff either, many of whom admittedly wanted him to fail. Hitler did have strategic vision and he was correct that most of the General Staff officers were unable to see the big picture. But Baku in the south was where the oil was, not in Stalingrad and certainly not in Leningrad.

The population metric

In the summer of 1942 *Greater Germany* (*Großdeutschland*) and its allies at last had a population greater than the Soviet Union; 140 million to 110 million. The Soviets were now without Ukraine and the Baltic States and Germany still had a good chance to win this war. When *Fall Blau* finally kicked off in late June 1942, *Army Group South* itself was dissolved and the new *Army Group B* (same organization, new name) was created with *6th Army* the main component. It was to advance *in the direction of Stalingrad* to protect the center. South of it, in what was *the main thrust*, a new army group was created from whole cloth: *Army Group A*. They were to take the oil fields. It sounded great, two new army groups, but it was all the same as it ever was. In the north, and to protect the far left, *Voronezh* was to be taken by 2nd Army and 4th Panzer Army. This was another wasted effort that took much longer than anticipated. It finally fell on July 24th and warning bells might have gone off right then and there. Maybe the Reds weren't that weak after all? The 4th Panzer Army was then expected to move south, (overland using up scarce fuel) to beef up

Army Group A. But they were never able to do much of anything. They began *Blau* in the center and should have stayed there. Instead Hitler and his staff had the 4th Panzer Army move all over the map. *Army Group A* did manage to take Maikop and its small oil fields. The Reds had burned them down and the Germans were only able extract 700 tons of oil before they were forced to retreat. At this point the German front-line was 2,500 miles long or the distance between New York and California. This would prove impossible to defend and supply. In this situation 6th Army got sucked into a city-fight that it couldn't get out of.

The Battle of Stalingrad

In *218 BC* the Carthaginian general *Hannibal* crossed the Alps from Spain and invaded Italy from the north. He famously had mounted Elephant shock troops and somehow brought them across the Alps with him. These were Asian Elephants whose range in those days (2,400 years ago) stretched all the way out to the Atlas Mountains in Morocco, then a part of Carthage's domain. North Africa was a lush paradise in those days which allowed Carthage to threaten Rome. Italy was a part of the *Roman Republic* back then. Two years later their army met Hannibal's at *Cannae* in southern Italy. Roman battle tactics were to hold the center with heavy infantry and then destroy the enemy's center with them. Usually they were unstoppable. However Hannibal, the toughest fighter anybody ever heard of, was able to surround them by maneuver and 86,000 Romans were killed to the last man. He and his army roamed about Italy for the next 15 years. They lived off the land, and killed off 20% of Rome's population. Hannibal was only forced to retreat when Rome attacked Carthage itself in 202 BC. The *Battle of Cannae* served as a model for the *double envelopment* ever since. The Roman commander was *Lucius Paullus*. He saw what was coming and tried to warn Varro, his co-commander, but to no avail. In a cruel twist of fate, Varro escaped while *Paullus* fell. In another interesting and eerie coincident, 6th Army commander *Friedrich Paulus* also saw that his army was in serious danger, but he too was ignored. Paulus the operational planner may have been in the wrong job as an army commander, but he could read a map. On his right were 4th Romanian Army and the under-strength, already shot up, low on fuel 4th Panzer Army. On his left were 3rd Romanian, 8th Italian and 2nd Hungarian armies all the way up to Voronezh, 400 miles away. Sad to say Italian 8th Army was placed between the Hungarians and Romanians to prevent them from attacking each other. In October the sky was permanently overcast and the rain began to fall. Paulus requested permission to withdraw onto a more manageable defensive position. Hitler said no; that Stalingrad must be taken and held. Grim in command, Paulus actually took the city; 90% of it: so much so that the Germans set up a city administration with a mayor and city council, police force and everything. They needed it because 40,000 civilians still held onto a precarious life in basements and bombed out buildings. There were instances where women and their children, on their way home from scavenging, wandered onto a battlefield. The men on both sides maintained their humanity, held fire and allowed them to pass. Among the legends that emerged from this battle was that the Red Army sent unarmed men in to fight. In fact, there was one Soviet division (*284th Batyuk*) that arrived without weapons. They were not sent into attack but were kept in reserve until their rifles arrived. This incident is falsely dramatized in the anti-Soviet war movie *Enemy at the Gates* (2001) and no, the poor fellows without rifles where not machine-gunned to death by their own officers when they retreated. It's all made up.

Ready, aim, fire

When Napoleon's *Grande Armee* marched to their doom in Russia, they fought one major engagement against the Russian Army at a place called *Borodino*, 70 miles west of Moscow. The battlefield is preserved and it's a nice day-trip if you are ever out that way. Russian soldiers were deployed in front of slopes to await the enemy's advance. Of course the French, knowing how to do it, would set up their artillery and bombard them with cannon balls that would start ripping off heads and limbs. The Russian men could only hope for the best as the cannon balls could be seen flying through the air like a flock of crows, getting closer and closer. They had to stand their ground. It wasn't something American college students would call a *safe space*. To stand and hold required iron discipline brewed by the fear of immediate execution if anyone broke and ran. The Duke of Wellington solved this dilemma by positioning his troops on the reverse slopes where the enemy couldn't see them. He only stationed officers forward to observe and they were allowed to dodge the balls; hence the beginnings of the game *dodge-ball*. But Field Marshall Blucher once famously told him; *I prefer my troops to be able to see the enemy*. So did the Russians. They stood fast and held their ground. When the French advanced, as they had to, Russian infantry then inflicted awful carnage on them. They fired their muskets *en masse* at close range. This kind of coordinated infantry shooting in unison, where an officer would command *ready-aim-fire*, is called *volley fire*. By the time the Russian Army fought the Japanese ninety-three years later in the *Russo-Japanese War*, they were still using it. The Japanese had machine guns.

The Battle of Khalkhin Gol

In 1938 the Kwantung Army that ruled *Manchukuo* decided that the interests of the Japanese Empire lay to the north in Russian Siberia. This faction had strong support in the Army and was named the *Hokushin-ron* (northern road). They aimed to conquer Siberia for its ports and resources and saw the Japanese Empire centered upon Manchukuo. They pointed out that one only needed to look at a map to see that the natural route of expansion for Japan lay to the north into an area that was vast and under-populated. In the end, and with hind-sight, it is evident they were right. Had they gone in that direction and avoided war with the United States, the Japanese Empire might still be on the map. They were opposed by the *Nanshin-ron* (southern road) that saw Southeast Asia and the Pacific Islands as the direction to go even though it would necessarily mean war with the USA and Great Britain. The Kwantung Army, as they always did, took matters into their own hands and invaded Mongolia and Siberia in 1938 even though Japan was already at war with China. They thought the conquest of Siberia would be easy. After all, they had beaten the Russians in 1904-05 and why should it be any different? It was completely different. They were up against the Red Army, a revolutionary army that fought differently than did the Tsar's army. The Reds had thousands of tanks and masses of Mongolian cavalry plus Georgy Zhukov, the most outstanding field commander of the entire war. Zhukov studied Hannibal's maneuvers and launched his own double envelopment against, interestingly enough, the Japanese 6th Army. Zhukov's army destroyed it at a place called *Khalkhin Gol*: the most famous battle nobody ever heard of. This loss helped convince Japan to take the southern road. Unfortunately for them, it would lead to Pearl Harbor and the Empire's eradication. On the other side of the world, and four years after *Khalkhin Gol*, Zhukov would plan the annihilation of German 6th Army at Stalingrad.

The Germans take Stalingrad

6th Army almost drove the Reds back into the Volga and got within 100 yards of it. The Reds were reduced to a small pocket that would soon fall. But as the weather got colder, the Reds got tougher. 6th Army was forced to withdraw their horses as the supply line was now too long to give them the fodder they needed. This was a big loss as the horses were one of the few links the men still had to any sort of rational world. They were now in the pits of hell, *Dante's Inferno* come alive; just as bad as Verdun or Gallipoli except that is was ever colder with the bleak gray and permanently overcast sky hardly allowing in a ray of sunlight. Illness, hunger and disease became ever-present. German metal helmets sucked the heat out of their heads. The Reds wore fur hats, as were their boots; stuffed with newspapers for extra insulation. The Germans wore leather boots and got frostbite. Food was getting scarce; the men began to eat the few horses left behind. Death by starvation was common. Suicide was prevalent and it happened every day: all a German soldier had to do was stand up and a sniper would get him. Winter gear was slow arriving as was anti-freeze. Starving field mice began to eat the wiring in the tanks. The snow and rain fell harder. Then, on November 19th, the Red Army launched its counter-offensive; *Operation Uranus*. Gehlen's *Foreign Armies East* said they didn't have the strength. They did. The problem with Gehlen's organization, aside from it being rife with traitors and informants, was that they relied on internal sources for information. They didn't have anybody infiltrated on the other side. On the contrary, the Reds had spies all over Germany at the highest levels of government and military. Gehlen and his people actually knew nothing of value and never did. When they invaded Russia in 1941, German military intelligence didn't even know the names of anybody on the Red Army general staff.

The double envelopment

The Germans at Stalingrad, like the Japanese at *Khalkhin Gol*, underestimated the enemy. A fixed situation had evolved and Field Marshall Zhukov could read a map better than anybody. As a military commander Hitler was comfortable in static positions as are most military men. They generally lack the imagination to correctly foresee the results that emerge from a fluid and rapidly changing situation. On the drive to Abbeville in 1940, only Guderian was able to see and understand what was happening. In 1942 on the Volga, 6th Army was in a static position. The whole German Army on a 1000 mile southern front was stationary. Zhukov could calmly pick out the weakest link in the German position that was evident to anyone with a map. The enemy had allowed their flanks to be protected by under-armed and under-strength foreign troops. Zhukov attacked the weak German left flank on November 19th, 1942. The Romanians had warned the high command something was afoot for weeks, but were ignored. They put up a good fight; some units refused to surrender and fought to the last man. They were simply overwhelmed by a vastly superior enemy force that included the *1st Guards Army* and *5th Tank Army*. The next day the Reds attacked south of Stalingrad and overwhelmed the *4th Romanian* and *4th Panzer Army*. The pincers linked up at *Kalach*, 50 miles to the rear and 6th Army was entombed. The Germans were never able to figure out a way to save it. They thought an airlift might supply 6th Army. Goering is always blamed for that failure but it was *Luftwaffe Chief of Staff Hans Jeschonnek* who suggested it to Hitler, backed up by Manstein who was flown in to save the day. He was however without his 11th Army that had been dissolved. With the small *ad hoc* force he scraped up, he couldn't break in and relieve Paulus. The main airfield used to supply 6th Army was named *The Tatsinskaya Airfield*. It is still there about 150 miles west of Volgograd. *Gumrak* was the last airfield inside the pocket to fall. It is now *The Volgograd International Airport* but most of the relics are demolished.

THE TRANSFORMATION OF THE WEST INTO A PERMANENT WAR ECONOMY

From Paris to Stalingrad

When the Stalingrad pocket finally surrendered in February, 1943, one hundred seven thousand Germans were captured. 6th Army and 4th Panzer Army would have twenty-one of their twenty-four divisions completely destroyed. Among them was the *44th Hoch und Deutschmeister Division* formed from the historic *4th Viennese Regiment* founded in 1526. Most of the soldiers in 6th Army were Austrian Germans. Those fellows were welcomed into the *Reich* in the famous *Anschluss* back in 1938. Of them, 95% would die in Soviet captivity. This was an extraordinarily high figure. Overall, only 15% of Germans died as Russian POWs after 1942. The Stalingrad prisoners were already near death from starvation when captured. That is why so many died, as those fellows weren't singled out for any kind of especially rueful treatment. In 1940, the 6th Army had a good time in Paris. Three years later they were in Siberia. Life out there is hard anyway, whether you are in a *Gulag* or not. German Army camps for Russian POWs were far worse and some of them, like *Dulag-205* (*Durchgangslager*), make the *Gulag Archipelago*, quite literally and without exaggeration, seem like an all expenses paid vacation at *Club Med*.

Unternehmen Zitadelle

Chastened somewhat by his utter failure in *Blau*, Hitler went back to listening to his Generals. Manstein had some successes taking and re-taking Kharkov a few times but there never was enough fuel to enable his fantastic maneuvers. Manstein could never grapple with this essential fact. For Hitler, he habitually sought static positions to hopefully recreate the western front stalemate of 1914-18. This would save dwindling oil supplies and might lead to some sort of renewed armistice. This was the appeal of the *Battle of Kursk* (July 1943) Germany's last strategic offensive on the eastern front. It didn't require the vast consumption of fuel across the endless steppe. The front was extremely narrow. Even so, they couldn't even break through the Soviet line into the operational depths as they easily had in 1941-42. Their dwindling reserves are best shown by the very fractional nature of this offensive and its resources. When the *Wehrmacht* attacked Russia in 1941 it did so with 3 million men in three different army groups on a front 1000 miles in width. In 1942 it was with one million men, in (essentially) one army group on a front 500 miles wide. In 1943 three armies (not army groups) attacked a salient 150 miles in width with the objective of taking a few prisoners. Was the war lost already? After losing his *Italian Expeditionary Force* out there in the frozen steppe, Mussolini nagged Hitler to seek peace with Russia. The question now was whether or not Germany could hold out for some sort of favorable or, at least, not terribly unfavorable, armistice. Negotiations did indeed take place in the spring of 1943, brokered by Sweden. Stalin was convinced that the west would never take Germany on directly. He wanted a return to the *status quo antebellum*. Germany asked for too much: they wanted Lithuania, western Ukraine, Poland, and Byelorussia as a buffer. The talks quickly broke down. Even after Kursk turned out poorly, Russian troops still had a long march to East Prussia and Berlin. The war did begin to look like a stalemate considering the vast distances involved. In the west, and after taking Sicily, the western allies allowed the Germans to set up narrow defensive fronts in very inhospitable Italian terrain. Bogged down in southern Italy, somebody should have told the western allies that the way to invade Italy was from the north: both Hannibal and Napoleon could have served as good examples. The allied air war against the Reich wasn't working either. By the end of 1943 it wasn't clear that Germany's war was lost. The German *Reichmark* was still a valued international currency. An ounce of gold was worth two weeks wage for an average German worker; a bit better than it is today. Bankers on both sides still made big capital gains. War was good for them. And of course, there was the bomb that history says Germany never had.

Germany's bomb

The Japanese delegation in Sweden reported to Tokyo that the German Army had deployed an *'atom-splitting device'* near Kursk in 1943. This is Japanese diplomatic signal # 232, intercepted in December 1944: National Archives, RG 457, and declassified October 1, 1978.

> *This bomb is revolutionary in its results, and will completely upset all ordinary precepts of warfare hitherto established. I am sending you, in one group, all those reports on what is called the atom-splitting bomb.*
>
> *It is a fact that in June of 1943, the German Army tried out an utterly new type of weapon against the Russians at a location 150 kilometers southeast of Kursk. Although it was the entire 19th Infantry Regiment [Vorezneh Rifles] of the Russians which was thus attacked, only a few bombs (each round up to 5 kilograms) sufficed to utterly wipe them out to the last man. The following is according to a statement by Lieutenant Colonel... Kenji, adviser to the attaché in Hungary and formerly... in this country, who by chance saw the actual scene immediately after the above took place:*
>
> *All the men and the horses [within radius of] the explosion of the shells were charred black and even their ammunition had all been detonated. Moreover, it is a fact that the same type of war material was tried out in the Crimea too. At that time the Russians claimed that this was poison gas, and protested that if Germany were ever again to use it, Russia, too, would use poison gas. Recently the British authorities warned their people of the possibility that they might undergo attack by German atom-splitting bombs. The American authorities have likewise warned that the American east coast might be the area chosen for a blind attack by some sort of flying bomb.*

The kind of bomb they are talking about is a Lithium-Deuterium bomb that *Enrico Fermi* proposed to the Americans at Oak Ridge. They weren't interested on account of the technical difficulties and also because it is a tactical nuclear weapon and costly. It weighs c. 10 pounds and will knock out a city block. The Americans wanted a big one. And so did the Germans.

Zinsser's Affidavit

Hans Zinsser was a Luftwaffe pilot who gave the following testimony to the USAAF (*military intelligence report of August 19, 1945, roll number A1007, filmed in 1973 at Maxwell Air Force Base in Alabama, declassified 1992*). In it

Zinsser describes a flight he took in October 1944. He perfectly describes an atomic bomb explosion that no person in the world had ever seen before. The Americans didn't test their bomb (in secret) until July 1945. Especially telling is his description of the initial purple mushroom cloud with small circular explosions within it. It is impossible to make this stuff up. He was aware of the test and flew as an observer:

> *In the beginning of Oct, 1944 I flew from Ludwigslust (south of Lubeck), about 12 to 15 km from an atomic bomb test station, when I noticed a strong, bright illumination of the whole atmosphere, lasting about 2 seconds. The clearly visible pressure wave escaped the approaching and following cloud formed by the explosion. This wave had a diameter of about 1 km when it became visible and the color of the cloud changed frequently. It became dotted after a short period of darkness with all sorts of light spots, which were, in contrast to normal explosions, of a pale blue color. After about 10 seconds the sharp outlines of the explosion cloud disappeared, Then the cloud began to take on a lighter color against the sky covered with a gray overcast. The diameter of the still visible pressure wave was at least 9000 meters while remaining visible for at least 15 seconds. Personal observations of the colors of the explosion cloud found an almost blue-violet shade. During this manifestation reddish colored rims were to be seen, changing to a dirty-like shade in very rapid succession. The combustion was lightly felt from my observation plane in the form of pulling and pushing. About one hour later I started with an He 111 from Ludwigslust and flew in an easterly direction. Shortly after the start I passed through the almost complete overcast (between 3000 and 4000 meter altitude). A cloud shaped like a mushroom with turbulent, billowing sections (at about 7000 meter altitude) stood, without any seeming connections, over the spot where the explosion took place. Strong electrical disturbances and the impossibility to continue radio communication as by lightning turned up.*

There is an article in the *Daily Mail*, Wednesday October 11th, 1944 that says Berlin lost its telephone service for 60 hours right at the same time Zinsser reported his observation. This was probably the result of an electromagnetic pulse as Berlin's telephone lines were not buried.

> *The whole point of the doomsday machine is lost if you keep it a secret!*   Dr. Strangelove

Did Zinsser observe a hydrogen bomb test? The hydrogen bomb was first patented by Dr. Karl Nowak of Germany in 1943 (*German patent 905.847, March 16, 1943*). If the Germans had one, and tactical nukes, as well Hiroshima sized bombs, the question always remains: why didn't they use them? The biggest problem was finding a delivery system that would work. The Russians were on the bad end of gas attacks in the 1st *War-phase*. They managed to retaliate and decided they weren't going to get caught napping again. In between the wars they amassed large stockpiles of gas bombs and had the delivery systems to use them. They were able to conventionally bomb Berlin and any Germany city because they had heavy bombers. When the Germans used tactical nukes against them, Russia threatened reprisal with gas. This forced the Germans to back off. The Germans weren't keeping their bomb secret either. The British had a plan called *Operation Vegetarian*. They were going to drop 5 million anthrax laced cattle cakes all over Germany to kill all the livestock, poison the land and kill off the entire population of central Europe. The Germans knew of this and threatened retaliation in kind. The August 11, 1945 *London Daily Telegraph* reported; *Nazis Atom Bomb Plans: Britain ready a year ago*. Both sides knew the enemy had weapons of mass destruction all set to go. What began as an ordinary European border war had evolved into a frightening science fiction scenario in five short years.

Delivery systems

Like the Japanese, the problem the Germans had was delivering the bomb. They also wanted a target that was undefended. This was why the Americans chose Hiroshima. It wasn't so easy for the Germans. London was the first city to undergo aerial bombardment in 1916. They then developed, over the next 30 years, the most effective system of air defenses in the world. The tactical nukes the Germans had in 1943 wouldn't do enough damage to end the war in their favor. The atomic bombs they had were too heavy for V-1 or V-2 rockets. The B-29 that flew the super-heavy Uranium bomb to Japan barely got off the ground. The Luftwaffe had some heavy bombers but could they get through RAF air defenses? Probably not. They scouted New York City in 1944. The gigantic 6-engined Ju-390 had flight characteristics actually superior to the B-29. A Ju-390 flight in August 1944 from *Mont de Marsan*, France, flew to within 12 miles of New York City. The crew took photographs of the New York skyline and returned to France. They tested air defenses and determined, correctly, that New York didn't have any. The Luftwaffe may have launched an atomic attack upon New York in September 1944 but the plane, a Ju-390 flying a polar route from Oslo, went down near Oak Ridge Maine. The trip from Oslo to New York was well within the range of the Ju-390 with a bomb-load. Three bodies were recovered and buried nearby. Luckily for the Americans the German Army collapsed none too soon. From the *Washington Post*, June 29, 1945:

> *RAF officers said today that the Germans had nearly completed preparations for bombing New York from a "colossal" airfield near Oslo when the war ended. Forty giant bombers with a 7,000 mile range were found on this base "the largest Luftwaffe field I have ever seen" said one officer. They were a new type of bomber developed by Heinkel. They now are being dismantled for study. German ground crews said the planes were held in readiness for a mission to New York.*

Some odd questioning: Nuremberg Trial Proceedings Volume 16: Friday, 21 June 1946

MR. JUSTICE JACKSON: *Now, I have certain information, which was placed in my hands, of an experiment which was carried out near Auschwitz and I would like to ask you if you heard about it or knew about it. The purpose of the experiment was to find a quick and complete way of destroying people without the delay and trouble of shooting and gassing and burning, as it had been carried out, and this is the experiment, as I am advised. A village, a small village was provisionally erected, with temporary structures, and in it approximately 20,000 Jews were put. By means of this newly invented weapon of destruction, these 20,000 people were eradicated almost instantaneously, and in such a way that there was no trace left of them; that it developed, the explosive developed, temperatures of from 400° to 500° centigrade and destroyed them without leaving any trace at all. Do you know about that experiment?*

SPEER: *No, and I consider it utterly improbable.*

Albert Speer was the famous architect and later Minister of (slave labor) Armaments. But he didn't know everything and by maintaining adherence to the standard official story he got off easy: twenty years of house arrest in Spandau Prison. Then came a life of fame and fortune, after the publication of his ghostwritten books. Like Sergeant Shultz; Speer *knew nothing*. The fellow actually in command of the secret projects was *SS Obergruppenführer Hans Kammler* who disappeared in 1945 and, like many war criminals, his body was never discovered. Kammler's HQ was at the *Skoda Works*, in *Pilsen, Sudetenland*. This was one the largest military industrial conglomerates in the world. It controlled the massive Luftwaffe underground factories and the uranium mines that were all over same area. It was here, and not Auschwitz, where a few hundred thousand Hungarian Jews were sent. General Patton's 3rd American Army captured it in April, 1945. What 3rd Army discovered there is unknown. Their war diaries are still classified top secret.

The American Bomb

Among the most persistent legends to emerge from the war is that the American bomb project was kept secret. It is often cited as an example of how a government can keep a large military mission undisclosed. If *keeping it secret* meant it didn't get into the newspapers and radio reports then yes, it was kept under wraps. The rest of the implication is complete fabrication. The *Manhattan Project* employed 120,000 people who were all in on it. Everybody knew they were working on a *big* project that would win the war. Most people figured it out. A steel cutter might not have any information for the enemy but a physicist would. Among them were hundreds of Soviet spies. Many of them were at the highest level: nuclear physicists like Theodore Hall, Morris Cohen and Klaus Fuchs relayed information to Moscow. However it is, the Soviet Union was not the enemy but an ally. None of the atomic spies relayed information to Germany, a nation that *was* the enemy. When the Americans began to share information with the British, who were infiltrated with nests of Soviet spies at every level of government, the atomic project news was on Joseph Stalin's desk as soon as it got to Churchill. There were at least 1,500 known data leaks.

The Rosenbergs get the chair

A further legend has it that the Russians would never have been able to build the bomb on their own without help from their spies. In 1943 Russia had its own set of problems, mostly that the European half of their country was occupied by marauding enemy troops. Even so, the Soviet Union built the best tanks in the war, the best ground attack aircraft, (the *Sturmovik Ilyushin Il-2*), the best infantry rifle, the best submachine gun, the best rocket launchers and much more superb military gear that defeated the German Army. They manufactured these designs themselves. They didn't need an atomic bomb because two years later they would be in Berlin. When peace finally came they built the bomb on their own, even though the Americans would never accept this. Instead they blamed Julius and Ethel Rosenberg, two New York Jews who were low level worker bees in the Soviet intelligence apparatus. The general principles on how to build a bomb were well known. The construction itself was a mechanical engineering problem that both Japan and Germany also solved. After the first explosion on Hiroshima there were no more secrets and the cat was out of the bag. Nevertheless, after a show trial worthy of Stalin, they strapped poor Ethel into an electric chair even though she never did anything but bake cookies. The couple was not even allowed a last meal together and Ethel, by design, took a long time to die.

Why do historians lie?

They don't lie as much as *dissemble* the truth (from Latin *dissimulare*: to hide or conceal). They do this because modern history has become a very lucrative socially constructed reality. Textbook sales in the USA amount to over *ten billion dollars* annually. Every academician wants a piece of that. The adage is *Publish or Perish*. Survival in the academic world is dependent upon recognition of and adherence to the prevalent ideology. Historians must present books and scholarly articles that conform to it and the system that emerges weeds out nonconformists. This includes the ever-present *World War* documentaries that dominate cable outlets. So for example, a television show about the *Battle for Italy* in 1943 shows footage of cheerful and even ecstatic Italians welcoming German (Nazi) soldiers with flowers and wine; but without any sort of commentary. This is how *dissimulare* works. The fact that northern Italians saw the Germans as saviors is hidden from the viewers by silence. The facts are shown but neither discussed nor elaborated upon. It's understandable especially in today's political climate. Very few can survive the fascist label in an academic and cultural system that is politicized in every field of endeavor.

Egyptology seems to have been at its peak in 1875   David Grant Stewart

One might think that the study of *Ancient Egyptian* history wouldn't be so political. It was a long time ago: over 4000 years. Very few people can grasp or care that *Egyptology* (the study of Ancient Egypt) is highly biased precisely because it is so obscure. A very select and specialized priest caste is this ancient civilization's sole purveyors of the truth. They present *Ancient Egyptian* culture, despite its fantastic monumental achievements, as fundamentally primitive. One need only observe the monuments at *Karnak* and *Luxor* (for example) to suspect that slaves armed with copper hammers and chisels didn't build them. Some other process was at work. But Egypt as a primitive culture with rudimentary tools conforms to the slow but steady evolution of all things from the Big Bang and Darwinian material origin right up onto modern society; one that is always presented as the inevitable highlight of world history. This ever upward arc of history towards present enlightenment is essential to our brave new reality. As a social science, *Egyptology* is controlled by the exceptionally few people who can read and decipher Egyptian symbolic writing known as *Hieroglyphic Script*. Nobody in the field may deny that *Hieroglyphic Script* is understood; that would negate an elaborate social construction. This would also mean professional ostracism for any *Egyptologist* who doubted the reality: no more textbook sales at $124.⁹⁹ each, no more career enhanced publications, and no more free eats at plush conferences in Paris. The final obstacle towards open inquiry is the Egyptian government itself; for if the monuments are indeed 10,000 years old (or older), it means that Egyptians didn't build them! This would further indicate that all of history is a misconstruction and that knowledge presented as fact is actually a fabrication.

The Rosetta Stone

The tablet was discovered by French troops in Napoleon's invasion of Egypt in 1798. It was a proclamation in Greek language about an upcoming royal festival (c.200 BC) because Egypt's rulers were Greek. Next to it on the stone were translations into both Egyptian written characters and symbolic (*hieroglyphic*) script. From this, various scholars felt that they were finally able to successfully translate the mysterious *hieroglyphics* that adored Ancient Egyptian monuments. This was and is very exciting. Up until then Ancient Egypt was a complete mystery wrapped in the proverbial enigma. Nothing was known about it. The pyramids are not dated and even though they are said to be royal tombs, no mummy has ever been found in one. How old were they? Nobody knew. Was the lion-like Sphinx constructed in the *Age of Leo*, 13,000 years ago? Nobody had the slightest clue. *The Rosetta Stone* seemingly changed that. Because Greek was known, the indecipherable hieroglyph symbols could apparently be translated. However it is not clear that an accurate translation was made and it should be discomforting that each *hieroglyph* may be any one of four things: a sound, a letter in an alphabet, an actual representation of the symbol itself or a conceptual ideogram: all of it dependent upon where each pictogram or symbol is placed in relation to the others. As a result, every assembly can mean almost anything the translator wishes. Naturally a coherent scheme was worked out. But is it authentic? Here are some brief but completely representative passages from the *Rosetta Stone* into English from the original Greek:

> *Whereas king Ptolemy, the ever-living, the beloved of Ptah…has been a benefactor both to the temples and to those who dwell in them, as well as all those who are his subjects, being a god sprung from a god and goddess… and whereas he has remitted the debts to the crown being many in number which they in Egypt and in the rest of the kingdom owed; and whereas those who were in prison and those who were under accusation for a long time, he has freed of the charges against them; and whereas he has directed that the gods shall continue to enjoy the revenues of the temples and the yearly allowances given to them, both of corn and money… and whereas he directed also, with regard to the priests, that they should pay no more as the tax for admission to the priesthood than what was appointed them throughout his father's reign and until the first year of his own reign; and has relieved the members of the priestly orders from the yearly journey to Alexandria…*

The entire proclamation is written this way and is why hieroglyphic translations all sound like this. There are no nuances of language; no similes, no allusions, no metaphors; how could there be? If you were visitor from another planet arrived on earth, and passages like this were your <u>only</u> lexicon in the English language (as the Rosetta Stone is for hieroglyphics) would you, along with any army of linguists, ever be able to translate and read this passage from Melville?

> *Call me Ishmael. Some years ago—never mind how long precisely—having little or no money in my purse, and nothing particular to interest me on shore, I thought I would sail about a little and see the watery part of the world. It is a way I have of driving off the spleen and regulating the circulation. Whenever I find myself growing grim about the mouth; whenever it is a damp, drizzly November in*

my soul; whenever I find myself involuntarily pausing before coffin warehouses, and bringing up the rear of every funeral I meet; and especially whenever my hypos get such an upper hand of me, that it requires a strong moral principle to prevent me from deliberately stepping into the street, and methodically knocking people's hats off—then, I account it high time to get to sea as soon as I can. This is my substitute for pistol and ball. With a philosophical flourish Cato throws himself upon his sword; I quietly take to the ship. There is nothing surprising in this. If they but knew it, almost all men in their degree, some time or other, cherish very nearly the same feelings towards the ocean with me.

If your dictionary was the landscape of the *Rosetta Stone* you could never accurately comprehend this. Another problem is that the hieroglyphs on the stone are a late translation, written, *at least*, 2000 years after the high culture of Ancient Egypt flourished. Consider our own language only 1000 years ago; *Old English* from the Epic Poem *Beowulf*:

Beowulf wæs breme (blæd wide sprang), Scyldes eafera Scedelandum in. Swasceal geong guma go de gewyrcean, fromum feohgiftum on fæder bearme þæt hine on ylde

This is English but who can read it but a specialist? We can figure out *Beowulf was* and a few other words but translation is only possible because the alphabet is the same and we also have *Old Norse* and *Old Frisian* to help figure it out. With the *Rosetta Stone* there is nothing like that; only vague supposition about people who, incomprehensibly, were technically, scientifically and spiritually far more advanced than we are. The Cairo Museum has hundreds of hard-stone artifacts from *"Predynastic"* Ancient Egypt that could only have been cut with steel and diamond-edged power tools. The Museum doesn't say anything about them; they are simply presented without commentary. Egyptology ignores them and also the mountain of evidence that suggests Ancient Egyptian history is far older than imagined. A 13,000 year old Sphinx would place it (and all Egyptian monuments) in the same timeframe as *Göbekli*

Tepe: a massive, but only partially excavated Neolithic city built, intentionally buried and abandoned by peoples unknown. The supposition presented is that "hunter-gatherers" suddenly discarded their spears and baskets and instead took up the advanced mathematics and geometry needed to construct essentially modern architecture. It's the same with Egyptology. Most people are not aware that Egyptian history *begins* with pyramid construction. There is no introductory phase; "hunter-gatherers" just decided to suddenly build complex monuments. It is as absurd as the Big-Bang. The masonry at *Göbekli Tepe* is very similar to Egyptian and all of it was probably built by the same peoples. But the strong possibility of a worldwide advanced civilization in the late Ice Age cannot be admitted. Our ancestral roots and true heritage is thereby desecrated and that makes our present wage-enslavement easier to enforce.

Chronological problems

There are only two trustworthy dates in ancient history. One is the first Olympiad in -776 BC. Since the last one was held in the modern era (AD 394) it is possible to accurately place Greek and Roman history within that timeframe. Egypt's only reliable date (from astronomical data) is the *Sack of Thebes* by the Assyrians in -664 BC. No event earlier than that can be accurately dated. But Egyptology presents its historical dating with the precision given a list of American presidents. The chronology of Egyptian kings is primarily offered by *Manetho* (c.300 BC). His list of Egyptian kings, and other extremely fragmented records, form the basis for dating Egyptian history and its monuments. But they do not, and cannot, offer dates as we know them. No records from Manetho himself exist and our understanding of his history comes from Christian historians five centuries later. *J. H. Breasted* (one of the giants) says Manetho's history is "mostly imaginary." Breasted:

> *Although we know that many of his divisions are arbitrary and that there was many a dynastic change where he indicates none... his dynasties divide the kings into convenient groups which have so long been employed in modern study of Egyptian history that it is now impossible to dispense with them.*

There's little to any of it beyond speculation. But since there is nothing else to go on it becomes the fact of the matter. All of contemporary history is constructed like this, especially the record of the *World War* since it is so vitally relevant to the manufacture of modern history.

Trinity

Robert Oppenheimer was the chief scientist on atomic bomb development and he informed new President Truman in May 1945 that the bomb wouldn't be ready until November, at the earliest. Then U-234 surrendered and that cargo of triggers was sent to Oppenheimer. Nuclear triggers, or how to make the thing go boom, was one of the big problems that the Americans couldn't solve. Here now they had working units thanks to the German war machine. Those 50 gold-lined tubes of Uranium 235 sure came in handy too; as the Americans had problems extracting the fissionable material from their limited stock of Uranium 238. So, a little more than two months after Germany's surrender, the Americans were ready to test their *Plutonium bomb* on July 16, 1945. *This was not the bomb type used on Hiroshima*. The first bomb dropped on Japan was a Uranium-235 device that the Americans never tested. The official myth is that the uranium bomb didn't need to be tested because *"everybody knew it would work."* Why and how is that? Nobody could know anything about these devices. The simple answer is that they didn't need to test it because the Germans already did. Without the German test the American military would not have used an untested bomb. That was far too risky. Suppose the thing was a dud? Then the Japanese could soon have a working model with bomb-grade uranium. This is the great secret of the Manhattan Project: *we got the uranium bomb from the enemy*. And that's why, three quarters of a century later, information about the German bomb is hidden and denied.

To bomb, or not to bomb

Harry Truman was the new American President upon Roosevelt's death in April 1945. Henry Wallace was Roosevelt's Vice-President in his 3rd term. The communists in Roosevelt's government wanted to be rid of him and

THE TRANSFORMATION OF THE WEST INTO A PERMANENT WAR ECONOMY

accused him of being a communist! It seems Wallace actually and passionately supported union workers and their right to strike. For this he had to go. Roosevelt's cronies picked a much more pliant and ignorant soul to replace him. Truman was a confidence man from the back woods of Missouri. He owed a lot to the *Pendergast Mob* in Kansas City. They appointed him an administrative law judge and got him started in politics even though he never had a college degree. That's how they did it back in those days. They still do, but nowadays they need to fake it with a law degree. Harry was quite a bit like Woodrow Wilson except that at least Wilson was, and looked the part of, a scholar. Truman looked and behaved like a pumped-up country bumpkin with no concept of anything outside the Ozarks. Quite a few said the same thing sort of thing about General Grant and still do. But when greatness was thrust upon Grant he assumed the mantle. Truman did nothing but drag the nation further into the muck of internationalism thickened by Wilson and Roosevelt. It was Truman, as commander in chief, who decided to atomic bomb a prostrate Japan. The warmongers cheered the decision and still do. Debate on the issue is usually summed up by the notion that there was no other choice. It was either atomic devastation or else an invasion that would cost one million American casualties. There was never, ever, any intention to invade Japan. Okinawa was subdued with tremendous cost. MacArthur's 6th Army was in an interminable struggle with Yamashita on Luzon. American leadership was not ready to spend one million casualties to subdue Japan. The third choice is never talked about. Normally, when one side wants to surrender and the Japanese did in May 1945, the losing side is offered terms and a surrender document is signed. In this case the Americans refused to do that. It was unconditional surrender or nothing. The Japanese weren't asking for much; only that their Emperor wouldn't be put on trial and declared a war criminal. That was all they wanted to stop the fighting; to be treated respectfully and not *lose face*. Japan's Emperor was regarded by most Americans (70%) as a war criminal and there was strong domestic feeling that he and his whole family should be hung. For a good old country swindler like Truman, nobody in Japan was going to get off the hook. As a new President he wanted to begin his term with a bang. Never mind the two hundred thousand women and children who would be blown away. Phil Sheridan and Sherman killed their share of mothers and their babies too. Truman wanted to be remembered like them. Plus, a lot of money went into building that bomb and the B-29 delivery system cost even more. The biggest problem for the Americans came when the Japanese Empire was suddenly and irrevocably eliminated from the international political arena. The power vacuum was quickly filled by the Soviet Union and Red China and you can read about those effects in today's newspaper. Somebody might have thought out this equation and did: Republican senators in the US congress tried to remind Truman it might be a good idea to leave Japan with perhaps some token of its empire intact, at least for the time being. There were undefeated cadres of communist fighters in the Manchurian back-country. Korea was another hot-bed of communist insurrection. Why not let Japan hold onto those places, or at least Manchukuo? But the guy they were talking to was thick as a brick.

Unconditional surrender

The unindicted war criminals Roosevelt and Churchill were both distant cousins related to the Duke of Marlborough just like Lady Diana and her kids. Funny how the same sorts of people always end up running the show? Churchill and Roosevelt both ran their respective navies when the *Lusitania* sank. They should have been hung. They met for a face to face early in 1943 and found a nice hotel in Casablanca, a city founded by the *Berbers* who, unbeknownst to most, are Caucasian. Nowadays, Roosevelt and Churchill are presented as shining lights of modern liberal democratic enlightenment. For Roosevelt, war was a way to get unemployed men off the streets and thereby reduce unemployment and stop the strikes that swept America in the 1930's. Massive sums borrowed from his close banking friends would finance the war and they already knew the enemy before the shooting started. It was going to be Japan and everybody in Washington knew it. Only the suckers in fly-over country didn't and they would be the ones paying for it with their blood. That's why you always see FDR smiling. Jolly as a lark, his theme song was *Happy Days are Here Again*. They were for him and his pals. War was good for business. Japan was literally on the other side of the world but easily provoked into war. All he had to do was threaten Japan with an oil and steel embargo by the world's primary producer of both commodities. Japan effortlessly fell into the trap and attacked Pearl Harbor because that's what happens when you don't have a government. For Churchill, who never offered the Brits anything more than *toil, sweat and tears*, war was a way to destroy Germany for his elite banking friends. They would keep him in power as long as they needed him. At Casablanca, they both got together to divvy up the post-war world. Churchill especially wanted to figure out how to screw the Russians out of everything he could. He hoped to put off an Atlantic invasion of France forever. Roosevelt's military, especially the Army, was keen to invade right away, in 1942. That was the American way of war: get right to it. They compromised and attacked North Africa first and France only two years later in 1944. Casablanca lay on the Atlantic Ocean with a lovely climate. After drinks one afternoon in the breezy part of the day, Roosevelt gathered his assembled minions and presented the notion of *Unconditional Surrender*; made famous by American *General of the Army* Ulysses Grant who ground the Confederacy into dirt. Germany wouldn't be allowed any sort of compromise peace like in 1918. The nation would be divided, stripped (again) of its ability to wage war and permanently occupied as they still are. Roosevelt was waiting for *The Bomb*. In the meantime the western allies would adopt Churchill's strategy and avoid direct confrontation with the German Army. They would attack them on its periphery and they'd let the Russians spill their own and as much German blood as possible.

The Road to Berlin

The Kursk 1943 Summer Offensive (*Operation Citadel*) was another failure for the German Army. They destroyed four times as many Russian tanks as they lost but the Reds had massive reserves that Germany didn't. Hitler's opposition to the offensive was seconded by Guderian who was now *Inspector General of Armored Forces*. But they were both overruled by the General Staff that kept delaying the offensive to allow the advent of more and better German tanks. This just gave the Red Army more time to dig in, lay more mines and beef up the infantry and armor for an attack they knew was coming: for while the Reds knew everything about them, Gehlen and his *Foreign Armies East* knew absolutely nothing about Red Army composition and plans. The Germans had the new *Tiger tank* that got one mile per five gallons of gas. With gas at critically low levels this sort of tank would, in the final analysis, be more a hindrance than a help. On top of that was its unreliability. If the transmission broke down, the part couldn't be fixed in the field but had to be sent back to the factory. The Russian T-34 could be repaired by its own crew and got 1 mile per gallon. The Tiger was a better tank with more firepower than the T-34. However, the Reds produced 50,000 of them while Tiger production was limited to 1,400. It was the same with the renowned *Panther* tank. It also had transmission and gearing problems. The Germans managed to produce 6,000 of them but the Americans produced more than 50,000 Sherman tanks. The biggest problem for German industry and military production was its reliance on slave labor. That's why those transmissions didn't work very well, and why so many artillery shells were duds. The German labor force was simply not motivated while the American workers wanted to kill the enemy any way they could and gladly worked overtime to do it.

Army Group Center is finally destroyed

The Red Army liberated Ukraine from the Nazi yoke at the cost of 3 million dead. You'd think the Ukrainians would have some sense of gratitude but they don't. With the Germans mostly driven out of Ukraine, *Army Group Center* was, again, in a precarious position. Hitler regained his confidence after Kursk when it became apparent that, strategically at least, the General Staff knew less than he did. They couldn't understand what he did: operations needed to be constrained on account of gas and oil. He strove to preserve a static position in the north and center while the south slowly retreat to Romania. This was the kind of war he understood. Manstein's massive mechanized maneuvers were impossible with oil at critical low levels. What Hitler didn't grasp in his world now fueled by methamphetamine, was that all those large divisions on the maps supplied to him by Gehlen weren't actually divisions anymore. Most of them had the strength of reinforced brigades. It looked good on paper but when the Reds struck the exposed flanks of *Army Group Center* in June 1944, it all fell apart. The Germans had taken Minsk in the summer of 1941 on their way to Moscow. Three years later, with the Luftwaffe no longer able to give support, the Reds retook Minsk on the main road to Warsaw and Berlin. Ten months later they would be in Berlin with Hitler a suicide; although neither they nor anybody else was ever able to produce the body.

The Longest Day

The region of France named *Normandy* comes from the Vikings who conquered it when the kings of France were both unwilling and unable to defend it. The name itself comes from *Northman* (*Nordmann*) or men from the north, *i.e.* the Vikings. They settled in and their ruler was the *Duke of Normandy* who was technically a subordinate (*fief*) to the king of France: although for a long time the Duke was more powerful. Normandy is a province rich from tangy alcoholic beverages, the best linen fabrics, as well as fish, agriculture and horses. It is also hard to get at and thus easily defended; which is why the Germans centralized their defense further north at Calais that lay in wide open plains. American General Eisenhower outmaneuvered them and attacked Normandy with three English speaking armies. It was the largest seaborne invasion in the history of the world and made the *Spanish Armada* look like a regatta. The invasion was preceded by night airborne landings in the rear and on the flanks of the German position. One of the enduring legends of the war is that the paradrop and daylight glider landings were a success. It was a disaster. American airborne divisions lost 50% of their strength; 3000 killed and wounded and 4,500 men who just plain disappeared. This makes it comparable to *Pickett's Charge* (65% losses). The night drop was scattered and the glider troops were never able to get organized. The Germans just brushed them aside. Luckily for the Allies, the main German reserves were near Paris and they were reluctant to commit them immediately. This delay is completely reasonable but is often blamed on Hitler who supposedly had a dream that the enemy would attack at Calais. It's all made up. German defensive positions in France were deployed by Field Marshalls Rommel and Gerd von Rundstedt. Rommel would have had them spread out and closer to the sea but he was overruled by von Rundstedt who wanted them centralized. When the landings did happen the Germans did not know what the Allied objectives were, or whether there might be another landing. No military commander in his right mind wants to commit reserves *willy-nilly* at the first sign of enemy activity. Only on the following day, June 7, 1944, did the reserve panzers mount up. By then the Allied armies, with command of the air, gained a foothold they would not relinquish. The overall success of the invasion deflected any criticism about the paratroop losses or the 3,000 men lost in dreadful practice landings on the Devon beaches the month before (*Exercise Tiger*). The Germans managed to maintain a static front for 6 weeks in the excellent defensive terrain. It was here that the Tiger tank proved its worth. Out in the open spaces of the Russian steppe the few Tigers could be easily outmaneuvered. In Normandy's bocage country filled with enormous hedgerows, woods and sunken roads, a single Tiger with infantry support could stake out a defensive position and hold up an entire battalion for a day. But the allies had overwhelming air superiority and the German defenders soon ran out of ammo, gas and food. In July the Americans broke out and drove the Germans out of France. A pretty good movie about this operation is *Patton* (1970). With the Americans approaching the Rhine, the Reds took Warsaw; 350 miles from Berlin with paved roads all the way to the Brandenburg Gate.

Mussolini is imprisoned (comfortably)

When Mussolini was dismissed on *25 de Julio* he was moved about from place to place because the new government wanted to be rid of him. But the King still had some semblance of honor and kept him alive. The Allies wanted him alive as well so they could roast and hang him. What nobody will admit now is that Mussolini, while somewhat unpopular in the south, still had a large base of support in the north of Italy. They finally settled on a nice hotel in the mountains not too far from Rome. The *Hotel Campo Imperatore* is still there and you can stay in Mussolini's room for a price. It's kept just the way he left it, even the bed sheets are in the closet. The one place German military intelligence actually did infiltrate was the Italian military and government, not that it ever did them any good. But with large bribes they did find out where *Il Duce* was held and organized a paratroop-manned glider rescue. German airborne troopers were among the best in the world.

One way they avoided the *Treaty of Versailles* restrictions on air forces was to form glider clubs. Those fellows made superb glider pilots for airborne operations. In 1940, *Operation Mercury* (*Unternehmen Merkur*) was a strictly airborne invasion of the large Greek island of Crete once home to the legendary *Minoan Civilization*. The airborne assault took the British Army completely by surprise. The Luftwaffe dropped the 7th *Flieger (Airborne) Division* and once they captured the small airfield at *Maleme* (it's still there, as tiny as ever), they air-landed the 22nd *Luftlande-Division* (*Air Landing Division*) and later the 5th *Mountain Division*. They overwhelmed the Brits who were forced to evacuate. The Germans suffered 33% casualties which made it comparable to the *Charge of the Light Brigade*. But the Light Brigade didn't take its objectives and the German *Fallshirmjäger* did. Unfortunately they forever stained their honor through the indiscriminate murder of civilians. For some reason that just seems to be the way the German Army does things. It's not like the Jews ever got any special treatment from those fellows: they killed everybody who might get in the way; race, color, creed or national origin didn't matter.

The Gran Sasso Raid

The *Hotel Campo Imperatore* is at a beautiful location high in the Apennines that run north to south along Italy's spine. There are plenty of open fields about it and for the Luftwaffe's crack glider pilots the air-landings were a piece of cake. They rescued the former *Il Duce* without firing a shot against his defenders who were obviously in on it as they were never disarmed. A character named *Otto Skorzeny*, a somewhat jovial assassin with a large dueling scar across his cheek is usually given credit for leading the mission. It was actually planned and commanded by Luftwaffe Major *Otto-Harald Mors* who died peacefully in his sleep six decades later. This was a high-profile mission with cameramen and film-crew. Skorzeny, who wasn't camera shy, attached himself to Mussolini like a limpet mine. This endangered the mission as the 2-seater *Fi-156 Storch* (*Stork*) flown in to extricate *Il Duce* was overloaded when Skorzeny insisted that he tag along. With three men in the cockpit the single-engined plane barely got off the ground but Mussolini was eventually reunited with an ecstatic

Hitler. Skorzeny got another medal and lots of face-time in the newsreels. Mors was forgotten. It was all probably arranged in advance with the Italians; who still weren't sure which side was going to triumph and they seemingly always manage to find the eventual winners.

Republica Sociale Italiana

With the Allied conquest of southern Italy and the German occupation of the north, the Italian nation that was forged in the prior century got dismembered. It didn't matter too much in the southern half that was the erstwhile *Kingdom of the Two Sicilies*. The people there were accustomed to foreign domination and it became the birthplace of the *Mafia* in Sicily and the like-minded *Camorra* in Calabria. These were self-protection organizations from overlords who were racially and culturally different. The Allied armies were just another in a long list of foreign invaders. The locals drank their dark wine and watched them drive by on the road to Rome and Naples; something everybody does. To them Mussolini was just another northerner telling them what to do. It didn't matter too much until their young men disappeared into Libyan wastes and the frozen steppes of Russia. The northern half of Italy was dominated by Germanic tribes and it was here that Hitler and the German Foreign Office established the *Italian Social Republic* with the newly liberated *Duce* as head of state. The new republic had its capital in *Saló*, a part of *Lombardy*; a Germanic province in the north, near and adjacent to other Germanic regions like the *Tyrol* and *Trentino*. All these states still have Teutonic eagles on their flags and coats of arms. The modern globalists in the European Union do not admit that there are racial tribes within Europe and actively work to destroy all memory of them. To them, human beings are commodities without roots or national identity. Resistance to European Union/Globalist extermination plans come from racial sub-groups like the Lombards. They are a German ethnic group that originated in northwest Germania near the Rhine and Denmark in a place called *Langobardi*. When the Roman Empire in the west collapsed, the *Langobards* moved south because there is a lot to be said for paved roads, marble baths, stone housing, hot and cold running water and other amenities they didn't have in the backwoods of *Germania*. The essentially Germanic *Italian Social Republic* is always described as a *"German puppet state."* It wasn't. It was a nation fighting for its survival and independence from enforced amalgamation with the *Kingdom of the Two Sicilies* and the *Papal States*. The Italian union was something they were never in favor of. Similarly, *Calabria* and the *Two Sicilies* viewed their conquest and loss of sovereignty to northern Germans in the same way. They were sold the new nation Italy, but it was a conquest by the north over the south, made palatable by the term *Italian Unification*. After the war in 1945 and with fascism extinguished, the victors enforced the legend that the victorious allies were all one big happy family, marching arm in arm to crush the fascists. Of course Italians weren't united, not then, nor ever. The *Italian Social Republic* willingly fought against the Allied enemy because the outcome was still in doubt and they wanted their own relatively wealthy industrialized, albeit still primarily agricultural nation, free from the poorer and racially distinct south. Thus we see nowadays that both Lombardy and Tyrol seek self-determination and independence from the chaos in the south that is already overrun by the Globalist funded invaders.

Forgotten armies

Fascist Italy surrendered on September 8th, 1943 but the Allies retained the king. They formed their own Italian puppet state with the obsequious Badoglio as Prime Minister. Not everyone was on the same page. Some Italian units fought for the Allies. Many other crack units fought for Mussolini and the Social Republic. Of course the Germans managed to make as many enemies as possible and demanded that all Italian troops disarm. The Italian *33rd Acqui Division* resisted and fought the Germans for a week before running out of ammo. When they asked for American and British air support they were ignored. The Allies wanted to see the Italians killed off just as much as the Germans did. Churchill summed it up: *I prefer a defeated enemy* he said. The German *1st Mountain Division* then began to massacre the *33rd Acqui*. When some of the Bavarian troops resisted the order, they too were threatened with summary execution. This was the most cruel and vicious war in the history of the world. Nobody on either side showed any mercy, not even to the utterly helpless; and to them even less so. Mad and psychopathic men had risen to leadership positions on all sides and the killing wouldn't stop even after the last round of ammunition was fired.

Operational zones

Mussolini was head of state again and faced the same problems as before. Very few people know now, and it's never mentioned, that when Mussolini took power in 1922, Lenin sent him a congratulatory note; one socialist to another. Mussolini was able to stave off armed worker rebellions through massive public spending. People in the countryside always did well under Italian Fascism because they had decent housing, fresh air, good pasta and practically unlimited reserves of cheap red wine. It was workers in the cities who didn't always have these luxuries. Mussolini bought them off but they didn't agreeably sign onto his grandiose vision of imperial conquest. War with the United States and Russia made sense only to the very few. Italy in 1940 had a standard of living superior to 90% of the world. Then the Americans and British began to bomb the worker's homes and Italy had no air defense. Italian warmongers thought hostilities with the USA would be something like Ethiopia; far away and trouble-free. When Italy surrendered to America less than two years later, resistance to the new *Social Republic* sprang up in the same places that revolted in 1920; up in and around the industrialized northern cities. They wanted a soviet-style worker's state. They were in the minority and would only be able to operate in the mountains. The *Social Republic* controlled the roads and cities until the very end. The Germans mucked things up for Mussolini by lopping of huge tracts of territory from the *Social Republic*. When Mussolini and Hitler met in 1934 the issue was German unification with Austria. Mussolini feared that an Austrian union with Germany would present Italy with a massive enemy on its northern border. They would naturally want a return of the Tyrol that was taken in 1919. It happened just that way. Nine years later Hitler technically resisted the lusts of the *Blut und Boden* factions by refusing to formally annex Tyrol and Trentino. But to prevent an Allied conquest of Italy, Germany occupied them anyway by declaring *Operational Zones*. They formed two: *Operational Zone of the Adriatic Littoral* and *Operational Zone of the Alpine Foothills* (*Operationszone Alpenvorland*): all out of territory that was a part of Italy and should have been part of the new *Social Republic*. Typically German they created the Social Republic and then immediately set about to weaken it. In Tyrol and Trentino the Germans completed a *de facto* annexation. In the Adriatic they occupied the coast; much of which is the present day *Republic of Slovenia*.

Is it Slovenia or is that Slovakia?

Many people nowadays have a little bit of difficulty discerning between Slovenia and Slovakia, not the least of which is that they both begin with S and are minor states forged by world war and its consequences. Slovakia was a part of Czechoslovakia and its present incarnation is a 1993 peaceable separation from the post-war re-created Czech state. The first Slovakian Rebublic (1939-45) was constructed by the German Foreign Office from the remains of the Czech cadaver they devoured in 1939. The Slovakians are decended from the *Wends*, dead and gone, who spoke a language similar to *Sorbian*; distantly related to Slovakian and presently spoken in southeast Germany and across the border in southwest Poland. Slovakian itself is a *West Slavic* language similar to Polish and Czech. Slovakia was always a firm ally of Germany. They declared war on Poland and they helped Germany consume it. They then invaded Russia with Germany in 1941 but were clever enough not to declare war. The *Slovakian 1st Division* made it all the way to *Maikop* and back which is quite a military feat. They got badly shot up and eventually Germany was forced to occupy Slovakia when the Reds approached. That was fair enough but problems arose when the German Army began to collect men and ship them back to Germany for slave labor. That's when Slovakian resistance began and of course, at the first sign of trouble, the Germans start shooting, thus creating more partizans. The Germans could never quite figure this out. Now in the 21st century, the radically globalist modern German nation is run by the anti-Hitler and communist Frau Merkel. Committed to open borders and the denial of nationality, Germany has lost her closest allies. Instead, Slovakia is now allied with Poland, Hungary, Austria and Slovenia in bloc-resistance to European Union *replacement migration* policies.

Slovenia suffers the fate of small states in world war

Slovenia lay about 250 miles to the southwest of Slovakia. Their language is also Slavic but not closley related to Slovakian but rather the Serbo-Croatian that was the official language of Jugoslavia. Versailles created Slovenia in 1919 and the treaty attached it to Jugoslavia as a province. They had large German minorities, some of which petitioned the United States to annex them. That didn't and couldn't happen but shows the desparation in people whose lives are thrown casually about by men in suits. When Germany destroyed Jugoslavia in 1941, they, along with Italy and Hungary, all annexed parts of Slovenia. Hungary had signed a *Treaty of Eternal Friendship* with Jugoslavia in December 1940 but just five months later invaded them alongside Germany. Unable to swallow his guilt, the man who signed the treaty, Prime Minster Pál Teleki, took his own life; thus the differnce between men of honor and virtue like Teleki and ruthless, atheistic marauders like Hitler and von Ribbentrop. Two years later, with (southern) Italy suddenly on the side of the Allies, Germany occupied the whole of Slovania. The *Social Republic* lost some more prime real estate as the Adriatic coast there is fabulously rich. By this time, the German Army's secondary mission was deporting civilians for slave labor back home. They were particularly brutal in this and didn't take no for an answer. Partizan movements then arose in Slovania as another one of Germany's once peacable rear areas became hostile. But the slave labor program took priority over military needs. Jugoslavia was destroyed again by the Americans in 1992 because they refused to abandon soviet style communism.

Yet who would have thought the old man had
so much blood in him? Lady Macbeth

On January 11th 1944 Mussolini murdered his son in law Count Ciano. He didn't pull the trigger but he may as well have. When Italy surrendered to the Allies, Ciano, Edda and their children sought refuge in Germany but were sent back to the *Social Republic* by the viper von Ribbentrop. There, the hard-line Fascists wanted the count tried for treason. They still hated him in revenge for his vote of no-confidence in the final meeting of the *Gran Consiglio del Fascismo* that saw Mussolini arrested and exiled. They put Ciano and four others on trial, all of whom had voted no-confidence; including Italy's most renowned soldier *Marshall of Italy Emilio De Bono*. Next day they were all tied to chairs and shot in the back. Mussolini could have put a stop to it; either to the trial or the sentence but he didn't. The nemesis of power was too shrill for him to defy. He clung to it until Red partisans tracked him down in April 1945 when he attempted to flee with his devoted girl friend Clara Petacci. The Reds were willing to let her go but she wished to die with him. They gunned them both down and hung their disfigured and mutilated bodies upside down on meat hooks from a gas station in Milano. Members of Mussolini's staff were shot and hung with him. They didn't choose to die for Mussolini. They were always motivated by the idea that he represented: that there is a way for the national state to survive within the capitalist system while avoiding the evident and ever counterfeit presentations of western liberalism. The Lombards believed this and still do. They defended their fascist republic but, undefeated, were forced to surrender when Germany collapsed. Italy was then permanently occupied by the Americans. In the seven decades since Mussolini's death, Italy never regained sovereignty and the Americans are deeply involved in rigged Italian elections to keep it that way. They also fund terrorist Red and Fascist Brigades to keep the populace on edge and in fear of the Stalinist (Red) menace. Presently there are more than 100 American military bases in Italy. The legend that Italy is a free and sovereign state is part of the ongoing *World War II deception*. This presents the victors as liberators when actually a more benign conqueror replaced a savage one. For Italians, who liked America and Americans anyway, as millions of their relatives had emigrated there, the new boss was way better than the old boss.

The Man of Steel

Joseph Stalin is the author of 146 books. You can find many of them on *Amazon* and they deal primarily with the soviet economy and the Russian Revolution in historical perspective. His books are not ghostwritten. He was a tireless reader with a personal library of 26,000 volumes and was an intellect of the first order. Sleazy professional politicians like Tony Blair and Barry Obama pale in comparison to him. Stalin was *General Secretary of the Communist Party* and over the course of the years offered to resign 6 times, four times in writing. There were moments when he got fed up with it all and just wanted to go home. His resignations were rejected because, like Hitler, he was the smartest guy in the room. The Revolution couldn't go on without them. Stalin was essential because, practically and often alone, he completely understood that classical Marxism could not and did not explain modern revolutionary movements. Stalin comprehended Lenin's analysis: that the triumph of class struggle must occur within the backdrop of western imperialism's outsourcing of capitalism to what we now call the *3rd World*. Stalin, and the people around him who created the Revolution, were committed communists. They interpreted history and society in terms of class struggle as did Marx. But for Stalin, only Leninism could show the way forward. Lenin proposed that world revolution would occur when the predatory effects of international-banking and its wars of imperial conquest for ever expanding markets and cheap labor would destroy the imperialist powers; first on the periphery and then from within. This is happening in the United States right now. But all this took a lot longer than Lenin thought it would. Unlike western politicians who are power hungry hucksters thirsting for the accumulation of wealth that government service brings them, Soviet Russian Communists were driven *solely* by Marxist-Leninist ideology. After the *Fall of the Soviet Union* in 1989 the secret political achieves from the 1920's and 30's were opened. They revealed that in private conversation, the Bolshevik and Soviet leaders spoke in the same language as in their public pronouncements: class struggle, wage-slavery, the soviet economy and the nature of western capitalism and imperialism. These themes were what they confidentially spoke about among themselves, *all the time*. This was how they saw the world, and is in sharp contrast to the vapid bourgeois licensed politicians in the liberal democracies who have one message for the little people and another true agenda they keep secret among themselves.

Kulaks

In 1928 the Russian Revolution was 10 years old. Communism was established in the cities but in the countryside, where food was produced, the means of production remained in private hands. Stalin asked the Politburo if the revolution could properly and correctly succeed in this way. They determined it couldn't but that confiscation of private property in the backwoods would create more problems than it solved. Stalin pushed ahead with it anyway because he was more committed to communism than anyone else around him. A national policy of collectivization ensued with personal possessions permanently commandeered by the state. This is the essence of Marxism. The *Kulak* was a pejorative term to mean a tight-fisted peasant; one who owned property and, for the most part, lived better than his neighbors. It was they who had to give up their homes and livestock to the newly formed collective farms. Them that resisted were harshly dealt with. Many did resist for the collective was essentially a slave-labor system. The sudden change threw the nation into turmoil; for while few wanted a return of the Tsarists, a new system where the individual had neither property nor fundamental rights is by definition slavery. Stalin couldn't see this as he was committed to the outcome rather than the process. The outcome he saw was a classless society based upon social justice and the end of petty human strife: a *nirvana* on earth. That never happened although the socialists didn't give up on it and still don't. This is not to say that Russian or Soviet agriculture was successful before collective farming. It wasn't. It is also a gross oversimplification to say, as many often do, "*Stalin collectivized the farms.*" There were 120 million people in rural areas and they were all collectivized within 4 years. One man didn't do this. Stalin obviously had some help from what was a revolutionary society. There were thousands of dedicated communists who formed worker's brigades called *the Twenty-Five Thousanders*. These were mostly young workers and students who were going out into the boondocks to show the local yokels how to be a good communist. That's when the shootings, arrests and deportations began. This sort of thing is already happening in the USA. The *Democrat Party* has a new terror arm called *Antifa*, short for *Antifascist* as well as the *Black Lives Matter Global Network Foundation (BLM)*. They dress in black (the harkening to Mussolini beyond their ken), wear masks and intimidate locals with looting, arson, shakedowns and murder; all with police and government support in Democrat precincts. For the young Communists in Moscow, the Kulak arrests empowered them. The slaves were sent to camps in the industrialization program. Commentators often say that Stalin killed 10-20 million people. If he did, he had a lot of help there too, especially from *Nikita Khrushchev* who pointed the finger at Stalin when he initiated *de-Stalinization* after Stalin's death (1953). Khrushchev was a tough fighter and serial-killer who got a thrill out of mass-murder. There is no doubt that *collectivization* in the Soviet Union saw the death of millions when *The Little Ice-Age* (generally 1350-1800) finally ended and a *planetary warm-period* ensued. This solar generated heat-wave struck the northern hemisphere hard in the 1930's.

He moved the sun and moon

Stalin was so powerful he could both change the direction of the wind and ocean currents to boot. He caused famines to appear with a mere wave of the hand. When a worldwide heat spell descended upon the northern hemisphere in 1932-36 it coincided with the Politburo's decision to collectivize farms. In Ukraine they now call this the *Holodomor* and hold Stalin responsible. This is all part of the *demonization* process to denigrate not only Stalin but the whole of Russia. Famines have always been common to the region and one every four years is a periodic constant in Russian history. A famine hit in 1927-28 just as collectivization began. The eastern Ukraine and the now famous *Donbass*, populated mostly by Russians, was hit the hardest in 1932-33. It is important to note that the *Holodomor* horror story was first presented by the virulently anti-Soviet William Randolph Hearst newspaper conglomerate in a series of lurid articles that used pictures of starving people from anywhere and everywhere, including the American Civil War. The *Holodomor* story was then taken up by German propaganda minister Joseph Goebbels with newspaper titles like *The Hidden Holocaust in Ukraine by Zionist Jews* and *10 Million White Ukrainians Exterminated by Jewish Bolsheviks*. After 1945, many Ukrainians who sided with the Germans were forced to emigrate out of Ukraine in fear for their lives. It was they, now ensconced in the liberal west, who invented the *Holodomor*; a term never heard before. The horror of mass starvation was not unique to Ukraine in the 1930's but was a worldwide social catastrophe. In America it is remembered as the *Dust Bowl*. Midwestern farmers, with their crops and topsoil blown away by the hot winds, lost their farms to banks. The week of July 7-14, 1936 was especially hot with 40 states suffering 100° Fahrenheit, 16 of them over 110° degrees and 90° F in the rest of the country. In this week alone *twelve thousand people* in 86 American cities died of heat exhaustion. The current *Climate Scare* tacticians often begin their graphs with the 1940's when temperatures got cooler again. They also like to wipe out the *Medieval Warm Period* (c. 900-1350) as it just doesn't fit the narrative. The 1930's was the hottest decade of the 20th century. In America the drought lasted years and millions of people abandoned their farms and moved to California. That was how collectivization was implemented in America. Small individually owned farms disappeared and were replaced by collectives owned by industrial conglomerates. In this process, millions of Americans died of starvation and starvation related illness as it coincided with a worldwide economic depression. It is possible to determine this through the USA census figures. Nobody ever does it because any scholar that did would be out of a cushy university job.

Borderlands

Soviet foreign policy under Stalin was the same as Tsarist foreign policy and is the same as modern Russian foreign policy under Putin. They want friendly nations that serve as buffer states on their borders. This provides protection from military depredations and hence the importance of Mongolia and Korea in the east. The states that border on Russia to the west are historically called *borderlands* in Russian and that is what the name *Ukraine* means in Russian language. When Vladimir Putin says that Ukraine is not a sovereign nation he does not mean they don't have a right to independence; only that Ukraine does not exist as a separate and self-sufficient military power. It never was and never will be. In the Russian mind, borderlands like Ukraine, Finland, Poland and the Baltic States exist *only* to be controlled by some military power. Either it will be Russians or the western imperialists. At present in 2020, these borderland states worry about Russian geopolitical power and seek aid and comfort from the west, especially the United States. This is always a mistake. Poland and the Baltic States are far away and America quickly dumps any ally on the basis of even minor contingency. For example, they abandoned South Vietnam after a 10 year commitment in blood, solely for a few dollars more on their budget. The cynicism was, and always is, astounding. If Poland thinks they are about to get better treatment they probably have another thing coming.

Der Ostsiedlung

Like Germany, Russia regarded the Treaty of Versailles' border revisions with distain. As the Germans pushed east with the conquest of Poland in 1939, Russia could only react by annexing eastern Poland and the Baltic states of Estonia, Latvia and Lithuania. These were all borderlands, both for the Germans and the Russians. German eastwards migration, *der Ostsiedlung*, began centuries before with the conquest of the region around Berlin from the *Wend*s. They were the Slavic peoples that used to live there but migrated south out of harm's way towards modern Slovakia. This conquest is the origin of Prussia, the eastern Germanic state known as *Mark Brandenburg*, from the Danish word *Mark* that also means borderland. For western Europeans, the Germans became a vanguard against the savage Slavs from the faraway eastern hinterlands. The *Mark Brandenburg* was a perfect buffer state for France and problems only arose when *Napoleonic France* expanded eastward across the Rhine. That's when things began to spiral out of control as Prussia felt threatened; and they were. It all reached a tripping point with Prussia's annexation of Alsace in 1871 that led to the 1st phase of the *General European War* (1912-1923). When the war began anew, and with the defeated France finally out of the picture, the newly formed *Third German Empire (das Dritte Reich)* continued the *Ostsiedlung* into Ukraine, eastern Poland and the Baltic States. That's when things got really nasty as the border wars became world war thanks to German stupidity.

The Polish-Lithuanian Commonwealth

Five hundred years ago Lithuania was the largest nation in Europe. Through royal births and marriages the *Grand Duke of Lithuania* became *King of Poland*

and a personal union became a legal nation by the *Treaty of Lublin* (1569). At its greatest extent it included over ten million people and stretched from the Baltic Sea to southern Ukraine 800 miles away. In 1795, weakened by wars and with no natural boundaries, it was conquered and partitioned by Russia, Austria and Prussia. It then ceased to exist although the modern nations of Poland, Lithuania and Belarus (the erstwhile *Byelorussia* or *White Russia*), are its successor states. When the Russo-German war began in 1941 it was within the confines of the former Commonwealth that most of the extra-judicial killings took place. These were murders, not casualties of war. This would be not only the 5 or perhaps 6 million Jews that everybody knows so much about, but also 9-10 million Ukrainians, Byelorussians and Poles. In the years 1942-45 the former *Commonwealth* was the most dangerous place to be alive in the whole world. *Byelorussia* (now *Belarus*) was particularly hard hit with more than 2 million dead. Over ten, some say twenty thousand villages and towns were looted and destroyed with most inhabitants killed by the German Army. They saw partisans everywhere even in cribs. Poland suffered a similar fate with more than 3 million dead in addition to 2-3 million Polish Jews; nobody can say for sure. In Ukraine there was another 3 million extra-judicial killings. You can pick up any of the literally more than ten thousand books on the Jewish Holocaust and not read one single word about any of these other human disasters; even though it all happened at the same time, in the same place, and with the same killers. There is a reason for this.

PART III

THE DARWINIAN REVOLUTION AND THE POLITICS OF MASS-MURDER

THE JEWISH HOLOCAUST is one of the most compelling events to come out of the 2nd War phase. There is no doubt about its authenticity. However, serious questions exist as to the method of its execution. The historiography of the event includes movies, as well as endless and omnipresent television shows and documentaries. In addition, thousands of books that include scholarly, pop fiction and non-fiction, as well as comic and picture books, adorn every book store. The literature is so expansive that almost everybody thinks they know something, if not everything about it. It would come as a severe shock to most of these citizens that until November 1938, almost six years after Adolf Hitler formed a government in Germany, not one single Jew had been arrested, shot, raped, murdered or forced to wear a yellow Jewish star. There are often documentaries about the 1936 Berlin Olympics that say the Nazis curtailed Jewish repression for the Olympics. Do they mean the kind of oppression that African-Americans were forced to endure in American states ruled by the Democrat Party? Do they mean lynching a black grandmother for verbally scolding white children? Or do they mean separate water fountains, separate lunch counters, and special seats in the back of public transportation? Jews were never forced to endure any of these things and since most of them lived in cities, they could, if they wanted, remain anonymous. It wasn't easy for Jewish professionals to lose their jobs in the new German racial state but there was an escape mechanism and many took it. It was hard for Jews in Germany but there were no camps for Jews until large-scale war began in 1940, and those camps were in Poland, for Polish Jews. Like in the *1st War-phase*, the Germans only adopted the camp system due to the blockade. They needed industrial and farm workers with the men far away in wars all over the place. This was how nations in the death throes of modern war dealt with industrialized and monetized warfare.

The evolution of modern warfare

When the *Emperor Napoleon I* created the French version of *Mitteleuropa* in 1806 he named it *The Continental System*. Europe was then almost entirely an agricultural society as it had been for thousands of years. Industrialized society, presented now as a boon to humanity, was still very small scale. The largest army Napoleon ever commanded was an allied multi-national 600,000 man army in Russia. Most of the time, the French armies he commanded were c. 200,000 men or less. They were equipped by local mills and cottage industries. Steel was only used for swords and bayonets. The rest of the weapons were made out of iron. As for explosives, there was only gunpowder to propel missiles of war. The high explosives and massive chemical industry that produced it didn't emerge until a century later. In 1806 there was no electricity and power came entirely from wind and water. Up until 1860 warships were made of wood and powered by wind. Fifty years later the first modern battleships, not much different from those built today, were built powered by coal and constructed with steel. Europe went to war soon after but not with the cottage industries that had propelled Napoleon. Europe was now an industrial machine, centered in large cities and funded by international banks that employed millions of workers and bureaucrats. The French, with its smaller population and industrial base, would have surely lost the *1st War-phase* had not powerful allies intervened. In 1940 she stood essentially alone and the Germans wiped them out. Now it was Germany and not France that established the *Mitteleuropa* economic community. But the Germans didn't have the population to man it while war-fighting. The answer was the camp internment system that they, and the French, had invented in the *1ˢᵗ War phase* to maintain industrial growth in time of war.

Poland stirs the pot

In November 1938 there were five concentration camps in Germany. By the end of the war in 1945, there were somewhere between ten and twenty thousand. The first five were not meant for Jews but for political prisoners. There were Jews among them who were political prisoners but, contrary to popular belief, German Jews actually had a special place in Germany. They were a part of *das Abkommen*. Jewish emigration was both financially and culturally enriching for both them and the National Socialist Party thanks to the *Haavara Agreement*. Even for those that remained, German Jews were far safer than Polish Jews. Poland in 1938 was no sweet haven of democracy but was a brutal military dictatorship and the single most anti-Semitic nation in the world. Pogroms, very similar to the Tsarist ones, were regular events and officially permissible phenomena. Local thugs, backed up by police and military would, like the Cossacks of old, ride into a Jewish quarter or village and shoot the place up. They might burn some buildings, desecrate a cemetery, rape some women, or kill a few men, depending on where their drunken rage took them. Then they would ride off and finish the Vodka. Nothing like that ever happened in Germany until *Kristallnacht,* an event precipitated by Polish anti-Semitism.

Herschel Grynszpan loses his cool

When Germany graciously welcomed Austria and Sudetenland into *the Reich*, Poland got a sudden case of the heebie-jeebies. They worried that all those Polish Jews that lived in Germany, some 50,000 of them, would hurriedly want to flee back into Poland. They didn't have anything to worry about. However bad it was for a Jew in Germany it was infinitely better than life in Poland. Just to be sure, the Poles then stripped citizenship from all Polish Jews living in Germany. Why Polish leadership continually wanted to create animosity with Germany is hard to fathom. Suddenly the German bureaucracies were faced with 50,000 Polish Jews in Germany who were stateless without passports. This was when the first roundup of Jews happened in Germany. Thousands of them were pulled out of their homes and taken to the Polish border empty-handed and destitute. This was a crime. Some Jews committed suicide rather than return to Poland: that's how bad it was there. The Poles then refused them entry. In this crisis atmosphere, a Polish Jew named Herschel Grynszpan gunned down and killed Ernst vom Rath, a low-level German embassy worker in Paris. Like 90% of all homicides, the parties knew each other as they both frequented the gay bar *Le Boeuf sur le Toit* (no longer at the original location). Herschel wrote his mother that he killed Rath in retaliation for the plight of Polish Jews but then, why didn't he shoot up the Polish embassy staff instead? He also said afterwards that he and Rath were lovers and that Rath had promised and then reneged on identity papers for the Grynszpan family. Thus Grynszpan was never put on trial as the ins and outs of the affair were too sordid for the staid National Socialist societal order. Incidentally, nobody knows whatever happened to Grynszpan. There is no record of his death anywhere. In 1946 he was last seen agitating for something or another in the lovely little *Frankish* town of Bamberg, famous for its *Rauchbier* (smoked beer). He then disappeared forever although there are rumors he ended up in Israel. However it was, the radical wing of the National Socialist party now had the opportunity they were looking for. These people included primarily *Reich Propaganda Minister* Joseph Goebbels, *Reichsführer der SS* Heinrich Himmler and his fanatical deputy Reinhard Heydrich, theoretician Alfred Rosenberg as well Field Marshal Goering and the infamous Adolf Eichmann; always a low level worker bee.

Kristallnacht

The standard story about *Kristallnacht* (*Crystal Night*, or *Night of the Broken Glass*) is that it was ordered by Hitler in some sort of fit. They say it was the first step in the direction of the Jewish Holocaust and maybe it was. *Kristallnacht* on a small scale actually began on November 7th in the German city of Kassel. On the news of Rath's shooting, local *Sturmabteilung* (political Storm-troopers) decided to retaliate. They busted a few shop windows in town and the violence spread to nearby villages. The *Jewish Virtual Library* and many other sources say: *more than 1,000 synagogues were burned (and possibly as many as 2,000).* To anyone engaged in any sort of critical thinking these figures might seem absurd. Were there even 2000 synagogues in Germany? Probably there were. Most people see a synagogue as a massive ornate stone building akin to the ones in Jerusalem. There weren't that many of those in Germany and the latest tally says 267 of them were burned to the ground on *Kristallnacht*. That is an astounding figure right there. However, keep in mind that there were thousands of smaller synagogues in Germany. Like a Christian preacher who can pitch a tent, punch a Bible, give a sermon and call himself a reverend minister; any Jew can become a Rabbi. All you need is a beard, a small to reasonably sized house to call a synagogue and hopefully, some knowledge of the *Torah*. These were the Jewish synagogues that were also attacked and so the figure of 2000 isn't ridiculous. But the major events attached to *Kristallnacht* are often misrepresented, although the final verdict; that it was a nightmare for thousands of German Jews, is unquestionably accurate.

A street-fighting man

In 1928 Adolf Hitler was a political rabble-rouser and gangster *par excellence*. He knew how to get a crowd worked up and his pal Joseph Goebbels picked up the technique. He learned that free and plentiful supplies of beer did wonders. November 9th, 1938 was the 15th anniversary of the *Beer Hall Putsch* that was Hitler's first failed attempt to seize power. They were both in Munich for the big celebration. It was often held at the massive *Bürgerbräukeller*. There were also limitless supplies of *Löwenbräu* for the always thirsty *storm troopers* who packed the house and every other bar in town. At 9 PM street demonstrations against German Jews began. Goebbels, who planned the whole thing, suggested to Hitler that some sort of *Aktion* against the Jews was necessary since Rath had died that day. Goebbels:

I go to the Party reception in the Old Town Hall. Colossal activity. I brief the Führer about the matter. He orders: let the demonstrations go on. Withdraw the police. The Jews must for once feel the people's fury.

Hitler understood *Aktion* to mean some sort of major demonstration; like in the old days, a good old fashioned street fight with a few busted heads and broken jaw bones. He was adamant that the demonstrations be *"spontaneous"* and not centrally planned. With no idea what was in the works he went back to his hotel. Shortly before midnight, Chief of Police Heinrich Műller, who was in on it with Goebbels, quickly sent a telex to every police station in Germany:

Actions against Jews, in particular against their synagogues, will very shortly take place across the whole of Germany. They are not to be interrupted.

It all happened, and got completely out of control, very quickly. Heydrich was forced to send out a telex at 1:20 AM that gave instructions on what was off limits and not. It was too late. Within two hours *synagogues* all over Germany were burning. Wealthy Jews especially were pulled out of their homes. That allowed thieves like Goering to steal what they could in the next few days. Vandals smashed in Jewish storefronts; hence the name *Kristallnacht* for the broken glass. With large fires across Munich and to the wail of fire-engine sirens, Hitler was aghast and called for Hess who then sent out a telex at 2:56 AM (November 10th):

On express orders issued at the very highest level, there are to be no kind of acts of arson or outrages against Jewish property or the like on any account and under any circumstances whatsoever.

Since Hess was *Deputy Fuhrer* and the 2nd highest ranking Nazi, *orders issued at the very highest level* could only mean one thing. Within an hour the outrages stopped. Most of what you read about *Kristallnacht* will say that it lasted two days and technically that is true: about 6 hours over a period of two calendar days, November 9th & 10th. Hitler in 1938 wasn't the street fighting man of yore. He was now Chancellor of the largest nation in Western Europe and went to great pains to keep it all orderly. In a few hours, all his efforts were dashed. Historically pogroms against Jews were rare in Germany, the last one had happened in 1819 in Bavaria. The last one before that was 1614 in *Frankfurt am Main*. Now, with *der Kristallnacht*, Germany was presented and exposed to the world as a savage medieval cesspool of intolerance. After he gave instructions to Hess, Hitler immediately called upon *Hjalmar Horace Greeley Schacht*, President of the *Reichsbank*. They met that afternoon and Schacht told Hitler that the *Haavara agreement* was too restrictive; that less affluent Jews should also be given the opportunity to leave with their assets intact. Hitler agreed and a new policy was immediately implemented. But in ten months the general European war would begin and with that, the end of *das Abkommen*. Thirty thousand Jewish men were arrested in the next few days and sent to labor camps where c. 2000 elderly died, mostly from exposure and shock. The rest were released in a few weeks and told to emigrate. By this time, 300,000 had already done that; which left c. 300,000 German Jews, or *Reich Jews*, in Germany. About half of them would die, some from the Allied bombing campaigns aimed at German cities where most of them lived. Many more were forcibly deported to work camps and some were machine gunned into open pits.

Lithuania goes full medieval

At the end of August 1941 it looked like the war in the east against Russia was a winner. The General Staff didn't know that Russia had another 10 million men in reserve so it wasn't even close to over. At this time the great humanitarian Albert Speer began to implement his grand architectural schemes for Berlin. He approached Joseph Goebbels who was *Gauleiter* (Governor) of Berlin about deporting some *Reich Jews* so he could have more flexibility in his plans. Speer wanted their apartments. Goebbels wanted Berlin to be *Judenfrei* (free of Jews) so he approached Hitler about it. *Der Fuhrer* gave the go-ahead because he, like many German officials, wanted to repopulate Russian cities like Minsk with *Reich Jews*. They felt *Reich Jews* to be a much better sort than the native Jews that lived out there. They in turn would be deported to Siberia. They saw what *Reich Jews* had done for Palestine. They were the people who built it into what it is today. After Minsk, where they might very well help rebuild the Ukraine as a German colony; *Reich Jews* would then be again deported farther east. Nobody in this chain of command thought for a moment that there might be something inherently and ethically wrong with this. Nor did they imagine that the Berlin *Reich Jews* would never get to Minsk and were all doomed.

To ravage, to slaughter, to usurp under false titles, they call empire; and where they make a wasteland, they call it peace. Tacitus

Lithuania was occupied by the Soviets when they and Germany split up the spoils of war in 1939. When Germany invaded Russia in June 1941 Lithuanian hard-liners began to murder the *Baltic Jews* that lived there. They saw Jews as *non-national* people, thus internationalist, which means communist. Therefore it was open-season on them. Naturally the German Army didn't interfere. There was a fourth army group that invaded Russia in 1941, the little known *Army Group Rear-Area Command.* Attached to them were four groups of killer commandos named *Einsatzgruppen* that always operated with the Army. They needed the Army's protection because they didn't have heavy weapons and could only defend themselves against the unarmed men, women and children who were their targets. Even these Teutonic heroes had to admire the Lithuanian efficiency in murdering disarmed and helpless Jews. There were more than 100,000 Baltic Jews in Lithuania and they were all murdered in a series of pogroms in 1941-42. When the *Reich Jews* from Berlin, Vienna and *Frankfurt am Main* incidentally entered this maelstrom they were taken off their trains and shot down like animals. An eyewitness:

> *The Gestapo men and the Lithuanians ordered the people to line up in a row. Most victims were shot after they had fallen into the pits. The shots were fired from machine guns set up on the wooded hill by the graves. Those who did not run or ran in another direction were shot on site by those Lithuanians and Germans who had earlier grouped them together.*

Many Germans faced ethical qualms about the killings because they perceived a difference between German Jews and others. This feeling was widespread. General Wilhelm Kube was a homicidal maniac who gave Jewish and White Russian children candy before he killed them. *What plague and syphilis are to humanity, are Jews to the white race* he wrote. Even so, he protested the killing of German *Reich Jews*:

> *Among these Jews are front veterans with the Iron Cross first and second class, war wounded, half Aryans, and even a three-quarter Aryan ... In repeated official visits in the ghetto I have discovered that among the Jews, who distinguish themselves from Russian Jews in their personal cleanliness, are also skilled workers, who are perhaps five times as productive as Russian Jews. I am certainly tough and ready to help solve the Jewish question, but human beings who come from our own cultural sphere are something other than the native bestial hordes. Should one assign the Lithuanians and the Latvians, who are even rejected by the population here, with their slaughter? I could not do it.*

But was it an accident that the *Reich Jews* were sent to Lithuania to be killed? That and questions like it always point to the personal guilt of Adolf Hitler, the man Jews, and admittedly many others, all love to hate.

The ideology of race

Hitler, and the entire National Socialist bureaucracy, tended to see human history as one of *racial struggle for existence*. This was the Malthusian-Darwinist creed in its essence. What Hitler and the academics that supported him did was take these ideas and turn Germany into the world's first national state whose laws, education, cultural infrastructure, national policy and identity were based upon *racial ideology*. This was the *Nazi Revolution* and it was the most radical upheaval in the history of western civilization and directly responsible for its apparent downfall in the 21st Century. The Communists, like the Nazis, also wanted to entirely transform society. They sought this by altering human thought. This is why there were never any racial purges in Stalinist Russia before the war. All people were equal in the Communist system; they only needed to *think* differently. Many communists like *Nikita Khrushchev* reckoned that a slave-labor camp was the best place to rethink reality. The National Socialists wanted to achieve another sort of conversion; one in which the physiology of the human species would be transformed into a higher state, one that had *previously existed* before recorded history at the dawn of humanity. To realize this, elements within the newly emerged Germanic racial state sought the physical eradication of races they not only deemed inferior; but inhuman as well: Jews, Gypsies, Slavic peoples. This made killing them easier to swallow as it was all proven true scientifically.

Adam and Eve had immortality in their grasp

The Jews were the main target as everyone seems to know. Interestingly there are some similarities between the Nordic and Jewish creation legends. In both, there was a time in the remote past when people had super-human powers and were immortal. Adam and Eve had all the powers of God except one physical/material limitation. They existed in a perfect world, warm and lush, one so friendly they didn't even need clothes. Why would they need them? They were not only immortal but invulnerable. The proto-Aryan superior human (*der Ubermensch*) lived in a harsh northern environment that hardened him through *the struggle for existence*. Then there was a fall from grace for both. For the Jews the fall was refusal to resist the moral and spiritual temptations of materialism. The perfect world God (*Yahweh*) the creator had fashioned for them wasn't enough. They wanted more and rebelled. The revolt was a spiritual insurgence, assisted by the Fallen Angel Lucifer; ruler of the material world. Directed upon God's perfection, their rebellion centered upon material desires and temptations. Post sin and now mortal, Adam and his descendants could only find redemption through personal righteousness and the advent of the Messiah: *The Redeemer*. For *der Ubermensch*, the fall was external through the intermixing of impure blood from *der Untermensch*; sub-human beings that looked human but weren't. Their true abode was deep within the darkness of the underground and not in the shining light of the Aryan race's mystical home among the cold white mountains of the north. Redemption for the Jews was living in *Yahweh's* grace and finding salvation in the afterlife. For the Aryan ideologues, deliverance was not on an individual level but would come when the physical manifestation (*der Volkskörper*) of the *Aryan race* as an organic corporeal being was purified. The transformation would be species wide: when the *Untermensch* were driven from Europe the Aryan race would be mystically, magically and instantly transformed as a single conscious sentient being. Every member of the race would have the supernatural powers of *der Ubermensch*. For the *Exterminists*, who were in a minority, this event would be accelerated when the Jews were wiped out to the last woman and child.

How old is the earth?

All these ideas seem horrific, strange and ridiculous compared to the rigors of modern science. This is why well-meaning people seek to severely limit and even eradicate organized religion as part of the modern war on spirituality. This war is the essence of *Humanism*. As part of this, ordinarily devout Jews and Christians seek to distance themselves from the apparent absurdities of Biblical history compared with modern science. Significant in this transformation was the film *Inherit the Wind* (1960) that chronicled the *Scopes Monkey Trial* (1928). It presented dedicated Christians, or anyone who doubted the efficacy of Darwinist truth, as stupid ignorant know-nothings. In a trial setting, Spencer Tracy (as Clarence Darrow) wondered and smirked about how in the world *Yahweh* could have created the universe in just six days? *Gee willikers*, in its essence the *Big Bang* proposes the same thing happened in less than a second! Yes, that is correct. According to the theory, fully the entire mass and matter of the universe was created in a *nanosecond* at the moment of the *Big Bang*; from nothingness into all-there-is from one moment to the next! How stupid does it get and how do they get away with it? They can preach this nonsense because laws dictate that it *must be* taught in schools. Christian texts, from the Jews, propose a young earth, created by a sentient spirit being not long before the first humans. Modern science proposes a practically immeasurably old universe created from nothing and by nothing except for the one eternal measurable force they know of: *gravity*. On the face of it, that's the single most absurd idea anyone has ever come up with. In truth nobody knows the age of the earth; except to say that the problem is highly political and not easily resolved. There is no reliable empirical method to accurately measure the age of rocks which is how modern science confirms its ideas. Radio-metric dating has numerous flaws inherent in the method. Significantly there is an inherent assumption, in all forms of radio-metric dating, that the rock has remained a *"closed system."* To be accurately measured, it must have remained stable *i.e.* nothing has gone in or out, nor has it ever been molten, nor reformed in any way. That is not only quite an assumption but utterly contrary to rational thought: both argon (a gas) and potassium (in potassium-argon dating for example) are mobile elements that often move freely in and out of rocks in a short period of time. All this *"knowledge"* about the age of the earth is actually impossible to know. It's not practical to assume any of this, except that it politically supports the theory of a slow 15 billion year *evolutionary development* of the entire Universe from the *Big Bang* to you.

What is the Sun?

The *Big Bang* creation theory assures us that all the matter now in the universe, (since matter can neither be created nor destroyed) was for one instance (15 billion years ago is the guess) compressed into a tiny point, no bigger than a pin point. You got that? All the matter in the universe compressed into a point smaller than the size of a pinhead. But at that point there was no matter. There were no atoms. It was a plasma; a kind of fluid gas without atoms. What? Atoms would come later. This *Singularity* then exploded and gravitational forces and unknown *"self-organizing principles"* created hydrogen atoms and gathered them all together to form galaxies, stars, planets like the earth and life itself; all from inorganic lifeless matter. Have you ever seen an explosion organize itself into anything? What's more logical; the notion that a cloud of hydrogen gas (on its own) coalesced to form Las Vegas or that *an eternal* and *all-knowing living being* that created a man and woman in its own image? In the beginning was *The Word,* an idea, says both the Bible and Quran. To say that *Big Bang Theory* is science and that everything else is discredited myth has no validity. There isn't one single person on the earth who knows what the Sun is. Many educated people think they know what the sun made of and therefore what it is. But all anyone can know is it gives off light and heat and is made of plasma. What it actually is in the larger scheme of things can only be a guess based upon materialism. How the sun produced light and heat is theoretical and unknown. The light photon is supposed to have no mass, is not matter, and always moves at the speed of light in a vacuum. It can be (theoretically) a wave or a particle. Which one is it? Nobody knows. This is the stuff they say negates God.

Who are you?

The vast expanse of inter-stellar and inter-galactic space is a recent discovery dating from the mid 20th Century. Prior to then, it was thought that the *Milky Way Galaxy was the universe*. With better telescopes astronomers could look outwards farther and see much more. They determined that the visible universe, now seen to be made up of millions, even billions of galaxies like our own Milky Way, was *expanding*. This too is questionable as light may not behave in inter-galactic space the same way it does in a cinema or in Einstein's brain. The Greeks thought the universe always existed and *Astronomer Royal* Fred Hoyle proposed the *Steady State Theory* where the universe created a few hydrogen atoms spontaneously every few seconds. Hoyle felt that the continuous creation of atoms in an eternal universe was more logical than the creation of the entire universe all at once from nothing. It was he who derogatorily coined the term *Big Bang*. The main evidence for it is something called *cosmic microwave background radiation* that was discovered in the early 1960's. It is interpreted to be the remnants of the fantastic explosion of the *Big Bang* that created the universe. However in 1926 Eddington (and others) accurately predicted the background radiation by calculating the minimum temperature space would cool to in a universe immersed in an environment of ultra hot-bodied stars and galaxies. This makes more sense than a primeval explosion. But the *Big Bang* gives the scientific community a date by which to fix the past and a neat replacement for God. Nor did they want to admit ignorance. But it's all made up. There is nothing to it. The bigger problem is that religious people run away from Biblical history and hide from these crazy theories. They don't know that modern science is all political and the politics of it is to destroy religion: the one and only force that has the power to demolish the prevalent Humanist society.

Goering's Jurassic park

The Białowieża Forest in Poland is the last remaining tract of primeval woods that once covered Europe. Poland wants to do some strip mining there now. This continent-wide *Urwald*, or primeval forest, was destroyed by the Roman Empire's military and commercial dominion over the whole Mediterranean region. They used up wood at an alarming rate. Roman armies built a wooden fort every night when they were on the march against enemies that excelled in night fighting and ambushes. Massive shipbuilding and architectural programs in North Africa caused the deforestation of Syria, Egypt, Libya and Morocco all the way to the Atlas Mountains. This was once the habitat for the Asian elephants that Hannibal used as mounted shock troops. They are all long gone as deforestation changed the moderate climate into the desert we see today. In Europe the alteration of the *Urwald* permanently changed the structure and attitudes of the races that remained and transformed them from hunters to farmers. Two thousand years later in 1915-18 the German Army and poachers violated the last pocket of the *Urwald* by hunting the European Bison to extinction and despoiling its habitat. When they recaptured the place in 1939 Herman Goering went about restoring the Bison. The standard story is that Goering wanted a big hunting preserve for himself and his pals. What he really wanted was to re-create of the habitat that, according to Nordic legend, supported *der Ubermensch*.

Heck cattle & horses

Lutz Heck was the curator of the Berlin Zoo that once held native Africans in a caged exhibit. They were well fed and could fornicate whenever they wanted. Goering wanted Heck to restore the *Auroch* (*Bos primigenius*) also called the *Urus* that once thrived in the entire *Urwald* out to Asia and North Africa. It was a wild cattle species somewhat similar to the *Texas Longhorn* but bigger. Hunted to extinction by loss of habitat, the last recorded *Urus* died in 1627. Using Longhorns and other wild species Heck recreated a creature that resembled the *Urus*. He also fashioned a breed of horses that looked a lot like the extinct *Tarpan* (*Equus ferus ferus*) that once roamed the *Urwald*. All these new breeds still exist and Goering stocked his primeval forest with them. Pity the human inhabitants; small farmers and forest dwellers that were mercilessly driven off or killed. The newly created *Urwald* would set the geological and ecological foundations for the re-emerged *Ubermensch*, a man that would have the power of 1000 ordinary men; hence the translation of *Ubermensch* as Superman; the Nordic ideal primeval *Mensch*: one with powers and abilities far beyond those of mortal men. Anticipating Rupert Sheldrake's *morphic resonance*, the ideologues felt his emergence would initiate an immediate species-wide transmutation. The *Ubermensch* would thus win the war and establish Nordic supremacy in a world without end.

Das Ahnenerbe

Nazi Germany had an organization named *das Ahnenerbe*. There is no direct English translation. The one often given; *Ancestral Heritage*, isn't quite right because modern translators reject the heart of *Pangermanic* ideology as impossible lunacy. For the people who created *das Ahnenerbe*, they felt that even they themselves couldn't understand the full meaning of *Ahnenerbe*; hence the impossibility of accurate translation since *Ahnenerbe* doesn't make sense even in German. In theory, only the Nordic race as a complete, physical, and conscious entity could grasp it. *Ahnenerbe* (vaguely) means a barely or scarcely comprehended human inheritance. Each and every race has its own trans-human consciousness (*der Volkskörper*) and its individual members go about life (for the most part) blithely unaware of their birthright and legacy. Modern humanity's lack of cultural cohesion results in attachment to technology and materialism. Cultural conditioning teaches there is no value to anyone's racial heritage; that human origins began long ago with ape-like creatures in Africa; themselves emerged from fish and slime over aeons of mindless cell division. The Jews and Christians (by implication) as well as the Nazis, didn't believe any of this baloney. For them, human origins began in the shining light of day, in the beginning, among the world the God(s) created for them. For Jews it was in a lush earthly paradise. For the Aryans, the world was harsh, one of ice and snow where survival was in no way guaranteed.

The Elimination of the Unwanted (der unerwünscht)

In 1893 an ardent academic supporter of Darwin's theory confessed:

> *...it is really very difficult to imagine this process of natural selection in its details; and to this day it is impossible to demonstrate it in any one point.*

More than a century later, this observation is as fresh as morning dew. Ingeniously, what the Darwinists do show is that their theory is not impossible. Thus they name it *Evolution* with the implication that *neo-Darwinism* is the sole course for the *creation* of new species. Everything else is impossible superstition, pseudoscience or some combination of both. This sort of arrogance can only occur when alternative theories are outlawed, as they are in American schools. When Herbert Spencer introduced the term *Survival of the Fittest* (1864) leading Darwinists were encouraged to adopt the catch-phrase as part of their credo. This (*at last!*) was something the average person could understand as the rest of it remains indecipherable. Yes obviously, when the weak, lame and slow-afoot are weeded out of an antelope herd by predators, those that remain are the fastest among them. But how land-animals shall transform into sea-mammals, or become lions and horses and things by this process is impossible to discern. But the general principle, *survival of the fittest*, gives a plausible rationale how this might happen; just as long as you don't delve into it too deeply. Most people don't. The Eugenicists didn't. The logic of weeding out anyone deemed unfit from the human population in order to enhance the breeding potential of the survivors became irresistible. *Three Generations of Imbeciles Are Enough* wrote American Chief Justice Oliver Wendell Holmes in *Buck v. Bell* (1927). This allowed the states to forcibly sterilize "*mental defectives*" with or without their consent. Because the new Nazi government wasn't in any way opposed to it, a similar law passed named *The Prevention of Hereditary Diseases* (*Gesetz zur Verhütung erbkranken Nachwuchses*). It was based upon *the Virginia Sterilization Act of 1924* and *the California Sterilization Act of 1909*.

Tiergartenstraße 4

By 1939 the German medical profession became convinced that sterilization wasn't enough. Germany had established the *Hereditary Health Court* (*Erbgesundheitsgericht*) in 1934. Between then and 1939 the doctors sterilized 400,000 people, 90% of them women. Hitler indicated he was all for it. Here he is at the Nazi party rally in 1929:

> *If Germany was to get a million children a year and was to remove 700-800,000 of the weakest people, then the final result might even be an increase in strength. The most dangerous thing is for us to cut off the natural process of selection and thereby rob ourselves of the possibility of acquiring able people. The first born are not always the most talented or strongest people... As a result of our modern humanitarianism we are trying to maintain the weak at the expense of the healthy*

How did he get away with it? In any case, when he became Chancellor in 1933 he had other things to think about. The doctors pressed for the right to kill whomsoever they wanted but Hitler was reluctant: not because he was philosophically opposed (see above) but because he was worried about public opinion. He judged, rightly, that Germans wouldn't go along with institutionalized murder. A short time after the war with Poland began, he changed his mind. He signed a degree (still extant in the archives) to allow the mercy killing (*Gnadentod*) of terminally ill (*unheilbare*) patients. His rationale was that hospital beds were needed for wounded soldiers. Now the doctors got everything they wanted. They would be responsible not just for sterilization but could choose who would live and who would die. They began killing children first. Both nurses and doctors were involved. The doctors would decide who to kill and nurses carried out the deed. Death depended on how many visitors the inmate had. Those with few were left outside to die from the elements or starved to death. Overdoses were given to those that had concerned parents. The doctors needed to fill out phony death-certificates to make it all legit. Eventually they evolved a scam to delay to process for parents and relatives that sent money for the (already dead) child's welfare. The *Gelt* would be pocketed with nobody the wiser. It was impossible to keep the gruesome program secret and public protests began, notably among Roman Catholics. Hitler then ended T-4 in August 1941. The German medical profession didn't care. They went right on with the murders and Hitler, consumed by his new role as Commander in Chief of the Army, was kept out of the loop. After the war, the program (*The Charitable Foundation for Institutional Care*) was dubbed *T-4* because the department that oversaw the process was located at *Tiergartenstraße 4* in Berlin. To keep this in historical perspective; from 1932-72, the American medical profession, among many other human experiments, conducted the *United States Public Health Services Study of Untreated Syphilis in Black Males* in collaboration with Tuskegee University. It would observe the natural history of intentionally untreated syphilis in African-American men even though a cure (penicillin) was available.

Life unworthy of life (*Lebensunwertes Leben*)

The German medical profession was waiting for Hitler because the foundations for medical murder were all there before him. The first professional chair for Eugenics was at University College (London) in 1909. Adolf Jost had already argued in *Das Recht auf den Tod* (the right to death) that when the state asked for the ultimate sacrifice from soldiers in war, the infirm and non-productive had no right to life. More ominously came; *Die Freigabe der Vernichtung lebensunwerten Leben* (the authority to destroy unworthy life). The title says it all. In 1905 Alfred Ploetz wrote *Die Tuchtigkeit unsrer Rasse und der Schutz der Schwachen* (the fitness of our race and the protection of the weak). He introduced the term *Rassenhygiene* (racial heath) and advocated, as did all Eugenicists, death in some form, be it murder or sterilization, for the helpless. This got him a chair at the University of Munich. Hereditary medical diseases eventually became a crime as did psychological disorders, enfeeblement, anti-social behavior (*asozialen*) and alcoholism. Anyone who didn't fully and gleefully participate in *die Volksgemeinshaft* could be and was disposed of. One of Hitler's physicians, Dr. Karl Brandt, said: *You can hang the Hippocratic Oath on the surgery wall but nobody reads it.* He was right. When they hung him at Nuremburg he had a speech prepared. He was cut off when the hangmen pulled a black hood over his head and opened the trap-door. Dr. Julius Hallervorden went along with the program and collected 690 brains from the 300,000 victims. He surgically removed most of them himself. He never did anything with them. He was a ghoul whose crimes never caught up to him. When he died in 1965 he was President of the German Neuropathology Society.

Gas

Psychiatric hospitals became killing centers and six were chosen. Patients were transferred from ordinary psychiatric hospitals into them to be killed. They were officially named *Tötungsanstalt* (Death Institutes).The one at *Hadamar* in *Hesse* was typical. Carbon monoxide in cylinders from I.G. Farben was used. The gas chambers were beautifully constructed with gleaming tile and marble. They are still extant and you can visit. The doctors and nurses there celebrated their ten thousandth murder with a beer and wine party. Again most of the victims were women. Somehow, many women had difficulty adjusting to life in Nazi Germany's *Volksgemeinshaft*. A good film about this era is *Never Look Away* (2018). Nobody knows the total number of victims since the death certificates needed to be falsified. The estimates range from 300,000 to 400,000. We don't hear about these processes vey much anymore. Much more attention is given to the *Todeslagern* in the east and there is a reason for this. The crimes against the weak were against Germans by German doctors in Germany. Race didn't have anything to do with it. Euthenasia and Eugenics are still essential to modern plans for population control. The film *Planet of the Humans* (2020) pitches drastic and merciless population reduction. The focus shifts depending upon the target population because after Malthus and Darwin redirected western civilization's *raison d'être;* there *always is a target population*: excess people who longer fit into the scheme the ruling elite have for them. When the killing fields shifted to the east in 1941, the object bcame racial reduction and eventual extermination. These ideas never go away. Aldous Huxley is considered one of the great minds of western civilization; a pacifist and ideal humanist: a man of the most profound *belles lettres* and paragon of academic virtue. Here is Huxley in 1958 and you won't find too much different from Hitler in 1929:

> *(In) the 20th Century, we do nothing systematic about our breeding; but in our random and unregulated way we are not only overpopulating our planet, we are also, it would seem, making sure that these greater numbers shall be of biologically poorer quality. In the bad old days children with considerable or even slight hereditary defects rarely survived. Today, thanks to sanitation, modern pharmacology and the social conscience, most of the children born with hereditary defects reach maturity and multiply their kind.*

Even before it became vogue, Huxley harkens onto Malthusian over-population. There is too much life he says. Death, for Huxley and his elitist pals, is the core tenant in the propagation of successful life; which is the kern feature of the Darwinian and Hitlerian worldview.

> *There is something at work in my soul, which I do not understand*   the Frankenstein Monster

The Americans have an organization named *DARPA* short for *Defense Advanced Research Projects Agency*. Most Americans have never heard of it. It was founded by a group of Nazi scientists brought into the United States as part of *Operation Paperclip*; a CIA plan to install anti-Soviet Nazi science and scientists into the fabric of American society. They did a good job: brought them in by the thousands, few questions asked. The most visible among them was *SS Colonel Werner von Braun* who built American rockets. He was often a smiling affable guest on Walt Disney's *Mickey Mouse Club* where he introduced enthralled young *Mouseketeers* into the wizardry of intercontinental ballistic missiles. The slave labor days were behind him. So too for the other jolly fellows brought in by *Operation Paperclip*, all of whom, they swore, were absolutely not involved in war crimes. *DARPA* was just another cool landing spot where the former *Blackshirts* felt right at home. They found employment in American war industries and universities building bombs and experimental death-rays as well as weeding out any law-abiding American who got in the way. The sort of thing that *DARPA* works on now include grand ideas like inserting insect brains into robots that can analyze their own source code to mate and reproduce with other robots. They call it *high-tech Darwinism*. What could possibly go wrong? There is no oversight whatsoever. There is never any oversight because the American legislative branch has no say in the matter, not that they ever would or could object as death by political assassination awaits. *DARPA* is a think-tank for mad scientists with absolutely no ethical or moral boundaries and is a microcosm for what every level of American society has become, thanks in part to *Operation Paperclip*. *DARPA* represents the anti-clerical triumph of the enlightenment over the *Rights of Man* that the American founders based their constitution upon, slavery notwithstanding. They felt there is a natural law present in the heart of every human derived directly from the godhead. Two hundred fifty years later, Judeo-Christian ethics and decency exist only in small pockets deep within the American heartland whose eradication proceeds like a harrowing and seemingly unstoppable nightmare. The atheistic ruling elite, centered on the coastal plains, direct their internationalist paranoia upon a world that must be *Americanized* for global redemption or else be annihilated for their own good. For them, the God of Abraham and Isaiah is a meaningless joke, and Jesus a biologically determined pathological freak. The military power that springs forth from *DARPA's* debased fountainhead of evil is the only policy they know. It mercilessly destroys any and all possible threats to their supremacy and allows them to suck the life force and wealth out of the American nation and its people free of charge. Even better, the fleeced suckers have no clue what is happening to them.

Flüssiges Brod

Amalie Emmy Noether was perhaps (after Newton) the greatest mathematician who ever lived. She was born and taught at *Erlangen*, a small provincial capital in Franconia (*Franken*), itself a part of Bavaria. Like nearly all Bavarians, the folks in *Franken* like barbecue and beer; a beverage they call *flüssiges Brod* (liquid bread). Most of them like to start the day with a cold one. The dialect they speak there (*Frankish*) is undecipherable to the people in the far north of Germany where they speak Frisian (*de friesischn Sprochn*); the tongue now spoken that most closely resembles *Old English*; the language of *Beowulf*. If you want to know what that sounded like, take a vacation in *Schleswig-Holstein* and *Ostfriesland* where they also just happen make the sweetest gin (*Doornkaat*). The speech that binds the various German regions, each with their own distinct dialect, is High-German (*Hochdeutsch*), spoken in central Germany. It is the common language in Germany; everybody understands it, and it is the lingo of televised newscasts and the educational system. If you want to get anywhere in Germany you have to be able to speak it. Emmy Noether's language was theoretical algebra and this got her in trouble with many of the leading big-wig German mathematicians and physicists. They felt that the modern prominence of theoretical approaches to understanding the world, and the corresponding emphasis upon the strict dogmatic interpretation of empirical data and math, would destroy not just the spiritual fabric of society but lead science down misbegotten paths. One only needs to take a quick look at the modern social order to see that maybe they were right. Emmy's problems were further exacerbated when the Nazis passed the *Nuremburg Race Laws* in 1935. There weren't many Jews in *Franken* but she was one of them and lost her job.

The Age of Relativity

Albert Einstein is the most renowned theoretical mathematician and most people are of the opinion that his proofs are unassailable. They never were and still aren't. Emmy Noether put time into proving some of Einstein's wilder propositions (no one else could) and he gave her some grudging praise considering that as a woman she was naturally beneath him (as was everybody else). The question never posed is: what *is* Einstein's actual contribution to civilization? Is it better than the people who built the great canals? How about the builders of the world-wide railroad net? What of the great bridges? Were Einstein's theories more important than the invention of modern refrigeration?

In truth Einstein's only contribution to society was the equation $E=MC^2$ that gave people the idea to build *the Bomb*. It would have been built with or without him. The equation's equivalent (mv^2) was originally proposed by *Olinto De Pretto* two years before in 1903. All the rest of it is theorems that very few people can even claim to understand. His notion that the speed of light is absolutely limited disconnected the universe from the sum of its parts. It made interstellar and intergalactic communication impractical and impossible. In a larger sense it meant that the universe, *the Cosmos*, had no larger identity than individual stars haphazardly coalesced into galaxies through the inexorable power of gravity. Even though Einstein's theory about the speed of light is still gospel, it has been often refuted (*Tifft's Data* on *quantized redshifts*; Halton Arp, [1986, 1998], Hoyle, Burbidge, Narlikar, [2000], for example). Newton's postulates are easy to understand. Why is it though, that there are hundreds of books and articles written to explain *Relativity* but none of them can do it? There is a reason for this. The assumptions that underlie *Relativity* may very well be wrong. *The Special Theory of Relativity* (1905) is all about the behavior of light and motion relative to it. Who can truly prove it? What is light? It was up to Einstein to define it and he proposed a physical impossibility; that light is made up of *photons*, actual physical particles that have energy but no mass. It's never been proven because still, at this minute, nobody knows what light is. Just as significantly, Einstein presented, with equations, that the *Luminiferous Aether* didn't exist: that light didn't need it to travel through space. The *Aether* was thought to be the physical body of space that we now regard (thanks to Einstein) as a vacuum. But is it? The *Aether* is a physical body that joins the entire universe into a connected and coherent system and makes interstellar and intergalactic communication feasible. Its negation was essential to Einstein's theories that establish an absolute and immutable value for the speed of light. One only needs to observe galaxies at vast inter-galactic distances that physically interact with one another to *intuitively know* that there must be some medium between them. Why shouldn't it be such? Even though the elimination of the *Aether* is necessary to Einstein's theories, science now implies it exists because, theory notwithstanding, it is essential to make sense of the Cosmos. The new *Aether* is called the *Higgs Field* as the search goes on for the elusive *Higgs Bison* as well as *quarks;* both of them invisible and indeterminable. Then there is that vast imperceptible body, *Dark Matter* and *Dark Energy*, thought to be 90% of the universe; both of them invisible and completely theoretical but (again) made necessary to exist only to make Einstein's theorems work.

> *What causes gravity and mass? These questions still baffle all of us.* The Astronomer Royal 2020

It is now indispensable to invent an imaginary universe to make *Special Relativity* seem valid. Modern research, centered upon Einstein's notions about the role of mass and gravity, depends upon it. Like Darwin's theory, itself a sociological phenomenon, Einstein's theories dictate the course of study and all results are interpreted according to it; even when it makes no sense. There is no proof that *Black Holes* exist except in Stephen Hawking's mind. The experiments said to prove them are fabricated in advance to confirm impossible observations. There are other explanations outside of Einstein's vision but those are (of course) discarded and suppressed. It's a sham centered upon Einstein's mystical vision of the universe in which gravity alone (as material god) determines the nature of everything. His obscure ideas became fact as western civilization discarded the Judeo-Christian cosmology of immutable God given decrees centered on the *Ten Commandments* and Jesus' *Sermon on the Mount*. The Laws set down by Moses and the creation of the cosmos by the God of Abraham, are replaced for one of overall cultural relativity and diversity as part of a larger sociological trend. Thus modern society emerged as one where there are no moral certainties, nor societal absolutes. Without clear-cut visions of right and wrong, anything goes. In the *Age of Relativity*, justice and cultural norms are viewed mutable and all human behavior depends upon relatively perceived environmental and social circumstances that have no lasting and intrinsic value. A civilization with these core values can evidently not last.

Deutsche Physik becomes Arische Physik

Obviously the invention of the door knob has far greater social impact than any of Einstein's theories. German physicists recognized this and promoted what they called German Physics (*Deutsche Physik*). This was practical physics applied to German engineering that led the world and produced (among myriad other things) the first ballistic missiles. But you don't need Einstein's math to shoot a rocket to the moon or the outer planets. Newton's *Philosophiæ Naturalis Principia Mathematica* (1687) and the invention of calculus (by Newton and Leibniz independently) gives you everything you need. Classical physics was based upon observation and the testing and verification of ideas by experiment. Einstein's theorems have none of that except for essentially inconsequential notions (that may nevertheless be wrong) about gravity's effect upon light. This annoyed quite a few German physicists who were more down to earth and (rightfully) didn't see any practical applications garnered from fellows before a chalkboard scribbling mysterious equations. When the Nazis took over and transformed German society into a racial state, *Deutsche Physik* was transformed into the absurdity of *Arische Physik* (Aryan Physics). This would eventually bring it into disrepute. As a race, Jews have the highest IQ in the world. They (and Indians) excel in theoretical math. The notion of an impenetrable Jewish Physics (*Jüdische Physik*) that led to nothing of practical worth was negated by the explosion of *The Bomb*. That seemed to settle the issue. But none of Einstein's ideas are essential to its construction. Newton could have done it given the material. The success of nuclear physics in winning the war undermined the essentially true nature *Deutsche Physik* when Germany lost it. All ideas even remotely associated with Nazi Germany were outlawed and culturally crushed. Einstein himself and his ideas (even though nobody understood them) attained cult status as the West rejected the notion of absolute Judeo-Christian ethical values.

Geopolitik

Geopolitics is the notion that geography determines the history of the world and modern Americans don't know a thing about it. They think the world belongs to them by the right of their perfection and in some respects they are correct. The American landmass lies upon a privileged position: it has 25,000 miles of navigable rivers; more than the rest of the world combined. They have vast population centers that sit upon two big oceans and their trade routes. American consumer economy is as large as the rest of the world combined. This is all due to their geographic setting. However, beyond all that is the dangerous expectation that the whole world must adopt not only superficial and transient American values, but accept the American political system, in its entirety, no matter where they reside. Geopolitical rational looks at the world differently. It isn't voting blocks in corrupt legislatures that decide how people think and behave. Rather, among the ruling elite that have the authority to move nations and people, geopolitical power directs them towards outcomes that are determined by geography. Largely, *Geopolitik* holds that civilizations draw their strength from a mystical base centered upon the earth and its soil. This does not negate the role of the individual. Rather, those societies and their leaders that recognize the role of geography will find an uncomplicated path to national security and stability. Geopolitical theorist Mackinder (1919):

> *I have no wish to stray into excessive materialism. Man and not nature initiates, but nature in large measure controls.*

This is foreign and impossible to the American mindset that is focused upon empirical rationality. What forces prompted American *Manifest Destiny*? Whatever it was, it is now largely forgotten and seldom discussed in any meaningful way, except under the generalized term *American Exceptionalism*. In today's political climate, this means that America has the right, geopolitically, to do whatever it wants under no physical or moral constraint. However, in the current *Age of Outsourcing*, American power is not centered upon its uniquely favorable geographical position. Instead an *internationalist worldview* now sees military might as the hub of its strength. Its economy is based upon that might but it is illusionary and can come and go. Geography doesn't change and neither do the principles of geographical power. With America's true source of power exported (its people's wealth and their well-being) America's innate geographical supremacy is squandered for the temporary assets of the few. This can only end in disaster. According to Geopolitical doctrine, the Eurasian landmass, or *World Island*, is the center of the world: not the Pentagon and Federal Reserve Bank. This idea was established in the 19th Century and, right for its time, it is now wrong. But nations act as if it were still true. One of the founders of the *Heartland* thesis was *Halford John Mackinder* whose theory he himself summed up in 1907:

> *Who rules East Europe commands the Heartland; who rules the Heartland commands the World-Island; who rules the World-Island commands the world.*

Since Germans ruled East Europe, this theory fit right into *Blut und Boden* and *Pan Germanic* notions that saw a magical interaction between humans and land; the one influencing the other on hallowed earth. Hence the Germanic drive to the east, the fabled *Drang nach Osten* that would control the *World-Island*. Hitler didn't invent this. He acted upon it because he was in a unique position of power to do so. If he didn't act, he would have been discarded. Trying to psychoanalyze Hitler's actions in terms of his *oedipal* relationship with his mother won't ever get to the point. Germany is an eastern European nation. It is western only in that American institutions were shoved down its throat upon catastrophic defeat. Eastward was the course they set for 500 years. If it weren't Hitler, some other Germanic nationalist would have invaded Russia. Never considering the possibility of defeat, they rolled the dice and came up empty. In 1939 Berlin was in the center of Germany and 350 miles from Warsaw. Geographically Berlin is (of course) still in the same place it ever was but not relative to Poland. Berlin is no longer in Germany's center but instead lies close to Germany's eastern edge; only 60 miles from Poland. The cataclysm of defeat in 1945 abruptly and violently shoved her borders and peoples westward away from the *World-Island*. Now the *Heartland* is owned by Russia and Ukraine with Poland close to them both. Thus we now see American military bases in Poland and the Baltic States as 19th Century minds direct their traffic. In the 21st Century, American political action behaves *as if* old-school Geopolitics directs it. And it does. But there is no sense of reality about it because the old theory is archaic. America (north and south) is now the *World Island* and has been since Hiroshima was obliterated. Thus we see *America First* as leading elements in the US Army (hopefully) want to withdraw to more sensible operational boundaries closer to home. Donald Trump is their candidate. Their opponents; the Globalist/communist/socialist elite, (as well as the Air Force and Navy that would see a reduction in their global power) are the ones obsessed with world dominion. Choking on their own ignorance, America's academic and socialist elite are suddenly obsessed with the Kiev-Moscow alignment like it's a new thing. They are willing to risk nuclear war to empower Ukraine while destabilizing Russia with blockades and embargoes. How can the fate of the Ukraine and the Crimea be of any geopolitical interest to the United States? Ignorant of historical developments because their jobs depend on it, and blinded by military omnipotence, America's ruling and academic elite behave like a gang of drunken louts.

Der Sonderweg

Nowadays the definition of *der Sonderweg*, the Germanic special, unique path forward in history, is given as one towards the establishment of democracy. Wikipedia:

> *the theory in German historiography that considers the German-speaking lands or the country Germany itself to have followed a course from aristocracy to democracy unlike any other in Europe.*

This is a joke; utterly laughable and pathetic. This kind of thinking, completely representative of American academic opinion and therefore its ruling elite, presents the notion that western liberalism is without question some magnificent goal that only the blessed may attain and one that every nation on earth aspires to whether they know it or not. Germany had to take a special path to get there. This is enough to make any German patriot want to kneel before a toilet and vomit. Surely abortion on demand, 24-hour live-streaming pornography, unisex toilets, surgically transgendered children, cross-sex hormones for 8-year olds and a smorgasbord of recreational drugs on every street corner are universal values that every nation on the face of the earth must have, no? Historically, since *Varus* and his three legions were annihilated in the *Teutoburg Forest*, Germany generally rejected the west until it was too often thrust upon them by Napoleon, Eisenhower and Stalin. At the same time, and only since Bismarck, they present liberal values to ordinary people; like the social security net that all western nations copied from them. Germany was always a world leader in every form of endeavor. You name it: forestry, engineering, applied or theoretical physics, literature, chemistry, architecture; the list goes on. Their only abject failure was in modern industrialized warfare. They were dismal at it and unable to comprehend its problems. In the end, the Red Army and American firepower was too much for them. That, along with Anglo-American duplicity, overwhelmed and, for all intents and purposes, exterminated the German nation. It's only a matter of time now.

The 8th Air Force re-enters the fray

German civilians got a reprieve from bombing when the defeated *8th Air Force* withdrew from the fight in 1943. When they attacked again it was against *Luftwaffe* targets with the aim of destroying it. The Germans had already figured this out and built massive underground factories out in the Harz Mountain staffed with slave labor. The 8th Air Force would achieve *Air Supremacy*, the next rung up the ladder from *Air Superiority*. They were able to escort their bombers with the improved P-51 that had extended range and a new English *Rolls-Royce Merlin* high performance engine. This sort of technological exchange between allies was something the Axis Powers never figured out. Under constant attack, *der Luftwaffe* began to run out of pilots and high octane aviation fuel. While they had some new and very hot interceptors, the Luftwaffe's main fighter was still the Me-109 that was operational in 1939 and now outmoded. Whatever they had, and that included too few Me-262 jet fighters, they couldn't compete with the P-51 that could hold its own with Russian jets in Korea, six years later. The Americans, who had support from the *Royal Air Force*, overwhelmed them with both quality and quantity. In the spring of 1944, 8th Air Force's mission shifted to support the Normandy invasions. But when the German Army was driven out of France in the fall of 1944, *around the clock terror bombing* of Germany would begin anew and continue to the very last days of the war in May, 1945.

WAR AND MIGRATION 1860-2020

There'll be blue birds over the white cliffs of Dover   Vera Lynn

What happened to Germany in the winter and spring of 1945 is impossible to describe. The films and images of the bombed out cities can never conceptually express the horror. One possible way is to imagine a situation where you have lost everything you ever had, even mementoes. There is nothing left. The house is gone. The spouse and children are gone; all in one day to the next. The civil and protective environment you grew up with is gone forever. There is an old woman down the street rummaging through garbage with a spoon. There is no running water, nor toilet facilities. Disease, especially typhus is rampant. Bodies lay in the streets. Rats that carry the typhus are everywhere nibbling at corpses. The stench of death is everywhere. The British Air Force, the *RAF*, seldom tried to attack military targets like the Americans. Their losses were just as awful. Their operational plan proposed that night bombing would reduce losses. It didn't. They lost over 8,000 bombers, 55,000 killed, 8,000 wounded, 10,000 prisoners; out of 125,000 crew for an astounding 58% casualty rate. Those are impossible losses. One can only continue with an operation like that if the men's lives mean nothing. And they didn't. What do you say to 110,000 parents of those 55,000 dead, most of them teenagers in the prime of life? The RAF's stated mission was to "*de-house*" workers. However that might be, most German men were away at the front somewhere; all 15 million of them. Germany had evolved the *camp system* in both world wars. Almost all the workers were slaves housed in camps and most of the industry was scattered outside cities. Thus German war production faced problems that the Americans didn't need to face. The American bomber factory at Willow Run Michigan churned out a fresh B-24 heavy bomber every 63 minutes, round the clock. The Germans couldn't concentrate production like that on account of American bombing. Even though the RAF couldn't hit anything they aimed at, Germany had to stop producing bombers altogether in favor of defense. Their best bomber, the twin-engined Ju-88, was converted into a radar-directed night fighter because it was that fast and versatile. With the entirety of Luftwaffe strength switched to the epic air battle *Defense of the Reich*, the army suffered from lack of ground support. So yes, indirectly, bombing did help shorten the war. The shocking losses are all rationalized because the mission was vital to the destruction of the most evil regime in the whole history of the world led by the most evil man there ever was. What could be more important than that? So they kept on with it, despite the losses, because, for the RAF, the mission object was purely destruction and annihilation. The RAF knew that while their planes were difficult to see at night, they also had no escorts and no defense. German searchlights were first-rate and once the bombers got lit up over a target, the flak decimated them. German night-fighters were radar equipped and shot the bombers down on the way in and on the way out again, just like they did to the Americans in the daytime. But unlike the Yanks, *RAF* bombers didn't have any escorts at night. It didn't matter. All those young men were expendable. It wasn't a military operation but a social one.

The destruction of German civil society

In 1945 they went after small medieval towns made of wood with incendiaries. Medieval universities, libraries, churches, farmer's markets; they were all targets.

> *You must understand that this war is not against Hitler or National Socialism, but against the strength of the German people, which is to be smashed once and for all, regardless of whether it is in the hands of Hitler or a Jesuit priest.* Churchill

In the end the Americans were no better. They ran out of real targets and joined the British in destroying Germany as a nation. Bayreuth was targeted because it was Wagner's birthplace. Nuremburg, another wooden medieval city with no military value, was hit with a 1000 plane raid on Hitler's birthday. Pope Benedict's 1915 forlorn plea to halt *The Suicide of Europe* only got worse. All sides in the war were now ethically indistinguishable as mass murderers rose to the top and stayed there.

> *We have got to be tough with Germany. You either have to castrate the German people or you have got to treat them so they can't just go on reproducing people who want to continue as in the past.* Roosevelt

The American President harkens to the Eugenist lobby and speaks to the castration of the German people; the ruination of their reproductive capacity. What sort of political geniuses were these fellows? Couldn't they imagine that the extinction of Germany and its thousand year old culture would have incalculable effects upon the rest of Europe and the world? As the last orange embers of the German inner cities slowly turned to ash, Churchill asked an aide: *What will we see between the snows of Siberia and the white cliffs of Dover?* He only began thinking about Russian hegemony in Europe as Germany lay in utter ruin resultant to his policies. There were people who understood what was happening. *The Lord Bishop of Chichester*: February 9th, 1944:

> *It would seem to be indicated that an effort, a great effort should be made to try to save the remaining inner towns. In the fifth year of the war it must surely be apparent to any but the most complacent and reckless how far the destruction of European culture has already gone. We ought to think once, twice, and three times before destroying the rest. Something can still be saved if it is realized by the authorities that the industrial centers, generally speaking, lie outside the old inner parts where there are the historical monuments.*

The bishop was vilified. In fact, his speech had the opposite effect. The ancient city centers, all made of wood, became the primary targets. Germany was to be obliterated. *Berlin Year Zero* (1948) shows the destroyed city from ground level. When the collapse came in May 1945, the victors refused to recognize that Germany even had a government. They accepted only the surrender of the German armed forces (*der Wehrmacht*). The *Allied Armies* became Germany's new administration and they were ruthless and vindictive. The bombing stripped Germany of its national and cultural inheritance. Still occupied by American, Russian and British troops, a legal surrender was not signed until 1990. Emotionally and psychologically ruined, the German rump state was, and still is, allowed only partial sovereignty. The god of American consumerism replaced the apparent malevolence of German national identity. Neutered militarily, Germany became a flaccid banker's paradise cheerfully subservient to American geopolitical whims. Their green, grim, but trendy pantsuit government now pimps the virtue of open borders. Ordinary Germans, dumbed down into historical ignorance and lethargy by decades of drug and alcohol fueled material excess, are passive and supine. Befuddled both emotionally and politically, they do not and cannot grasp the completely evident scheme to physically eradicate them from the face of the earth.

The curious case of Anne Frank

Anne Frank was a beautiful darling Jewish girl who died of typhus in 1945. Most people know she kept a diary that chronicled her arrest and journey to Auschwitz. When she got there, with her sister Margot, mother Edith and father Otto, they were all immediately tattooed with a number so the camp authorities could keep track of them. Auschwitz was the only camp where prisoners were tattooed. So the first question one might logically ask is: why tattoo people who are going to be killed? This is a death camp right? Otto was 56 and sickly. Why wasn't the old Jew sent directly into a gas chamber? Instead, Otto was kept under care *for six months* in the camp infirmary and brought back to health. Liberated by the Red Army he eventually settled in Switzerland and died there in 1980. Anne herself was skinny as a rail and not much good for anything except calligraphy. She, her sister and mother all quickly ended up in the infirmary where Edith died of disease or starvation, or probably a combination of both. Why weren't they all just gassed? It is a documented fact that of the 13 people arrested with Anne, none were gassed. Why were these essentially useless Jews nursed back to health? At this point in time, a typhus epidemic swept Europe and food was scarce. Auschwitz is supposed to be the ultimate Darwinian death-trap. Nevertheless, the Frank family was kept alive. Anne and Margot, weak and for all intents and purposes helpless, were transferred to Bergen-Belsen in northwest Germany so as to save them from the barbaric Red hordes. Once there, she and her sister weren't gassed because there were no gas chambers at Bergen-Belsen, nor at any other camp in Germany. Legend has it that the place was a death camp. It wasn't pleasant but people weren't murdered there. The camp was, however, routinely bombed and strafed as Germany was a free-fire zone for Allied fighter-bombers. Josef Kramer, Commandant of the Bergen-Belsen camp:

The camp was not really inefficient before you [British and American forces] crossed the Rhine. There was running water, regular meals of a kind. But then they suddenly began to send me trainloads of new prisoners from all over Germany. It was impossible to cope with them. Then as a last straw the Allies bombed the electric plant that pumped our water. Loads of food was unable to reach the camp because of the Allied fighters. Then things really got out of hand. I did not even have sufficient staff to bury the dead, let alone segregate the sick. I tried to get medicines and food for the prisoners and I failed. I was swamped.

Anne and Margot, weakened by starvation, died of typhus few weeks before the British Army arrived. There were 60,000 prisoners alive there when the British liberated the place in April 1945. They then took over administration of the camp. Within three months, 30,000 of the prisoners were dead from starvation and disease.

Psychopaths in uniform

Amon Göth was the antagonist in the film *Shindler's List* (1993). He was a sadistic homicidal maniac and serial killer. There were no gas chambers in Göth's camp and he murdered prisoners indiscriminately with gunshots. Obviously he was insane. Most people think a serial killer is some sort of social outcast who lives in his mother's basement with a pet hamster. Much more often than not, the serial killer wears a uniform and is part of a large organization. Every year, *one million, five hundred thousand people* die in American hospital. *Two hundred and fifty thousand* of them have no medical problem when they enter hospital. Places like this are very fertile ground for serial killers, and killer doctors and nurses are well documented. In some cases their victims number in the hundreds. Those excessive medical murderers are the ones caught. Many more, one might assume, who kill only a few innocent victims per year, remain on the job. Nurses are afraid of them and often refrain from reporting repeated malpractice lest they themselves lose their job (or their life). However it is, the death toll is astounding. Every 10 years, and the numbers remain consistent, *fifteen million people* die in American hospitals.

THE DARWINIAN REVOLUTION AND THE POLITICS OF MASS-MURDER

This is why there are so many *good doctor* shows on television. There are many documented killer cops as well. Cop shows fill the airways and not without purpose. Killer soldiers are out there too. Every sociopathic commander who ordered a frontal assault against dug-in Vietnamese machines guns is one. Serial killers can find themselves promoted and admired in any organization where death abounds. It happens all the time and the *Nazi SS* was not an exception. Studies show that psychopaths tend to be very glib and convincing in their oral presentations. It's how they gain advantage over people to gain respect and advance to the top in organizations like banking, government, the corporate world in general as well as the prison system. Göth was the commandant of the *Kraków-Płaszów* labor camp. The *Schutzstaffel* (protection staff) had many people like Göth at the top because traits like vicious ruthlessness were admired in that organization. But the systematic random murder of people who were in the camp system as laborers was obviously counter-productive. The German Army hated their roundup mission and had no interest in creating partisan problems for themselves by sending workers to be murdered by scum like Göth. In a letter dated December 28, 1942 (*Nuremberg document PS-2171, Annex 2. NC&A "red series," Vol. 4, pp. 833-834*) the head of *SS* camp administration writes to all the camps:

> *Camp physicians must use all means at their disposal to significantly reduce the death rate in the various camps. The camp doctors must supervise more often than in the past the nutrition of the prisoners and, in cooperation with the administration, submit improvement recommendations to the camp commandants. The Reichsführer SS (Himmler) has ordered that the death rate absolutely must be reduced.*

Göth terrorized everybody before he was finally relieved of command and *arrested by German authorities* in September 1944. You didn't see that part of the story in the movie. He was charged with methodical violations of regulations regarding the care, treatment and punishment of prisoners. Göth was a very dangerous man. Nevertheless, some officer, or group of officers, had to risk their own lives to circumvent the chain of command and get this fellow dismissed. It took courage to get paperwork completed and sent to the proper authorities without the sadistic killer finding out about it. Once he was replaced, the new camp commander ended all the extra-judicial killing. Göth was due to be tried before SS judge *Georg Konrad Morgen* who was noteworthy in his attempts to clean up the camps, many of which were ruled by psychotic sociopaths. Göth was eventually hung by the Poles in 1946. Situations like this prompted a number of group experiments after the war. *The Stanford Prison Experiment* and the *Milgram Obedience Experiment* and many others showed that ordinary people will not only *quickly* adapt to authoritarian penitentiary systems, but will often be prepared to administer lethal punishments upon orders from some authority figure with only an imaginary title and white coat.

Holocaust denial

One may freely admit that five million Jews were murdered in Eastern Europe and still be sent to prison for it. The Holocaust chronology requires absolute strict conformity as to the nature and mechanism of the crime. The machinery *must be* systematic murder with gas. Any deviation from the standard story is met with howling abuse, intimidation and finally arrest in most European countries. The crime *Holocaust Denial* or *Incitement to Racial Hatred* depends on which country you are in. What's even more astounding is that once accused of *Holocaust Denial*, the accused may not defend the allegation! The logic is irrefutable: to defend one's self against *Holocaust Denial*, and to present evidence in defense against the charge, would be, *ipso facto,* Holocaust Denial, which is a crime. Welcome to the rabbit hole. The essential ingredient, the *sine qua non*, is that Auschwitz was a systemic murder factory and the central organ in the execution of the atrocity. The problem is little direct evidence supports the standard chronology. Deborah Lipstadt:

> *Our objective should be to create a society where denial of the genocide is seen as so outrageous and so despicable that anyone who engages in it would be rendered a pariah.*

Well they've done that. It is now practically impossible to talk about the Holocaust rationally. Twelve European countries, many of them historically involved in the process, have outlawed the dissemination of revisionist research results on the internet. A big problem with the Holocaust legend is that the story keeps changing, and not just slightly. *Falsus in uno, falsus in omnibus* said the Latins. It's a principle of jurisprudence: *a witness who testifies falsely about one matter is not credible to testify about any matter.* When the Poles first turned Auschwitz into a tourist attraction, the sign at the entrance said 4 million Jews were gassed and incinerated there. Good for business. Slowly, coherent people came to the conclusion that in two and a half year's time it was physically impossible to kill that many people within the facilities in Auschwitz. So then the figure was reduced to 2.5 million. That was still impossible to swallow. Now the tally is 1.1 million: all gassed (except for the Frank family & friends). But the problem now is the admission that the gas chamber in Auschwitz is a "*reproduction*" built by the *Red Army* in 1948. The sign at the entrance says so in very small print. *David Irving* spent one year in an Austrian jail for saying that. While in prison he discovered, interestingly enough, his own books in the prison library. There were two genuine gas chambers at Auschwitz. They were named *The Red House* and *The White House*. Both were small buildings now in ruins. They were used to delouse clothes with the infamous Zyklon-B gas or to put dying people out of their misery. You won't see them on a tour of the camp, but the guides will show you them if you ask. Rudolf Hoess was commander of the Auschwitz camp. He was put on trial at Nuremburg and admitted to overseeing the murder of 2.5 million Jews. He also later testified that he was tortured and this was admitted by his captors in 1983. In his final weeks alive he confessed that he had told the victors what they wanted to hear. In translation:

> *Certainly, I signed a statement that I killed two million Jews. But I could just as well have said that it was five million Jews. There are certain methods by which any confession can be obtained, whether it is true or not.*

In his final disposition to the *Polish Supreme National Tribunal* before he was hung, he admitted to 350,000 deaths at Auschwitz by starvation and disease.

> *Every Jew, somewhere in his being, should set apart a zone of hate-healthy, virile hate – for what the German personifies and for what persists in the German.* — Elie Wiesel

There are many logical inconsistencies in the Auschwitz story that offend any righteous Jews who remain among the rational. How is it that over a million Jews calmly walked into a gas chamber without offering any attempt at revolt? This part of the story, and the victim mentality that goes along with it, really ticks off a lot of ordinary Jews. Why was there a nursery and kindergarten in the camp and why did the midwives there celebrate the one thousandth birth? The legend says that any Jew who got pregnant was immediately gassed. Why was there a swimming pool for the prisoners? With two thousand people, on average, gassed and incinerated every day for years on end, all in full view of the pool; who would want to go for a swim? Why were there theater productions and an orchestra for the prisoners? Or a sports field where prisoners would play the guards in soccer? The camp held 35,000 prisoners and many of them went to work each day next to the alleged gas chamber they could easily see. Wouldn't they hear the screams in the night from a genocidal process that went on around the clock? Detailed aerial recon taken in 1944 and declassified in 1979 show no trace of corpses, smoking crematoria chimneys nor masses of silent Jews sheepishly awaiting death. Why only 12 standard individual crematoria like those used in funeral homes? The legend has it that thousands of bodies were hauled *manually and individually* on large stretchers up stairs from the gas chambers to the furnaces. To make the numbers work, the official history says up to six bodies were stuffed into funeral home crematoria designed for one. It takes two hours to incinerate a single human body. The narrative has it this was the most elaborate mass-murder facility ever constructed. If the death toll were true, why didn't German engineers build instead a conveyer belt and a blast furnace for the massive piles of corpses that needed to be disposed of in a round the clock operation? If you look at some of the construction programs organized by the German Army this would have been an *easy* building project. These were the people who invented modern mechanical engineering. Why did Auschwitz remain essentially a low-tech operation when the whole of the German Reich was supposed to be transporting millions of Jews there just to be killed and disposed of? The more you delve into the story the more implausible it becomes; and therefore the more violent the reaction to any opposition. Rational discussion about these issues is a crime and *Wrong-Think*. There can be no questions asked and silence is the ultimate safety net for dissenting voices.

Lamp shades

Karl-Otto Koch commanded the *Buchenwald* labor camp near Weimar. He was another murderous psychopath arrested and shot by the *Schutzstaffel* for crimes against the prisoners. His wife, *Ilse Koch* sometimes called *The Bitch of Buchenwald* (it's alliterative), is famous for constructing lampshades from the tattooed skin of prisoners whom she personally murdered for their skin-art. What she actually had were some lamp shades made from goat skin. American General Lucius Clay, military governor of the American zone of occupation:

> *There was absolutely no evidence in the trial transcript, other than she was a rather loathsome creature, that would support the death sentence. I suppose I received more abuse for that than for anything else I did in Germany. Some reporter had called her the "Bitch of Buchenwald", and had written that she had lamp shades made of human skin in her house. And that was introduced in court, where it was absolutely proven that the lampshades were made out of goatskin. In addition to that, her crimes were primarily against the German people; they were not war crimes against American or Allied prisoners ... Later she was tried by a German court for her crimes and sentenced to life imprisonment. But they had clear jurisdiction. We did not.*

Another story that emerged from the war was that the Germans manufactured soap from the bodies of dead Jews, women and children especially chosen on account of their high fat content. This was similar to French and British propaganda against them in the *1ˢᵗ War-phase* that proved completely untrue. Seventy five years later the latest allegations are again shown to be lies. *The Jewish Virtual Library*:

> The leading scholars of the Holocaust are of the opinion that the Nazis did not make soap. It was a cruel rumor at the camps. Available documentary evidence and eyewitness accounts have been unable to corroborate in a conclusive manner reports that the National Socialists and their collaborators used human fat from their victims in the manufacture of soap. Rumors that Germans made soap from human remains originated in French propaganda from the First World War.

Soft Holocaust denial

In *The War Against the Jews* (1976) Lucy Davidowitz proposed that Hitler's invasion of Russia didn't have anything to do with *Blut und Boden*, *Pan Germanism*, *Geopolitik* or anything else but the complete annihilation of the Jews. Davidowitz:

> Hitler had embarked on an ideological war, to achieve ideological/racial goals, but to win that war he also had to fight a conventional war.

She proposed that Hitler may have conceived of the war against the Jews as early as 1919 and certainly as soon as he was named *Reich Chancellor* in 1933. Thus all his plans and actions must be seen as directed against the Jews. The evidence that swayed Davidowitz was the German Army's desperation when the war went against them. They needed railroad rolling stock to fight the war against the Reds. The German Army never ran out of ammunition; not even on the last day of the war. However, they did have problems getting the right kind of their plentiful ammo to the front where it was needed. This was a German problem throughout the war in the east. They were told by the high command that the transport of prisoners to the camps was of equal importance to their resupply requisitions. Well why should that be? And that begs another extremely serious question seldom ever asked; to wit: *If the object of the war was to kill Jews, why was it necessary to ship millions of them all over Europe to do it?* The Lithuanians did it the old fashioned way; just round them up and march the poor souls into a wood and machine gun them into pits. It didn't take them long to figure this out. They began killing Jews the day after the Germans invaded Russia in 1941 as did Latvia. They are both in *NATO* now and all is forgotten and forgiven. Even the mention of their involvement in the massacres that killed 250,000 Baltic Jews is now referred to as *Soft Holocaust Denial*, and that's bad; so don't even think about it. The term was invented by Deborah Lipstadt who has it all figured out. Any reference to the nations that took part; Romania, France and Ukraine especially, along with the Baltic States is *soft Holocaust denial*. It has to be Germans, it has to be gas, and it has to be *them* alone. This is why internet reference to *Holocaust Revision* is blocked in these places and slipped into the memory hole. Everybody can feel safe and warm because it was that homicidal maniac Hitler and all those nasty pure-bred Nordic white men who did it.

The Holocaust by Bullets

As the death toll in Auschwitz was lowered from 4 million, to 2.5 million down to the present 1.1 million the revised figures presented a problem. How to make up the deficit, assign guilt to the Germans, and make sure the victims were gassed as well? Never mind the 1.5 to 2 million Jews killed in the Ukraine with lead poisoning. It's called *The Holocaust by Bullets* (2008). But that is unfortunately, *soft Holocaust denial* so it doesn't count. It's got to be gas. An interesting film about the Jews in Ukraine is: *Everything is Illuminated* (2005). The need for gas was centered upon the requirement that the Jewish deaths were different and special. There were 75 million people (*minimum*) killed in the six years of the *2nd War-phase* and if Jewish deaths were just like all the others; well then those 5 million or so would be lost in the astronomically high general mortality of the war. Thus, Jewish dead needed to be the result of a mechanical and very German industrialized murder machine. There were 15 million unarmed civilians killed in the little corner of the world that now make up Poland, Lithuania and Belarus. The only deaths still remembered are the Jewish ones. Jewish historiography did a good a job: they protected their own interests and justified not only Israel's creation but continued cash payments from Germany (what's left of it). Who can blame them? They also made the other casualties not only irrelevant, but erased from memory. Israel isn't the first nation to do that, nor is it presumably the last. Who remembers that Canada wiped out the *Beothuk* in Newfoundland, or that the British Army tried to exterminate the entire population of Tasmania, every last man, woman and child in a systematic slaughter? Nevertheless, more death camps were needed to make the numbers good. Necessarily, a new term was invented by the Allies: the *Vernichtungslager* (extermination camp) or *Todeslager* (death camp). The terms were a post-war creation. The Germans never used them. The terms didn't exist because there were no death camps; all the killings took place in the field by *Army Group Rear-Area Command* (*Befehlshaber des rückwärtigen Heeresgebietes*). The invention of the death camps insured that the German Army's reputation remained as pure as the driven snow. They were to be a part of *Operation Unthinkable*, the Allied invasion of the Soviet Union in 1945.

Vernichtungslagern und Generalplan Ost

One might think that with all the atrocities committed by the German Army and its attached *Sonderkommandos* there would be no need for embellishments. Who remembers the massacres in Danzig and Pomerania (*Darżlubska Wilderness*) where 15,000 Jews, Czechs and Poles, as well as those deemed *unerwünscht* (undesirable) were murdered in 1939-40? This was all part of *Generalplan Ost* that included the deportation of *65 million people* to settlements in Siberia. The details were worked out in the oft noted *Wannsee Conference* in January 1942 and the famous *Final Solution* (*Endlösung der Judenfrage*). What is noteworthy is the list of people who did not attend this one-day (three-hour) symposium: Hitler, Goering, Himmler, Rosenberg and Goebbels; even though it was right there in Berlin. On the contrary, the attendees were all low level bureaucrats like Adolf Eichmann who, in 1962, was ritually executed by Isreal. There wouldn't be any inquisitive reporters asking him silly questions. Undoubtibly Reinhard Heydrich, who presided at *Wannsee*, was one of those people among the Nazi hierarchy who sought the complete eradication of the Jews. In October 1941, the Germans rounded up, among thousands of others, 2000 Spanish Jews in retaliation for an attack on some German soldiers. The Spanish government wanted them released and they were willing to take these Spanish Jews and ship them to Morocco, at their own expense. Heydrich denied them:

> *These Jews would be too much out of the reach of the direct measures to be taken after the war regarding the fundamental solution to the Jewish question.*

Even here he admits it is not policy but somethiing to do later on. But his personal madness is evident and is often exemplified on the eastern front, not only by Germans but by their allies as well. That murderous process was already well underway when those men met at Wannsee. But they made no reference to killing Jews or anyone else. The murders did in fact happen but on an individual unit level and not as a nationally directed policy of extermination. There is no evidence from the Wannsee Conference that there ever was one. The notes from the conference, not minutes, and in translation, were all suddenly produced at Nuremburg. They make one single reference to the *final solution*, and mention deportations. We are supposed to all know, *as if the participants understood postwar concerns*, that *final solution* means gas in death camps. But does it make sense in any kind of objective historical analysis? Let's say it again: *why do you need to round up millions of Jews from all over Europe and ship them to camps to be murdered when you can do it right on the spot?* The German Army never had any problem murdering Ukrainians and White Russians right where they found them. What is the actual historical evidence that it all happened this way; with gas and incineration?

The historical method

The first Europeans to land in the *New World* were Norse adventurers from Greenland. For a long time there was vehement denial that this happened. The *Icelandic Sagas* told that *Leif Erikson*, his brother *Thorwald Erikson* as well as his pal *Thorfin the Valiant* had all landed and discovered three distinct places: *Helluland* (the Land of the Flat Stones), probably Labrador, *Markland* (the Land of the Forests), probably Newfoundland and the famous *Vinland* (the Land of Grapes), probably Nova Scotia where they still grow grapes and make wine. It was an easy voyage for those fellows. The climate was mild, somewhat like *Long Island* today, and warmed by a very strong and friendly *Gulf Stream*. The northern hemisphere was still in the *Medieval Warm Period*. Grapes for wine were cultivated in England. Crops in Europe were bountiful and there was a population explosion in the years 1000-1300 that helped account for *The Crusades*. Greenland's glaciers had receded and the island sported all sorts of wild berries and tropical birds. It was possible to grow hay and keep livestock in Greenland which is impossible today. The *Skálholt Map* (1570) also confirmed the Norse discoveries. But it wasn't enough evidence to convince the skeptics. All these sources are considered *secondary sources* as the authors were not there themselves. There was no direct physical evidence until the discovery of a Viking settlement at *L'Anse aux Meadows* on Newfoundland in 1960. That settled the argument.

Assemble the facts

Leopold von Ranke (1795-1886) was the first of the modern historians. He advised gathering the facts and for him these were state archives; letters and testimony written at the time of the event by people who were there. Do that he said, and it would be possible to see history, *how it actually was* (*wie es eigentlich gewesen*). These are called primary sources. *Luigi Albertini* (1871-1941) did this and quite literally assembled all the facts, as defined by Ranke, in his astounding and massive 3 volume *The Origins of the War of 1914* (spoiler alert: the Austrians did it). The problem with this method is that it cannot explain events that lie outside state archives. For example, most of the generals and statesmen in 1914 seriously doubted that many men would actually show up to fight. Albertini doesn't talk about this. The men did show up, even though *Das Kapital* was in print for close to 50 years. Most of the men knew, even if vaguely, that war served the interests of the banking elite and not them and their families. The men were willing to be shot at and killed because nationalism motivated them more than communist/socialist theory. Mussolini recognized this and created *fascismo italiano*. This is why Donald Trump is often refered to as a fascist or nazi. He, and the people behind him, are nationalists who oppose the communist international now euphimistically sold as *Globalism*.

Anecdotal material

Testimony after the fact, that is to say *anecdotal material* or personal stories, is the least reliable historical evidence. Shumel Krakowski, the director of the *Yad Vashem Holocaust Institution* in Jerusalem:

> *Many were never in the place where they claim to have witnessed atrocities, while others relied on second-hand information given them by friends or passing strangers…A large number of testimonies on file were later proved inaccurate when locations and dates could not pass an expert historian's appraisal.*

All the evidence for the gas and incinerate hypothesis is based upon anecdotal material. This is hard to swallow for people who think the evidence is overwhelming. Early eyewitness reports told of Jews being burned alive in the camps, or electrocuted, or killed with steam and buried alive. Finally everybody just settled on gas and the other stories were forgotten. There are no state archives that can be used as evidence for the systematic murder of Jews in *death camps* specifically designed for that purpose. The usual explanation is that the documents were destroyed. In fact, there are literally tons of documents from the *Third Reich* located in the victor's vaults. One problem is that few people can any longer read German Gothic script; printed or written. Those that do have determined that written orders don't exist. Raul Hilberg, in his massive *The Destruction of the European Jews* (1961), explained the lack of *primary source material* this way:

> *But what began in 1941 was a process of destruction not planned in advance, not organized centrally by any agency. There was no blueprint and there was no budget for destructive measures. They were taken step by step, one step at a time. Thus came about not so*

much a plan being carried out, but an incredible meeting of minds, a consensus – mind reading by a far-flung bureaucracy.

What is no longer extant is the physical evidence. The gas chambers exist only in imagination. They are gone, including the one in Auschwitz. It was all based on Allied war propaganda designed to demonize the enemy because some story had to account for all the dead; and the Allies weren't going to blame their own policies for the typhus epidemic that killed millions in 1945.

All war is based upon deception   Sun Tzu

Perhaps the starkest image to emerge from the 2nd War-phase was that of a bulldozer pushing piles of emaciated corpses killed by the Germans into a ditch at Bergen-Belsen, the place where Anne Frank died. In fact, it was a British bulldozer, driven by a British soldier pushing some of the 30,000 dead that died of typhus during the British administration of the camp in the summer of 1945. It's easy to caption a photograph of this and write *"Jewish victims at Bergen-Belsen."* Or take a shot of Jewish children and write *"awaiting death on the selection ramp at Auschwitz."* Yes the children are Jewish: we can see the yellow star on their coats. But where is it taken? How do we know by implication that they will soon be gassed? Maybe they are getting on the train. Why did the Germans at Auschwitz bother to give children identification tattoos at all? The story goes that children were immediately gassed there. When the Red Army liberated Auschwitz there were thousands of children. Nazi Germany was one of the most oppressive and violent governments in world history. It is easy to ascribe any crime to them. A recent documentary tried to show the bodies burned at Treblinka. The picture showed a forest with some smoke in the distance. It could have been a forest in British Columbia. But the image is accepted by the casual viewer not trained in the historical method. They are not aware that *historians and documentary filmmakers* might try to mislead them. Another revealing misrepresentation is the picture of 3000 corpses lined up in rows at the *Nordhausen* camp. The caption in Wikipedia reads:

THE DARWINIAN REVOLUTION AND THE POLITICS OF MASS-MURDER

Rows of dead inmates fill the yard of the Boelcke Barracks, a sub-camp of Mittelbau-Dora in Nordhausen, 12 April 1945

In fact the dead were all killed by Allied fighter-bombers on an early morning raid a few days before. The bombed out buildings are plainly visible. Nevertheless one site (*Jewishgen.org*) blames the Germans:

This effective bombing killed a great many of helpless inmates because the SS forced them to stay in the hangars which were set ablaze by the bombs.

Who will want to walk outside of a concrete hanger when 6-ton fighter bombers armed with heavy machine guns, bombs and rockets are shooting up the place? They say the attack was a "*mistake.*" It wasn't. Germany was a free-fire zone. They bombed everything. The guards were huddled up in fear against a wall inside the hangers just like everyone else. The hard evidence for the gas and burn Holocaust isn't there. There were no gas chambers at Bergen-Belsen, nor Nordhausen, nor Dachau, or any place else. The only gas chambers still extant are the artfully constructed ones at the *Tötungsanstalten* in Germany connected to the T-4 murder program. That is where the gas chamber stories originated. Everybody knew about them and that's why the T-4 program was halted. *David Irving* questioned the standard story and spent most of his adult life harassed and threatened by Israeli agents. In Israel, Holocaust denial is worth 5 years in jail. Denying God will get you one. That might tell you something about the priorities. Others like *Elie Wiesel* just make it up as they go along. In his own hand:

What are you writing?' the Rabbi asked. 'Stories,' I said. He wanted to know what kind of stories: 'true stories.' 'About people you have known?' Yes, about people I might have known. 'About things that happened?' Yes, about things that happened or could have happened. 'But they did not?' No, not all of them did. In fact, some were invented from almost the beginning to almost the end. The Rabbi leaned forward as if to measure me up and said with more sorrow than anger: 'That means that you are writing lies!' I did not answer immediately. The scolded child within me had nothing to say in his defense. Yet, I had to justify myself.

'Things are not that simple, Rabbi. Some events do take place but are not true; others are – although they never occurred.

He knows he will never be called to account for the lies. He can't help but perpetuate the hate as it means so much to him. It is easy to understand it. He had a good life in Hungary. He was suddenly rounded up, probably by Hungarians, and sent to Auschwitz. Then he's sent to Buchenwald. All these places were awful. Nobody he knew got gassed but, for a time, his life was ruined. Then he turned it all into fabulous wealth and the Nobel Peace Prize.

Lucy Davidowitz's consternation and Hungarian Jews

Wiesel was caught up in the German Army's arrest of Hungarian Jews and anybody else local Hungarian officials wanted to get rid of: mostly homeless vagabonds and Gypsies (now named *Roma*). They helped the Germans round them up. This was in the spring and early summer of 1944. An interesting Hungarian film about this is: *1945* (2017). The figure generally given is 447,000 souls. The legend says these people were loaded into over 100 separate train sets, sent on a single RR line across the Slovakian mountains, unloaded at Auschwitz and then walked immediately into the gas chamber. They quickly killed 400,000 people, mostly Jews, and disposed of the bodies so that there isn't a trace left over. There were no records of their arrival even though the Germans took meticulous account. There is no documentation for additional coal to feed the furnaces that were now going 24/7. There is no evidence whatsoever. Fully 1/3 of all Jews killed at Auschwitz were supposedly killed in this 3-month spasm of violence. In the meantime, General Eisenhower's three armies landed in Normandy and the Red Army launched its summer offensive that would destroy *Army Group Center* and bring them to the Vistula, only 250 miles from Berlin. Davidowitz looked at this situation and came to the logical conclusion that, for the Germans, killing Jews was more important, or at least of equal importance, to winning the war. If all the circumstances were correct, how could she be wrong? First she had to unquestionably accept the gas and incinerate hypotheses or else be driven out of academia and quite possibly jailed. She couldn't dispute the numbers either as they were needed to confirm the astronomically high death rate attributed to Auschwitz. Well, she could have been misled about the numbers. *Istvan Deak*, leading American expert on Hungarian history:

> *Let me note here that statistical data on such things as the number of Second Army soldiers and forced laborers, or the casualties they suffered, or the number of Hungarian Jews gassed at Auschwitz, or the total number of Jewish dead, are not much better than guesses. There exists no reliable information on these subjects.*

However many there were, there is no evidence they were all shipped to Auschwitz, nor that they were all killed. Many retuned to Hungary. Many didn't want to go back and who could blame them? Thousands died in the vast underground factories the Luftwaffe built in Bavaria. If General Patton's war dairies were not sealed until 2046 there might be more information about that. Davidowitz:

> *The Final Solution had top priority, even at a time of military exigencies. The need for railroads to transport Jews to their deaths often competed with the need for railroads to transport soldiers and military supplies to the front. Both received equal consideration.*

She was and is absolutely correct. They did all receive equal consideration because they weren't shipped off to be gassed but rather to be worked as slave laborers in German war production.

Treblinka

In the days before *Photoshop* a photograph or film image could be solid evidence. Thus we know that the multitudinous massacres in the east are not exaggerated. Cameras were ubiquitous among German military personnel. They snapped away, often sending the photos back home. *Babi Yar and thousands of other massacres happened.* But Auschwitz, Treblinka, Sobibor and the other *Todeslager* remain a mystery. Where are the pictures of the mass graves, the exhumations, the gas chambers, the functioning crematoria for millions of hapless prisoners? They don't exist. Do an internet search for *Treblinka images*. You will see a series of stock photos from various locations. They say now 900,000 Jews were killed at *Treblinka* but there are no remains. The total has widely fluctuated from 3 million steadily down to the present figure. There are tours, day trips, everything you need if you want to visit. There is hardly anything there actually from the camp. You can buy an inexpensive lunch and souvenirs but the camp is gone with the wind. Allied air recon showed nothing there at the time in question. That's when supposedly close to a million people were gassed, murdered, buried, exhumed, piled up on massive bonfires and burned once again, all in about a year's time with alarming Teutonic efficiency. One *"eyewitness"* said women and children were used as kindling because their high fat content burned better. The fantasies are astounding. Human bodies don't burn easily and you can't use them as kindling. Then, so they say, after burning a million exhumed bodies into ash on open pits, those utterly efficient Germans destroyed it all; every brick and timber. There are no bodies to dig up, not a trace. No bones, not even teeth. There should be at least 25 million teeth out there at Treblinka but there are none. They say the Germans invented a machine to destroy the teeth and bones. No longer extant, the single picture of it looks like an ordinary ball mill. Researchers for a television documentary found *a single tile* and some fragments at Treblinka that had a Star of David embossed upon it. *There's your gas chamber* they proclaimed! The very one where so many Jews shuffled silently along on the assembly line of death. The Star of David tiles were supposed to lull them into passivity as they entered the gas chamber. Other *"eyewitnesses"* say SS thugs beat the naked Jews with whips and drove them along like cattle. A Star of David on a floor tile is supposed to calm the nerves? What's really a wonder is how they get away with it. The filmmakers found a single shinbone and wept accordingly and dramatically for the cameras. The bone was found right near an old Christian cemetery. The film-crew desecrated that while the search went on for the Jewish bodies they never found. Wait. Maybe the bone wasn't Jewish after all; don't all shin bones look alike? No time for stupid questions. Soon after, the world media proclaimed that the Treblinka gas chamber was found!

Sobibor

They say 250,000 died at *Sobibor*, it too down from 3 million. Nobody even knows where that camp was exactly, except that it was somewhere near the village of Sobibor in Poland. Only three people are known to have ever seen it. The process is: find someone, anyone, who call themselves a *forensic archeologist*, give them a shovel and a job to dig around where the camp might have been, find a few bricks, or the foundation of a building, any building, and call it a gas chamber. No bodies, no teeth, no bone, no mass graves there either. The *"eye witnesses"* said the prisoners at Sobibor crushed the bones and teeth with small hammers. Imagine it. The stories keep changing. In 2004 and 2014 single core samples were taken with a core drill and the analysis showed human remains. Was there a massacre there? Maybe; there were lots of massacres. How many people? Unknown. Were they gassed and burned? That could not be determined. The place is near the *Pripet Marshes* (sometimes *the Pinsk Marshes*) where thousands of Jews formed communities that resisted the Germans. They built small towns in the wetlands, with schools and libraries. They fought with Russian partisans as the German Army, with reason, didn't like going in there. You won't find too much information about this because it doesn't fit the victim narrative. A film that touches these subjects is *Run Boy Run* (2013).

Falsus in uno, falsus in omnibus

French priest Jean-Paul Renard promoted the deliberate lie that he saw "homicidal gassings at Buchenwald." When former Buchenwald inmate Rassinier pointed out to him that there were no homicidal gas chambers or murderous gassings in the camp, Renard replied: "Right, but that's only a figure of speech…and since those things [Hitler's gas chambers] existed somewhere, it's not important. Paul Grubach.

The camp at Buchenwald had absolutely no gas chambers. There is no question about this now. However "eyewitness" Charles Hauter told a different story:

An obsession with machinery literally abounded when it came to extermination. Since it had to occur quite rapidly, a special form of industrialization was required. The gas chambers answered that need in a very different way. Some, rather refined in conception, were supported by pillars of porous material, with which the gas formed and then seeped through the walls. Others were simpler in structure. But all were sumptuous in appearance. It was easy to see that the architects had conceived them with pleasure, devoting great attention to them, gracing them with all the resources of their aesthetic sense. These were the only parts of the camp that had truly been constructed with love.

"*Eyewitness*" Georges Hénocque on Buchenwald:

On the ceiling at irregular intervals were seventeen air-tight, sealed shower heads. They looked like ordinary shower heads. The deportees assigned to the crematorium had warned me of the manner in which the victims, to mock them, were all given a towel and a small bar of soap before entering the shower. The unfortunates were thus brought to believe that they were entering a shower. [...] the gas descended to the floor, so that none of the victims could escape what the Germans called the 'slow and sweet death.' Everything was organized on a strictly scientific basis. The Devil himself could not have planned it better.

At the Chelmno (Kulmhof) death camp there is also nothing except a few foundation stones of the '*gas chamber*.' They say all these camps were meticulously deconstructed by the Germans because the war was lost and they wanted to hide what they had done; as if they all foresaw the Nuremburg Tribunals. Who would win the war was the only thing nobody knew in 1943. The German Army was still intact and packed a lot of punch. The Red Army was still 750 miles from Berlin. The war was a stalemate and expected to last another ten years. In 1943-44, Auschwitz still employed (as slaves) 35,000 people and turned out enough synthetic fuel and rubber to keep the German Army rolling. The working conditions were awful and food scarce for everybody.

Thousands died of disease and misery. They constantly needed more workers. That's why the trains kept rolling into Auschwitz. It was the biggest industrial conglomerate in the world. *I.G Farben* owned the plant complex and saw its profits soar; same with Krupp, Daimler-Benz (now Mercedes-Benz), and Porsche, Beyer, ITT, Bosch, Siemens, Oskar Schindler and many more. They all used slave labor. War was good.

War Crimes

Spencer Tracy played the American Chief Justice at the *International Military Tribunal (IMT)* that tried German politicians, military leaders, doctors, lawyers and judges as war criminals. Tracy was the kindest man you'd ever want to meet and exemplified the fair-minded American jurisprudence at the trials. Unfortunately for the fellows in the dock, Tracy was an American actor who dated Katherine Hepburn and was the star of the film *Judgment at Nuremburg* (1961). In the film, justice was served by the unselfish and benevolent Americans. In real-life, most of the guys who should have been hung walked away scot-free. Franz Halder, the man who planned and executed *Operation Barbarossa*, now worked for the Americans and was therefore not indicted. Gehlen also worked for the Americans and supposedly tracked down the communists he never found when he worked for Hitler. No need to charge him with anything either. The fact that Gehlen was a charlatan interested solely in personal power was of no account. The other high-profile Nazis were either already dead or soon would be. The *IMT* was a *Kangaroo Court* that made up its own laws and tried the defendants upon *ex post facto* laws that were non-existent when said crimes were committed. It's true that the Kellogg-Briand Pact urged nations to renounce war as a legitimate means of national policy. But the authors never considered that individuals might be tried and executed for it. Admittedly, *Julius Streicher* was a loathsome character who was the editor of the virulent anti-Semitic *Der Stürmer*. The tribunal invented the crime of *incitement to racial hatred* and hung him for it. Many defendants were charged with waging war or *crimes against peace*. First off, Britain and France declared war on Germany, not the other way around. In addition, if this were a real charge and criminal act then every American

President since 1946 would be a war-criminal. Most significantly, the *IMT* was, all at once, the Prosecutor, the Plaintiff and the Victim. Being the prosecutor and plaintiff is not unusual. The American *Department of Justice* (DOJ) is often the prosecutor and plaintiff at the same time. They win 99% of those cases; which is a better conviction rate than enjoyed even by Joseph Stalin who only won 90% of them. Problems must arise when both prosecutor and plaintiff are presented as the victims at large as well. Finally, the prosecutors were also the judges. This strongly indicated that the outcome of the tribunal was never in doubt. It wasn't. In addition to the main trial that sentenced Goering, von Ribbentrop, Rosenberg and eight others to death, there were twelve separate trials associated with the *IMT*. They were all held at the *Palace of Justice* at Nuremburg. One hundred forty people were hung, some of them deservedly so. The industrialists and corporate managers that built Auschwitz and other slave labor camps were sentenced to relatively short prison terms. Most of them were acquitted. By April 1949 all the show trials were over and it was back to business as usual.

Prussia is extirpated

Harry Truman, the original *Flimflam Man*, met with Uncle Joe Stalin and Winston Churchill's replacement Clement Attlee in the summer of 1945. The meet and greet was at Potsdam, playground of the Royals just outside Berlin. Churchill was now out of power again. Once the war was over, Attlee's Labor Party promised better jobs, more pay and more welfare. They coined a phrase; *cradle to the grave* state sponsored welfare for all. With native Britons on the verge on national extermination we can see now how well that all worked out. At the time it sounded great. Truman was a polished con artist but he was in over his head with Stalin. He and Eisenhower were both threatening Russia with nuclear war (*Plan Totality*) that was leaked to the Reds. Stalin withdrew from Iran and Greece (as he promised he would at Yalta) but would never surrender Eastern Europe. That was good enough, so the Americans backed off. Like most Americans, Truman couldn't understand that Russia had a foreign policy centuries old they weren't going to change because some fresh-faced American gangsters were in town. What is still not recognized is that Russia had Japanese nuclear technology captured in Korea and the Americans knew it. American nuclear bombs didn't scare them because they had their own albeit not yet announced. Truman and Stalin did see eye to eye about one thing and that was Germany's destruction. With the German Army utterly ruined it was now easy. *Law # 46* was passed by the *Allied Control Council* on February 25th, 1947 and it simply stated: *The Prussian State together with its central government and all its agencies are abolished.* East Prussia, the revered *Ost Prussen*, was given to Russia and Poland. West Prussia was amalgamated into preexisting German states. Prussia was no longer on any map. Agencies like the *Prussian Academy of Sciences*, that saw Max Planck, Albert Einstein, and Fritz Haber make major contributions to modern science, were renamed. Prussia ceased to exist and is barely remembered. Poland emerged as one of the big winners. Its borders were shifted westwards and it gained the very rich provinces of Pomerania and Silesia as well as Danzig (now *Gdańsk*) and Stettin (now *Szczecin*). If the game were chess, Germany lost its Queen and was hereafter rendered defenseless, groveling on the back rank to await its inevitable extinction via racial termination by replacement migration.

The Iron Curtain

Churchill continued to frantically stir the pot for more war. He met Truman early in 1946 and since both sincerely and firmly believed in the old adage *there's a sucker born every minute* they found themselves in complete *accord*. Now the enemy was to be Russia. But it had to be sold to British and American people who were tired of the killing. In America especially, the war machine was not to be wound down but ramped up. Big bombs and big bombers were the order of the day. No peace, but more ships and more guns; eternal war and easy money from Aunt Nelly down on the farm who would pay for it through her nose. Withholding tax was now the law so Americans would shell it out with earned money they were never allowed to see or feel. Just a few years before there were some great questions about whether or not an income tax could even be legal. It had to be settled with some political assassinations and a constitutional amendment; the 16th: *the Congress shall have power to lay and collect taxes on incomes, from whatever source derived*. This gives the government and its representatives the right to not only appropriate your property and set the price you must pay for it, but to even use it against you when they see fit. The Democrats and Progressives were heartily in accord and the *"soak the rich"* amendment passed. For the average working man and woman, they would soon be paying far more proportionally than the rich. In any case, the money was there for the massive arms buildup and war maintenance we see today. Churchill had a way with words and issued the clarion call:

> *From Stettin in the Baltic to Trieste in the Adriatic, an iron curtain has descended across the Continent. Behind that line lie all the capitals of the ancient states of Central and Eastern Europe. Warsaw, Berlin, Prague, Vienna, Budapest, Belgrade, Bucharest and Sofia, all these famous cities and the populations around them lie in the Soviet sphere and are all subject in one form or another, not only to Soviet influence but to a very high and in many cases increasing measure of control from Moscow.*

Americans were now asked to spend more of their blood and national fortune on international crusades to grant freedom and democracy to the displaced and oppressed. What could be better than that? But was any of this true, and did any of the oppressed want anything that the west had to offer? The iron curtain was the perfect metaphor: a vast metal wall *descending* upon Europe where the barbaric Reds imposed their horrific ideology onto the hapless survivors of the war. For a huckster like Truman, who didn't know the very first thing about Romania, Hungary, or Poland it seemed very real. They weren't allowed the blessings of democracy. That was *prima facie* evidence. Isn't democracy not only what everybody wanted but needed for freedom and security? Americans primarily wanted a good burger and shake at the drive-in and trusted their representatives to do the right thing.

The Cold War

The west never gave Poland anything but misery. The Red Army and Soviet Russia gave Poland three fabulously rich German provinces: Silesia rich in coal and iron ore, Pomerania with Danzig and Stettin, and East Prussia. Poland got all this in return for some swamps. This was the best thing to happen to Poland in 300 years. In the meantime, the Red Army protected them for the next 50 years. Now Germany and France want a combined *European Army*. Against whom it might be set upon is not yet clear; but Poland has what many Germans want returned to them. Modern historians and commentators of all sorts often state that Poland was '*thrown under the bus*.' In what way except that Poland was denied the glories of western liberal democracy? Millions of Poles didn't want it, nor anything else the west might have for them (except money). An interesting film about this era in Poland is *Cold War* (2018). Why would Albania, for example, want to go with the west in 1946? The Italian occupation was brutal. They would take 200 Albanians hostage for every Italian soldier killed by partisans and gun them down. They wiped out whole villages. The image most people have of Italian soldiery is a smiling fellow eating a cannoli and strumming a mandolin. The Italians made the German Army look like *Snow White and the Seven Dwarfs*. Should it be any wonder that when the Italians were driven out, Albania might want to reject the west? And indeed they did. What about Romania? They had a whole generation of young men slaughtered in Russia. Stalin returned Transylvania to them. Hungary lost two wars fighting with Germany. Czechoslovakia was brutalized by the west at Munich. They should want more western values, more liberal ideals? When the Red Army liberated these nations from fascist bondage the people wanted something different. One thing they wanted was land reform and they got it. The communists broke up the large estates and redistributed the property. France and Italy would have gone the same way but for the American occupation and material support. The winters of 1946-47 were harsh. France and Italy got plenty of food while two million Germans starved to death by design. The Americans wanted Italy as an unsinkable aircraft carrier in the Mediterranean. There would be no military tribunals for Italian war criminals. Their war crimes were covered up and Field Marshall Badoglio, who had personally mustard-gassed Ethiopian farmers, children and soldiers, died comfortably in his bed and was buried with full military honors.

The Demonization of General Tojo

Aung San Suu Kyi is a Burmese (now Myanmar) heroine. She is currently (2020) Prime Minister. Her father *Major General Aung San* fought with and for the Japanese Army that liberated Burma from British rule. The British later killed him. *Aung San*:

> *The training in the Japanese Army was so harsh I almost committed suicide. However, when Rangoon fell, we were convinced that what we had been doing was right.*

Hideki Tojo was a soldier who fought for his country and carried out policy orders from the Emperor's Privy Council, known as *The Supreme War Council* and later the *Supreme Council for the Direction of the War*. He willingly took the rap and died for them. Tojo is currently the most popular political figure in Japanese history even though he was hung by the Americans after a mock trial. He is held in esteem by many former adversaries as well. *Ba Maw*, Burma Head of State (1943-45):

> *The true friend of independent Burma was General Tojo and Japan.*

Seni Pramo three times Prime Minister of Thailand:

> *Asia gained independence because of Japan.*

Goh Chok Tong Prime Minister of Singapore (1990-2004):

> *The Japanese occupation was harsh but it was the Japanese Army that terminated the western domination of Asia. That gave Asia the confidence. Within fifteen years of the war all Asian colonies were freed.*

In the western mind, Japanese Prime Minister Tojo was part of a *triumvirate* that included Hitler and Mussolini. The three of them provided good

THE DARWINIAN REVOLUTION AND THE POLITICS OF MASS-MURDER

and instant visual war propaganda. All three are still fervently demonized. A casual internet search for Tojo reveals:

> *Tojo is responsible for the deaths of more than 5 million civilians during World War II – including unprovoked attacks on the Americans at Pearl Harbor, plus non-military casualties in China, Korea, the Netherlands, France and countless other nations in the Asian Pacific*

That's a long list of atrocities. It is impossible to blame all that on one man. The Imperial Navy planned and executed the Pearl Harbor attack that was provoked by an embargo. But the object of demonization is to simplify the war and present it to the liberal mind as a conflict between good and evil. That seems to work 100% of the time. The war wasn't Tojo's invention. The process was well underway when he assumed a limited command. Hideki Tojo was one of many ministers that carried out an imperial war directed by Japan's Emperor and his family. Just before the kangaroo court that killed Tojo, General Bonner Fellers (MacArthur's aide) told Admiral Mitsumasa Yonai:

> *It would be most convenient if the Japanese side could prove to us that the emperor is completely blameless. . . . Tojo, in particular, should be made to bear all responsibility at his trial.*

Chosen as the fall-guy for the Emperor, General Tojo was tried and hung at the *International Military Tribunal for the Far East*. All the laws that convicted him were *ex post facto* laws. The verdict was known in advance. Once during questioning Tojo reminded the court that the Emperor bore some responsibility for the conduct of the war. The proceedings were <u>*immediately*</u> halted. Tojo was whisked away and given a good talking to. He was persuasively reminded (as were many wayward Nuremburg witnesses) about what might happen to his wife and family if he persisted in this line of reasoning. Tojo returned the next day and informed the court that he had been mistaken. The Emperor was wholly innocent, purely passive and primarily interested in marine biology as well as the welfare of his beloved people. It wasn't his fault that so many millions of them got incinerated. In *The Manchurian Candidate* (1962) Captain Marco's platoon all said the same thing about Sergeant Shaw: *Raymond Shaw is the kindest, bravest, warmest, most wonderful human being I've ever known in my life.* It was like that with Hirohito; once word got out bad things would happen if you said anything different. Denied his uniform, General Tojo was pulled into a basement hole at midnight and hung in a prison jumpsuit.

The war is prolonged

Among the legends that emerged from the war was the absolute necessity to atom-bomb Japan in August 1945. Very few people know that Japan wanted to capitulate in May, three months before. After Germany's unconditional surrender, Japan knew the game was up. Concentrated around central Europe the Red Army was not in any position to attack Japan. Had the Americans accepted the Japanese offer to negotiate, there would have been no Soviet invasion of Manchuria and Korea. There would have been no Korean War, no 5 million Korean dead, and no 150,000 American losses either. President Truman called that war a *Police Action*. In 1952 the quack was forced to retire but by then it was too late; America was already embarked on imperial ambition. The wars were always defined as protective measures and police actions to defend poor, desperately impoverished natives from the threat of communist aggression. Far too many of those helpless natives were armed with AK-47 machine guns who wanted to kill the Americans that had replaced the Japanese as colonial masters. The death toll was, and still is, astounding.

The Philippines in the Japanese scheme of things

When Japan took the *Southern Road*, the central position of its empire became the Philippines as a glance at any map will tell. General Douglas Macarthur was the American commander in the island nation that the Americans took from Spain. Admiral Dewey and his fleet just happened to be out there the day war was declared by the USA in 1898. For the Pilipino people the Americans were just another colonial overlord that replaced the Spanish;

only worse. The Spanish Catholic ruling elite maintained their positions of power and best accommodated themselves to American rule. The rest of the population had been fighting the Spanish for independence and just continued that war against the Americans. The ensuing *Pilipino-American War* (1899-1913) is one few American have ever heard of. The American Army was mostly southerners who, like most of their compatriots, never quite adapted to losing the Civil War to those damn Yankees. Out in the Pilipino boondocks they could kill darkies with impunity and did. In a prelude to Vietnam they killed them all and let God sort them out. Was it a million Pilipino civilians who died, or was it two million? No one can say for sure. With the society's infrastructure obliterated by design, disease took a devastating toll. America then installed a malevolent police state marked by intrusive surveillance, incarceration and torture. Since Filipinos did not enjoy the individual protections of the United States Constitution there were no constraints. When the Japanese took over in 1942 nobody was too upset. They were welcomed as liberators as people lined the streets and waved Japanese flags.

The Far East Air Force

General MacArthur's strategy to defend the islands was to protect every square inch of ground. The War Department approved this madness. Therefore, *the Generalissimo* dispersed his supplies. Food, fuel and ammo were cached all over the Philippines. His air force, *au contraire*, some 300 planes including 24 magnificent B-17's that could attack Formosa, was concentrated at Clark Field in northern Luzon. They were destroyed on the ground nine hours after Pearl Harbor. MacArthur was a political general officer who had proven his worth when he helped gun down *American Bonus Marchers* and their wives in Washington DC back in 1932. The American ruling elite knew they could count on Doug. His plan for the overall defense of the Philippines failed upon first contact with the enemy. The US Army Forces in the Far East consisted of 31,000 US Army troops and 100,000 Filipinos. They were driven back into the small *Bataan Peninsula* where they waged an amazing and heroic delaying action for *5 months* against overwhelming force. Unfortunately Doug's strategy of dispersing his supplies meant his men had little food, no fuel and were permanently low on ammo. In the end there were 50,000 casualties and 100,000 captured: the worst military disaster in the history of the United States Army. The Japanese Army marched then already weakened and starving prisoners back towards Manila. They shot or bayoneted any man who couldn't keep up. This was the infamous *Bataan Death March*. By this time though, *the Generalissimo* had yellow-bellied out of there on a speed-boat. The apologists say he was ordered to escape and had no choice. No military commander is obligated to accept an order to abandon his men. On the contrary he is morally obligated to share the fate of the men he led into disaster. For the Generalissimo, morality never entered into any of it. Self-absorbed to a degree that ordinary people cannot comprehend, he vowed to return. When he got to Australia he opposed awarding the *Medal of Honor* to General Wainwright whom he left in the lurch with the Bataan defenders. Doug felt they all should have fought to the last man and shot themselves with their last bullet. Somehow he is proclaimed a hero.

The Destruction of the Imperial Japanese Navy

When the Empire of Japan commenced hostilities against the United States in December 1941, its fleet was the most powerful navy in history. They had ten aircraft carriers manned by 1,500 of the finest naval aviators in the world. Their planes were better than anything in the British or American fleets, the British still flying bi-planes, for example. The eleven, shortly twelve, Japanese battleships were as good as the enemy and Japanese cruisers and destroyers, armed with the unerring *Type 93 Long Lance torpedo*, were also the best in the world. In all, the IJN put 2,500 ships to sea including transports. Three and a half years later, almost all those ships were sunk or rendered out of action by the United States Navy. This is the greatest naval disaster ever. In retrospect, given the tremendous advantage the United States had in economic and industrial resources the defeat seems inevitable. Yet, through two years of war, it was a fair fight, and even into the third year, the Japanese Navy still had chances to even the score. They failed miserably. The sheer immensity of the defeat boggles the mind and cannot be blamed upon the individual sailors and airmen of the *IJN* who fought with astounding courage and fanatical determination to the bitter end. The rout rests upon the leadership of the *IJN* who adopted and maintained illogical strategic objectives until it was too late to avoid Armageddon.

Ironbottom Sound

Two months after Midway in August 1942, the Americans astoundingly went on the offensive. They landed the *1st Marine Division* on a small island at the eastern tip of the Solomon Islands. The Japanese reacted quickly and sent a fleet of seven cruisers under *Admiral Gunichi Mikawa* to intervene. The Americans and their Australian allies had a covering force of eight cruisers and fifteen destroyers. They didn't think the Imperial Navy was any good. The Solomons are an island chain and the route from the Japanese base at Rabaul to Guadalcanal was named *The Slot*. The closely arrayed islands interfered with the radar that the Americans depended upon. The Japanese relied instead on the best night optics ever made. Near *Savo Island* they made visual contact first, lit up the enemy with star shell, and raked them with accurate fire and torpedoes. The *USN* lost three heavy cruisers and the Australian Navy one heavy cruiser, all in just a few minutes. The covering force was scattered and the route to the transports that supported the *1st Marines* lay open. They were just over the horizon 25 miles away. At this moment Mikawa's intellect failed him. He thought the battle was won and his job done. He turned his fleet around and withdrew to Rabaul. He didn't know that the purpose of his sortie was the destruction of the unarmed transports. This was the failure of the Japanese naval mind, indoctrinated by years of adherence to the *Decisive Battle* concept. Too often they could not grasp the complexities of naval combat. The aim of all naval operations is to support operations on land. For the confused Mikawa the destruction of the enemy fleet was the object of his mission. That was just part of it. The American Marines only had a 14 day supply of food and 20% of them already had dysentery. The complete annihilation of the *1st Marines* was at hand. Yamamoto, as always, was strategically asleep at the switch. He might have sent two battleship divisions down *The Slot* to finish the job but couldn't. All his precious battleships were back in Japan and not centrally located at *Truk* (now *Chuuk*). This allowed the Americans to slowly consolidate their position. The Japanese missed their chance and were never able to drive them off.

> *The fiercest serpent may be overcome by a swarm of ants*   Yamamoto

Japan emerged as one of the big winners in the Versailles raffle/giveaway. They had conquered German *Peleliu* directly in 1914 and it was theirs by right of conquest. That gave them 30 years to dig in and make the place practically impenetrable. In 1944 the Americans needed their Marines and Army to take the place in one of the most vicious and deadly battles ever fought. Versailles gave the Japanese all the other German island chains north of the equator. Under the rules of the game set up at Versailles, these territories were to be '*mandates*' for the benefit and cultural enrichment of the natives. That was a joke. In fact the *Caroline, Marshall and Mariana Islands* and their inhabitants served as slaves for the Japanese Army. Japan now had an empire that stretched 3,000 miles east towards the United States and astride all the American sea-lanes to China, the Philippines and East Asia. America wanted free-trade with China. They could only establish that if the Japanese let them. Japan wanted to dominate the region and could limit American trade any time they wanted to. They saw the Americans as just another western imperialist power looking to horn in on their territory. Conflict was inevitable.

Japanese leadership wonders; Total war or limited war?

When the *1st War-phase* wound down in 1919, Japan suddenly found itself, by default, the dominant military power in the region. The Russian and Chinese Empires were no more. Britain and France were destitute. The *1st War-phase* was total in that the entire resources of the combatants were mobilized for victory. The losers were either dismembered or annihilated. When a great power like Germany could be made to grovel, Japan saw that the same fate might await them. They imagined two ways forward. One was limited war and in truth all their wars up until 1937 were limited and successful. Along with that was the need for alliances with other great powers. Like the Soviet Union, they might seek safety through the prevention of enemy coalitions against them. Obviously this school of thought didn't prevail and Japan ended up fighting the whole world practically alone.

Naval treaties

For a time the limited warfare model got precedence. Japan joined the 5 great naval powers (USA, England, France, Italy and herself) in limiting the number of battleships allowed; *The Washington Naval Treaty* (1922) established the once famous 5-5-3-1.67-1.67 ratio model for new construction. Japan at *3* was placed between England/USA at the top and Italy/France at bottom. This was very advantageous for Japan since the top two powers were scaled at well below their actual production potential. The treaty was signed in 1922 but Japan's warmongers saw it as an affront. When they withdrew from the treaty obligations in 1936 the USA immediately went on a massive naval construction program that would doom Japan. This was just what the doctor ordered for Roosevelt's job programs and war planning. As always, the warships were bought with money borrowed from the privately owned *Federal Reserve Bank*, paid back with income taxes from a now perpetually fleeced American public. A continually cheapened dollar emerged as the national debt exploded.

Treaty cruisers

The Washington Naval Treaty limited primarily battleships. While the Republican Presidents from 1923-1933 actually sought limited expenditures, Japan looked to find any loopholes they could and avoid compliance. Since there was no limitation on cruisers of 10,000 tons or less, or on aircraft carriers, the *IJN* focused on those. They would have been wise to continue in that direction but didn't. Instead they built *Yamato-class* super-battleships that never sank an enemy ship and were a stupendous waste of resources. *The Doolittle Raid* really shook things up. Here it was only four months after Pearl Harbor and Tokyo was bombed. The disaster at Midway followed and saw the watery demise of four out of the only six Japanese fleet carriers. Japan should have had ten or more and a vastly expanded naval air arm. Instead they had 65,000 tons of '*Hotel Yamato*' gathering barnacles in Tokyo harbor while it served as a massive and luxurious floating HQ for the admirals of the *Combined Fleet*. Two months later the Americans went on the offensive that would take them to Okinawa. Yamamoto wasn't ready for it. *Truk* in the Caroline Islands was a bigger and better anchorage than Pearl Harbor. It was invulnerable to American attack and would be until *Tarawa* in the Gilbert Islands fell in November 1943. More than that, it was centrally located right smack-dab in the middle of the main theater of operations. It wouldn't have taken a strategic genius to recognize this. But Yamamoto was a charlatan. When the Guadalcanal Campaign began his fleet wasn't poised for action from a central position. At this point in the war, Japanese battleships were less vulnerable and potentially more effective than at any other time in the war. The Americans didn't have a massive air fleet yet and had only one carrier operational after *Wasp* (CV-7) and *Hornet* (CV-8) were sunk. From *Truk* Japan's battleships might have rapidly intervened and crushed what was a premature American counter-offensive. Instead, the Imperial Navy was in home waters protecting Tokyo from another Doolittle style raid that would never come. This was completely irrational. The Doolittle Raid was a suicide mission. All Japan needed to do was conduct more and better aerial searches and maintain additional patrol boats as pickets. A nation cannot suspend a war against the world's greatest industrial power to defend against possible minor incursions. How many Doolittle style raids did Japan think the Americans capable of? In the only one carried out; the Americans lost an entire squadron of medium bombers piloted by their best aviators (most of whom survived but never re-formed as a squadron). They did some damage to heavy industry works in Tokyo, as well as the light carrier *Ryūhō* that kept her out of action for 6 months. But the only real value was psychological. *Let* them come, *let them* make more costly raids, should have been Japan's thinking. But they didn't have a government that could make these kinds of coordinated cogent decisions.

The Guadalcanal Campaign

The Japanese Army became committed to the defense of Guadalcanal as a point of honor. The area around Guadalcanal and *the Slot* near *Savo Island* got named

Ironbottom Sound. It became, as Mikawa would repeatedly tell his superiors, *a black hole* for the men, ships and aircraft of the Imperial Navy. Yamamoto didn't listen and reluctantly decided to support the Army. It was too dangerous to send transports by day to reinforce the island so the Army asked the Navy to transport infantry in fast destroyers by night. In that part of the world, night and day are 12 hours long; so there was enough time to move the troops to Guadalcanal down *the Slot* and then get away before daybreak. These actions were named *The Tokyo Express* by the USN. Admiral Yamamoto didn't have to go along with this. It was of no help as the destroyers could only carry men and small arms. The Japanese on Guadalcanal became isolated, outnumbered and short of ammo and heavy weapons. Without them the Japanese defenders were forced to rely on *Banzai* frontal assaults and ambushes. That couldn't work on a small island against defenders that fully understood the principles of concentrated firepower.

> *So will you please say hello, to the folks that I know, tell them I won't be long*   Peggy Lee

Guadalcanal was occupied by Japan in May 1942 as part of its general eastward expansion in hopes to cut off Australia. Around the same time, they drove towards Midway and the Aleutian Islands 4,000 miles away. The Doolittle Raid forced this massive dispersal of force. If Japan had a government they might have concentrated their effort. The Aleutian Islands do lead straight to Japan. But they are shrouded in fog 355 days a year, not to mention snow, sleet, hail, rain, frozen rain, heavy winds, frozen ground, permafrost, and sub-zero temperatures that make any kind of construction project (like an airfield or harbor) hazardous. All military missions are equally perilous. Any serious American thrust had to come through the central and southern Pacific. This was spearheaded by the United States Marines (founded 1776) divided into six divisions. It was they who would carry to fight right into the Tokyo Prefecture (*Iwo Jima*) while the Army drove towards the Philippines through New Guinea. On Guadalcanal the *1st Marine Division* found out that Japanese troops didn't surrender and seldom took prisoners. They began to do the same. A film about this is *The Thin Red Line* (1998). Luckily for the Marines, Yamamoto had his fleet all over the ocean and never grasped the strategic significance of the Guadalcanal Campaign. Instead of the absurd phantasm of Midway, it was here that he could have forced, and found, the elusive and decisive fleet engagement he forever vainly sought. But by this time Yamamoto had lost his nerve if he ever had any. It was he who forced war upon the United States over Tojo's objections. When he got the war he wanted Yamamoto committed the Imperial Navy sporadically when a thrust with the entire fleet would have wiped out an under-strength American counter-offensive. Instead he used destroyers and cruisers and only two battleships (*Hiei* and *Kirishima*) both of which were sunk by superior American firepower. Unlike land combat where adversaries may keep reserves hidden by undulating terrain, naval forces must all be committed at once because on water there is no terrain. Yamamoto kept his best battleships in reserve where they were useless and sent out two fine ships to be overwhelmed by an enemy that better understood the principles of naval combat.

For want of a destroyer, the fleet was lost

Japanese destroyer losses became incommensurable with the losses sustained by the Americans. In the Guadalcanal Campaign, from August 6 until November 15, 1942, the Americans lost 15 destroyers to Japan's 11. At the same time, the USN commissioned 62 new destroyers to Japan's 7. Japanese construction could not make up for these losses, as in all of 1943 the Japanese launched only 15 new destroyers. By then, the tactic of using destroyers for combat supply had evolved from expediency to standard operational procedure. The *Battle for Guadalcanal* (August 1942-February 1943) was the most viciously sustained naval campaign in the history of military operations. In these seven months the American Navy lost 14,000 men, 29 ships and 615 aircraft. The IJN lost 20,000 men, 38 ships and 685 airplanes. But the Solomons Campaign still had almost a year to run! When it was over at the end of 1943, the IJN lost 40 destroyers, which was 2/5 of the prewar inventory. All this while American submarines were wreaking havoc among Japanese merchantmen from the lack of escorts. Refined oil became a rare commodity because the Japanese weren't interested in anti-submarine warfare, or in establishing a convoy system, until it was too late.

The benefits of self-sealing fuel tanks

The Americans code-named enemy fighters after men. Bombers had lady's names like *Betty* for the almost famous *Mitsubishi Navy Type 1 attack bomber*. Admiral Yamamoto went down in one after being ambushed by a squadron of American P-38s. Some say he was assassinated but it was war. The official Japanese propaganda had him found upright in his immaculate white uniform, still clutching his Samurai sword. In actuality he took a 50 cal. bullet that almost tore his head off. It was quick and probably only hurt for a split-second. He died in one of the most beautiful aircraft ever built. The *G4M1 Betty* was very similar to the older Mitsubishi *G3M Nell*. Sadly for the crew, it was unarmored and lacked defensive armament. One of its nicknames was *the flying gas tank*. Regrettably for the men who manned it, *Betty* didn't have self-sealing gas tanks: hence another of its many other monikers; *the flaming coffin*. But armor and self-sealing tanks are heavy and they were sacrificed for range and speed, somewhat like the similar German *Schnellbombers*. Japanese Betty's suffered grievously at Guadalcanal. The day after Mikawa failed to conclude his mission, the Navy tried again with 27 Betty's of the *1st Chutai 4th Kokutai* (1st Squadron, 4th Air Army). These were many of the same fellows that sank the *Prince of Wales* and *Repulse*. They were the best bomber pilots the Japanese had; the crème of the crop that took years to train. They didn't know that each American transport was now armed with more anti-aircraft weapons than either battleship *Prince of Wales* or *Repulse*. They soon found this out. The *1st Chutai* got shot to pieces, losing 6 *Betty's* without scoring a hit. The next day the *1st Chutai* tried again, this time armed with torpedoes. They got wiped out with 18 of 24 bombers shot down with only one hit recorded. One hundred twenty officers and men drowned and there were no replacements. Military organization cannot proceed with losses like this. The *Betty* squadrons were withdrawn and except for occasional surprise raids in west Australia, they were forced to engage in night missions only. For the Americans, the Guadalcanal airstrip was quickly made operational and the transports departed, giving the Japanese the false impression that their attacks had driven them off. They thought that the *1st Marine Division* was now vulnerable. They weren't and the *Tokyo Express* strategy of reinforcing the island in small increments became, as predicted by Mikawa, a black hole for the Imperial Navy and Army.

The Zero and Kamikaze Nation

The *Mitsubishi A6M Zero* was the most famous Japanese aircraft ever built. American military nomenclature called it the *Zeke*. Like the *Betty*, the *Zero* was unarmored and without self-sealing gas tanks. In the vast eternity of the Pacific Ocean range was paramount. The Americans were willing to sacrifice range for armor protection of pilots and gas tanks. They had the best combat engineers in the world (still do) and would advance in stages: conquer an island and quickly build an airbase. It was a methodical advance clear across the Pacific. Since Japan was victorious in the early going they had plenty of time to build bases and never emphasized combat engineering. With fewer airbases their planes needed range. The *Zero* (at 1,600 miles) had almost twice the range of American fighters. The Hellcat's range was 945 miles and the Wildcat, 100 miles less. The Zero's extremely light weight meant it could out-turn and out-climb any opponent. Introduced in 1940 when the Chinese air force was still flying bi-planes it had a kill ratio of 12-1. Later on, the very durable American *P-40 Warhawk* and *F4F Wildcat* held their own. What the Americans didn't know, and it took them quite some time to figure this out, the *Zero* was most effective at low altitude and lower speed. It didn't have hydraulically operated flaps and rudder because dang it, they were too heavy. This omission made the plane lighter but it had to be steered manually. The higher the speed the more difficult it became; kind of like when your *Silverado* loses power-steering. When the Japanese changed their naval air tactics to suicide bombing, films often show *A6M Zero* attackers diving straight into the sea. The pilots didn't have the strength to control the plane in a 350 mph crash dive. But earlier in the war the *Zero* fought mostly at sea-level protecting and attacking aircraft carriers. That's why the lumbering American torpedo bomber squadrons were completely wiped out at Midway. Those fellows were first-rate pilots but stood no chance against the nimble *Zero* piloted by the best naval aviators ever assembled. But in mid-1942 the Americans captured an intact *Zero* and restored it. With what they learned came the *Grumman F6F Hellcat*, an *F4F Wildcat* upgrade that was a flying *Brink's armored truck* with speed and firepower.

Tawi-Tawi

The Americans ground on inexorably westward. General MacArthur took New Guinea supported by crack Australian infantry whom he would never directly credit. When the Americans won a battle it was an American victory. When the Australians did, it was an Allied victory. He generally and studiously avoided contact with the front lines except if a camera crew was at hand. With the American 5th Fleet island-hopping to the north, Doug ordered they outflank and bypass the heavily fortified and defended Japanese naval bases at *Rabaul* and *Truk*. This was a part of Doug MacArthur's strategic genius and he was one, despite all the personal faults. Both Rabaul and Truk became *de facto* prisoner of war camps for Japanese troops that never would or could be evacuated. Japan had to fall back to what they named *The Inner Defense Perimeter*. The Americans set their sights on the Mariana Islands and landed in July 1944. The Japanese saw what happened to Germany and knew that the islands were within heavy bomber range of Japan. The *IJN* had to contest this invasion. By this time the Imperial Navy had centrally located to the Philippines. They chose a gigantic open anchorage at *Tawi-Tawi* near Borneo, an immense island that had lots of oil. It was *sour crude* that didn't need to be refined. Just pump it right out of the ground into the warships. What could be better than that? The one problem was *sour crude* has a high sulfur content that not only corrodes boilers but is also highly inflammable. The unrefined sour-crude was tolerated because boilers can be repaired after an operation. On the downside, Japanese warships began to explode from the highly volatile unrefined sour crude oil fumes, mixed with the steam from leaky boilers that could be set off from even one enemy hit. The casual observer might very well feel sorry for them.

The Battle of the Philippine Sea

When the Japanese fell back to the *Inner Defense Perimeter*, they reassembled their fleet at *Tawi-Tawi* with a reconstituted naval air arm. After Midway the Japanese figured they would someday need a fighter to replace *the Zero*. They might have thought about that the day they bombed Pearl Harbor. By

1944 it was finally ready: the *Nakajima Ki-84 Hayate*, named *Frank* by the Americans. It was the best Japanese fighter of the war. *Frank* was unfortunately not designed to operate from aircraft carriers since it was an Army project. What a pity. Interestingly, in 2020 the *USN's* most advanced carrier (*Ford class*) can't operate the Navy's most advanced fighter (the *F-35*) and won't until 2027. In Japan's case it is difficult to discern who or what organization was making the final verdict on projects like this. They didn't have a government, but rather like the United States in the 21st Century, a large group of competing bureaucracies. The Japanese Army wanted a new fighter and left the Navy out of the decision making process. The Navy did the same to them with the Zero. The Army never got their hands on one.

The lovely Taiho blows up

Flying the now obsolete *Zero* instead of the very hot *Frank*, the *IJN* assembled nine aircraft carriers for the decisive battle to defend the Marianas Islands. They had a new carrier Admiral; *Jisaburō Ozawa* who was the best the Japanese ever had. Unlike Nagumo at Midway who rushed forward, Ozawa coordinated his attacks with Army long-range bombers and launched his own attacks out of the range of American counter-attacks. His plans were quite brilliant but three of his carriers blew up on account of volatile oil when struck by American submarines. This included the esteemed *Shokaku* and their only wartime carrier designed as one from the keel up: the sleek *Taiho* with its armored flight deck. The scores of escort destroyers Japan lost transporting troops might have saved them but couldn't.

Turkey shoot

Benjamin Franklin wanted to name the *American Wild Turkey* as the national bird instead of the *Eagle*; the symbol of every repressive monarchy and dictatorship throughout world history. The whole history of the United States might have been different were he listened to. Like the *American Buffalo*, the wild turkeys were easy targets for men with guns. In a battle that came to be known as a *Turkey Shoot*, Ozawa was able to launch a 1000 plane attack upon the American fleet in combination with land-based Betty's. In the old days the American carriers would have been doomed. But now they were defended by massive anti-aircraft cannons and the Hellcat. They did what they were designed to do and completely wiped out Japan's naval air arm. The Americans named the battle *The Great Marianas Turkey Shoot* and shot down 750 Japanese warplanes to 130 of their own (80 of which crashed attempting night landings). For the Americans, the Marianas operation coincided with the D-Day landings in Normandy. From this point onward, the US Army would suffer 65,000 casualties a month in all theaters. They named it *The Casualty Surge* and were not prepared for it. Japan came away from the Marianas calamity with two realizations: if the Americans could ever be defeated at sea it would have to be with surface units, preferably at night and in constricted waters like the Solomons where the IJN was often very successful. Finally they slowly and reluctantly came to the conclusion that any conventional air attack on American naval units was akin to a suicide mission.

The Central Location

General MacArthur could read a map. He finished first in his class at West Point so was able to recognize topographical features and calculate time and distance; something the German Army never quite properly understood. Considering the awful jungle conditions on New Guinea he constantly outmaneuvered the Japanese. He was able to establish landward defensive perimeters with repeated seaborne invasions to the rear of Japanese positions. Instead of directly attacking the enemy, General MacArthur thus made the Japanese Army march hundreds of miles through the jungle to attack him! He gained a thousand miles in two months; something no military commander in world history has ever done. With New Guinea taken, the Americans were ready to thrust northwards towards Japan; but how and where? At the *Pacific Strategy Conference* (26-27 July 1944) Doug convinced President Roosevelt that the Philippines reconquest would best further American interests. The islands were and are an American possession he reminded the President. Admiral Nimitz wanted to bypass them and attack Formosa instead, and then Japan. MacArthur countered that there were half a million Japanese troops defending the Philippines and that it was now the central position of their empire. Japan needed it and the loss of 500,000 troops there would further reduce the number of defenders for the home islands. Roosevelt concurred but Doug neglected to tell him that he wanted to retake every island, every inch of ground and wipe out the entire Japanese garrison to a man. He couldn't do it but leveled Manila in the process. Manila was a thriving city in the summer of 1944 and undamaged by war. It was known as *The Pearl of the Orient*. When Doug was through with it a few months later, it was worse than Hiroshima after the atomic attack. There were 200,000 dead and a million homeless. Now they blame it all on the Japanese. But they didn't have the firepower to turn Manila into a wasteland. Their air force attacked the American invasion, not Manila. The little heavy artillery they had was in the north. But for Doug, every battle was *the Alamo* and Manila was the center of Pilipino collaboration with the Japanese. For him this was not only a personal affront, it was treason and he was going to make them pay for it.

Petticoat junction

Nowadays, *Pilipino* people like Americans. After serving for nearly a century as an American *puppet state*, the last American military base was gone in 1992. The Americans now come as tourists with money to spend. There is also a market for young *Pilipino* women as brides for American men of all ages. The men must come to the Philippines, join the woman in an arraigned contractual marriage and take her home. You could say this is human trafficking but there is no deception involved in the process. Everybody knows what they want and everybody has a pretty good idea about what they will get. The women want a new home and life in America. The men, fed up with radicalized American feminism, want a *young* wife not ideologically committed to her husband's emotional, psychological and physical destruction: hence a charming trans-oceanic *quid pro quo*. Manila is the center for this trade. When war broke out in 1941, the situation was completely different.

The 2nd Philippine Republic

Among the legends that emerged from the war was that the Pilipino people loved Americans and therefore, *ipso facto*, hated the Japanese conquerors. The truth is the exact opposite: most Filipinos passionately hated the Americans and welcomed the Japanese as liberators. The *Sakdalista* party was formed to legally resist American occupation. Once Japan took over they were supported by the *Ganap Party* led by pro-Japanese general Artemio Ricarte, *the Father of the Philippine Army*. His organization was a part of the *Katipunan* or *KKK* (Supreme and Venerable Association of the Children of the Nation) founded in Manila in 1892. These pro-Japanese groups were active throughout the nation and fought with Japan against the Americans. The Japanese had never done anything horrible to them and the Americans had. The vast majority of Americans never hear of the *Philippine-American War* (1899-1913) where millions of Filipinos died awful deaths. The combat on both sides included terrifying atrocities that went far beyond the capacity of any civilized people to comprehend. This is why the war in unknown in American history; it's not clean, nor easy to understand. When Spain was overcome in 1899, Filipinos established the *1st Philippine Republic* under President Emilio Aguinaldo. The Americans crushed them and created the puppet *Insular Government* and later *Commonwealth* as euphemisms for an American military dictatorship. Artemio Ricarte was another founder of the doomed 1st Republic. Forty years later, Ricarte would invade the Philippines with Japan. The Japanese were smart enough to let the Filipinos govern themselves and gave them formal independence in 1943; something the Americans had promised but didn't deliver. Both Aguinaldo and Ricarte were firm allies of Japan as were many other founders of the *1st Republic* who didn't want to see the Americans return. They formed the *2nd Philippine Republic* centered in Manila. The Japanese had problems relating to most of the people they conquered which is why they often and sensibly took a step back and allowed home-rule. One thing they didn't like was short-wave radios. If the Japanese military police (*Kempeitai*) found someone with one, they were in very serious trouble because it was a tool for spies and sabotage. For most ordinary Filipinos though, if you kept your head down it was possible to lead a normal life: hold a job, have a home, a wife and children. This is something most Americans often hope for as well. In regions of the Philippines populated by Muslims there was the constant threat of rebellion and massacres. This was the *Moro Rebellion* and it continues to this very day. The areas in revolt weren't a good place for Japanese Army troops and there was butchery on both sides. There was also a resistance unit led by *El Supremo Luis Taruc*, a communist and chief honcho of the *Huks* that operated in a central Luzon enclave north of Manila. Named *Hukbong Bayan Laban sa mga Hapon* (*People's Army Against Japan*) the *Huks* were fierce fighters who took no prisoners. The Japanese did the same. But the area around Manila was good duty and a safe place for Japanese soldiers and Imperial Marines on shore-leave. In Manila, an off-duty Japanese soldier could go out at night in dress uniform with a buddy and not worry that he might get his head cut off. He could go in a bar, have a few friendly beers and maybe even find a real girlfriend. If not, there were thousands of prostitutes patrolling the narrow and dimly lit streets of *Old Manila* and hundreds of bordellos. Manila was a peaceful place and the Japanese authorities wanted to keep it that way and did.

Little China girl

In *Shanghai Express* (1932) Marlene Dietrich remarked: *It took more than one man to change my name to Shanghai Lily*. On one of the many occasions that General MacArthur returned to Washington from the Philippines, he brought a sweet young lady out of Shanghai with him. Doug set his girl up in a nice Washington hotel but neglected to provide her with any outdoor accessories like an overcoat. He told her: *There is no need for you to ever leave the hotel room my dear*. She soon did and Doug, miffed, sent her a one-way ticket to Manila along with a help-wanted list. She was smarter than he thought and rightly squeezed $15,000 out of him (real money in those days) before she moved on. The truth is, and it's often neither acknowledged nor properly understood, soldiers need women. It's what the fighting is all about.

That is why the men have dress uniforms made from the finest fabrics and trimmed with enough regalia to make the last joined buck private look as sharp as a gold-braided General Field Marshall. Military commanders want their soldiers to look good on leave. The fact is there are millions of women who are attracted to a man in uniform and will often bestow sexual favors upon them. It's one of the reason men join-up and also why the United States Marines have the sharpest dress uniforms ever invented. They do this so that the men can connect with women or; *get laid* in the *vernacular*. If the men cannot form liaisons with women, however brief they might be, authority breaks down. Rapes occur, then robberies and break-ins, even arson and murder. Pretty soon a disciplined combat unit becomes an armed mob. This sequence of events is as old as warfare and might be why prostitution is called the world's oldest profession.

The world war still shapes today's human perception

Even now we continue to demonize Japan as one of the major perpetrators of evil in the war. Russia, a nation that sacrificed a whole generation of young men and women (27 million of them) in the fight against fascism, is now counted among the enemies on account of the failed peace. China too is placed on the wrong side of history as their socialist/communist state emerged from the war as a permanent enemy. Only the victors have remained pure in their ideals say the prevalent legends. The victorious Allies; England, France and the USA are simply *morally good*. This allows them to keep killing and at the same time permits them to ignore their own place in the process that killed 75 million people, most of them unarmed women and children. The killing continues daily but the legend of the righteous war makes it all sweet as Danish pastries at *Dunkin' Donuts*. For Germany and Japan especially, their deeds are criminalized. American laws are still ratified to punish them. Witness California's *Hayden Act* (1999) that allowed any disgruntled Korean-American or Asian-American of any nationality, to sue Japan for war crimes, real or imagined, for up to *one trillion dollars*. This was eventually ruled unconstitutional. Then there is *House Resolution 121* (2007):

> *Whereas the "comfort women" system of forced military prostitution by the Government of Japan, considered unprecedented in its cruelty and magnitude, included gang rape, forced abortions, humiliation,*

and sexual violence; resulting in mutilation, death, or eventual suicide in one of the largest cases of human trafficking in the 20th century.

Neatly overlooked are American comfort women in Japan, Korea and Vietnam that involved millions of women in a worldwide *human-trafficking* operation that dwarfed Japan's. Three days after the Japanese surrender on August 15, 1945 the United States military set up the *RAA* organization (*Recreation and Amusement Association*) to gather Japanese women into brothels to provide sex services for the entirely American occupation troops. Eventually 500,000 Japanese women were recruited to work these brothels. Japan was overwhelmed by war with millions of dead men. For many families and young women it was either submission to American troops or else watch mother eat dinner out of a garbage can. We don't see any American congressional inquiries about this; nor will we ever. But the US Congress still seeks to criminalize Japan's organization of prostitutes for their own troops as illicit and grossly immoral. This is because the issues of Japan's war were never resolved in a realistic way. Instead, the post-war treaties were only ratified as retribution against an Asian nation that dared usurp the power of the west.

Japan liberates Southeast Asia

The *Imperial Japanese Army* was centered upon ironclad discipline that showed no mercy to slackers of any sort. When they conquered all of Southeast Asia in the matter of a few months they were greeted enthusiastically as liberators by the native populations. Indonesia fell quickly as did Malaya. The *Kingdom of Siam* (Thailand) swiftly became an ally. *Tun Muhammad Ghazali bin Shafie*; Malaysian Foreign Minister (1981-84):

> *Why does Japan have to make an apology? In the war Japan got rid of the British didn't they? We should not forget we welcomed the Japanese Army with such joy. Without Japan there would have been no independence for Southeast Asia. If we try to deny the precious sacrifices the Japanese made it is like looking only at the back mirror.*

After the war, 945 Japanese were executed for war crimes, not against the natives but for alleged crimes against the former colonial masters. The Japanese didn't take and murder hostages like the Germans and Italians. When there was a problem the *Kempeitai* took care of it, usually with bribes. Their methods were sometimes brutal but whole villages weren't wiped out in retaliatory massacres like in Albania, Russia, Greece and countless other places under Italian and German occupation. For the western colonialists in Southeast Asia, no native had any rights whatsoever. The British, Dutch, French and American colonists were only interested in rubber, oil and opium for re-sale in the west. The natives were enslaved to get it. The Dutch in Indonesia were particularly brutal. The Americans thought themselves the best of the lot and let the Spanish elite do some of the dirty work. But you couldn't tell that to the *Huks* who are still fighting, as are the *Moros*. Some say the Japanese enslaved up to 500,000 *comfort women*, a euphemism for sex-slave. This doesn't make sense. In places like Bangkok, Hanoi, Saigon, Rangoon, Singapore and other large cities there were plenty of native prostitution services and bordellos by the thousands. Yes *comfort women* were sent to posts out in the backwoods and the conditions were not good. There are thousands of prostitutes working legally in Nevada right now who can say the same thing. The Japanese occupation was looked upon as a temporary situation that would end when the war was over. And in truth, all of Southeast Asia was in fact liberated from the former colonial masters by 1960. The Japanese showed the natives not only how to do it, but that it could be done, and easily.

Nanking

Japan's war in China was a horrifying race war, very different from anywhere else in Asia. The image we have of the *Imperial Army* is that of a malevolent force that didn't take prisoners and enjoyed atrocities. That comes from the war in China. The incidents at Nanking are particularly well known. Iris Chang (*The Rape of Nanking*, 1997), who literally devoted her life to the massacre, concluded that up to 400,000 died concurrent with thousands of appalling and terrifying atrocities. Japan's Hata Ikuhiko (*Nankin jiken* [*The Nanking Incident*] 1986) says far fewer died, perhaps 10% of Chang's estimate. What people don't take into account was that *the Imperial Army* was medieval in command structure. It was not a modern army. And Japan didn't have a government. Nobody was in direct command and control except for local commanders. And keep in mind; no Japanese soldier or sailor ever did anything in this war unless ordered to by a superior officer.

The Rape of Zara

In 1202 the *4th Crusade* set out to retake the *Holy Land* from the godless Saracens. On the way to Jerusalem, the holy knights sacked the Christian city of Zara (now the Croatian city of *Opsada Zadra*). Units from Venice felt they were owed money. They deemed the rich city theirs for the taking and got other Crusaders to join in. Nobody was in overall authority and nor could they be, as that was the nature of medieval command and control. Some units participated while others didn't. Pope *Innocent III* excommunicated the perpetrators (later rescinded) but it was too late. Something similar happened at Nanking in 1937. The city lies on the Yangtze River, the 3rd longest in the world and the Japanese thought that when they took it, China would surrender. They didn't and never would. It was defended by some of the best units in the Chinese Army (*The National Revolutionary Army*) including the elite German trained *86th* and *87th Divisions* (Germany still train Chinese troops) as well as squadrons of fighters and bombers of the independent *Soviet Volunteer Group*. The problem was that the Nanking defenders never surrendered. The main defending force pulled out but left behind a rear-guard, some uniformed and some not. The shooting let up but never stopped. Had there been some sort of formal surrender things might have been different. For the *Imperial Army* they thought the campaign was going to be easy. It wasn't and the men began to take revenge upon the civilian population. In Russia there were many massacres of Jews where some individual Germans refused to participate. The deeds were carried out anyway. No German soldier was ever punished for refusing to kill Jews. In Nanking it was the same. Some Japanese units, often led by psychopaths, raped and murdered thousands of innocent Chinese women and children. Thousands of young Chinese men were put to the sword. Other Japanese units stayed clear of it. Some tried to help but we never hear about them. However it was, the Nanking incident was deemed typical and established the *Imperial Army* as a vicious and murderous organization capable of any and all atrocities. But was Nanking any more representative of the *Imperial Army* than *My Lai* for the American Army?

> *I sent them a good boy and they made him a murderer*   Mrs. Myrtle Meadlo

Paul Meadlo was 22 year old farm boy from Indiana. He was a member of Charlie Company, *20th Infantry Regiment, 11th Brigade* attached to the *23rd Americal Division* (established 1942). Their average age was twenty. Charlie Company was in Vietnam for three months when they attacked *My Lai* on a March morning in 1968. They had already suffered 35% casualties but never actually engaged the enemy. The losses were all from sniper-fire, mines and booby-traps. Many of the men were fearful, lost close friends and wanted revenge. When they were ordered to attack the village of *My Lai* in a *search and destroy* mission they were told that elements of the *48th VC Regiment* (*Viet Cong* guerilas) were in the village. Officers also said that since it was a market day, the villagers would be away. Looking for their first real fight, Charlie Company didn't get any return fire because there weren't any *VC* in *My Lai*. Nor were the villagers at market. They were still there eating breakfast while the *48th VC* had left the night before. Enraged, the unit proceeded to kill everything alive in the village including farm animals, dogs and cats. Many young women and prepubescent girls were brutally and unspeakably raped and then murdered. There were 504 dead and observers stated there were no military age men among them. They were *all* women, children, infants and old men. Meadlo participated as did most of the company. He died a broken man. Some Americans like Harry Stanley refused to shoot. Michael Bernhardt wouldn't fire and planed to assassinate the entire American chain of command, starting with Lt. Calley when he returned home. Hugh Thompson and his helicopter crew rescued as many Vietnamese as they could. Ron Ridenhour wrote a 5-page letter that was largely ignored, but finally acted upon. It got the massacre investigated. Nobody in the chain of command was ever punished except for the company commander, Lt. Calley who led the massacre. He served 3 days in jail and was released. A good film about all this is *Four Hours in My Lai* (1989). The American hypocrisy is especially evident when only 22 years before they hung Japanese General *Tomoyuki Yamashita* after a mock trial for simply being who he was. The charge and verdict was that Japanese troops not under his command allegedly committed similar atrocities. In fact it was just another post-war show trial and judicial murder.

Yamashita takes command

In September 1944 it was evident that Japan might very well lose the war. Prime Minister Tojo tried to end the war in China but the Imperial Army was unwilling to make any concessions. Somebody needed to tell them to wake up and smell the coffee. But there wasn't a governmental agency that could do that and Emperor Hirohito was a war monger. Japan should have shortened the line and withdrawn to northern China and Manchukuo. But when a nation decides to fight the whole world, viable options become limited upon looming defeat. When the Marianas fell General Tojo was asked to resign and was replaced by General *Kuniaki Koiso*. The new PM looked at a map, saw what was coming, and recalled Japan's best General Officer from isolation in Manchukuo. *Tomoyuki Yamashita* was put on the first plane to Manila. Named *The Tiger of Malaya* after his conquest of Singapore, he took command on October 10, 1944. Yamashita was the toughest General anybody ever faced and he would hold off MacArthur until the Emperor Hisself surrendered in August 1945.

Saratoga becomes an American template for war

Years ago all American school children learned about the *Battle of Saratoga* (1777) many times over. Nowadays it isn't taught anymore because it was won by all those nasty white men that are erased from history, one monument and curricula at a time. *The Saratoga Campaign* was noteworthy because the elaborate multi-pronged British attack plan showed how silly they were from the American perspective. Yes, *Gentleman Jonny Burgoyne*, who was a playwright of some note, did follow through on the plan (his own actually) to march south from Canada and split the colonies in two. But General Howe, who was supposed to march north from New York in support, instead went south and took Philadelphia whose inhabitants, to Howe's utter disbelief, did not cheer upon his arrival. Barry St. Leger, who was to drive east in support of *Gentlemanly Jonny*, did not make haste and never got there either. Burgoyne was then isolated and destroyed by the ever so practical and concentrated Americans. Through their own experience, complicated and far-flung plans thus became a direct contradiction to *the American Way of War*. That method was: locate the enemy, attack the enemy, defeat the enemy and then go home. They don't do it that way anymore. But in October 1944 the Americans attacked the Philippines with everything they had including the most powerful navy ever to sail. Their aim was the utter destruction of the Japanese Empire.

Leyte Gulf

The *Imperial Japanese Navy* was, beyond all doubt, the most superbly trained naval force in the world when the war began. They enjoyed complex plans because their rigorous preparation and attention to detail allowed them to coordinate intricate maneuvers in a vast ocean sea. At Midway it all fell apart. After that their strategy became more straightforward. At the Philippine Sea they concentrated all their naval air forces but were shattered nonetheless. Forced to retreat, Admiral Ozawa tried to reconstitute the naval air arm in home waters. The surface fleet sailed to Singapore and Tawi-Tawi and waited there in relative safety. MacArthur's 6th Army of 200,000 men invaded the Philippine island of Leyte ten days after Yamashita's arrival. Doug chose Leyte because he knew the terrain and Leyte Gulf was itself a vast and attractive anchorage. More importantly Leyte was the central position of the Philippines and from there the Americans might attack in any direction. Leyte was already occupied by the Japanese *36th Division* (11,000 men) and Yamashita rushed in six more divisions and two independent brigades of the *14th Army*, including the renowned *1st Division*. Leyte is a relatively small island and General Yamashita recognized that it could be better defended than a large one. Why not stop the enemy there he reasoned? Since the Japanese had two years to build defensive emplacements they put up a good fight. They used wood and earth rather than concrete and let the jungle overgrow it to make them all but invisible. American units were in for some nasty surprises. Field Marshall William Slim fought the Imperial Japanese Army in New Guinea. Slim:

> *He fought and marched until he died. If 500 Japanese were ordered to hold a position, we had to kill 495 till it was ours. And then the last 5 killed themselves.*

Lingayen Gulf

Yamashita's defenders would all be wiped out after a three month battle. Leyte was eventually declared secure in late December 1944 with some individual Japanese soldiers fighting onward until the 1970's. Stymied by fanatical resistance on Leyte, General MacArthur was in a hurry. He thought he'd have the whole thing wrapped up in three months. The next step was Luzon and indeed he would never take it. On January 9, 1945, American 6th *Army* landed 200,000 men at Lingayen Gulf north of Manila. This was one of Doug's patented sea-borne maneuvers to the enemy's rear. They drove south to take the city and General Yamashita decided to abandon it and fight on undefeated in the mountainous north. What he didn't know was that 12,500 *Imperial Marines* in Manila decided they were going to defend the place. They were joined by 4,500 Imperial Army soldiers who didn't want to retreat anymore either.

The Battle of Manila (February 3-March 3 1945)

When General MacArthur's 6th *Army* invaded Leyte they saw themselves as liberators. That's the common and overwhelming historical interpretation of the event. It makes the whole thing into a morality play for public consumption. It was a righteous war and Americans paid a high price in blood to help them dang Filipinos gain the freedom they so justly deserved. In truth, Japan didn't have too many allies in their struggle against the West but the 2nd *Philippine Republic* was one of them. Back then, most of Japan's allies were

German satellites like Slovakia that could never offer any help whatsoever. Germany did occasionally send, via the polar route over Siberia, long-range Ju-390's with weapon designs, aircraft engines and nuclear technology. Closer to home Japan's only allies were Manchukuo, a vassal protectorate, Thailand and the Philippines. The *2nd Philippine Republic*, when rarely mentioned at all, is always listed as a Japanese conquest and puppet state. As it were, most Filipinos hoped to have seen the last of the Yankees forever when they were ignominiously driven out in 1942. The American invasion in 1944 was against a primarily hostile population. The American Army had killed millions of their friends and family. The center of Filipino resistance to the Americans was in the capital of the *2nd Philippine Republic* at Manila. There were more than one million civilian residents including 100,000 Japanese *émigrés* who were small business owners, shop-keepers and fishermen.

Victory or Death

When a small force of Spartans, Thespians, and Thebans defended the pass at Thermopylae against Xerxes' Persians, there were no women among the defenders. The women were home with their families caring for the children and elders. That was their job. The Greek men died protecting them. That was their job. Women are something men die for. When Col. Travis sent his famous *Letter to all Americans* he wrote; *I shall never surrender or retreat*. The 182 men at the *Alamo* decided to die with him because death was preferable to being pushed around by scum like *Antonio López de Santa Anna*. For the *Imperial Marines* in Manila, they and their buddies were part of the long retreat from the Gilbert and Marshall Islands, from the Solomons and all points east. They too were tired of being pushed around. They blew the bridges and set up defensive positions as best they could. The Imperial Marines got these orders:

> *Manila Naval Defense Force Order No. 43, dated 3 Feb. 1945.*
> *1. The South, Central and North Forces must destroy the factories, warehouses, and other installations and materiel being used by Naval and Army forces, insofar as the combat and preparations of Naval forces in Manila and of Army forces in their vicinity will not be*

> *hindered thereby. 2. The demolition of such installations within the city limits will be carried out secretly for the time being so that such actions will not disturb the tranquility of the civil population nor be used by the enemy for counter-propaganda. Neither large scale demolition nor burning by incendiaries will be committed. "3. A special order will be issued concerning the demolition of the water and electrical installations.*

For Japan, Manila was a friendly city. You can read that in the orders. Japanese demolitions were confined to the docks and tactical strong points. They did not destroy the water and electrical installations. The Americans did that. They did not massacre the civilians who were brutally hogtied and murdered by Filipino guerillas fighting for the Americans. The slain civilians were primarily Japanese émigrés.

Manila Defense Force Order 13, Feb 1

> *The Americans who have penetrated into Manila have about 1,000 army troops, and there are several thousand Filipino guerrillas. Even women and children have become guerrillas. 2. All people on the battlefield with the exception of Japanese military personnel, Japanese civilians, and Ganaps will be put to death.*

As the Americans moved south into Manila they took along with them *Huk* guerrilla fighters who usually armed women and children. They were ruthless and wanted revenge upon the civilian population of Manila. American resistance leader John C. Hunt:

> *My experiences with the Huks were always unpleasant. Those I knew were much better assassins than soldiers. Tightly disciplined and led by fanatics, they murdered some Filipino landlords and drove others off to the comparative safety of Manila. They were not above plundering and torturing ordinary Filipinos, and they were treacherous enemies of all other guerrillas (on Luzon).*

These were the people the *Imperial Marines* were up against. Warring with Japan were the anti-American Filipino *Ganap* troops. They saw the Americans as oppressors and they too defended the 2nd *Republic* to the death. They knew what the Huks would do to them if they were taken alive. The *Battle of Manila* lasted one month. When it was over, all Japanese and Filipino defenders were dead. Manila was completely destroyed by constant American air and artillery bombardments. Doug's apologists say he forbade all air-strikes on Manila because he loved the Pilipino people so deeply. Put into American military jargon; that's just a lot of bullshit. Manila was bombed, strafed and pounded by artillery for one month solid. Among the cities destroyed in the whole extant of the *World War*, only Warsaw suffered greater destruction than Manila. Warsaw was *systematically* eradicated house to house by highly skilled German Army demolition troops. This was the kind of destruction suffered by Manila. To blame this kind of city-wide devastation upon a few thousand *Imperial Marines* with no heavy artillery and no extensive demolition experience, is one of the big lies to emerge from the war.

> *Never send a man where you can send a bullet*   US Army tactical doctrine

What happened to Manila is similar to the fate of *Saint-Lô* and hundreds of other French cities, towns and villages in the *Normandy Campaign*. The American tactic was called *putting the city into the streets*. American artillery and carpet bombing would shower the target until the buildings would collapse as rubble into the streets. This then blocked enemy wheeled and tracked vehicles. *This is a defensive tactic.* It was used to prevent German mechanized units from mounting counter-attacks. It didn't matter if the Germans were in the town or not. The tactic is to just destroy the buildings and block the roads. Good luck to the people who live in the town. Much smaller than Manila, the French medieval city of *Saint-Lô* stood as a major road hub in Normandy. In July 1944 the Americans carpet-bombed and shelled the city for two days. They destroyed 95% of it. The death toll record is kept artificially low, some reports suggesting only 352 civilians died or maybe 800 at most. *Saint-Lô* was otherwise untouched by war. However, the population of *Saint-Lô* in 1936 was c. 12,000. In 1946 it was c. 6,000. You figure it out. Only now in the 21st Century is it slowly revealed that at least 60,000 French civilians died in the two-month *Normandy Campaign*. All those photos and films of smiling French women kissing and ecstatically greeting American troops are carefully stage-managed photo-ops. The American Army, the fabulous *Band of Brothers*, cut a swath of devastation 200 miles wide across the heart of France. It was war. The French still show distrust and this is one reason why. In this relatively short campaign, French courts sentenced 29 Americans to death for rape (punishments carried out) and 124 other soldiers for prison terms. The problems arise when Americans try to sugarcoat it as they always do. That's how all the myths, lies and legends emerged from this war as gospel truth. Since the war never ended, the myths need to be perpetually maintained and sold to a reluctant population because the current and future wars aren't about freedom but markets.

> *War is hell*   William Tecumseh Sherman

When General MacArthur looked down upon Manila and saw the desolation he had wrought, he knew he had to blame someone other than himself. Manila just suffered more damage and more deaths than Hiroshima or Nagasaki combined. A light went on! Why not pin it on General Yamashita and the goddamn Japs? His sycophantic staff backed him up all the way. With the upmost sincerity they explained how deeply Doug loved the unfortunate citizens of Manila who were viciously gunned down by a fanatical enemy known to often go berserk. The *Imperial Marines* and *Ganap* troops were all dead anyway so who could know what really happened? What Filipino would dare dispute him or the American version of events? Anyone who did would be quickly and quietly murdered by cutthroat Filipino-American guerillas. The Americans were in charge again and they occupied the Philippines as a puppet state until 1992. Japanese resistance in the north of Luzon would keep MacArthur occupied and out of the coming Okinawa operation. This also kept Doug out of the headlines. For this, he would see to it that General Yamashita be hung.

THE DARWINIAN REVOLUTION AND THE POLITICS OF MASS-MURDER

*No captain can do very wrong if he places his
ship alongside that of the enemy*   Nelson

There were four instances in the *Pacific War* when the *IJN* might have turned the tide and at least delayed the seeming inevitable. Had *Admiral Nagumo* ordered a 2nd strike at *Pearl Harbor* he might have rendered the American base inoperable. Instead he ran. At Midway, a strike with the 63 aircraft available to him might have lessened the catastrophe. In those early days, carrier borne strikes upon enemy carriers were <u>always</u> successful. With the American strikes already on the way, there was nothing Nagumo could have done to protect *Akagi*, *Kaga* and *Soryu*; they were doomed. But the early launch surely could have sunk one enemy carrier and perhaps two, leaving him with *Hiryu* and the soon to arrive *Zuikaku* to carry on. Instead he dithered and saw his fleet destroyed. At Savo Island *Admiral Mikawa* turned away at the decisive moment. He feared an air attack that never came. The entire Solomons campaign was in his hands and he let it slip away. The fourth instance was at Leyte Gulf.

Fast Carriers

As the United States *5th Fleet* approached Japanese home waters they began to encounter the vast armada of war planes assembled by the Imperial Army for the final defense. There was the redoubtable *Kawasaki Ki-61 Tony* and the *Nakajima Ki-43 Oscar*. So too was the *Nakajima Ki-44 Tojo* as the American signal corps maintained a sense of humor throughout. All these Army planes had the same flight characteristics as the *Zero* with the same defects; lack of armor and self-sealing tanks sacrificed for range and speed. The Army had a bomber the Americans had yet to encounter, the Mitsubishi Ki-21 *Sally*; once *Jane* but that was Doug's wife's nickname and so it had to go. *Sally* was a bit faster than *Betty* with more defensive armament; but like *Betty*, a flying gas tank with no armor or self-sealing tanks. When American *6th Army* prepared to land at Leyte, the Japanese Army launched a series of large-scale air attacks with 200 bombers against American *Task Force 38*. Attached to *3rd Fleet*, it was the most powerful flotilla ever assembled. *TF38* included 17 fast carriers, 6 fast battleships, 13 anti-aircraft cruisers, 58 destroyers, and over 1,000 aircraft. Among them were five *Atlanta* class light cruisers with eight dual 5-inch/38 caliber gun mounts that could fire over *17,600 pounds* of radar directed proximity fused anti-aircraft shells *per minute*. The American aircraft carrier personnel were now as skilled as the early flight crews of the *1st Air Fleet*. In those days the attack had primacy and was indefatigable. Now, no conventional air attack could break through American defenses. The Army's attack lost 80 aircraft or 40% losses. The returning pilots however were ecstatic. They claimed to have sunk 11 American carriers and 5 battleships. There was jubilation in Tokyo. The Emperor was beside himself and composed a poem.

The Imperial Navy's dilemma

Admiral *Soemu Toyoda* was now commander of the *Japanese Combined Fleet*. He was at least competent and an improvement over Yamamoto and Nagumo. Admiral *Mineichi Koga* had replaced Yamamoto whom the Americans ambushed in April 1943. *Koga* was, unfortunately for Japan, unable to end the suicidal use of destroyers as transports. He died in March 1944 when his heavily armed Kawanishi H8K *Emily*, the best flying boat in the world, crashed in a storm. *Toyoda* was then named commander and he had the good sense to make Jisaburō Ozawa the *3rd Fleet* commander that comprised the naval air arm. He then had more good sense not to accept Ozawa's resignation after the debacle in the Philippine Sea when the naval air arm was routed. It's not like nobody saw this coming. *Kōichi Kido, Lord Keeper of the Privy Seal*, was Emperor Hirohito's closest advisor. Before Pearl Harbor he advised Hirohito that the Army's ambition to invade and annex the Dutch East Indies for its oil was an over-reaction to the American embargo. Already bogged down in China, he suggested there were other ways to secure oil and husband resources short of world war. He correctly assessed that the embargo might not work. *Royal Dutch Shell* was an independent mega-oil corporation. They operated independent of state control (still do). They sell oil to the highest bidder. Like the misbegotten attempt to cripple Mussolini's Italy with an oil embargo in 1935, this one probably wouldn't work very well either. He argued that it was 3,500 miles from Indonesia to Japan through passageways of constricted waters that are typically haunted by submarines. He predicted that tankers might become easy targets in a war with America that would surely ensue. He was right and by October 1944, Japan had lost more than 50% of its already limited merchant and oil-tanker fleet. Admiral Toyoda now knew he had to fight the Imperial Navy's final battle for the Philippines; for were it to fall, Japan would no longer have access to either Indonesia's nor Borneo's oil. The Imperial Navy would have to give up deep water naval operations entirely and conduct costal defense only in home waters. Thus the Imperial Navy would have to be prepared to sacrifice the entire striking power of the fleet to defend the Philippines and destroy the American landings at Leyte.

Toyoda commits the naval air arm reserves

The Admiral didn't entirely believe the Army's exaggerated reports but suspected that at least *some* USN carriers were lost. He couldn't know it, but the Army's attack hadn't sunk a single enemy ship. Nevertheless he had to go all in. The naval air arm reserves were committed. These were the men who could take off from, and land, on moving aircraft carriers. This is still the most difficult feat in all of aviation. Finding and training the fellows who can do this isn't easy. Toyoda also committed 100 bombers of the *Tkōgeki Butai*. This was *la crème de la crème*, the T-Air Attack Force with radar equipped Betty's and the new radar guided Army Mitsubishi Ki-67 Peggy bombers of *Sentai 98*. Armed with torpedoes, the T-Attack Force specialized in night attacks at zero altitude. They lost 42 planes and got one hit on the cruiser USS Canberra that damaged her. Of the 400 naval aviators, 300 of them were lost. Admiral Shigeru Fukudome:

> *Our fighters were nothing but so many eggs thrown at the stone wall of the indomitable enemy formations*

Admiral Ozawa's 3rd Fleet now had only 100 pilots to man the four aircraft carriers left to him. It included three light carriers: plus the esteemed Zuikaku and two hybrid and makeshift half battleships with tiny flight decks. Those two ships, *Ise* and *Hyūga* were useless as attack carriers and would have been better left as battleships. Their attempted conversion only shows how desperate Japan was. As the seaplane tenders they turned out to be, they would have been much better assigned to *Center Force* that had no air support whatsoever. With no viable attack formations left to it, Japanese 3rd Fleet was a decoy. As it was, Japan no longer had a naval air arm and the final battle would be fought with surface formations.

The Naval Battle of Leyte Gulf

Leyte Island lay on the eastern shores of the Philippines facing the colossal and planetary Pacific Ocean. To the north was Luzon Island, where in 1942 Doug MacArthur's doomed army fought its last battle at Corregidor on the Bataan Peninsula. The *San Bernardino Strait* separates the two islands and it was through this narrow body of water that Japan sent *Center Force*, one of the most powerful surface fleets ever assembled for battle. Their mission was to destroy the invasion transports attending American 6th Army's Leyte invasion. *Admiral Takeo Kurita*, a grizzled veteran of the Solomon's Campaign, commanded *Center Force*. Five modern fast battleships were the backbone of the fleet. They included sister ships *Yamato* and *Musashi*, the largest and most powerfully armed battleships ever constructed. Their main armament was nine 18.1-inch guns. Their secondary armament, twelve 6-inch guns and twelve 5-inch guns, was equivalent to a heavy cruiser and a light cruiser combined. In terms of firepower it was three ships in one. *Center Force* had in addition 10 heavy cruisers, including *Atago, Takao, Chokai, and Maya;* all modern fast sister ships with ten 8-inch guns. A single salvo from them could realistically fire 3,000 pounds of ordinance at a moving target 15 miles away. There were two light cruisers and fifteen destroyers as a screen. Because of Japan's chevalier use of destroyers, *Center Force* didn't have nearly enough of them.

The Plan

Japanese *2nd Fleet* divided its force as there are two approaches to the anchorage off Leyte. The *Southern Force* was to probe the *Surigao Strait* that divided Leyte from the much larger island of Mindanao. The USN *7th Fleet* was laying in wait. *Southern Force* ran straight into an American trap set with battleships as well as four destroyer squadrons and 59 torpedo laden patrol boats. The main *USN* force was six old battleships; *Pennsylvania, Maryland, West Virginia, Tennessee, California,* and *Mississippi,* the first five veterans of Pearl Harbor. Two of them (*West Virginia* and *California*) were sunk at Pearl Harbor by Japanese torpedoes and raised. This was the last battle ever fought between big gunned battleships. In a night action, old battleships *Fuso* and *Yamashiro* were heavily outgunned, torpedoed and sunk, as were 2 cruisers and 5 destroyers, including the venerable heavy cruiser *Mogami*, veteran of Midway. 7th *Fleet* then gave chase leaving MacArthur's invasion force to its own devises. Surely they assumed that Halsey's fleet was protecting the northern route to Leyte. No?

> *I am hurt, but I am not slain; I'll lay me down and bleed a-while, and then I'll rise and fight again.*   Sir Andrew Barton 1511

In the meantime *Center Force* had its own set of problems. Since Japan's air fleets were aimed at the enemy carriers, *Center Force* had no air support. This meant that American submariners could brazenly operate on the surface. Where were *Ise* and *Hyūga?* They were providing air recon for 3rd Fleet that didn't need it. Seaplanes armed with depth charges are the bane of submarines. Two them, *Darter* and *Dace*, spotted Kurita's battleships at midnight with radar, reported the location and were able to position themselves for an attack at dawn. Like the attack on Lusitania, the submarines were able to freely maneuver on the surface and plot an intercept. *Center Force* lacked sufficient destroyers so the American boats got close enough to sink heavy cruisers *Atago* and *Maya* and heavily damage *Takao*. For some unknown reason Admiral Kurita had his flag in *Atago*. She was a sleek and beautifully powerful ship. But why didn't the Admiral have his flag and staff with him in the legendary and breathtaking *Yamato*, pride of the Imperial Navy? At Trafalgar, Nelson was in the 104 gun *HMS Victory*, the most powerful ship in the Royal Navy. Why was Kurita in a lesser and much more vulnerable ship? Did he think himself unworthy of the great ship? When *Atago* capsized from four torpedo hits, she took 360 men down with her. Kurita was fished out of the water. With his flagship shot out from under him, he finally transferred his flag to

Yamato. Most of his staff was killed and the Admiral needed them to maintain first rate communications. Later that day, 259 dive and torpedo bombers from *Task Force 38* attacked Yamato's sister-ship, the magnificent *Musashi*. She took 11 torpedo and 16 bomb hits and went to the bottom. She never got to fire her batteries at an enemy ship. *Captain Inoguchi* and 1000 men went down with her. Heavy cruiser *Myoko* was blasted into impotence and limped home. Admiral Kurita surveyed his shattered formations and ordered a *battle turn-away*. They ran and apparently made for Singapore and safety. But it was a ruse of war. He had no intention of withdrawal.

Halsey takes the bait

Admiral Ozawa's *3rd Fleet* lay to the north and hadn't been spotted by the Americans yet. But he knew where the enemy was. With the last of Japan's naval air arm he launched the final Japanese carrier attack of the war. They were shot to pieces and didn't record a hit. But now, *Admiral William F "Bull" Halsey* knew where Ozawa was. He turned *Task Force 38* northward towards Ozawa's carriers to get in range of the enemy. But this took *TF-38* away from General MacArthur's landing zone, leaving him defenseless! Halsey had been one of the loudest voices condemning Admiral Spruance who, rather than pursue Ozawa after *Philippine Sea*, stayed to protect the landing zones in the Marianas. Spruance understood that the whole point of naval operations is to support operations on land. Halsey forgot this and got wrapped up in his own quest for glory. He then went after Ozawa's ghost carriers with everything he had. He didn't even leave a few destroyers as pickets to patrol the *San Bernardino Strait*; much less his splendid fast battleships that could and should have been left behind, just in case. But he had the name *Bull* for a reason. He didn't know that his airmen greatly exaggerated Japanese *Center Force* losses, much like the Japanese Army airmen had done a few days before. *Center Force* still had four fast battleships, six heavy cruisers, two light cruisers and all its destroyers. Kurita shrugged off his losses and when the last of the enemy airplanes flew away over the horizon, he turned again towards the San Bernardino Strait and Leyte Gulf.

THE DARWINIAN REVOLUTION AND THE POLITICS OF MASS-MURDER

All those moments will be lost in time, like tears in rain   Roy Batty

At dawn, with *Southern Force* destroyed, Kurita's *Center Force* was Japan's last hope. However the battle was all going according to plan. American *7th Fleet* was off chasing down the shattered remnants of *Southern Force*. Halsey's *3rd Fleet* was hot in pursuit of Ozawa's phantom carriers. *Center Force* then emerged unseen from the San Bernardino Strait. They turned south toward the American transport fleet and were 50 miles away from a decisive victory. The only enemy force in the way was *Taffy 3*, the call name for an inconsequential group of 6 escort carriers and 7 destroyers, four of them light. American escort carriers (*aka* jeep carriers, or baby flattops) were merchantmen with a flight deck. They were slow, without armor, had a single 5 inch gun, and carried only 20 planes that didn't have armor-piercing bombs or torpedoes. *Center Force* should have sunk all of them and brushed the destroyers aside. *Yamato* weighed more than all the ships in *Taffy 3* combined. The route to Leyte Gulf lay open. Once there, *Center Force* would *effortlessly* sink the anchored transports and MacArthur's flagship as well. That would have killed him as Doug was aboard. At this critical point, in the one moment of time he was born for, and with victory his, Admiral Kurita had a nervous breakdown. He emotionally collapsed and ordered *General Attack*, an order that sent all the ships of his fleet to be on their own in two-ship divisional command and initiative. Kurita's battleships would attack the enemy individually and not in force! He immediately lost command and control of his big ships! *General Attack* is an order left over from *Galley Tactics*: when warships propelled by oars and slaves sought to close with the enemy and ram them. In the *Age of Sail*, it might be ordered when ship captains wanted to close with the enemy and capture prizes. Its only modern usefulness is to send lighter ships to cover heavy unit withdrawal in a desperate situation. The Germans ordered such an attack at Jutland; the famous *Death Ride of the Battlecruisers* (*Todesritt der Schlachtkreuzer*). That's the extent of it. Kurita needed to order *Line Ahead*. This is not a difficult maneuver and is as old as the day ships were equipped with cannon. It is orderly and is the fundamental naval tactic in the *Age of Steam*. When Mikawa smashed the American fleet at Savo Island, his ships were in *Line Ahead* formation and it was at night. This is something those fellows practiced all the time and getting into *Line Ahead* is about as difficult as backing your car out of the driveway. In *Line Ahead* the fleet's firepower is concentrated and maximized. There is a methodology: the ships line up, one after the other, and *all its guns* can be brought to bear upon the enemy. Targeting and range-finding is accomplished as a group and hit percentage is increased dramatically. *Center Force* had a massive firepower advantage. First contact was at 20 miles. Their ships were twice as fast as the enemy and only needed to quickly close to within 15 miles to begin deadly accurate shooting. Kurita's destroyers would have methodically placed themselves between *Center Force* and the enemy fleet to prevent torpedo attacks. In *General Attack* there is no formation, no method. Swiftly, battleship *Haruna* almost collided with her sister ship *Kongo*. It's not easy to maneuver 45,000 tons of steel moving at 35 miles per hour when nobody knows where anybody else is going. *Haruna* had to drastically alter course away from the enemy to avoid the collision with *Kongo*. She never fired a shot that scored. In *Line Ahead*, all the anti-aircraft guns of *Center Force* would have been concentrated as well. American air attacks in this battle were harassment and not a mortal danger. In any case, all their carriers would have been sunk in just a few minutes; like shooting fish in a barrel.

> *Reason and calm judgment are the qualities that belong to a leader.*   Tacitus

Taffy 3 was commanded by Rear Admiral Clifton Sprague. He made optical contact with Japanese battleships that have a distinctive silhouette. Being Japanese, the designers shaped their battleship's conning towers to look like a pagoda; very unique and beautiful ships. When Sprague made visual contact he knew he was in serious trouble. His entire force and the 10,000 men under his command faced imminent death because the Japanese weren't going to stop and pick up survivors. Nobody would. As it was, 1,500 men would soon be dead and another 1000 wounded. This was the deadliest naval battle of the war for the Americans thus far, with the exception of Pearl Harbor. He stayed cool and made one correct decision after another. He immediately turned into the wind and launched all aircraft while scanning the horizon for rain squalls and cloud cover. *Taffy 3* was part of *7th Fleet* and so he radioed *Taffy 2* and *Taffy 1* that both lay to the south. He told them his predicament; that an enemy surface fleet was about to blow him out of the water. *Taffy 2 & 3* immediately launched planes. They had no armor-piercing bombs or torpedoes as these light carrier groups were there for anti-submarine, and combat air patrol only. Sprague then ordered his destroyers to lay smoke-screens while he ran his carriers toward the closest squall. Had the Japanese been in *Line-Ahead*, Sprague would have found himself already under fire. Nevertheless, with the battleships closing fast Kurita then stupidly ordered his destroyers to the rear. When American destroyers entered the fray they would have been forced to engage them instead of taking hundreds of shots at Japanese heavy cruisers.

At sea one day, you'll smell land where there'll be no land, and on that day Ahab will go to his grave, but he'll rise again within the hour. He will rise and beckon. Then all – all save one shall follow

While Sprague ran the carriers, American destroyer captains decided to attack the enemy. They didn't need an order from Sprague to do that either. As Nelson once said; *a captain can't go wrong attacking the enemy*. With Kurita fouling his command, there were no enemy destroyers to hinder the American attack. Destroyer escort *USS Samuel B. Roberts* (DE-413), named for a seaman who heroically died in the *Naval Battle of Guadalcanal*, took on the Japanese heavy cruiser *Chikuma*. It should have been no contest. Lieutenant Commander Robert W. Copeland radioed his men: *This will be a fight against overwhelming odds from which survival cannot be expected.* They went ahead at full-steam. *Chikuma*, armed with eight 8-inch guns, should have blown *Roberts* out of the water. Instead, *Roberts* armed with only two 5-inch guns rapidly fired off all 600 rounds onboard and raked the heavy cruiser at close range. Chikuma, like the rest of the Japanese fleet that day, fired but missed too often. Destroyer *USS Hermann* (DD-532) joined the fight and caught Chikuma in a deadly cross-fire that would eventually sink her. Things were happening fast as they do when warships moving at 40 mph are shooting at point-blank range. It was like the 30-second *Gunfight at OK Corral*; seven men standing a few feet apart and firing 30 shots at each other. Most of those shots missed. Cmd. Ernest Evans made for super-battleship *Yamato* at 65,000 tons. Evans' ship, the destroyer *USS Johnson* (DD-557), displaced only 3,000 tons but she too had 600 rounds of 5 inch ammunition and she just kept shooting. *Yamato* began blasting her with its secondary armament but couldn't fire accurately nor hit anything consistently. Evans wanted more speed and ordered a volatile fuel mixture. A junior officer pointed out how harmful to the engines this was. Evens told him; *Son, I don't expect to be alive in 3 hours.* He knew his fate but before he went down with the ship, Evans launched all of the 10 torpedoes *Johnson* had. That forced *Yamato* to turn away. The great ship would not return to the battle, nor would it ever fire upon an enemy ship again. As *Johnson* sank, Japanese crewmen saluted her. Kurita's order to his destroyers was obviously the wrong one; presumably made to give his heavy ships clear fire. Even more sorrowful was that Japanese destroyers were the best in the world and well practiced at close range engagements in their often victorious battles in the Solomons. Undefended by destroyers, *Center Force* lost heavy cruiser *Chokai* when a single 5-inch shell from an escort carrier's solitary gun exploded her torpedoes. Luck always seemed to favor the Americans.

> *There seems to be something wrong with our bloody ships today*   Beatty at Jutland (1916)

Why was Japanese gunnery so bad? The attacking American destroyers should have had no chance of survival. The problem was Japan used their computerized range-finders when they should have sighted the guns manually. Each gun on a battleship may be fired individually by its *Gun Captain*. They instead used electromechanical analog computers; the *Type 92 Computer* or, on the *Yamato class*, the *Type 98 Director*. High atop the Pagoda, course and speed were entered manually and the computer's results calculated each gun battery's shot. But Japanese heavy ships were not practiced in point-blank gunnery at small ships moving at 40 mph. For decades the Japanese navy practiced long-range shooting out of *line-ahead formation* at enemy battleships. They designed their computerized gunnery control for the *Decisive Battle*. That was the kind of encounter they envisioned. They could have had that against even easier targets; the slow moving American escort carriers. Instead, Japan's big ships weren't prepared for the *general melee* that followed when Kurita ordered *General Attack*. Japanese ships continued to use range-finder calculations that could not accurately gauge a haphazard melee. Kurita then continued to panic and when two other destroyers also attacked he misidentified them as cruisers. He also misidentified the escort carriers as fleet carriers. This led him to believe he was up against the entire *USN 3rd Fleet*. He then ordered *Center Force* to withdraw. They scuttled three more heavy cruisers that were badly shot up by small caliber gunnery and aircraft armed only with depth charges. In the end, Sprague and his subordinate captains did everything right and Kurita did everything wrong. Again, like Nagumo at Pearl Harbor and Midway, like Mikawa at Savo Island, and like Yamamoto at Guadalcanal; Kurita didn't understand the strategic value of his mission. None of them could see the larger scheme. Kurita should have pressed onward at all cost. The attempt to halt the invasion was worth every ship in his command. Had even one heavy cruiser broken through to the undefended American transport fleet, the United States would have suffered its very own Stalingrad-like disaster. They still would have won the war out there, but at the cost of General MacArthur's entire 6th Army. Instead Kurita ran. The battle was lost and with it the Japanese Empire.

> *If we're going to die, let's die like men.* General Patrick Cleburne's last words. Franklin (1864)

The term *Kamikaze* was an American mistranslation of Japanese characters for *The Special Attack Corps*, itself a euphemism for human guided bombs. When the Americans attacked first the Philippines and then later the home islands at Okinawa, *the Special Attack Corps* seemed that it might be the only way out of a lost proposition. The Americans tend to see the *Kamikaze* as a product of ingrained Japanese fanaticism. This is how we continue to see the war. Japanese soldiers and airmen didn't desire to die in battle nor were they fanatical. They viewed life, duty and death in a different way. They wanted to win battles and were prepared to fight to the death for it. That's not an attribute unique to Japan. But they hadn't won too many battles since the *Solomons Campaign*. Suicide bombing wasn't based on a desire to *die for the Emperor*. By this time in the war, most Japanese didn't give a hoot about him. The distant and remote Hirohito was someone they increasingly began to blame for a war that had come home very suddenly, unexpectedly and horribly wrong. The formation of *the Special Attack Corps* was based upon sound military precepts. Many of the deficiencies that the Japanese faced, like fuel, ammo, a shrunken pool of qualified pilots and outmoded airframes, could be rectified by a change in tactics. The high command was reluctant to adopt suicide bombing but did so only when the first units, formed as an impromptu reaction to overwhelming American firepower, had some successes in sinking an American escort carrier in the extended battle for Leyte. Suicide bombing was a directional shift in strategy and once adopted, became the method the Japanese used to counter American material advantage. It was logical not fanatical. The Japanese did try to compensate families for the loss of their sons. When a *Special Attack Corps* pilot died in action, his family was compensated 10,000 Yen or about $38,000 in today's currency. This was a lot more than the British or Americans gave to their sons who died on suicide missions.

Suicide missions

Field Marshall Montgomery sent the British *1st Parachute Division* on a suicide mission to take *Arnhem Bridge* far behind enemy lines. He knew the *2nd SS Panzer Corps* was there waiting for them. He rolled the dice and sent them in anyway. The 10,000 paratroops had few heavy weapons and took 80% losses. Less than 10% of German fighter pilots survived the war. Every time a young German pilot strapped himself into a *Ju-87 Stuka* ground attack aircraft it was akin to a suicide mission. Those *Stukas* flew at 90mph at the completion of a dive. They were a realistic target for anyone with a gun. American *8th Air Force* crews that flew unescorted missions over Germany in 1943 suffered 90% losses and the average life-expectancy was 6 missions. German submariners suffered 70% losses, yet the men went to sea anyway. For Japan, conventional attacks upon American targets had become *de facto* suicide missions that took disastrous losses. Why not make suicide attacks standard operational procedure? In fact the Japanese lost fewer pilots when they adopted suicide as policy. They actually overwhelmed American air defenses. Kamikaze tactics, while deadly for the individuals involved, protected the interests of the nation and caused the enemy to suffer at a catastrophic rate. The Japanese simply didn't recognize the sanctity of the individual. For the *Kamikaze* pilot, his sister and mother were far more important than he. He died to protect them. If his mission required less fuel because it was one-way only, he was happy to make the sacrifice. Because the mission was one-way, targets that would normally be out of range were now in range. That was excellent compensation for his life that now had tangible value. The kamikaze pilot didn't need to be as well trained. There was no need to try and hit a target with a bomb. The airplane itself had a 1000 pound bomb attached to it. The aircraft was an instrument to stop the slaughter of innocents burned alive in American terror bombing. While a damaged airframe would stop a conventional pilot and force him to abort, the *Kamikaze* pilot continued the mission, often successfully. They had no fear because their first combat mission was their last. The *Kamikaze* attacks were the only rational means the Japanese had to prevent the invasion of their homeland and the physical eradication of their race. It was a trade-off they felt worth it. A good short film about this is *Victory at Sea* episode 25 (1952). It's scary.

Kamikaze tactics

Westerners think Kamikaze assaults were individual aircraft making lone-wolf attacks because in the west suicide is an individual decision based upon utter despair. For the Japanese it was war. The raids were well thought out and meticulously planned. A typical raid would consist of c. 300 fighter escorts along with a like number of suicide bombers. Some planes would drop *chaff* to baffle American radar. The first big raid was on April 6, 1945 off Okinawa. The great ship *Yamato*, with only enough fuel for a one-way sortie, was used in conjunction with it. She was lost with 3,000 men. The air attacks got through though. On the approach, the attacking force changed course frequently and weaved in and out of cloud cover to confuse the defense. When intercepted they split into smaller groups; the escorts engaged with enemy *Combat Air Patrol* while the suicide bombers dropped to sea-level to commence the attack. In suicide attacks off Okinawa the *IJN* had 2,525 naval pilots killed and 1,387

Army pilots lost as well. In return, more than 400 Allied vessels were struck by *Kamikazes*. The problem for Japan was that while the *Kamikaze* attacks caused a lot of damage and mayhem, they were never able to completely disrupt American air operations, which was the point of it all. Nor could individual suicide attacks upon B-29s over Japan stop those deadly fire-bombers. Tokyo was razed in March 1945. Like German medieval cities, Tokyo was primarily made of wood. They are all gone now, forever lost without a trace. Nor did it prevent the defeat at Okinawa with half its population dead (150,000 civilians) along with three full divisions and six independent brigades of 100,000 men. With Okinawa taken, and Germany's defeat, Japan tried to surrender in May 1945. The Americans wouldn't let them.

> *There is no instance of a nation benefitting from prolonged warfare*   Sun Tzu

The Battle for Okinawa is listed in the books as a victory for the United States. It was a strategic victory that put the Japanese home island of Kyushu within range of American single-engine warplanes. But it was the last US military operation of the war. They couldn't go on taking losses at this level. The US Army suffered between 50,000 and 75,000 casualties in Okinawa, nobody knows for sure. Thousands of bodies were never recovered, lost in the mud. The carnage was worse than in the Argonne 26 years before. For the United States Navy, Okinawa was the single greatest and only catastrophic defeat it ever suffered. The Okinawa disaster is forgotten because everything tuned up roses when Hiroshima went up in smoke. The *USN* had some bad days against Japan but nothing that came close to Okinawa. At Pearl Harbor 4 battleships went down along with 13 ships damaged and 3,500 casualties. Savo Island saw the loss of four heavy cruisers and 1000 dead. Taffy 3 got beat up badly and lost four ships. At Okinawa the *USN* lost 34 ships, with 368 damaged, 4,900 sailors killed with over 4,800 wounded. Admiral Nimitz warned Washington that the Navy could not continue operations with losses like this and they didn't. The next proposition was the invasion of Kyushu that neither the Army nor the Navy was ready for. This was especially true since Doug MacArthur's 6th Army was still engaged with General Yamashita and would be until the final surrender. Okinawa was protected by three divisions and six independent brigades. Kyushu would be defended by at least nine divisions and perhaps as many as twenty. No Japanese unit of any size ever surrendered in this war. Every man was expected to fight to the death and did. In addition the Imperial Army had another 10,000 *Special Attack* aircraft in reserve. The early completion of the atomic bomb project was an unexpected get out of jail free card for the Americans. There was never any serious intention to actually invade Japan. When U-234 surrendered and gave up its cargo of nuclear triggers, the American bomb was ready.

None dare call it treason

An enduring legend is that the Americans only used atomic bombs as a last-ditch alternative to an invasion that would cost one million American casualties. This is based upon the generally accepted notion that it was impossible to offer the Japanese anything other than abject capitulation. This *either/or proposition*; unconditional surrender or else nuclear annihilation is now unquestioned. It didn't have to be that way. *The Manhattan Project* was very resource intensive as was the even more expensive B-29. It is understandable that people involved in the engineering realm wanted to see them used. But there is no conventional or rational political motive that can otherwise explain the utter American refusal to negotiate after Okinawa. *Unconditional Surrender* wasn't written by Moses on stone tablets. It was conceptually aimed at Germany; told quite explicitly that 1945 wasn't going to be like 1918 all over again. Germany was to be vanquished and the problems associated with the eradication of Prussia are still felt, even if not comprehended, today. Japan was another story and having borne the brunt of the war against them, the Americans strangely decided they needed Soviet help. *The Flimflam Man* never met anybody like *Uncle Joe Stalin*. Nobody ever did. Here we have a true country bumpkin from the backwoods of the *Ozarks* in negotiations with a political genius who, in addition to all else, was at once a poet and a real-life gun-toting bank robber just like Bonnie and Clyde. Even a conman like Truman, who was at his best fleecing ordinary Americans, had to be impressed. They say Stalin killed 20 million people. That's a lot of death warrants to sign. Actually, Stalin signed fewer than 900 death warrants for counter revolutionaries; and there were plenty of them inside Russia all paid for by the West. If 20 million did die then obviously he had a lot of help. Look no further than the people who denounced him led by the madman *Khrushchev* and his cronies. The edge Stalin had over Truman was that he was a straightforward man who meant what he said and kept his promises. The last honest man Truman ever met was long ago when he stopped going to church. In the end he was overwhelmed, not by Stalin but by the traitors in his midst. Fellow Soviet agents and communists like Averell Harriman and Dean Acheson, who was Truman's Undersecretary of State, all agreed that the Soviet Union should enter the war against Japan three months after Germany's surrender. Whatever for? The Imperial Navy was at sea-bottom. Japan was already reduced to her pre-war boundaries. Let them keep some of that. The problem with understanding American strategy is the blanket acceptance of the notion that not only wouldn't there be any negotiations; but that there never could be any. The Americans refused to make any serious concessions. It was complete surrender or else. The Japanese refused to capitulate when that was the only option. When we look back upon it all now, the end is known and that end is a fireball over Nagasaki. Were it not, America's position in Asia would be far stronger than it is today with Communist China a mortal enemy and an economic and military superpower that has infiltrated the highest reaches of American government and society.

Unsustainable losses

After Okinawa's fall in May 1945, some in Japan schemed for a long, perhaps interminable war, fought to the death of the nation and the race. They still had 1,200,000 troops in Manchukuo. They planned for an inevitable Soviet invasion and would concede the north but fight it out in the mountainous south and Korea. Every unit would fight to the death as they always did. The Red Army never encountered this kind of opposition and, after four years of brutal race war against the Germans, they could not have been ready for it. At this point in the war 400,000 Asians died, on average, each month. The American Army losses (65,000 casualties per month) were not sustainable. Those losses didn't count Navy and Marine casualties. The Americans wanted to double draft quotas to make up the deficits. They also wanted to move twenty full divisions over from Europe. Those fellows didn't want to die in Japan. They'd done their job and wanted to go home. There were threats of mutiny. Logically it was time to take a step back and leave Japan with a small remnant of her empire intact. There were many ways to keep pressure on Japan. The B-29 attacks were unstoppable. Curtis LeMay wanted twice-daily 1000 plane raids. He had the planes. Blockade was already in place. With the American Navy and Army unable and, in the Navy's case, unwilling to conduct further operations, why not negotiate? The American communists got their way because Truman should have been managing a chicken & pancakes joint in Joplin Missouri. He couldn't understand that ever since America embarked on empire and made the Philippines, Cuba (in effect), Puerto Rico and the Kingdom of Hawaii possessions; then *ipso facto* American foreign policy was anti-nationalist and anti-monarchial. It would be forevermore. Both were the main threats to the international bankers that controlled the American government since 1913 by virtue of their monopoly over America's money supply. In 1945, communist Secretary of the Treasury Henry Morgenthau, Jr. and his communist deputies Harry Dexter White, William Ludwig Ullmann, William Henry Taylor, Harold Glasser and Irving Kaplan, as well as Bela Gold (Agricultural and Foreign Economics), Nathan Gregory Silvermaster (War Department), Schlomer Adler (Treasury), Launchlin Currie (Special Representative to China), *Alger and Donald Hiss* (State) and thousands of others, worked tirelessly to destroy Germany while supporting Stalin and *Mao Tse-tung* in China. These fellows also coordinated espionage rings like *The Silvermaster Group*, the *Golos Group*, the *Soble spy ring*, the *Perlo Group* and many other organizations working within the United States government. They were all directly controlled by Soviet assassination teams (*Ignace Reiss* murder, *Juliet Stuart Poyntz* disappearance for example) and the *NKVD* (KGB). The American government wasn't infiltrated by Communists; it was being run by them. It still is. They supported first Soviet Russia because there were no labor unions there. They promoted and supported Communist China because there wouldn't be any labor unions there either. A soviet state where all workers are slaves is an ideal banker's paradise run from afar in London and New York. *Mao Tse-tung* was at the head of a hardened army of one million ideologically committed soldiers. Manchukuo as a supply hub in the hands of the *Soviet Red Army* would secure the northern flank of Mao's *Red Chinese Army*. This would ensure the defeat of *Chiang Kai-shek's Chinese Nationalist Army* four years later. There is no other explanation for American rejection of any realistic terms in May 1945 and to instead purposefully allow the *Soviet Red Army's* easy conquest of northern Manchukuo from the already demoralized Japanese. Stalin, no fool, quickly promised he would declare war on Japan three months after German capitulation. Exactly to the day, the *Red Army* invaded Manchukuo. The Soviet supply line east along the single track Trans-Siberian RR was tenuous and slow. Instead, this invasion was primarily supplied by the Americans through Vladivostok on Liberty Ships re-flagged with Soviet colors (*Operation Milepost*). It included 45,000 trucks, 1000 tractors, over 1000 motorcycles, 2,400 Jeeps and tons of RR equipment. This was all part of the *Lend-Lease* giveaway (70% of which went to England). If the legion of communists working for Truman wanted what was best for America, they would have done all they could to keep the Red Army out of Manchukuo. They had something else in mind and that was the destruction of Chinese nationalism. To do this, American internationalists kept Japan's war going to create the *Chinese People's Republic* as the densely populated nation of slave laborers that it is today. After all, Japan only asked for the continuation of the Imperial System. Let them hold and administer Manchukuo and Korea for the time being. Considering that the Americans eventually granted *Hirohito and his entire family* blanket immunity soon after their surrender in September, why was it impossible to consider this just a few months before? The standard explanation is that it would have been political suicide for Truman to accept terms from the Japanese in May 1945. He was told that too many Americans wanted Japan thoroughly squashed. The snake-oil salesman bought it from his Communist cabinet. He would have been a hero had his nation defeated both Germany and Japan in the same month. Instead the Japanese Empire was given away to the Communists. What the American public actually wanted was a victorious peace and the safe return of their sons. Give Japan Manchukuo so what? Who might care that it was promised to China? If China wanted it, let them take it. Why not let Japan keep Korea too? At least it would be out of the hands of the Reds. North Korea wouldn't now be the most repressive government in world history threatening Los Angeles and San Francisco with nuclear annihilation. For American Reds this was impossible to entertain because they wanted Japan's nuclear secrets in Korea to be captured by the Red Army. And they were. No patriotic American cared if Japan were to retain partial control of her empire. None of them cared when Japan continued to administer the whole of Southeast Asia after their actual surrender. Instead the Red Army was allowed to take both Manchukuo and Korea and Communist collaborators continue their treachery unabated to this very day.

The Hirohito crime family

Japanese military expansion in Asia was under the complicit direction of Emperor Hirohito and his family. They had more than cordial relations with *Yoshio Kodama* who ran all the rackets in Japan. Hirohito's brother *Yasuhito, Prince Chichibu* directed the looting of banks throughout Southeast Asia. He and *Kodama* made Al Capone look like a piker. Most of the theft was gold holdings from western banks or else from rich religious orders that accumulated gold in support of the western colonists. In the early going the gold was transported directly to Tokyo. From 1942 onwards, American submarines began to sink the gold transports and so the loot was centrally located in the Philippines. They call this hoard *Yamashita's Gold*, although the General arrived too late to bury all that gold or even be involved at all. He was a soldier, not a conman. The loot was disposed of by the *Yakuza* (the Japanese mafia) directed by *Prince Chichibu*. The gold is said to equal the value of the entire United States expenditures to fund the war, or $120 billion ($12 trillion today). Some of it was buried in the Philippines and some sunken into Tokyo harbor. Doug took over as Emperor *pro tem* by conquest in 1945. In one of history's biggest payoffs, he gave immunity to Hirohito's family when they should have been imprisoned, tried and hung. This made the Australians extremely angry. Their prisoners of war were often murdered in cold blood by Japanese small unit commanders. In some instances, Australians were used as live targets for gunfire and bayonet drills. Nevertheless, Hirohito and his brother had connections to the *Yakuza* which Doug used to pacify Japan and quell communist resistance. Like all crime syndicates, the *Yakuza*, as well as Kodama's organization (the *Kantō-kai*) are fiercely patriotic and anti-communist. They couldn't get away with their crimes in a communist police state. Stalin recognized American suzerainty over Japan because he was always careful never to overextend Russian influence. He agreed to split Korea down the middle with the Americans even though they didn't even have any troops there. Here the Americans spill all their blood and treasure but are forced to accept *largesse* from Stalin in nations that should have rightfully been theirs by conquest. What was important in Korea was Red Army control of *Hungnam* and its atomic secrets. Cautious with limited financial resources, *Uncle Joe* didn't support the large homegrown Japanese labor union communist movement. They were left in the lurch to be murdered by Japanese organized crime and their American allies. Stalin was committed to traditional Russian foreign policy and the island nation of Japan was irrelevant to that. He had Manchukuo (now *Manchuria* again), Mongolia and Korea as buffer states, and would soon have all of China too, or so he thought.

American Caesar

The myth has it that Hirohito was revered and loved by the Japanese people. Therefore, if General MacArthur, who was *de facto pro consul*, prosecuted him as a war criminal the Japanese people would have revolted. The truth is the Japanese people hated Hirohito's guts. He brought unfathomable disaster upon Japan. Most importantly he had permanently *lost face* when he surrendered. Not only was his surrender *dishonorable* but he had brought *dishonor* upon his whole family and his ancestors as well. This was the code the Japanese lived by. He had asked millions of young and vibrant Japanese men to throw away their youth and commit suicide rather than surrender. He continued a lost war while millions were incinerated. Yet in the end, he took the coward's way out and hid in the basement rather than fight to the death. The films of adoring mobs admiring him after the war were all stage-managed with paid crowds. Japan was never a rich nation under his rule. It was a brutal police state. All resources went to the military and all profits went to the ruling elite who supplied them. Scarcity abounded as millions of young girls were sold into the poverty of wage-slavery and prostitution. Hirohito got immunity precisely because he was a coward and war criminal. He was easy to control and intimidate. It was Hirohito who insisted that three Doolittle raiders be executed for war crimes. Tojo tried to talk him out of it but the little rat refused. In the end it was Tojo who was hung for Hirohito's crimes. MacArthur murdered patriots like *Hideki Tojo* and *Tomoyuki Yamashita* since they represented the nativist faction; the one force that could stall the American military dictatorship. Japanese nationalism was replaced with representative democracy as a supposed cure-all for militarism. Burned-out Japan was partially rebuilt with Hirohito's stolen gold and American venture capitalism. Like in Germany, consumerism, drugs, pornography and alcohol soothed and dulled the senses of anyone who thought independently or who might've harkened back to *Shintoism*. It worked like a charm.

French Indochina

The Vietnam War began the day Japan surrendered aboard the battleship *USS Missouri* on September 2, 1945. There was never a single moment of peace. Doug was the *Master of Ceremonies* at the formal surrender. He gave a speech that asked for world peace and then *roughly and sternly* ordered the Japanese delegation to *sign NOW!* Doug hated their guts and showed it. As they say nowadays, the optics weren't good. The Americans were always wonderfully beneficent once the bomb-bay doors slammed shut and there is something to be said for that. However, Doug's cruel and vindictive rendering to the humbled and withered Japanese delegates dressed in top hats has been edited out for posterity. The surrender ceremony now has a new camera angle from high and above. Doug's close-up is edited out so you can't read his lips. A dubbed and conciliatory MacArthur voiceover gently and respectfully now asks the Japanese to please sign. They do this sort of deception because they can. Everything about the war needed to be cleaned up, falsified and rectified in every way imaginable. And it was. The Japanese troops in French Indochina weren't imprisoned but immediately put to work by the Americans and British. They would continue fighting *Ho Chí Minh* and the nationalist troops under his command. *Ho* had been fighting the Japanese for the last five years. That didn't matter to the Americans; although *Ho*, in his essential naiveté, thought it would. The French would not allow what was *French Indochina* to become what it is today; the three independent nations of Vietnam, Laos and Cambodia. It would cost 40 years of bloodshed, millions of dead and massive long-term destruction to end the wars caused by French, British and American intransigence. To justify the war, the French and then the Americans sold it as an anti-communist prophylactic. The real war was against Asian nationalism.

Dien Bien Phu

The Vietnam War was just as unpopular in France as it was in the United States. The French were up against the military organization formed by *Ho Chí Minh* named the *Viet Minh*. They would later become the regular *North Vietnamese Army* (*NVA*) and the *Viet Minh* irregulars; afterward to be named the *Viet Cong*. Like the Americans later on, the French couldn't figure out how to corner them. With support at home fading fast and in desperation, the French decided to build a massive set of mutually supporting fire-bases replete with an airstrip in northern Indochina. Since the position controlled the flow of supplies and military movements in northern Indochina, the plan was to draw the Vietnamese to attack them, and then defeat them in a defensive set-piece battle. The French hoped to replicate the victorious *Battle of Verdun*. They assumed the primitive Vietnamese Army couldn't lug artillery through the jungle, just like the British assumed General Yamashita's troops could never advance through the jungle to take Singapore from behind. They were both all wrong. The French fire-bases were built in a valley and the Vietnamese could and did bring up massive firepower in the surrounding hills. They encircled the French and bombarded them day and night. Some men went mad. The French artillery commander took his own life. Vietnamese artillery destroyed the airstrip and prevented the arrival of supplies and reinforcements except by dangerous paradrop through enemy fire. The battle lasted two months (March-May 1954). The French surrendered and their troops were ridiculed and stoned when they returned home. The Americans thought they could do better.

The Munich Syndrome

Alexander subdued Afghanistan on his way to India in 330 BC. The Greeks stayed there for 300 years and there are still some cities named after them. From *A Journey around Parthia* by *Isidore of Charax* (early 1st Century AD):

THE DARWINIAN REVOLUTION AND THE POLITICS OF MASS-MURDER

Beyond is Arachosia at 36 schoeni. And the Parthians call this White India; there are the city of Biyt and the city of Pharsana and the city of Chorochoad and the city of Demetrias; then Alexandropolis, the metropolis of Arachosia; it is Greek, and by it flows the river Arachotus. As far as this place the land is under the rule of the Parthians.

He gives the distances in *schoenus* (ropes) an ancient Egyptian unit of distance that varied according to whoever used it. *Arachosia* is in ruins at *Ulan Robat*. The river *Arachotus* is probably the *Arghandab River*. Before the Soviet invasion (1980) there was once a weekly bus (*the Magic Bus*) from Amsterdam to India that passed through Afghanistan no problem. Now, such a journey is impossible and none of these sites are accessible. The Russians invaded to protect the then communist government in Kabul, limit Islamic tribalism within the Soviet Union, and test the military equipment since they hadn't been in a real shooting war since 1953 (Korea). Afghanistan isn't known as *The Graveyard of Empires* for nothing. The Soviet Empire collapsed ten years after the invasion. The Americans invaded in 2001 and it's been 20 years now; the longest war in American history. It is doubtful they will have any cities named after them. The population is extremely hostile. American soldiers cannot take any leave in the capital city Kabul unless they want to be cooked alive in hot oil, a fate suffered by some unfortunate Russian soldiers on leave. They don't have any contact with the natives except in full battle gear and only when out on mission. American soldiers live in large fortified compounds in communal tents that are air-conditioned. All food is flown into them, catered in the Philippines by corporate America. The air-conditioning costs billions as does the chow. Thus far the total cost is *one trillion dollars* or 5% of the national debt. The rational is they wanted to kill *Osama bin Laden* who supposedly ran an international terror organization out of a cave in Afghanistan. The now dead but legendary *bin Laden* is somewhat akin to *Dr. Fu Manchu*, a Hollywood movie villain who directed the vast tentacles of his depraved crime syndicate from *The Cave of the Golden Dragon* in China. The Americans can't get out because the *Munich Conference in 1938* was proof positive that America and the West can never afford to take a step back against evil. Until the world is totally disarmed and pacified and all nations given the blessings of the American way of life, constant warfare against any nation not in accord with representative democracy (and freedom as its necessary corollary) must therefore be destroyed. Thus, foreign policy is made simple and historical interpretations of it in academia and media nicely uniform. Even better, Afghanistan's occupation (when rarely mentioned) is easy to sell on all those Sunday morning political talk-shows. The fact that opium is the world's most lucrative cash crop, and that Afghanistan produces 90% of it, is never mentioned.

Vietnam

After the French were driven out, there was supposed to be a plebiscite in Vietnam. Since *Ho* was going to win it, the Americans set up the *Republic of Vietnam* without him. *Ho Chi Minh* and the nationalists communists ruled in the northern half of the country named the *Democratic Republic of Vietnam*. They wanted control of the nation's resources as opposed to internationalist ownership by bankers. That's what *Mohammad Mosaddegh* wanted in Iran until the Americans organized a coup in 1953. They labeled him a communist and installed the Shah. This is called *Regime Change* now. As a result, fanatically anti-American Mullahs are now in charge of Iran. That's called the law of unintended consequences, an older idea. The Americans labeled *Ho Chi Minh* a communist too, even though the first lines of the Vietnamese declaration of independence are written by Thomas Jefferson. War between north and south was inevitable and the Americans invaded Vietnam in 1965 with an army that eventually numbered close to 550,000 troops. Like the Germans in *Operation Barbarossa*, the Americans didn't know anybody on the North Vietnamese Army (*NVA*) general staff, or anybody in the government except *Ho*. Like German intelligence services they didn't have anybody on the inside and didn't care either; they thought it would be easy.

The Republic of Vietnam had popular support

The *Viet Cong* guerillas terrorized the civilian population of South Vietnam. They lived off the land, stole whatever they needed and that included young women whom they usually murdered when they were done with them; sometimes after a few months. The American Army they were up against in 1965-67 was a professional one. One of the myths of the war is that the American Army never lost a battle. Barry Obama actually said that as did other American general officers. It's just not true. The army covered up lost battles by calling them *engagements*. There are more than 100 lost *engagements* (some divisional level) amid heavy losses: 5,600 helicopters and 3,700 fixed wing aircraft were shot down. Some company level units were wiped out. They were up against not only the *VC* but also the *NVA* and those fellows had been fighting the French and Japanese for decades. They knew how to do it. It was a fair fight, but slowly the veteran American professional soldiers became casualties. They were replaced by young draftees, many of whom didn't want to be there. American atrocities and especially multitudinous massacres by their *ROK* (Republic of Korea) allies against the civil population began to mount up. But the South Vietnamese only slowly turned against the Americans. However bad the American method of war was, it was nothing compared to the *VC* who were utterly lawless and without any sense of decency. The *VC* hated everybody.

Saigon

It's called *Ho Chi Minh City* now which can tell you how it all turned out in case you don't already know. In the 2nd *War-phase* American infantry combat soldiers were, on average, engaged with the enemy 10 days out of 365. In Vietnam it was 240 days out of 365. Even so, American WW II vets had the gall to denigrate Vietnam combat soldiers. Returning Vietnam veterans wanted to join *Veterans of Foreign Wars* (*VFW*) social clubs. The fat old WW II vets rejected them for not fighting in a '*real war*.' Generally unknown is that most soldiers in both wars did not see combat duty. In them, 75% of the force is in supply, or logistical support. In Vietnam there were usually c. 100,000 combat soldiers. Another 400,000 men kept them supplied. Most of those fellows lived in Saigon and it was good duty. Like Imperial Japanese soldiers in Manila or Singapore, Americans in Saigon could go out and have a beer, find a girl and not worry about getting knifed in the throat. Combat soldiers could take leave in Saigon and even shack-up if they had a girlfriend. Not so in Iraq and Afghanistan, where they cannot mix with an exceptionally hostile civil population. That makes all the difference in the world to a *Grunt*. In many ways the American situation in Vietnam was like the British position in the *American Revolutionary War* (1775-1783) with the roles reversed. The British Army (like the Americans in Vietnam) occupied the coastal cities while the American Colonists controlled the countryside (like the *VC*). The Brits were up against General Washington's *Continental Army*, which was a regular army dressed in bright powder blue with white stripes. They fought a conventional war using ordinary volley-fire tactics. It was General Washington's regular army that won the war with French help. The Americans also had irregular armies commanded by *Light-horse Harry Lee*, *Swamp Fox Francis Marion* and others who would make raids and ambushes like the *VC*. Nowadays they would call those fellows terrorists. It got so bad for the British they had to import firewood when their foraging parties were too often ambushed. In a densely forested land, the Royal Navy had to organize a convoy system to bring in firewood from Canada and England to their armies trapped in American cities. In a complete about-face, the Americans in Vietnam were in a similar position. They would build massive airbases throughout South Vietnam to airlift in the necessary food, fuel, ammo, beer and cigarettes to soldiers confined to fortified fire-bases. Combat soldiers would spend a week *in country* and then return to a fire-base for two days of barbeque and female companionship with flown in prostitutes. The food was plentiful and if not mom's home-cooking it was prepared by real cooks who tried their best when the army still had *KP* (kitchen patrol). Beer and cigarettes were unlimited. They don't have that anymore. Unfortunately for American platoons on mission, the *VC* could smell their cigarettes from miles away and always knew where they were. In the end though, it wasn't the *VC* with irregular tactics that won the war. The regular *North Vietnamese Army* simply outlasted the Americans who wanted to go home. Like the French, the Americans couldn't figure out how to beat them in the ten years they were up against them.

Attritional warfare

The war was lost when American commander William Westmoreland decided to the only way to defeat the enemy was to kill more of them than they could reasonably replace. It's called *attritional warfare* and it is the last gasp of an army bereft of ideas. The Army instituted *Search and Destroy* missions, invented by the British in their (losing) war against *Malayanese* guerillas (1948-60). With helicopters, the Americans would fly in a brigade (1000-1500 men) and try to isolate and overwhelm an enemy force with air support in a quick battle. Very often the *NVA* would be dug in and they had really good Russian-made automatic weapons. Like the Reds in Stalingrad, they would try to achieve and maintain *close combat* to negate American artillery and air support. In a battle come to be known as *Hamburger Hill* (*Hill 937*) the *3rd Brigade* of the *101st Airborne Division* suffered 84 dead and 480 wounded for 60% casualties in an eleven day battle (May 1969). The enemy managed to slip away at night. The 101st took the hill, and then left two days later never to return. The Army called it a victory because, (they said), 630 enemy were killed. The real estate meant nothing. There were hundreds of battles like this and it was the entire war in microcosm. This battle caused consternation back home as thousands of people wrote their congressmen to ask what it was all about. A really good film about battles like this and American civil reaction is: *Two Days in October* (2005).

Body counts

The civil population of South Vietnam began to turn upon the Americans when they commenced to indiscriminately kill Vietnamese males, somewhat like the Imperial Japanese Army in China. This was around the time when the protesters back home began to frequently use the word *immoral*. It was. For many American commanders the path to promotion was to present inflated body counts when the number of dead became the full measure of success. This meant killing all males encountered in the field, any age and any occupation. Pity the poor farmer's family when the Americans killed first his buffalo and then him and then his sons. They had the firepower to do it and they were above any law including the sham of military justice. For many Vietnamese, who would never have dreamt of joining the *VC*, they began to join up. It became both a survival mechanism and revenge motive all at once: may as well have a gun in your hands if the Americans were going to kill you anyway. Air Force General *Curtis LeMay* advised that the way forward was to *bomb them back into the Stone Age*. He'd done that to Germany and Japan; why not these guys? What LeMay and others like him didn't understand (and still don't) is that the object of the war was not the complete destruction of Vietnam like it was with Germany and Japan. This is why the same military machine that defeated the two greatest military establishments of the 20th Century in 3 ½ years, could not defeat Vietnam in ten. Leadership didn't want to, as irradiated and immolated people don't make good slaves.

War without end

Even today, it is practically impossible for an American, even those few patriots in the government itself, to understand the nature of American strategy. In 1917 the war against Germany was fought not only against an overseas foe, but against the Germanic nativist population of the United States as well. Twenty five years later, and thrust again into *World War*, American foreign policy since December 7th 1941 has been the destruction of all nativist movements. That is what Nazi Germany and Imperial Japan were, and why their suppression was particularly brutal. All American war since then has been against nationalist movements nominally defined as communist for the public. The United States overthrew the nationalist government of Guatemala in 1954. Guatemalans wanted the resources of the country to serve them and not American capital investment. A 36-year civil war followed that pitted the Guatemalan military funded by the USA against anyone who didn't keep their head down. Ofttimes that wasn't enough. It never is. More than 700 villages were wiped out in massacres with at least 200,000 dead. In the metro setting, 40,000 students, lawyers, teachers and labor leaders were kidnapped and killed. Their bodies were made to *disappear*. A film about this is: *Finding Oscar* (2016).

Baseball and Beer

Cheap fruit, sugar and coffee for breakfast, along with an all-encompassing televised sports industry are one of many ways that keep the American populace pacified. The American *lock-down* in 2020 threw a monkey wrench into this scheme. With no more televised sports and no jobs, the people revolted. Up until then the American communists in command of the nation used private equity firms to conquer and enslave: first their own people, and then the rest of the world. *United Fruit* (now *Chiquita Brands International*) in Central America or *Anaconda Copper* in Chile (both for example) are nominally independent capitalist monopolies. They and other massive international conglomerates are allowed dominion over small nations as they literally strip them of their wealth. The American people's (relatively) high standard of living is supported by this since they pay for it. Suffocated by visual and physical addictions Americans can't understand it. The American Capital-Communist system supports friendly foreign police states backed by American financed military death-squads. American domestic police are now fully militarized too. The military factions on both sides are given lots of guns and ammo as well as the promise of a fairly lucrative lifestyle as long as they support American capital interests. Labor leaders in Guatemala and other Latin-American nations *disappear* when they are thrown out of helicopters. American labor leaders just lose their jobs when the industry they want to unionize is outsourced to China, Mexico or India. When those firms eventually return, but now owned by foreigners, American workers are happy to land any job at lower pay and without union representation. As this happens, American wages are slowly lowered to that of the rest of the world; which is subsistence. This is the nature of modern industrial communism. The election of American nationalist Donald Trump in 2016 met with such astounding and sustained resistance from American institutions because it represents perhaps the last gasp of an anti-communist *Nativist* uprising in the nation that is now the heart of international communism.

Cultural Marxism

After the *1st War-phase* (c.1912-23) and its astounding cruelty, a group of sociologists in Frankfurt Germany, called appropriately *The Frankfurt School*, determined that the Germanic patriarchal family, with its strict hierarchical male dominated structure, was to blame. Their source was one of the original Marxists, Friedrich Engels in his The Origin of the Family, Private Property and the State (*Der Ursprung der Familie, des Privateigenthums und des Staats* [1884]). Most people believe that *Das Kapital*, the source of Engels' ideas, was only economic theory. It was that, but also as an absolutely necessary corollary, demanded the destruction of not only the family but the religious and national structures that supported it. Hitler didn't fall for any of it and since they were all Marxists, he threw them out. They landed in an America that had taken a sharp left-turn with Franklin Roosevelt's election and inauguration in March, 1933. Their course in the infiltration of American society was configured by *Antonio Gramsci*, an Italian communist who was murdered by Mussolini's Blackshirts in 1937. Gramsci was a delightful fellow with a keen sense of humor who liked red wine. He understood that Communist Russia's experiment in socialism had failed miserably. He also correctly recognized the deep flaws in the western bourgeois social order that he was a part of. He saw that war would come again, and proposed that the only way forward was to overthrow bourgeois society from within. He knew this would be a long process; one that he would never see culminated. For the *Frankfurt School*, their members got jobs in the American university system, promoted their friends and weeded out their enemies. With a play on words mimicking *Mao Tse-tung*, cultural Marxists Rudi Dutschke, Herbert Marcuse, and Ernst Bloch named the process *The Long March through the Institutions*. Taking their cue from European Reds, American education stressed *critical theory*: the notion that America was all wrong and in need of re-evaluation and re-structuring. For American sociologists, the primary cause of all social ills, both presently and historically, was the *American Family* that needed to be dismantled and destroyed in its present form. This is why prepubescent children in American public schools are now taught dildo use in what used to be playtime. The infiltration of American society by Marxists is now openly acknowledged by the

THE DARWINIAN REVOLUTION AND THE POLITICS OF MASS-MURDER

American communists who call themselves *Democratic Socialists*. Their leaders know the way forward is not standing on a street corner selling copies of the *Daily Worker*. Their way is to attain success in government, media and academia, insert themselves there and assist a revolution that is barely perceptible in its stages. The end result is now (2020) plainly visible as American media (itself dominated by Socialists) gleefully support an American Maoist revolution. Americans discovered Gramsci in the 1960's. What Gramsci presented was a path towards a *shift in consciousness* away from Christian structured family values that had been the *norms* of American culture. Gramsci proposed that when these *cultural norms* are first challenged and then changed, the composition of the old bourgeois familial order will collapse as the society adopts *new norms*. So for example, attitudes about homosexuality and *same-sex marriage* shifted from 75% opposed in 1980 to 80% in favor by 2015. There is a kind of moral rectitude about this shift in opinion because one's sexual preference ought to be an individual and inviolate choice. But it places Christians and Jews into a moral bind as the Laws of Moses leave no doubt about it. However it is, over such a relatively short period of time, this sort of dramatic reorientation in traditional *norms* doesn't take place by chance. It can only happen as the result of a sustained, intensive and centrally controlled campaign directed at the entire populace by media, academia and governmental institutions now controlled by Marxists. Modern revolution doesn't have red flags and kommissars marching in the streets. It instead stifles dissent and requires uniformity of thought in a quiet but intensely sustained cultural and social revolution. Any deviance from the preferred ideology is a thought crime that can and does lead to political and social ostracism. Significant in this process is to allow and promote Howard Zinn's *A People's History of the United States* (1980) and *A Young People's History of the United States* (2007) as standard texts for American schools. Written by a self-professed anarchist and communist, it chronicles everything that was ever wrong with America. God knows Zinn had an expansive litany of material to choose from. However, when only the negatives are emphasized, young students have nothing else to draw upon. Millions of them now hate America and want to destroy it. The end result is plainly visible as American media institutions gleefully support an internal and violent Maoist revolution by (mostly white) American urban youth.

Margaret Meade visits Fantasy Island

Franz Boas was a West Prussian (*Westphalian*) who landed at Columbia University in New York well before the *Frankfurt School* got there. He is known as *The Father of American Anthropology* (*Humanism*). His students and ideas eventually dominated American Anthropology. They promoted the theory of the *Blank Slate* (Tabula rasa) and *Cultural Relativism*. This idea is that humans have *no innate fixed identity* but one that is solely determined by environment. Race has no reality and does not exist except as a social construction. This is now the single dominant theory in American Anthropology and it is impossible to oppose it. People who try are ostracized. *Margaret Mead* was a young graduate student from Pennsylvania who studied with Boas. In 1928 she set off to *American Samoa* to find out if his theories were correct. She did, for to find the contrary would have been an academic dead-end and career suicide.

Samoa

The islands are way out there near New Zealand. When she got there, the population had been Christianized for over 100 years. She never learned to speak nor read Samoan. Nevertheless she came to the astonishing and remarkable conclusion that Samoan girls all practiced *free love* before marriage with no social consequences. Just on the face of it, the proposition is rooted in the most abject folly. Mead:

> But the seventeen year old girl does not wish to marry – not yet. It is better to live as a girl with no responsibility, and a rich variety of experience. This is the best period of her life. She wants as many years of casual love-making as possible.

Mead never interviewed Samoan men but came to the astounding conclusion that rape was unknown:

> *Samoans are one of the most amiable, least contentious and most peaceful peoples in the world. In Samoa love between the sexes is a light and pleasant dance, and male sexuality is never defined as aggressiveness that must be curbed. The idea of forceful rape or of any sexual act to which both participants do not give freely is completely foreign to the Samoan mind.*

It was all hearsay and fantasy. What else could it be? Not fluent in Samoan, Mead spent just 5 months with the possibly 25 subjects of her study; some of whom later claimed (one of whom swore on her Bible) that they were just pulling her leg. None of her subjects ever got pregnant, nor were they ever pregnant, even though they practiced, according to their own testimony, unabated gratuitous sex for years on end. Mead conducted no follow up and never returned to Samoa. In reality, and before colonization (1900), adultery of any kind was punished by death in Samoa. Young girls in Samoa were and are closely guarded by their parents and brothers, just like in every other culture throughout the world. Like in Western Europe before *The War*, young Samoan men kidnapped girls of higher social status and upon ravishing them, could force a desirable marriage. Both then and now, rape in Samoa is actually more prevalent than in the USA, as is violent crime, especially adolescent crime. Samoans are just as messed up as we are. No matter. Mead rushed home and quickly got her findings published: *Coming of Age in Samoa* (1928). Because her ideas conformed to and enhanced the theory of *cultural relativism*, and at the same time served as a vehicle to break down American *mores* and *norms*, Mead's madness was protected and promoted. Anyone disputing her work still risks professional banishment. There followed *The Kinsey Report* (1948) that endorsed homosexuality, pedophilia and bestiality as healthy lifestyle choices. Save bestiality they are now American *norms* under the banner of *inclusivity*: witness the well-attended *Drag Queen Storytime for kids* at your local public library and grade-school. *Playboy* (1953) adorned the newsstands and *The Playboy Philosophy* stressed hedonism over marriage and family. *Masters and Johnson* (1966) and *The Hite Report* (1976) glorified not the quest for *spiritual redemption*, but rather *multiple orgasms* as the scope, source and object of life. Pornography was legalized and then abortion in 1973. Sixty million babies were dismembered, a holocaust communist America not only don't care about, but promotes and celebrates. They refer to the murdered children as *the removal of uterine content* and the body parts, surgically removed while the fetus is kept alive, are sold for profit. At least in *Baal* they just threw the babies into the fire. The myth of overpopulation in *The Population Bomb* (1968) predicted worldwide starvation and encouraged abortion and contraception. O*verpopulation* is endorsed as a universal truth. None of the book's prognostication ever came true as the problem isn't numbers but inequality of justice and poor resource management. Not too long ago, large traditionally constructed families were an American *norm*. Now the *norm* is a single mother struggling at the lowest rung of the American social hierarchy. With the American family deconstructed and customary male behavior ridiculed as *toxic masculinity*, wars should have stopped with a bright new era of peace ushered in like a golden dawn. It hasn't happened and things are worse than ever.

PART IV

THE FAILURE OF LIBERAL DEMOCRACY

HOMAS HOBBES PROPOSED in *Leviathan* (1651) that in the construction of government, humans give up *all their natural rights* (freedom) in defense from *The State of Nature*: wherein life is (famously) *nasty, brutish and short*. He called this a *Social Contract*: loss of freedom in return for government security and protection. Royal families didn't like this idea because their proposition was that a king's power to govern came from God and not mortal men. Later Jefferson, Madison and Franklin would offer that government exists only by and through the consent of the governed in a democratic republic. When Wilson decided that it was his personal mission, and by extension that of the United States, to destroy monarchial government he looked in the mirror and saw that it was good. After all, the image he saw was the smartest person there ever was or could be. Since he was the duly elected President of the world's most powerful state, the American system must therefore not only be superior, but righteous. So Wilhelm II, Nicholas II, and poor old cranky Franz Joseph, all of whom were moronic at best if not imbecilic, had to go. There was no room for the *Sultan* either and Wilson proposed that Turkey be an American mandate. From this point onward, in the western mind at least, monarchy was presented as the least effective form of government where brutal maniacs like *Vlad the Impaler* and *Ivan the Terrible* ruled by whim. This is the current state of affairs and to question it invites ridicule. But is any of it true? Is western liberal democracy the best, or even a good form of government? Or is it the worst sort of regime ever created and a nightmare for humanity?

The false premises of liberal democracy

Without the right to secede, no democratic form of government is essentially different from monarchial or princely rule. In America the right to secede was effectively crushed when General Grant rode into Richmond. American democracy is therefore a compulsory one. The legislature may vote to change the mechanics of oppression but not the rule itself. Under the guise of protection, the people may not question government's right to tax; only how much will be taken from them. Even though the regime should exist to protect everyone's property rights, American democracy reserves its right to take anyone's property if any bureaucracy rules it so. No American owns their home. They rent it from a government that can take it at any time. *The Sicilian Black Hand* called this system *Pay or Die*. Americans are taxed not only by the federal government but by state and local municipal government as well. They bear all the characteristics of a nation and people defeated in war: heavily taxed, occupied by an omnipresent and ruthless army of police, and often imprisoned at the whim of local authorities. They find themselves victims of a two-tiered system of justice; one for the little people and another for excessively paid government agents who are essentially immune from any sort of prosecution no matter what crimes they commit; even cold-blooded murder. Many Americans begin to see this now, but find themselves in a *Hobbesian* world in which they have no rights whatsoever and are practically if not completely at the mercy of the state's protection racket. A tax-funded collection agency created allegedly to look after the people's interest is an incongruity. That agency will always demand more funds, and in the end will confiscate the entire wealth of the nation in order to defend the transfer of wealth from the tax payers to either the government agents themselves, or to some other favored group. This is why the ultra-rich often invest their resources offshore: the rest, the fellows Adam Smith called the wealth of the nation, just have to sit down, shut up and take it.

Princely rule must be superior to ~~mob~~ democratic rule

Modern people see princely rule as archaic and fundamentally unfair because participation in government is limited to the princely caste. Liberal democracy is deemed obviously better because it allows everyone to play a part: anyone among the masses may not only vote (*hallelujah*) but can actually become part of the ruling bureaucracy as well. But in truth, in liberal democracy the worst sorts of people rise to the top. Most of them are *conmen* who have never held a real job. The people who rule in the liberal west are primarily callous sociopaths whose only quest is political power and the good life that comes with it. Dr. Martha Stout, clinical psychologist:

> *Politicians are more likely than people in the general population to be sociopaths. I think you would find no expert in the field of sociopathy/psychopathy/antisocial personality disorder who would dispute this... That a small minority of human beings literally have no conscience was and is a bitter pill for our society to swallow — but it does explain a great many things, shamelessly deceitful political behavior being one.*

Dressed in silk suits and briefed in talking points for the crowd, the erstwhile rights and hereditary privileges of *the Prince* can now be attained by anyone ruthless enough to get them. The difference is that *the Prince* viewed the nation and everything in it as his personal property. Thus he would, unless mad, be careful with the resources at his disposal. The elected official, *au contraire*, correctly sees himself only as a temporary caretaker. He becomes *a provisional prince* with transitory ownership rights of *property that is not his*. He/she then proceeds to exert monopolistic control of the nation's resources. However, unlike the *hereditary prince*, the *provisional prince* actually owns nothing and never did. Government becomes a business where every elected official tries to take advantage of the nation's wealth in the (relatively) short time they are in power. As a result, taxation in the liberal west is far beyond anything ever seen under monarchial rule. This is why the national debt of every nation ruled as a democracy today is irredeemable. The wealth of the nation is used to secure the *provisional prince's* maintenance of power. The designated *provisional prince* will use taxes to enhance his own personal wealth through various scams and misappropriations. Even more disastrously, he will use it to transfer assets from one group to another to secure votes and re-election. In our modern *Age of Egalitarianism* this takes money from people who have it and gives it to people who don't. The innovative spirits that create wealth are shackled by excessive license fees and taxation. Whatever assets exist is transferred to the indentured social classes for use in their perpetual quest for abject survival. This rejection of the Malthusian social state is thought to improve the overall quality of life. But it doesn't. In the United States 50 trillion dollars was transferred by taxes to the inner cities over the past 50 years. They are the same as they ever were, rife with crime, dilapidated housing and disease. Not only that; it's now worse than ever. Individual property rights have no meaning in the egalitarian social democratic state either. All property becomes public property that can be confiscated at any time by the all powerful *provisional prince caste* and it happens all the time.

Psychopaths in Suits

Envy and greed are two of the *Seven Deadly Sins*. Every society, no matter where or when, is populated by people who desire other men's property. In monarchial rule this problem is mitigated by the fact that property is owned by *the princely caste*. Their wars and appropriations tend to be small as they can only steal from each other. Since there are few of them and everybody knows who they are, they tend to be careful about who they step on. In the liberal democracy, where all property essentially belongs to the state (and therefore to no one in particular), fraud and misappropriation are endemic. *Scientific American*:

> *Superficially charming, psychopaths tend to make a good first impression on others and often strike observers as remarkably normal. Yet*

THE FAILURE OF LIBERAL DEMOCRACY

they are self-centered, dishonest and undependable, and at times they engage in irresponsible behavior for no apparent reason other than the sheer fun of it.

Since government employment can be and is a corridor to the massive accumulation of wealth, liberal democratic rulers tend to be that element of society that has the least scruples and moral constraint; for indeed robbery in the guise of a government agent is infallible. Honest people are slowly weeded out of government and often imprisoned. Political elites emerge who hold ordinary people in contempt since they are viewed as prey. When this happens, as it must, society begins to degenerate and disintegrate as a criminal element slowly but inevitably rises to the top and takes control of the nation. In monarchial government there is a cross-section of types due to the vague and capricious nature of birth. The ruling family may beget a bad prince but even if they do, he can easily be assassinated by his own family (usually by poison) when his rule becomes harmful to their station and property. Most of the time however, the prince is not evil but is very often a mediocrity who just wants to go hunting. The nation's stability stays constant as wiser heads prevail. The wealth of the nation remains within and not transferred to the unproductive, foreign hands or hopeless ventures. Assassinations in democratic states are far less frequent because nobody really knows who to dispose of. Hannah Arendt, *On Violence*:

> *In a fully developed bureaucracy there is nobody left with whom one can argue, to whom one can present grievances, on which the pressures of power can be exerted. Bureaucracy is the form of government in which everybody is deprived of political freedom, of the power to act; for the rule by Nobody is not no-rule, and where all are equally powerless we have a tyranny without a tyrant.*

Since the whole of the democratic state is a criminal enterprise one simple political murder cannot alter the fundamental decadence of it. This is why the monarchial imperative in Europe lasted for 1400 years but sadly, and after only 250 years, democratic rule in Europe and America is in free-fall collapse.

Rivers of Blood

Enoch Powell was an English gentleman of the finest sort. Educated in the classics he fought the good fight against Hitler. In the twenty years after the war he witnessed the massive influx of Pakistanis into England. The first among them were fellows just like himself; educated men who played and loved cricket. Pakistan was a part of India until the Partition in 1947. England had turned a once prosperous India into a hell-hole so who can blame the hundreds of thousands who wanted to flee the place? They thought to settle in the lush green fields of England. That was the idea anyway. In reality they dwelled in the awful mill towns of central England just when those jobs dried up. By 1968 the cultures; one pale and Christian, the other dark and Muslim, began to clash. Powell, now a leading political figure, gave speech in which he outlined the problems facing his native born constituents:

> *For reasons which they could not comprehend, and in pursuance of a decision by default, on which they were never consulted, they found themselves made strangers in their own country. They found their wives unable to obtain hospital beds in childbirth, their children unable to obtain school places, their homes and neighborhoods changed beyond recognition, their plans and prospects for the future defeated; at work they found that employers hesitated to apply to the immigrant worker the standards of discipline and competence required of the native-born worker; they began to hear, as time went by, more and more voices which told them that they were now the unwanted. On top of this, they now learn that a one-way privilege is to be established by Act of Parliament; a law which cannot, and is not intended to, operate to protect them or redress their grievances, but is to be enacted to give the stranger, the disgruntled and the agent provocateur the power to pillory them for their private actions.*

Nowadays this sort of talk is not allowed in Great Britain. They call it *Hate Speech*. At the time, polls showed 75% support for Powell's speech. If the average Briton supported this today with a *like* on social media, he would find himself interviewed by the police. If they didn't like the answers he'd be arrested. Powell's talk came to be known as the *Rivers of Blood Speech* although he never used that term but rather made allusion to Shakespeare and the *River Tiber* in *Julius Caesar*. Nevertheless, Powell could never have imagined that in 50 years, every native European alive would witness the subjugation of their heritage right before their eyes. It's not a process that takes centuries. Native European familial birthrates are like an upside down pyramid: four grandparents on top, two parents in the middle, and one lonely child at the bottom. The replacement population is the exact opposite. The ruling elite tell us the migration from south to north can't be stopped. It is *natural* they say. These governments possess the most powerful military machines ever assembled yet profess helplessness to defend borders. At the same time, they tell you they have the power to alter and control the weather. *Climate Change* is presented as the gravest threat to civilization. Never mind the weekly beheadings, disembowelments, acid attacks, honor killings and other massacres in European cities. It's just too hot outside. What Enoch Powell didn't articulate was that while these migrant groups are *different* from the prevalent culture they are not *inferior*. Most do want to become Britons but only so long as Britain offers a better life than from whence they came. As the west declines, that is no longer the case. As their numbers increase, and the quality of life deteriorates, immigrant groups have no recourse other than tribalism. The migration is now primarily (90%) military age men who have very slim prospects for marriage, family, employment and constructive life. Hundreds of studies show that this sort of situation, with males outnumbering females, can only lead to criminal violence. This is all well and good for the globalists that seek the destruction of all ethno-states like Britain, Germany, Sweden and the USA. The subsequent dissolution of power from the ethnic nation-states into global Marxist, Leninist and Stalinist communities will, it is hoped, destroy whatever is left from Western Civilization. Some races will have to be exterminated in this process but that's acceptable collateral damage for the Marxist mindset.

Apathy and tolerance are the last signs of a dying society   Aristotle

Powell never could have imagined Great Britain now inundated with foreigners from places not ever remotely a part of the British Empire. The native born are against it, yet the ruling elite are all for it. They completely accept the notion of *Cultural and Moral Relativism*. The current invasions of Europe are a part of Adolf Hitler's lasting legacy. If he and the nationalists were for *ethnic* (i.e. *racial*) *determinism*; the notion that racial heritage determines fate: then *ipso facto*, our current university educated rulers are against it. Race is deemed a social construction with no scientific validity. Since all races are therefore in every way equal, the assimilation of foreigners must proceed apace since its success is preordained and guaranteed. Even in 1968 Powell recognized this wasn't true. The original Pakistani émigrés spoke perfect English and loved football, tea and crumpets. Their sons less so and eventually, with unemployment rife, a criminal underground formed: no surprise there, as there wasn't any work in central England where they settled. From Rotherham to Oxford, right down the spine of England, Pakistani gangs gathered young girls (as young as 12) from broken homes, addicted them to drugs and formed prostitution rings. The police, social workers, politicians and magistrates looked the other way. They didn't care because they were all just as corrupt as the émigré gangsters. The saga continues with no end in sight.

Conspiracy theories

The term was invented by the American *Central Intelligence Agency* (CIA) after President John Kennedy was gunned down in broad daylight. The shooter was immediately named as Lee Oswald who was connected to *US Naval Intelligence* and the Russian spy agency *KGB*. Just on the face of it, the official story didn't make sense with mountains of contradictory evidence standing in the way. They say Oswald acted alone and used a short-barreled variant (*Modello 91/38*) of the Italian *Carcano Modello 1891* infantry rifle. Like it says on the label, the rifle was introduced in 1891. The *Modello 91/38* was an upgrade when long barrels were phased out with volley-fire. Since most people don't know too much about military gear, the average person can't understand that this rifle was not primarily designed to actually kill anyone. Over 99% of all casualties in modern war are caused by artillery, automatic weapons fire and bombing. The *Carcano* is a defensive small arm issued to make the foot-soldier feel better about his chances for survival in a hostile environment. The designer's principal goal was to create a rugged all-weather gun that Italian infantry could employ in the ice cold Alps and the searing hot deserts of Africa when they set up in defensive positions. It didn't matter if they could really shoot anyone. With a telescopic sight that Oswald used, the *Carcano* has only one good shot at a moving target (the first one) and that's dicey. For the 2nd and 3rd shot, manual sighting is better and faster. Oswald would have known that. Bolt-action infantry rifles aren't designed for rapid-fire, sharp-shooting, or accuracy. There are other rifles specifically designed for that. If Oswald wanted to kill Kennedy he would have gotten one of those considering his extensive contacts with people and agencies that routinely practice assassination and murder for hire. Also, Oswald (himself a sharp-shooter) would have chosen a better location. From the depository building the target was moving away from him through an obstructed view. A much better spot would have been *the grassy knoll* that presented a clear field of fire with the target coming towards him. Americans seldom ask the question *Cui bono*; who gains? *Cicero* repeatedly asked that question in the course of legal proceedings. It always leads to the perpetrator. Kennedy was shot dead in Texas. *Cui bono?* Lyndon Johnson, former Governor of Texas and himself Texan, then became President. He and his pals tied up all the loose ends. It's not that tough to figure out. The term *Conspiracy Theory* is now a general term used to denigrate any interpretation of an event that might question the government's own conspiracy theory that is always presented as absolute irrefutable fact.

> *Who do you believe? Me or what you see with your own two eyes?*   Groucho Marx

Most people don't know that *three* steel and concrete high-rise buildings collapsed in the 9-11 terrorist attacks: the famous and iconic *North & South Towers* and the lesser known *47 story high Building #7*. They remain the only steel and concrete constructed buildings to ever disintegrate from fire. All three collapsed as if they were intentionally demolished. According to the official theory, the massive *Building #7* imploded from an ordinary office fire; it was never hit by an airplane. The next day, work crews began destroying all forensic evidence as they cleared the site as fast as humanly possible. Just like in 1963 when Lee Oswald was instantly blamed, the perpetrators were immediately identified. It was all directed by ~~Dr. Fu Manchu~~ *Osama Bin Laden* from his cave in Afghanistan, a country that needed to be invaded pronto. The Federal Government's conspiracy theory was presented as the only possible explanation even though it is *evident* that all three buildings were destroyed by controlled demolition. There were two other airplanes involved and they '*vaporized.*' The *War on Terror* was then declared by President Bush. *You are either with us or against us* said the little fellow who ducked for cover when service in the *National Guard* was a ticket out of Vietnam. His problem is with eternity. America's problem is the obliteration of its values that the *War on Terror* finally accomplished. Utterly brain-washed by endless media exposure and capped off with daily, even hourly pharmaceutical cocktails, Americans cannot grasp that the fabulous and mostly secret war-making and psychological warfare engines that their taxes pay for are now directed back at them. The attack is relentless. The average American child views 40,000 homicides on media by the time he is 18 years old. The talking heads then wonder why there are mass shootings. Most Americans no longer know or understand their birthrights outlined in the *Bill of Rights*, nor that they even have any. Their inherent freedoms are willingly surrendered to government agents who promise protection and free benefits to whatever social subgroup they belong to. *Al Capone* never suspected that his racket would become a nationwide policy directed from the top. The liberalized metro-sexual city slickers and collegiate elite swallow it whole.

> *In a country where everybody has a gun,*
> *I don't need one*   M. Kiva Dion

Many Americans are confused about the 2nd Amendment because they don't know what a *Militia* is.

> *A well regulated militia, being necessary to the security of a free state, the right of the people to keep and bear arms, shall not be infringed.*

A Militia is an armed group that is not attached to, nor a part of any larger traditional military organization. It is not the National Guard. Militias don't wear uniforms. It is not the Army although they often work with and support a national army. The Viet Cong were militiamen. *The Swamp Fox*; *Francis Marion* led a group of men without uniforms against the British Army in South Carolina. They brought their own guns to the field. They followed Marion because they wanted to. Crazy Horse and Sitting Bull led the militia that beat Custer. Most of the Ethiopian units that fought Mussolini's army were militia. In Europe, militiamen are called Partisans. They made life extra miserable for the German Army. Militias are the final defense of a nation beset by invasion or tyranny. This is why the American 2nd Amendment to the Constitution guarantees the right to bear arms. It's not there for drunken cowboys to go duck hunting on the weekend.

> *Guns are our friends because in a country without guns, I'm prey. All females are*   Ann Coulter

Alexander Kerensky's last act as Minister President of the Provisional Government was to hand out guns to the workers and soldiers of the Petrograd Soviet. The agenda wasn't gun control. His last ember of support came from the *1st Petrograd Woman's Battalion of Death*. That was a tough outfit. Those ladies didn't advocate for gun control either. Lenin and Stalin both did. Guess who won?

War and Migration

Way back when, at the beginnings of the American Republic, the novelist Hawthorne told poet Longfellow a story. Passed down in oral tradition, a young girl named *Evangeline* was violently separated from her betrothed on their wedding day. She searched for him the rest of her life. Interwoven in the tale was the story of the Acadians: French people who lived mostly in Nova Scotia and eastern Canada generally. Nova Scotia is like an island and far away from anyplace important. Often cold and dreary but warmed by Gulf Stream winds, it is nevertheless vastly beautiful. In the end its remoteness didn't affect the Arcadian's fate. Some bureaucrat in London decided to deport them just because they spoke French. They call this *ethnic cleansing* nowadays. Thousands of Arcadians would die and the rest stripped of their possessions and sent to live in faraway lands. Some of them settled in Louisiana. Their descendants still live there and speak a French-English dialect called *Cajun*. Now, in the beginning of the 21st Century, the entire population of Europe is scheduled for an ethnic cleansing that goes beyond deportations. Rather, it entails the substitution of the native European inhabitants with African and Middle Eastern *migrants*. What's interesting is that the doomed Caucasian-Christians cannot grasp what is happening to them. Some do but many among them, tired and forlorn, welcome their own eradication. It is difficult for them to understand the effects of the permanent warfare state that they live in. Their leaders, elected in a liberal democratic system thought the finest form of government ever imagined, bomb and ruin small nations in what was once the vast Ottoman Empire. It's all far away and on television. Then those same politicians invite the bombed out and homeless refugees into Europe and America. It's all an immense sociological experiment gone terribly awry for the target population.

Advanced Civilization

Today, there is a common assumption that we live in a highly technical and very advanced society that is the most complex and wondrous ever existed. Like in most things sold by federal bureaucracies, the truth is the complete opposite. Civilization is in a steep decline over the past 10,000 years and has now reached its lowest point; one where there is more slavery, cruelty and wanton destruction than ever before in human history. Cursory research can show that entire nations like Saudi Arabia and China keep millions of people living and working as slave laborers; conditions so brutal that *suicide nets* are constructed to prevent workers from hurling themselves to death out the factory windows. China is in the business of *organ harvesting*. There are sickly but wealthy people (mostly American) willing to pay for human internal organs. China accommodates them. They keep the organs fresh as they slice them out of living *Turkic* political prisoners who are then disposed of as trash. Workers in Korea, both north and south, routinely immolate themselves to protest labor conditions. Millions of young women, girls and boys are enslaved in a massive worldwide sex industry with no escape. In America, millions are in debt slavery and find themselves trapped in marginal communities policed by militarized ruffians dressed in combat gear. They are subdued by an array of laws that criminalize almost all aspects of human behavior. The stress overwhelms ordinary people who often suffer from continual *post traumatic stress disorder*. Many need a constant diet of drugs just to cope. In truth, more than half of America is addicted to prescription opium; gleefully given out by doctors in a medical system devolved into a holocaust. The laws don't protect the common people either but rather control them to be taxed; while another class of people with more wealth live freely outside the law in walled villas. Yet the common assumption is that this is as good as it gets; never been better. To argue otherwise can lead first to ridicule and then isolation as friends disappear. The final stage of separation is medicated incarceration for the mentally deranged as the list of official mental illnesses grows exponentially year by year.

Caligula's children

Europe and America are like the Roman Empire in the west; so long ago we scarcely remember it. They too fell apart from within. Like modern Euro-Americans, its people ceased to reproduce. In 1950 white Europeans were the largest ethnic majority in earth: 30% of the world's population. East Asians were close behind while Africans numbered only 10%. In 2010 the percentage of whites had amazingly shrunk to 16% while the African population had doubled. It takes a coordinated effort to affect change like this in only 60 years. In 1923 when *Count of Coudenhove-Kalergi* introduced a plan to breed the Caucasian race out of existence he named it *Paneuropa* or *The International Paneuropean Union*. Eventually it became *The European Union* or *EU*. The Count was influenced by *The World War* that was a bloody and super-destructive European civil war. He blamed it on the white race and not without reason. The way forward he thought, was to import North Africans into Europe. This would promote the inbreeding of the races, and promise the creation of a new race; one less warlike, less white and much more manageable. *Houari Boumedienne*, President of Algeria, in 1974:

> *One day, millions of men will leave the Southern Hemisphere to go to the Northern Hemisphere. And they will not go there as friends. They will go there to conquer it. And they will conquer it with their sons. The wombs of our women will give us victory.*

The native Caucasian populations of Europe and America are slowly and silently replaced, driven from their homeland in the name of *multi-culturalism.* This is through the *social construction of reality*. We are taught at every level of education that humans *evolved* in Africa over millions of years and then rather suddenly, and less than 100,000 years ago, migrated north to Europe. There they incredibly turned white with multi-colored hair and eyes. The truth to this story is presented as *scientific.* Therefore it must be factual. Whites are now presented as recent late-comers to history; a people with no real rights to their own land, cultural integrity or identity. *Diversity* is presented as a boon to European society. But it is something that only the whites must concede. All other cultures around the world are protected.

Diversity and inclusion

Demographic studies now show that by the end of the 21st Century the Germans will be reduced to 20 million; essentially exterminated in their own country, overwhelmed by the reproductive power of 80 million migrants. *Muammar Gaddafi*:

> *There are tens of millions of Muslims in the European continent and the number is on the increase. This is the clear indication that the European continent will be converted to Islam. Europe will one day be a Muslim continent.*

This fate awaits the rest of Western Europe. *Diversity* has become an international code word for the eradication of the white race: but only for those in the know; and the whites aren't. They are intellectually unable to recognize that the genocidal processes they lived by are now directed back at them. The *Globalists* call it *the browning* of Europe and America. Many native white leaders are all for it; as most of them are sterile and ideologically internationalists. Nativist impulses are denigrated as *racist*. They speak of a *new world order* that won't include whites; a people too heavily armed and historically very dangerous. In fact, the *cultural relativists* say, every other culture in the world needs protection from *them*. There is more than some truth to that. The French President Emmanuel Macron: soft, smooth and childless, married to a woman his mother's age, calls for the creation of *Eurafrica*; where he says:

> *Mass migration creates a welcoming multicultural Europe; one that would fully embrace a mixed-race land of immigration and interbreeding.*

In a world literally engulfed in weaponry, what could possibly go wrong?

Marx didn't see this coming

The western political class gave up on class warfare as a way change society for the better. Marx, in *Das Kapital*, predicted that workers fighting for their rights against a destructive capitalist class of money-managers would be the decisive agent in the evolution of an ideal human society. It didn't work out that way. Instead, western rulers now see the quickest way to engineer social change is to allow foreign invaders to infiltrate native Euro-American society and take it down from within. To most Americans the country they grew up with is already gone and what's left of it is slated for destruction. With *The Kalergi Plan* in full swing, the Globalist calculations show that Europe and the United States will have a native Caucasian minority in 50 years, if not sooner. In America, the demonization of white Christians and their families began openly and in earnest with President Barry Obama. *They cling to their Bibles and guns* he said; and he got that part right because religion and plenty of ammo is their only protection against people like him. The war against the American family that began with Franz Boas, Margaret Mead and the Frankfurt School continues one mural at a time, one statue at a time, one painting at a time. When the English Department of the University of Pennsylvania removed a painting of William Shakespeare, the greatest playwright and poet in the English language, and replaced it with an obscure black lesbian poet, cultural genocide is imperceptibly apace. Authors are written out of curriculum because of their white pigmentation. Murals with white children that accurately reflect past reality are destroyed for multi-cultural scenes that didn't exist. We only allow the cultural destruction of native Caucasian heritage. Only whites have no allowable protected habitat. They are not permitted cultural defense organizations either. Attempts to defend their traditions are demonized and labeled *White Nationalist*. Slowly and indiscernibly the white race is eradicated; often by one prescription bought opioid suicide drug at a time.

We are not allowed to openly talk about it. *White Genocide* is a *paranoid conspiracy theory* says Wikipedia. For the Globalists, America is too heavily armed: not just the small arms held by individuals but all those nuclear weapons and their fantastic delivery systems as well. The Euro-American political elite, *the provisional princes*, can't ever be safe in their gated compounds in Dubai with warlike American men on the loose. Hopefully the Nordic savages will finally be driven out of their homelands through *Replacement Migration*. The *United Nations* issues regular and updated reports on it: they propose quite openly that the white races no longer adequately reproduce; they need to be substituted with races that do. The need for obedient slaves is vital for the maintenance of Globalist society. When Kalergi's plan is finally implemented the Globalists may then feel secure. They are generally childless and see the genocide as what's best for planet earth. Save the earth is the message. At the same time they envision the natural end to a European civilization that has run its course. In *The Decline of the West* (1918) Oswald Spengler defined a civilization as a living organism that goes through life cycles; vibrant youth, wise maturity, decline and fall. It happens to every one of them.

July 20th

In the summer of 1944 the war turned badly for the Germans. *Army Group Center* was on the verge of dissolution. The western allies had landed in Normandy and were about to break out. In Italy, the Langobards were holding on but only with German assistance. At this point the German Army high command decided to kill Hitler. As usual they botched the job. Lt. Col. *Claus*

THE FAILURE OF LIBERAL DEMOCRACY

Philipp Maria Schenk Graf von Stauffenberg volunteered to do the deed. He was a regular attendee at Hitler's military conferences, was fearless, and the best man for it. He didn't want to just draw his pistol and gun the man down. That would have meant his own instant death from Hitler's goons. Instead he chose an elaborate time-bomb scheme that would ensure a getaway. Ever since Stalingrad Hitler did not spend much time in Berlin. Obsessed with military command he passed almost all his time at his massive *Führerhauptquartier* just outside *Rastenburg* (now *Kętrzyn*). That was way out there in the part of *Ost Prussen* that is now Poland. The massive compound covers two and a half square miles. There are more than 30 gigantic reinforced concrete bomb-proof buildings. It's still there, a bit overgrown and spooky, but accessible with restaurants, hotels and guided tours. A nice time to visit is in September and October when warm breezes from the Baltic Sea make the former *Ost Prussen* one of the most beautiful places there is. His HQ was named *die Wolfsschanze* or *The Wolf's Lair* as both Hitler and Stalin seemed to be somewhat preoccupied with wolves. Hitler was broken down by this time, fed and injected with daily and often hourly stimulants and depressants. His mad personal physician Theodor Morell juiced up strange vitamin concoctions with methamphetamines and cocaine. Hitler's mind was numbed and his body almost permanently encased in damp, smelly concrete bunkers. Pale and sickly he had less understanding of the Reich's internal affairs than a *Hausfrau* in Dusseldorf. He would sleep till noon and then pore over maps and the military situation for the next nine hours. It was all fantasy wargaming but with real people at the other end of it. After that he would sit around watching movies, munching *apfelstrudel* and *kibitzing* with his entourage until three in the morning. Then the process would repeat, day after day, month after month. Count von Stauffenberg carried a bomb-laden briefcase into a meeting with Hitler and 23 other officers on July 20th 1944. When von Stauffenberg excused himself the time-bomb went off. It didn't kill the target. Someone inadvertently moved the briefcase behind a big table leg that deflected the blast. Had von Stauffenberg been prepared to make the ultimate sacrifice he could have prevented haphazard events. But he wasn't. He might have thought about the men at Stalingrad and Kursk who willingly gave their last measure of valor. But he didn't. In a short time he a few other plotters were shot dead by firing squad. In the aftermath, over 7,000 people were arrested with 4,980 gruesomely tortured and killed. A good film about the conspiracy is *Valkyrie* (2008). What the conspirators wanted was a separate peace with the western allies. That was never going to happen because by 1944 the United States had become the world's leading communist power. Their alliance with the Soviet Union was paramount because it was ideological. Both communist powers aimed unequivocally at Germany's complete and utter destruction. American interests, throughout the war, were subverted for Soviet aims. For most Americans, this was, and is, incomprehensible because the true history of the war is hidden.

A Communist is what communists do

Franklin Roosevelt is the single most important President in American history and one of the greatest scam artists ever. He served three full terms (12 years and 1 month) and in that time was able to transform American civil bureaucracy into a communist organization. He was inaugurated in March 1933. Within two months of taking office, he confiscated individual Americans' gold holdings by executive decree. Generally, what communists do is steal wealth from people that have it and ostensibly give it to people who don't. In American communism the wealth is taken by the ruling economic elite to control and consolidate it. This leaves the middle class impoverished. Americans are law-abiding people. They try to be compliant and most often are. In 1933, and it's hard to believe this now, American money was backed by gold. The average person used gold coins and gold certificates for common transactions every day. Gold currency was the only currency in use except for silver and copper coins. Roosevelt demanded that Americans hand over almost all their gold to him and the federal government; except for jewelry and numismatic collections. They did it. A citizen was only allowed to keep five ounces in personal wealth. Thievery is how the communist state works. At the time of confiscation the federal government owned 6,000 tons of gold that was pegged at $20 per ounce. In a slight of hand worthy of Houdini, Roosevelt then raised the price of gold to $35 per ounce after the gold was stolen. Thus he doubled the price of the government's gold holdings and fleeced ordinary Americans who were forced to sell at $20. Artfully and with the stroke of a pen, they practically and legally doubled the price of the gold they stole and impoverished the suckers they stole it from. This is always the scheme as destruction of the middle class is essential to the establishment of the slave economy. Three years later they opened the gold depository at Fort Knox and deposited 13,000 tons of gold. By doubling both their holdings and its price, Roosevelt was legally able to quadruple the amount of paper money in circulation. This is now generally celebrated as the way out of the *Great Depression* and a glorious part of Roosevelt's unique genius. But it wasn't. Even the world war didn't end the depression. His banking cabal was however enriched. In a sop to the internationalists now in complete control, he maintained the dollar on the gold standard for international transactions. The little people were issued silver certificates in exchange for their gold since holding it was now illegal punishable by ten years in prison and stiff fines. He and his globalist bankster pals laughed all the way to the mint. Ordinary Americans had kept gold not only as a hedge against inflation but as secure savings after thousands of banks failed in the market crash of 1929. Now they had to keep and save paper. Soon, immediately in fact, they would see constant inflation and rising taxes just as they feared. The depression persisted until the 1950's.

> *We can ignore reality, but we cannot ignore the consequences of ignoring reality*   Ayn Rand

Six months later in November 1933, Roosevelt recognized Stalin's Soviet Union. This was a boon for them. It allowed Soviet Russia to staff embassies with spies all across America. Soon they would control the State Department and United States Treasury. They would also shortly dictate policy to a compliant Roosevelt. Loy Wesley Henderson (for example) was a career diplomat who saw through the sham of the Soviet worker's paradise. Roosevelt sent him to Iraq when ordered to by Stalin. The shift to communism happened fast. American capitalists, investors and bankers had already supported Soviet Communism since before the Revolution in 1917. They approved of a system where workers had no rights to anything but a low paying job. They tried to achieve this in America but were met with strikes and revolts. The soviet system gave them an alternative path towards tyranny and they thought they could direct the revolution. Somehow they weren't worried about a rope around their necks. Karl Marx showed the workers how to string that rope. What made *Das Kapital* unique was its conclusion: that the neurotic oppression of the working class by capitalists could only be alleviated by violent revolution. Prior analysis by Smith, John Locke, and J.S. Mill (for example) only hoped to improve the lot of the working class within the maintenance of the prevalent capitalist structure. Essential to all of them was the sanctity of individual liberty and property. Marx would have none of that. He proposed the abolition of property rights and the establishment of the famous *Dictatorship of the Proletariat*. This, he predicted, would create a classless society, the end of racism, wage-slavery and national states. This would naturally evolve into a paradise on earth. It never worked out that way.

The American republic is transformed

Before long, people had figured out that the mighty *Industrial Revolution* did not improve the life of ordinary people. Serfs didn't have a whole lot of rights and pity them if the king's hunt rode through their cabbage patch. But they did have a right to the land they lived on and the house they lived in; rights that most Americans don't have any more. Serfs couldn't be sold or forced to relocate and they had water-rights as well. There were no prisons. They had lots of holidays too; over 200 of them. That had to stop. The shift from common law to codified civil law gave the landed aristocracy the legal right to evict them. Landless serfs were forced to migrate into the new industrial cities. Once there they didn't have rights to anything except the *Law of the Jungle*. Critiques of the system soon emerged. The Goode Reverend Malthus advised simply kill them all and let God sort them out. That proved impractical. Hoping to forestall revolution, Count Bismarck introduced the social welfare state. Roosevelt would copy him and introduce *Social Security* and use it as an excuse for the massive tax increases that followed. *I will gladly pay you tomorrow for a hamburger I can eat today* boasted Wimpy. Roosevelt would propose the same as the *Social Security* payouts would come many years down the road. The new taxes were for war. The long march to the socialist and permanent warfare state began with the intellectual class who wrote stories about the plight of the working man. It was awful so they had lots of grist for their mills. Workers formed powerful unions and the *Socialist Labor Party* (1876) as well as the *Socialist Party of America* (1901) drew a lot of votes. Eugene Debs ran for President and won almost a million. But it was never enough to end capitalism by ballot box. Allied with the *Frankfurt School* and the notion of *critical theory*, they instead infiltrated American institutions from within; as later outlined by Gramsci. In 1905 the *Intercollegiate Socialist Society*, founded to indoctrinate college students in communism, morphed into the League for Industrial Democracy (1921) and then in 1960 into the Students for a Democratic Society (*SDS*). These formed the core of million strong student cadres. We can see the final result in 2020 as *Antifa* and *BLM* (mostly white unemployed college students and intellectuals) strive to overthrow American culture and history. Many of their members have sincerely held belief in the primacy of the classless society. They seek cultural change by dividing society into victim groups; black *vs.* white, men *vs.* women, gay *vs.* straight, liberal socialists *vs.* everyone else who is *ipso facto* a fascist. The racial aspect is primary; thus we see *Whiteness Studies* that encourage whites to be enthusiastic participants in their own decline and eradication. *White Privilege* re-education camps (that white corporate workers are forced to attend) teach that conceptual frameworks like hard work, planning for the future, science, rigid time schedules, aesthetics, justice, competition, and individualism are inherently white and therefore racist. This is not the kind of revolution envisioned by Marx and Lenin. They predicted an economic insurgency led by *the working class*. America's 21st Century cultural revolutionaries don't care about working people, wage-slavery or altering the terms of exploitation. The revolution is now cultural and entails the mandatory destruction of the prior (white) society's norms. Thus it enfolds with target group erasure and the destruction of idols. This is the essence of Maoism. Interestingly they are funded and supported by *The Rockefeller Foundation, the Ford Foundation, Nike, Apple, Microsoft, Hollywood,* to mention only a few. The average American cannot understand that these are *American Communist* institutions that seek the overthrow of free peoples for compliant, cowed and surgically masked perpetually humiliated servants.

Meet the new boss

These revolutionary groups originally gained strength when the *Great Depression* (1929) ruined American cites. To many people it seemed evident that the capitalist system didn't work. Roosevelt was among them and began staffing his administration with socialists and communists, many of them already in the employ of Soviet Russia. Within a year they implemented *American Communism*. The gold confiscation and recognition of Soviet Russia were the first steps. Next Roosevelt instituted *the camp system* under the guise of organizations like the *Civilian Conservation Corps* (*CCC*), *National Recovery Administration* (*NRA*) and *Public Works Administration* (*PWA*). They gave destitute men low paying jobs in camps. At the same time it not only separated families but insured that the men in camps wouldn't start any. This was one small part in the larger scheme to end the patriarchal family system. Like the Japanese dams on the Yalu, the *Tennessee Valley Authority* (TVA) primarily provided the electricity needed for the centrifuges at Oak Ridge that would build *The Bomb*. Roosevelt's American communism saw the banking elite favored and maintained while the government set prices and production, limited wages, destroyed unions and prepared for war. The same group of people who grew rich financing the *1ˢᵗ War-phase* geared up for more of it. Like a good short-order cook, Roosevelt took Wilson's leftover hash-browns and served them up as *Potatoes au Gratin*. The *14 Points* became the *Four Freedoms*. *The only thing we have to fear is fear itself* he chimed and the people surrendered into tax servitude. The buffaloed little people financed the eternal internationalist wars to come. When an aide pointed out to him that Americans might not care about people on the other side of the world, Roosevelt coolly replied; *they will have to*.

The more corrupt the state, the more numerous the laws   Tacitus

Roosevelt's *New Deal* copied Mussolini's fascist economic program. So did Hitler's *Volksgemeinshaft* whose ultimate aim was an agrarian communal society. All three of these economic plans were communist; they all strived for a *Gemeinshaft* or a communal endeavor. They sought to overthrow the individually run capitalist structure through control of the economic system by central banking systems run by the internationalist economic elite. Expediency drove this because the cashless and digital society was still decades away. But at the same time, Roosevelt, Hitler and Mussolini all sought the destruction of organized labor and the nation's indigenous small business capitalist class that paid and employed them. Finally the individual entrepreneur would be replaced by state-run corporations. We can see this scheme played out in America today as large-scale retail conglomerates that sell *everything* drive small individually owned business into oblivion. In the current Coronavirus scare the big-box enterprises are allowed business while mom and pop stores are shuttered and forced into bankruptcy. The revolution comes in stages or as the *Wicked Witch of the West* told Dorothy: *All in due time my Pretty, all in due time.* Suddenly and perhaps irrevocably on account of a seasonal flu, Americans lost the right to travel, assemble for religion, and freely walk in public without a mask; while others are allowed mass-gatherings dependent upon one's point of view and social status. As *Gramsci* predicted, the Revolution is ongoing through the slow but barely perceptible modification of norms. The Caucasian race is now presented as an incurable pathological disorder and anti-white education is openly taught through *Critical Race Theory*. From *White Fragility (2020)* the manifesto reads:

> *A positive white identity is an impossible goal. White identity is inherently racist; white people do not exist outside the system of white supremacy.*

Americans, 72% of whom are of European heritage, have freely surrendered their birth-rights. They now live in fear of some vague disease and watch indifferently without a whimper as their way of life is terminated forever.

Defund the Police!

The first police force in the USA was the *Pennsylvania State Constabulary* established in 1905. They were strike breakers. Before that the county sheriff, (from Old English *scīrgerefa* and Middle English *shirreve*) was not much different from the infamous *Sheriff of Nottingham*. Historically the sheriff and not uniformed police would take care of the local criminal element. There was no organized crime in America except for local ethnic and family gangs. Prohibition changed all that. The 1920 passage of the 18th Amendment to the US Constitution (by overwhelming margins) prohibited the manufacture, sale, or transportation of alcoholic beverages. This turned millions of extremely law-abiding Americans into criminals. It's a forgotten memory now but prior to the 18th Amendment women did not frequent bars or saloons. It was off limits to them and neither did they want to go there. Bars were a male-only sanctuary. *Women of the night* were the only females one could find in bars. American women drank at home and alone. With a cold beer outlawed, a vast criminal conspiracy emerged to supply *everyone* with whatever they wanted. Naturally the local, state and federal governments followed suit with expanded police powers to get in on the action. Eventually, local uniformed police became a vast army of occupation with practically unlimited powers to confiscate property, as well as life and limb. Prohibition died but soon *The Drug War* took its place. Police were militarized and given ever more expanded powers. Right now, Maoist gangs, funded by Red China and various *Open Border* organizations seek to reduce what was clearly an over-funded and over-armed police presence in the United States. Unfortunately *Defund the Police* does not mean eliminate the police. It means replacing them with armed gangs of disgruntled college students and anarchy in the streets.

Tail-gunner Joe

Most people think that Senator Joseph McCarthy invented anti-communism by committee in the 1950's. He didn't. *The House Committee on Un-American Activities (HCUA)* was founded in 1938. Roosevelt let out a howl. People were on to him. Later on and more famously, Senator Joseph McCarthy tried to warn America about the Communist takeover. Unfortunately Joe was addicted to alcohol and an easy target; especially since he didn't have the support to go after the real criminals in the American government. Instead he targeted easier prey like minor officials. Eventually his tactics resembled those of the Communists themselves and were seen as anti-American. Joe was also addicted to illicit sex (in all its forms) as was his chief law council Roy Cohen. Drunk with power they both allowed their peccadilloes to dictate strategy. For personal reasons they chose to target the Army which wasn't a good idea since General of the Army Eisenhower was now President. Joe and many others were fueled by the revulsion they felt when the fruits of victory over Japan were stolen by Soviet Russia and especially Red China. Joe watched Mao's *Peoples Liberation Army* (*PLO*) triumphant and knew why they won: Mao had the support of both Communist America and Soviet Russia. The Chinese Nationalist Army (*National Revolutionary Army*) was abandoned to its fate. They fought a rear-guard action, escaped total destruction, evacuated to Formosa and took over the formerly Japanese possession. That was really tough luck for the native Taiwanese. Imperial Japan gave them representation in the Diet. When China invaded (1946) Taiwanese natives were quickly disarmed and gunned down by Chinese troops. The *February 28 Massacre* (1947) claimed 25,000 dead at least. This is what Americans can expect when *United Nations Peacekeepers* patrol Los Angeles, Chicago and New York.

> "It's a white whale, I say," resumed Ahab, as he threw down the topmaul: "a white whale. Skin your eyes for him, men; look sharp for white water; if ye see but a bubble, sing out."

Joe was allied with Doug MacArthur who wanted to be President but wouldn't do the dirty business of political infighting. He expected to be ordained. Doug was a vindictive bully but he was an American patriot. The *Flimflam Man* relieved Doug of command when the General recognized and publicized that the American State Department was (and is) infiltrated by communist cadres. Doug saw that Communist China was America's real enemy (still is). When he pushed for war against them and their million man army, he quite reasonably lost American Army support. He and *Tail-gunner Joe* were defeated and literally relegated to the dustbin of history. This allowed the communist takeover of the United States' government to proceed apace without any further hindrance. Indeed, American nationalism is come to be maligned. Any attempt to rationally understand *American Communism* is labeled *McCarthyism* and therefore anti-American. Civil war looms and everybody is well armed. An interesting film about the McCarthy era is *Goodnight and Good Luck* (2005).

The Mount at Zion

President Trump is a Christian Zionist. He moved the American embassy from Tel Aviv to Jerusalem and recognized the city as the capital of Israel. The UN vote was 128-9 against. The American Democrat Party was against it. Every American President since the *Flimflam Man* promised it but none did the deed. According to Scripture, Jerusalem is where the Messiah; *The Redeemer* will appear to be anointed. For Christian Zionists occupation of Jerusalem represents a fulfillment of Biblical Prophecy. For most American Jews however, Zionism is anathema. They don't even know what it is except that the Marxists say it's bad. American Jews are the most educated class and therefore most under the influence of Cultural Marxism whose power they neither recognize nor admit. That's how successful American educational indoctrination has been. Trump not only recognized Jerusalem as Israel's capital, but also that the *Golan Heights* is theirs by right of conquest. Trump is beloved in Israel, but American Jews (a separate animal) still hate him. Does he need to sign a notarized affidavit that says he's a Zionist? The whole point of Zionism isn't only the creation of a Jewish state. It is about Redemption. The American Marxist educational system says that's just a lot of hocus-pocus. They teach God doesn't exist. This is how and why there is a Zionist American President whom American Jews hate. Lost in a political netherworld, most American Jews can tell you more about Heinrich Himmler than they can about Theodor Herzl. Do they suppose the Zionist movement was about another phony liberal democracy in the Middle East? If it was they got that. Zionism is about the creation of a Jewish theocratic state dedicated to the *glorification of God!* It is about Israel as a divinely guided nation devoted to the God of Abraham. The only hope for Israel is under the Davidic line of Kings. It follows then that the survival of the Judeo-Christian ethos is centered upon a spiritual revival in Israel. Liberal democracy is a sham. Every Jew in the world should be committed to crowning the King of the Jews. King David has literally millions of descendants. Pick one. They are named Davisson, or Davidson. It doesn't have to be difficult. According to Scripture, this must come. In the holy books Jews are told: *You are either with God or against Him.* There is no fence. There is no middle ground. Completely contrary to their own interests, American Jews support the atheistic Globalists whose aim is the destruction and utter ruin of Israel and Judaism. Some American Jews begin to see this now but the indoctrination is persuasive, especially since much of it comes from Jews who deny God. Carl Sagan was a slick and smooth talking atheist whose God was *Materialism* and whose influence was generational. The Holy Scriptures say quite clearly that *Satan* is the ruler of the material world. Sagan, a *Philistine*, couldn't understand his own place in it. Another atheist, Stephen Jay Gould, had it all figured out. God might exist but doesn't have any influence over the material world. God is out there somewhere just watching. Maybe, but that's not going to save either Israel or *Judentum*. If God didn't exist why would Israel exist? There is no other reason to suppose its creation out of the World War's chaos. Israel is the only stable nation to emerge from the *War of the Ottoman Succession*. Justifiably armed to the teeth with stockpiled *fifty megaton hydrogen bombs*; who can think Israel doesn't have them? Jews invented the hydrogen bomb. They also have thousands of miniaturized tactical nuclear weapons and delivery systems for all of it. The military situation is unstable worldwide and the *War of the Ottoman Succession* remains unrecognized and unreported. With the Valley of Armageddon but a short hike away, Jews need to wake up and soon. Israel is the West's only hope. Besieged by the forces of intolerance and evil; if she falls so does the West. It is all written. Like Casey Stengel used to say; *you can look it up. FIN*

Some Sources

An ordinary internet search on Jewish Holocaust historiography leads only in one direction. For alternative theories or interpretations try the following:

Primary: the Institute for Historical Review:
http://www.ihr.org/

Neatly organized by: The Unz Review: An Alternative Media Selection: A Collection of Interesting, Important, and Controversial Perspectives Largely Excluded from the American Mainstream Media
https://www.unz.com/publication/jhr/issues/
https://www.unz.com/publication/jhr/author/david_irving/
https://www.unz.com/publication/jhr/author/robert_faurisson/
https://www.unz.com/publication/jhr/topic/holocaust/
https://www.unz.com/book/arthur_r_butz__the-hoax-of-the-twentieth-century/
http://holocausthandbooks.com/index.php?page_id=29
https://www.unz.com/announcement/the-remarkable-historiography-of-david-irving/
https://www.unz.com/runz/american-pravda-post-war-france-and-post-war-germany/

Pearly Harbor
https://www.unz.com/publication/jhr/author/james_j_martin/
https://www.unz.com/publication/jhr/author/percy_l_greaves_jr/
https://www.unz.com/publication/jhr/topic/pearl-harbor/

Alternative History:
https://www.unz.com/runz/american-pravda-holocaust-denial/

www.ingramcontent.com/pod-product-compliance
Lightning Source LLC
Chambersburg PA
CBHW030901080526
44589CB00010B/90